Asset Management

PUBLISHED AND FORTHCOMING TITLES IN THE UK SIP SERIES

Series Editors: John Goodchild and Clive Callow

ASSET MANAGEMENT
Equities Demystified

Shanta Acharya

JOHN WILEY & SONS, LTD

Published in 2002 by John Wiley & Sons, Ltd
Baffins Lane, Chichester,
West Sussex PO19 1UD, England

National 01243 779777
International (+44) 1243 779777

e-mail (for orders and customer service enquiries): cs-books@wiley.co.uk
Visit our Home Page on http://www.wiley.co.uk

Other Wiley Editorial Offices

John Wiley & Sons, Inc., 605 Third Avenue,
New York, NY 10158-0012, USA

Wiley-VCH Verlag GmbH, Pappelallee 3,
D-69469 Weinheim, Germany

John Wiley & Sons Australia, Ltd, 33 Park Road, Milton,
Queensland 4064, Australia

John Wiley & Sons (Asia) Pte Ltd, 2 Clementi Loop #02-01,
Jin Xing Distripark, Singapore 129809

John Wiley & Sons (Canada) Ltd, 22 Worcester Road,
Rexdale, Ontario M9W 1L1, Canada

Library of Congress Cataloging-in-Publication Data
Acharya, Shanta.
    Asset management : equities demystified / Shanta Acharya.
        p. cm.
    Includes bibliographical references and index.
    ISBN 0-471-55791-9
    1. Portfolio management. 2. Investment analysis. 3. Investments. I. Title.
    HG4529.5 .A24 2002
    332.6–dc21
                                                              2001055918

British Library Cataloguing in Publication Data

A catalogue record for this book is available from the British Library

ISBN 0-471-55791-9

Typeset in 11pt Rotis serif by Deerpark Publishing Services Ltd, Shannon, Ireland
Printed and bound in Great Britain by CPI Antony Rowe, Eastbourne
This book is printed on acid-free paper responsibly manufactured from sustainable forestation, for which at least two trees are planted for each one used for paper production.

For my father, who died unexpectedly
during the writing of this book
and in memory of my
grandparents

All men are liable to error; and most men are, in many points, by passion or interest, under temptation to it.

John Locke

If a little knowledge is dangerous, where is the man who has so much as to be out of danger?

Thomas H. Huxley

What we anticipate seldom occurs; what we least expected generally happens.

Benjamin Disraeli

A foolish consistency is the hobgoblin of little minds.

Ralph Waldo Emerson

No man is an *Island*, entire of it self; every man is a piece of the *Continent*, a part of the *main*; any man's *death* diminishes *me*, because I am involved in *Mankind*; And therefore never send to know for whom the *bell* tolls; It tolls for *thee*.

John Donne

Contents

Contents

Preface

This is the third title in the UKSIP/John Wiley series on contemporary investment themes. Its publication is timely: a study of the industry was overdue.

Over the past ten years there have been developments in information technology, globalisation, demographics and trade liberalisation that have combined to produce a revolution in capital markets. That revolution has taken the form of an integrated global market economy, and Dr Acharya's study assesses the implications for both private and institutional investors. It examines the changes that have occurred and considers the role of governments, regulators and individuals in defining the future pattern of markets.

Shanta Acharya has contributed essays to many journals, including *Professional Investor*, and her latest book offers a perceptive analysis of the changing face of the asset management industry.

John Goodchild
Clive Callow

Acknowledgements

I owe thanks to all those who helped, encouraged and sustained me over the past two years in the writing of this book. They all contributed in their myriad ways in transforming my learning curve into a stimulating and rewarding experience. They were generous with their time, in answering my questions, correcting transcripts of the interviews, providing me with data and research, reading parts of the book and offering their invaluable critical comments. I would particularly like to acknowledge the help offered by Simon Abrams, Diane Alalouf, Rupert Allan, Charlotte Amiri, Mark Archer, Mark Boylan, Sally Bridgeland, Alan Brown, Stephen Butt, Dominic Caldecott, Clive Callow, Peter Chambers, Chris Cheetham, Mike Clark, Kevin Coldiron, Allan Conway, Charles Cortese, Willie Cotter, Stanislas Debreu, David Dobson, Jill Dodds, Harald Egger, Nick Ferguson, Simon Fraser, Tim Gardener, Alastair Ross Goobey, Leslie Hannah, Peter Hodgman, Daniel Hodson, Peter Hopkins, Alex Ineichen, Bozena Jankowska, Simon Kenny, Rob Leary, Joseph Leung, Mario Levis, James Lyle, Bill McQuaker, Nicola Meaden, Nitin Mehta, Dimitris Melas, Suzanne Mitchell, Crispin Odey, Stuart O'Gorman, Liam Pagliaro, Martin Phipps, Nicola Ralston, Andreas Ritzi, Chris Samuel, Penny Shepherd, Clive Sherling, Fred Siegrist, Andrew Skirton, Russell Sparkes, Raymond Stokes, Chris Sutton, Peter Thompson, Tony Watson, Steven Wiltshire and Brian Woods-Scawen.

I am grateful to John Goodchild for his original suggestion and to Sally Smith for commissioning me to write this book and to both of them for their editorial support.

Without the unfailing and unconditional support of my family and friends, this book could not have been completed.

List of Abbreviations

ABI	Association of British Insurers
ACCA	Association of Certified Chartered Accountants
AIM	alternative investment market
AIMR	Association for Investment Management and Research
AOL	America Online
AUTIF	Association of Unit Trusts and Investment Funds
B2B	business to business
B2C	business to customer
BGI	Barclays Global Investors
BIAM	Bank of Ireland Asset Management
BiC	Business in the Community
BiE	Business in the Environment
BP	British Petroleum
BT	British Telecommunications
BVCA	British Venture Capital Association
CFA	chartered financial analyst
CalPERS	California Public Employees' Retirement Scheme
CAPM	Capital Asset Pricing Model
CAPS	Combined Actuarial Performance Service
CEO	chief executive officer
CFO	chief financial officer
CFROI	cash flow return on investment
CIO	chief investment officer
CML	capital market line
CPP	capital-protected product
CSFB	Credit Suisse First Boston
CSR	corporate social responsibility
DB	Defined benefit
DC	Defined contribution
DeAM	Deutsche Asset Management
DJ	Dow Jones
DT	Deutsche Telecom
DTB	Deutsche Terminbörse
DTI	Department of Trade and Industry
EBIT	earnings before interest and tax
EBITDA	earnings before interest, tax and depreciation allowances
EIRIS	Ethical Investment Research Service

EM	emerging markets
EMH	efficient market hypothesis
EMAS	Eco-Management and Audit Scheme
EMS	environmental management system
EMTN	euro medium-term note
EPS	earnings per share
ERISA	Employment Retirement Income Security Act
ETF	exchange-traded fund
EUREX	European exchange
EU	European Union
EVA	economic value added
EVCA	European Venture Capital Association
FDI	foreign direct investment
FESCO	Forum of European Securities Commissions
FIS	Friends Ivory & Sime
FSA	Financial Services Authority
FTSE	Financial Times Securities Exchange
GAAP	generally accepted accounting principles
GARP	growth at the right price
GDP	gross domestic product
GE	General Electric
GM	genetically modified
GNP	gross national product
GIGN	Global Institutional Governance Network
GRI	Global Reporting Initiative
GSTP	global straight-through processing
HFR	Hedge Fund Research
HNW	high net worth
HSBC	Hong Kong & Shanghai Banking Corporation
IAFE	International Association of Financial Engineers
IBE	Institute of Business Ethics
I/B/E/S	International Brokers' Earnings Estimates
IFA	independent financial adviser
IBO	institutional buyout
ICCR	Interfaith Centre on Corporate Responsibility
ICFC	Industrial and Commercial Finance Corporation
ILO	International Labour Organisation
IMF	International Monetary Fund
IPO	initial public offering
IRR	internal rate of return
IRRC	Investor Responsibility Research Center
ISA	individual savings account
IT	information technology
JIG	Jupiter International Group
KKR	Kohlberg, Kravis, Roberts
LEC	London Environment Centre
LIBOR	London interbank offered rate
LIFFE	London International Financial Futures and Options Exchange
L&G	Legal & General

LSE	London Stock Exchange
LTCM	Long-Term Capital Management
MAR	managed account reports
M&A	Mergers and acquisitions
MBI	management buy-in
MBO	management buyout
MFR	minimum funding requirement
MSCI	Morgan Stanley Capital International
MNĆ	multinational corporation
NAPF	National Association of Pension Funds
NASDAQ	National Association of Securities Dealers Automated Quotation
NASDR	National Association of Securities Dealers Regulation
NAV	net asset value
NGO	non-governmental organisation
NIM	Nordea Investment Management
NVCA	National Venture Capital Association
OEIC	open-ended investment company
OECD	Organisation for Economic Cooperation and Development
OTC	over the counter
PIRIC	Pension Investment Research Consultant
PPP	principal-protected product
PSBR	public sector borrowing requirement
PwC	PricewaterhouseCoopers
R&D	research and development
REO	Responsible Engagement Overlay
ROCE	return on capital employed
ROE	return on equity
SAN	Shareholder Action Network
S&P	Standard & Poor's
SEAAR	social and environmental, accounting, auditing and reporting
SEC	Securities and Exchange Commission
SEE	social, environmental, ethical
SERM	safety and environmental risk management
SG	Société Générale
SIA	Securities Industry Association
SIF	Social Investment Forum
SIM	Schroder Investment Management
SIP	statement of investment principles
SMEs	small and medium-sized enterprises
SML	security market line
SOFFEX	Swiss Options and Financial Futures Exchange
SRI	socially responsible investment
SSB	Salomon Smith Barney
SSGA	State Street Global Advisers
T-Bill	Treasury bill
TMT	technology, media and telecommunications
UBS	Union Bank of Switzerland
UKSIP	UK Society of Investment Professionals
UN	United Nations

VCT   venture capital trust
VIS   Voting Issues Service
ZCM   Zurich Capital Markets

CHAPTER 1

Capital Market Revolution

INTRODUCTION

During the 1990s, developments in information and communication technology, globalisation, demographics and trade liberalisation brought about a revolution in capital markets. They delivered an integrated global market economy, encouraged governments to address their fiscal imbalances, prompted central banks to reassess their reigning paradigms and forced multinational corporations (MNCs) to seek ways of capturing market share in an increasingly competitive global environment. The creation of the euro-zone intensified industry consolidation, while increased competition from the Far East triggered an era of mergers and acquisitions (M&A), unprecedented in corporate history. The performance of most industrial sectors started to depend more on global economic factors than national ones. While quantum theory and game theory influenced market economics, wealth became more concentrated in fewer MNCs, individualism and the profit motive gained ascendancy but the course of democracy or collective decision-making at the grass-root level faced a crisis.

Leading companies today operate across national and geographic boundaries in product, capital and labour markets. This consolidation and rationalisation of business is reflected in the explosion of cross-border M&A activity (Table 1.1). The increasing importance of mergers within the same industry also indicates that the productive capital stock of industries has become global. Differences in security prices today reflect diverging expectation of future earnings across

Table 1.1 *Cross-Border Mergers and Acquisitions*[a]

	1989–1993	1994–1998	1999–2000
	IN BILLIONS OF DOLLARS		
Similar product lines (Intra-industry)	100.5	488.7	1123.9
Across product lines (Inter-industry)	97.1	311.4	468.5
Total M&A	197.6	800.1	1592.4
	AS A PERCENTAGE OF TOTAL		
Similar product lines (Intra-industry)	50.9	61.1	70.6
Across product lines (Inter-industry)	49.1	38.9	29.4
Total M&A	100.0	100.0	100.0

[a] Source: Phillips & Drew, *Pension Fund Indicators 2001*

global industries.[1] The asset management industry is no exception. However, as its underlying business consists primarily of buying and selling shares of other companies, be they listed or in private ownership, the asset management sector is highly sensitive to changes in global corporate trends.

According to research conducted by William M. Mercer, during 1998 there were more cross-border and cross-segment deals than ever before, with over a quarter of the investment managers, operating in 30 countries, being involved in such activity. Corporate transformations were all part of the industry's move towards greater globalisation and establishing an international standard.[2] M&A activity continued at the same pace through 1999–2000. Restructuring of the ownership of the fund management industry has been significant, particularly in the 1990s. Many of the firms, which were once independent, are now part of wider financial services organisations – Mercury Asset Management is now Merrill Lynch Investment Managers (having been owned by SG Warburg and then by Swiss Bank Corporation), Morgan Grenfell is embedded within Deutsche Bank, Gartmore is owned by Nationwide Mutual Insurance of the US, and Phillips & Drew is part of UBS Asset Management. The list goes on and on, and by all accounts this consolidation is set to continue.

The relationship between economic growth, technological development and capital markets is not new. But it has become one of the most contentious issues in asset allocation today due to the increased concentration of wealth at the top. Some 86% of the world's wealth is held by the richest 20% of its population and the poorest 20% own a mere 1%. The largest 100 companies account for more than 25% of global trade, and the 10 largest traders in the world, consisting of some 78% of total exports, are all the developed nations – the euro area, US, Germany, Japan, UK, France, Italy, Netherlands, Canada, Belgium and Luxembourg. The top 75 companies have assets that rival the combined GNP of Germany, France and the UK. Global pension assets have reached $13 trillion, 80% of which is concentrated in the US, UK and Japan. European pension fund managers' assets amounted to $1.8 trillion. The top five managers' worldwide assets amounted to over $4 trillion, which is more than the GDP of Germany and the UK (Table 1.2).[3] Worldwide, pension funds own some 15% of the largest MNCs. The top 500 global fund managers collectively managed some $33.6 trillion of assets in 1999, which was larger than the GDP of the world. Their collective decision has a profound effect on our lives.

Table 1.2 *The ten largest fund managers in the world: total group assets ($bn) as at 30 June 2000*[a]

Parent Company	Assets
Fidelity Investments	1,000.0
AXA Group	845.5
Barclays plc	833.0
Zurich Financial Services Group	821.0
Allianz Asset Management [4]	781.7[b]
State Street Corporation	738.4
Deutsche Asset Management	595.0
Vanguard Group, Inc.	561.3
Merrill Lynch & Co, Inc	554.7
Mellon Financial Corporation	521.4

[a] Source: William M. Mercer, *European Pension Fund Managers Guide 2001*

[b] The figure given above includes assets under management with Allianz Asset Management ($492.5 bn) and AGF Asset Management ($49.8 bn) as well as that of PIMCO Europe ($199.3 bn) and Oppenheimer Capital ($40.1 bn), which were both taken over by Allianz AG in May 2000.

The question that is paramount from the investor's perspective, in light of such massive changes in global industrial structures, is whether these developments are contributing to market efficiency – improved transparency, liquidity, competition – or whether they are working against an optimal market process. And to what extent are these global investors behaving as responsible shareholders? While developments in technology are generally perceived as positive, the greater concentration of wealth among MNCs and pension fund managers raises concerns, salient among which are issues surrounding efficient asset allocation. In an environment that is ostensibly market-oriented and market-dominated, ensuring an optimal level of efficiency in the market mechanism cannot be over-emphasised. The question then arises, Who exactly is supposed to ensure that and how is that to be delivered? If you subscribe to the theory that the market is the ultimate arbiter of efficient asset allocation, then is intervention by an external market regulator even desirable? If so, who then regulates the regulator? What role do investors play in such a process because they essentially define the nature of the market?

Before we embark on an analysis of market efficiency, we need to examine the role played by the dominant market participants. In order to do so, we must bear in mind the environment in which they operate – for example, the impact of technology, globalisation, demographic changes, and related financial issues, such as low inflation in the developed economies – as all that clearly influences their business model. The two other major factors that we also need to understand when assessing what shapes the decision-making process of these market-makers are legislation and what is commonly known as the rise of the cult of the equity. In fact, the importance of free market theory originated from the rise in equity investing. The mismanagement within the banking sector and the crisis that ensued led to the rise of equity investing, where risk was transferred to the investors. While banks still have an enormous role to play in the economic growth and development of any nation, UK banks hold less than 1.5% of the UK equity market.

THE RISE OF INSTITUTIONAL INVESTORS

In 1963, individual investors owned around 56% of the UK equity market; institutional investors owned 30%. With the rise in occupational pension fund schemes, individuals now own 16%, but institutional managers' share has risen to 47% (Table 1.3). Pension funds' share has gone up from 6.4% in 1963 to 17.7% in 2000, having peaked at 32.4% in 1992. Insurance companies have more than doubled their share from 10% to 21% and unit trusts/investment trusts and other financial institutions have lost some of their share, declining from 12.6% to 8.4% over this period. The other significant development is the rise in the ownership of the UK equity market by overseas investors, which has risen from 7.0% in 1963 to a staggering 32.4% in 2000.[5] Of the total £587 billion owned by overseas investors as at 31 December 2000, 33% were US-based and 39% were investors in Europe.[6]

One of the historical attributes of the UK economy has been the prevalence of funded occupational pension schemes. 'Retirement was not invented in the twentieth century;' wrote Leslie Hannah in the preface to his study of the development of occupational pensions

Table 1.3 *Percentage ownership of the UK equity market[a]*

	1990	2000
Overseas investors	11.8	32.4
Insurance companies	20.4	21.0
Pension funds	31.7	17.7
Individual investors	20.3	16.0
Unit trusts	6.1	1.7
Investment trusts	1.6	2.1
Other financial institutions	0.7	4.6
Charities	1.9	1.4
Private non-financial companies	2.8	2.2
Public sector	2.0	0.0
Banks	0.7	1.4

[a] Source: Office of National Statistics, *Share Ownership: A Report on Ownership of Shares as at 31st December 2000*, p. 8.

in Britain, 'but it did then become the eventual lot of the majority of British employees and its terms were then fundamentally rewritten.'[7] Thanks to the steady rise of occupational pensions, over 65% of all funds under management are on behalf of UK institutions.[8] Competition for the management of assets today has prised open the market; the top 20 managers in the UK accounted for less than half the pension fund assets estimated at $1,403 billion in June 2000 (Table 1.4).[9]

In 1999, UK insurers had £1.1 trillion of assets, of which £977 billion was accounted for by life insurance. Between 1989 and 1999, the life

Table 1.4 *The 20 largest pension fund managers in the UK: value of UK pension assets managed ($bn) as at 30 June 2000*[a]

Manager	Assets
Merrill Lynch Investment Managers	92.8
Schroder Investment Management	90.3
Barclays Global Investors	77.7
Hermes Pensions Management	65.7
Deutsche Asset Management	56.1
UBS Asset Management	48.7
Goldman Sachs Asset Management	41.3
Zurich Scudder Investments	27.6
Henderson Global Investors	23.7
First Quadrant	23.3
Fidelity International	20.0
Capital International	17.1
Foreign & Colonial	13.8
HSBC Asset Management	13.0
JP Morgan Investment Management	12.9
Baillie Gifford	12.8
Baring Asset Management	11.1
Morley Fund Management	10.9
Prudential M&G	10.2
Newton Investment Management	10.1
Total	679.2

[a] NB: Gartmore Investment Management is excluded from this list as it was undergoing a restructuring during that time and did not wish to be included. As at 31st December 2000, Gartmore managed $65.8 billion of UK pension assets. Source: William M. Mercer, *European Pension Fund Managers Guide 2001*.

insurance sector's investment holdings rose from £388 billion to £977 billion. Unlike pension funds, insurance companies compete openly in commercial markets and are thus influenced by profitability considerations and competition issues. The assets managed by the largest life insurance companies in the UK are given in Table 1.5.

Pooled investment vehicles such as unit trusts, open-ended investments companies (OEICs) and other institutional investments such as investment trusts together form a third and smaller category of institutional investors. The largest unit trust/OEIC managers are given in Table 1.6

With increasing affluence, changes in employment patterns, rise in self-employment along with changes in pension legislation, it is likely that individual investors will be able to claw back some of

Table 1.5 *The 20 largest life assurance companies in the UK: value of assets (£bn) in 2000[a]*

Group	Assets
CGNU	143.1
Prudential	132.3
Legal & General	101.1
Standard Life	75.8
Lloyds TSB	56.3
AMP	52.7
Barclays	47.4
AXA	46.4
Royal & Sun Alliance	41.1
Zurich Financial Services	38.9
Equitable Life	33.8
Friends Provident	30.3
Royal London	26.3
Halifax	25.7
Abbey National	23.5
Aegon	22.2
CIS	19.7
Britannic Assurance	11.4
GE Insurance	9.7
National Westminster Life	8.6

[a] Source: Association of British Insurers

Table 1.6 *The 15 largest unit trust or OEIC managers in the UK: total assets under management (£bn) as at November 2000[a]*

Group	Assets
Fidelity	16.4
Schroder	12.6
Threadneedle	11.3
M&G	10.8
Gartmore	9.9
Perpetual	9.6
Scottish Life	8.8
Merrill Lynch	8.0
Scottish Widows	7.4
Barclays	6.3
Aberdeen	6.1
HSBC	5.9
Friends Provident	5.8
Jupiter	5.3
Invesco GT	5.3

[a] Source: AUTIF

their influence in the market. But that process has only just begun and it will take decades for it to filter through. Also, individuals will continue to channel their investments via institutions, although direct investment in the stock market may well rise. From stakeholder pensions to hedge funds, individuals will continue to invest in institutionally managed funds, simply because they do not have the time, the skill or the desire to manage their personal investments with due care and diligence. Individual investors constitute the largest owners of investment trusts in the UK, at 37%.[10] The role of institutional investors will therefore continue to influence the market as it is unlikely that their accumulated wealth and skill will be denuded by greater competition from individual investors. Most of us have come to appreciate the importance of pension schemes along with other investments in the distribution of wealth, in social welfare policy and in the capital markets. Considering the rise of pension assets over the past 50 years, its impact on capital markets and in an efficient asset allocation process need not be spelled out.

The funded occupational pension scheme is driven by asset allocation being determined primarily by the trustees of these sponsored funds with input from their advisers and investment managers. With the decline in defined benefit pension schemes and the shift towards defined contribution schemes, the asset allocation decision will in time also shift towards the individual owner of the scheme, although current practice indicates that these schemes actually offer very limited choice to the individual investor. The stakeholder pension offers even more limited choice. In effect, asset allocation decisions by institutional investors continue to send strong signals to the market. The retail investor has not had much influence in determining asset allocation over the past decades although, at the last count ownership of the UK equity market by individuals only marginally lagged behind that of pension funds. It is true that, in markets, the marginal investor often dictates the price and in the US, for example, the retail sector did contribute significantly to the asset bubble. But in most parts of the world, direct market ownership by individuals has been significantly lower. With greater restructuring in Europe, a higher exposure to equity assets – at the institutional level and the retail level – is expected over the next decade or so.

Globalisation and market liberalisation have meant that overseas investors, particularly US institutional investors, have increased their share of UK and European capital markets. Even within the short space of time that US investors have been established in the UK, the market has experienced the rise in what one chief investment officer called the 'Americanisation' of fund management. However, this influence is not just confined to the fund management sector or to the financial services sector. Restructuring of the ownership of the UK asset management industry is also an effect of globalisation. Among the top 20 in the industry, only Schroder, Hermes, Baillie Gifford, Morley and Prudential are the ones whose ownership remains largely UK-based. The rest have been acquired, partly or wholly, by overseas interests. The process of consolidation in the asset management industry is far from over.

However, it remains to be seen how exactly clients benefit from it while the merger process is still on, as it takes a long time for the results to feed through. In the interim, it distracts management attention away from genuine value addition, which essentially resides in better analysis of information and improved processes that reflect in optimal investment performance and client servicing. For Tim Gardener, global head of investment consulting at William M. Mercer Limited, none of the recent mergers have yet delivered anything of real value to the client:

> You could argue they delivered cost savings internally and thus have prevented fees from going up. But there is no evidence that the mergers have had any real beneficial effect on the client. For example, it has not yet resulted in higher-quality information coming through into the investment process because the focus of the mergers seem to be on issues such as distribution, cost savings, etc. So from the client's perspective, the mergers in the industry may seem inevitable, but are not seen as the best means of adding value. However, we haven't had enough time to see the benefits of these mergers come through. The last round of mergers in 1987 did improve the quality over time; it just took a long time to get there.[11]

For Nicola Ralston, head of investment management at Schroder Investment Management (SIM) until September 2001, the jury is still out. In May 2000 the Schroder group completed the sale of its world-wide investment banking business to Salomon Smith Barney, freeing it to concentrate on the asset management franchise. SIM's strategy is to establish itself as one of the world's leading asset managers by developing its position as a domestic or specialist international manager in the principal savings markets of the world. Nicola Ralston believes that by merging, clients can

> benefit from economies of scale through reduced costs and additional resources to enhance investment performance and client service. However, it has more to do with leveraging resource to best effect rather than the quantity of resource in itself. Corporate activity can also destabilise companies. Management attention can be dominated by integration issues and lead to staff departures. Thus, on balance, clients have had mixed experiences to date; but many mergers are still in their infancy in terms of full integration. So the jury is still out.[12]

It is not surprising that asset managers who have not yet been publicly engaged in mergers espouse such a view. William Cotter, chief executive at the Bank of Ireland Wealth Management Services, advocates a similar opinion:

> For many fund managers, access to increased financial resources means that they can provide broader product choice. It can also facilitate investment in client servicing – both in 'old' and 'new' economy ways. Greater scale should also produce other savings that can be passed on to clients. However, from a client's perspective, I think many of the positives are outweighed by the uncertainty change creates.[13]

Alastair Ross Goobey, who retired as chairman of Hermes Pensions Management at the end of 2001, believes the mania for mergers has more to do with the ability to offer a wider product choice. For him, the high level of M&A activity in asset management stems from two things:

- There is a need for fund managers to offer a much wider range of products than traditionally have been the case. The model in the 1960s and 1970s was balanced pension fund management, both in the US and the UK. That model has been under serious threat because the old defined benefit schemes are not the power they were.
- The trend is very much towards individuals making decisions about their own savings. As a result, asset managers need to provide a wider range of products.

But have clients benefited? Ross Goobey reserves judgement:

Well, as Chou En Lai said of the French Revolution, 'it is too soon to say.' There are two business models emerging today in fund management. One is to be hyperbig to be able to invest in the wide product range and in the IT that is needed to be able to deliver these products to the client, online. The other model is the 'specialist' factory for investment products. They don't need to have all the products but concentrate on their strengths in creating a niche product. The distribution can be achieved in a different way – open architecture from some of the banks using other people's products to sell through their distribution network. We clearly fall into the second category and believe the 'specialist' model to be as valid as the first supermarket one. The advantages are that you can keep your costs under control and thus supply good value products to your clients.[14]

While clients may benefit indirectly via cost control and wider product choice, the consolidation in the sector is far from client-driven. As one CIO pointed out, the corporate activity in the industry is clearly 'consultant-driven'. However, long-term success in the field of investments comes not from just cost control and branding power, but crucially from the ability to deliver consistent top-quartile performance.

The major uncertainty triggered by large-scale mergers arises from staff turnover or the inability of firms to retain their human capital. Large investment firms, regardless of their talk of building teams and established investment processes, end up creating 'star' managers. This kind of branding obviously has its nemesis when the stars walk out, and set up their own hedge fund boutiques or niche investment management practices. Considering there can only be a limited supply of stars, the competition for experienced staff has resulted in significantly higher costs to the industry. As asset management is a very specialised business where a small team of experts can thrive independently and are capable of reaching out to clients either directly or through a network of consultants and distributors, it is not unusual for experienced and well-connected managers to set up their own firms.

The other factor driving up costs has been the changing organisational structures as a result of globalisation, increasing the number of offices around the world. Although half the managers in UK/Europe are centralised in one country, on average the number of offices per firm has risen. In 1998, for example, one-fifth of the firms covered by Mercer's research in Europe, operated out of five or more countries. As a consequence, the number of investment professionals employed also rose, with the bulk of the growth coming from the establishment of overseas offices. The number of fund managers, analysts and research staff virtually tripled during

1998, giving rise to greater complexity in managing staff, due to the geographically dispersed locations.[15] Managing the information that is generated from global operations is also one of the major challenges for fund managers.

The consolidation in the industry has helped in containing costs. According to a study by PricewaterhouseCoopers (PwC), average profit margins for fund management have remained constant at around the 30% level over the past five years, in spite of stable fee levels, rising assets under management and higher stock markets.[16] This suggests that managers have found it difficult to keep costs under control, the most corrosive being employment costs. Compensation level for fund managers has also been driven by the spectacular rise in executive pay within other financial services, particularly in investment banking and information technology. Fund managers on average still earn salaries well below that of their investment banking peers. This has been one of the factors behind the rise of hedge funds, where both client fees and employee compensation are directly linked to performance. Upgrading and implementation of the new network technologies has been a major driver of cost escalation within the asset management industry. Ironically, fund management has become more labour-intensive as a result. While outsourcing of various non-core activities has risen, the growth in product complexity, risk monitoring, marketing and client servicing, along with compliance and corporate governance issues, has increased costs, mostly as a result of higher employee-related costs.

The trend towards unbundling the various competencies within the asset management business along the value-added chain may have something to do with competition, thanks to the rising influence of US investment firms in the UK. When the Americans arrived on the scene in the mid-1980s, the prevalent practice in the UK pension fund management sector was the so-called balanced asset allocation approach, which meant that a single manager was often given the responsibility for the entire portfolio. Trustees and their consultants assessed performance with reference to the peer group benchmark. The high level of concentration in the industry as a result of such a practice began to unwind after the mid-1990s, by which time US managers had established their presence and a track record in the UK market, which was in any event poised for a change. It is estimated that the big five pension fund managers in the UK, Mercury Asset Management, SIM, Phillips & Drew, Gartmore and Morgan Grenfell, controlled approximately two-thirds of externally managed pension fund assets. New entrants had difficulty in making any headway into that fortress. Today these same firms dominate the sector. But apart from SIM, the other fund managers are owned by overseas firms. And, the big five's share of the market has declined significantly.

While the UK institutional fund management sector is characterised by a higher level of concentration, in the US there was a significantly high level of fragmentation. In the early 1980s, thanks to the Employment Retirement Income Security Act (ERISA) legislated in 1974, many pension plans restructured their fund management arrangements and outsourced to a host of specialist money managers. The specialist system spawned a multitude of competitors and over the past couple of decades it has been possible for individuals, groups and overseas fund managers such as the Bank of Ireland Asset Management, for example, to win large pension fund mandates in the US. New firms enter the industry regularly; in 1999 there were more than 30 start-ups. While many have sold out to larger organisations, there are still between 2,000 and 3,000 firms active in seeking investment management business, including at least 700 managers dedicated to the pursuit of pension mandates. In fact, there is a swing back in the US to reducing the number of suppliers while there is a rise in the use of specialist managers in the UK. According to Alastair Ross Goobey:

> Most reasonable-sized pension funds in the UK are now on a 'specific' or customised benchmark and as a result many more are looking at core–satellite structures. Interestingly enough, in the US, many of the larger pension funds are reducing the number of suppliers they have used in the past. There is a debate going on whether there is any advantage in having two different styles in the same area – for example, growth and value in US equities. Both sets of managers have too much business risk to ignore the other's universe entirely; so there are a lot of mutual shareholdings. [17]

The rise in the use of specialist and core–satellite structures in the management of pension funds, which was clearly established in the US, enabled US managers to win market share as well as consolidate their presence in the UK. Increased competition also forced UK managers to concentrate on their core competencies and niche markets, rather than be all things to all people. This rise in product and market specialisation is also an indication of a higher level of investor sophistication. Globalisation in the industry has also meant the rise in best practice standards within the investment industry, something which may have been ushered in via their consultants to a great extent. From asset allocation to performance measurement standards, there is a perceptible rise in standardisation within the industry.

Such was the need to examine investment techniques and take an audit of one's internal practices that in 1997 Gartmore initiated a major review of its growth philosophy and to benchmark its investment process against global best practice. This project was completed in 1998, resulting in the reinforcement of its investment philosophy, strengthening its buy and especially sell disciplines, as well as in the separation of research from portfolio construction and the creation of a pan-European research team. Based on external research and feedback from major UK consultants, Gartmore concluded that the changes resulted in one of the most innovative and robust investment practices in the UK and one which compares favourably to best practice in the US. In fact, one of the major factors driving the success of Bank of Ireland Asset Management in winning pension fund mandates in the US was its ability to establish its internal asset management processes in compliance with US best practice at an early stage of its development. However, it was less able to replicate that success in the UK:

Our success in the US reflects a combination of factors that were working in our favour when we made the original decision to 'export' our investment expertise. Fourteen years ago, when we took the first steps to establish in the US, we encountered a number of positive factors, including the fact that:

• The market was undergoing fundamental change, with public sector funds for the first time exploring the potential for international investing.

15

- The market was receptive to new ideas and new providers who had something unique to offer.

I think it is only recently that we have started to see a similar pattern emerge in the UK. Historically, the market has been a very traditional one, with the bulk of funds going into balanced portfolios managed by a small number of well-established UK managers. This is now changing – not just in terms of the movement from balanced to specialist funds but also in the way plan sponsors are actively seeking out good firms that have the potential to add value in other ways. What we are now seeing in the UK is a similar pattern of change to the one that developed in the US over 10 years ago. We now find ourselves benefiting from this structural change.[18]

While European asset managers have also established themselves in the UK market, they have been relatively self-absorbed in sorting out an array of issues at home, issues ranging from the introduction of the euro to changes in pension legislation (Table 1.7). The uncertainty surrounding the UK's adoption of the euro has left overseas investors unable to bet one way or the other as there is advantage to be had either way. In any event, pension fund assets as a percentage of gross domestic product (GDP) in various European countries is substantially lower than in Anglo-Saxon countries, suggesting that with greater restructuring in Europe there will be a significant rise in assets under current management. With a continuing cultural shift towards equity investments among European fund managers, overseas investment in the UK market is set to rise.

Fund management is one of the success stories in the UK; over £2,500 billion of assets are managed for domestic and overseas clients, including retail and institutional.[19] The strong tradition of international investment in the UK has helped it secure such an eminent position in the industry globally. UK plc has more invested in foreign securities than foreigners have in the UK. Between 1987 and 1997, for example, the Office for National Statistics counted more than three times as many British acquisitions abroad as foreign acquisitions in Britain.[20] Overseas acquisitions by UK firms reached a record level of £108.8 billion in 1999, almost double the amount in 1998, which had itself been a record.

Table 1.7 *The Pension Fund Industry in Europe*[a]

Country	Value of Pension Assets		Dependency Ratio (%)	Equities (%)[b]
	$bn	% of GDP		
Austria	28.0	12.0	22.1	20.0[c]
Belgium	29.7	11.0	26.2	42.8[d]
Denmark	186.0	100.0	22.4	20.5[d]
Finland	52.0	36.0	22.4	2.0[c]
France	82.0	5.0	24.6	0.6[c]
Germany	288.0	13.0	23.5	16.3[c]
Ireland	49.0	43.0	16.4	37.0[c]
Italy	275.0	22.0	25.0	1.4[c]
Netherlands	695.0	162.0	20.9	29.3[d]
Norway	43.3	24.0	23.1	22.0[d]
Portugal	12.0	10.0	22.1	6.0[c]
Spain	32.0	5.0	23.2	10.2[c]
Sweden	308.0	112.0	26.6	16.0[d]
Switzerland	318.0	111.0	22.4	11.0[d]
UK	1403.0	91.0	24.6	23.1[d]

[a] Source: William M. Mercer, *European Pension Fund Managers Guide 2001*
[b] Average pension fund asset allocation
[c] Non-Eurozone only
[d] Including Eurozone

The largest reported transaction was the acquisition of AirTouch Communications Inc. of the US by the Vodafone Group. Acquisitions in the UK by overseas companies also reached a record level of £60.1 billion, twice that in 1998. Once again, the major acquisition was of Orange plc by Mannesmann AG, which in turn was acquired in 2000 by Vodafone AirTouch for a reported £101.2 billion.[21]

The sheer size and diversity of the US economy traditionally discouraged US fund managers to invest overseas. Even with the Big Bang in 1986 and the liberalisation of the market in the UK, the concept of international diversification among US pension fund managers was relatively low. However, today corporate America has taken the lead in directing some 80% of its foreign direct investment (FDI) into areas such as Western Europe, Japan and Canada. US companies are the largest investors in Britain and are among the country's largest exporters. In fact, the UK currently accounts for 25% of all inward investment into Europe. This was being gradually reflected in portfolio allocations. A change in investment strategy by US fund managers, such as a rise in overseas investments, will have a significant impact in markets worldwide. With $18.5 trillion of assets under management, US investors wield enormous power on a global scale. While this wealth is technically the savings of individuals, it is the collective decision of a select group of institutional investors that has become critical to the future of our world.

Institutional investors are too powerful and their interests too vested. There are endless examples of the power exercised by fund managers in deciding the future of companies. The moral hazard problem is also reinforced when one institution is saved for fear of contagion and another is left to survive any way it can, simply because it does not pose such a threat to global economic stability. Thus, salvation is more inherent in size and ability to upset the status quo than in efficiency, integrity, transparency and other key features of an efficient market. Fund managers have a fiduciary duty to their clients and MNCs are accountable to their shareholders, although it is sometimes difficult to enforce these obligations. While the long-term interests of all these groups should be shared, conflicting short-term interests often blur that vision. More importantly, it is not always self-evident that the interests of all these groups are necessarily aligned in the best interest of the market. On the contrary, it can safely be argued that a high percentage of decisions reflect a need to manipulate the efficient market process.

THE IMPACT OF TECHNOLOGY

Harold Wilson's dream of a Britain that was going to be forged in the white heat of the technological revolution[22] is closer to reality today than ever before. The technology sector accounts for some 20% of the world's stock market value. Although recent US technology spending has declined sharply, most people recognise that the new technology has increasingly acquired 'public good' characteristics. Whether we like it or not, technology has altered the way we communicate. Not only has the cost of transmitting information around the globe declined sharply, globalisation could not have occurred without the development of powerful telecommunications technology. Likewise, it is computer technology which facilitates the instantaneous dissemination of information, thereby enhancing opportunities for investing on a global scale. Developments in programme trading, currency hedging, indexation, enhanced indexation, evolution of derivatives and their application across all asset classes, not to mention e-commerce would not be possible without technology. The technological convergence of telecommunication, broadcasting and the internet has applications and economies whose scope is already revolutionising the marketplace.

Today information technology (IT) affects all aspects of our lives. While the cost of acquiring networked technologies is falling, the fact remains that over the past few years investment in such technology by asset management companies has been high, almost one-quarter of overall expenditure for some firms. According to industry analysts, major fund managers are IT-enabled, but their use of IT as a means of client servicing and business development is at an early stage of the cycle. As most of the mergers are geared towards scale efficiencies in the distribution of investment products and services, it is in this area that the biggest changes are expected. The onus today is on the consumer in understanding the investment product he/she is buying, often at a front-end charge of 3–5% on top of the annual management fee. The steady rise in retail investing, combined with the power of technology, will empower the individual consumer to determine the product as much as its cost structure. Never before in the history of mankind did such a confluence of factors as diverse as technology, demographics and legislation come together in shaping the future quality of life of individuals on a global basis.

For Morgan Stanley Capital International (MSCI), a leading provider of global indexes and benchmark-related products and services, among the new products being developed is a 'life-style index' for the retail investor in the US. Such services would be inconceivable without the widespread use of computer technology. The regulatory framework in the US has been supportive of individuals' planning their financial future. While the big issue relating to the future of pensions provision is being debated in Europe, a combination of developments in demographics, globalisation and technology implies that long-term future trends in Europe may eventually follow developments in the US. Although in the short term there will be considerable resistance to implementing changes that may appear to threaten the financial security of some sectors of the population.

Concerns about costs and other burdens arising from the Pensions Act 1995 requirements already influence the trend towards defined contribution (DC) pension plans in the UK. Typically, sponsors set up such plans for new employees where the investment vehicles are usually pooled or mutual funds. Within DC plans, the 'lifestyle' approach has found favour with plan members as well as trustees. This approach involves investment in an equity-oriented growth fund during the early stages of a member's working lifetime and automatic switching into less volatile bond and cash funds as the member approaches retirement. With the gradual rise in stakeholder pensions and self-employment, individuals will end up taking greater control and responsibility in managing their financial affairs. Once again the impact of technology in this area of individual financial planning will be profound.

One does not have to be a new economy fanatic to acknowledge that technology is helping to reduce costs, raise productivity and increase competition. After all, there is no such thing as new economy, only new technology. While the institutional fund management sector may have been slow to embrace technology, the impact of IT is not confined to any one industry. Depending on the individual user's ability to deploy the new technology, it either threatens or promises to benefit all producers and distributors of goods and services with lower prices and new methods of selling and distribution. In the emerging digital economy, companies and individuals have to adapt or risk being overwhelmed by competition. Luckily, there is a learning process and often it takes years to get to use a new technology productively, particularly network technologies. The new technology's multivariable access and dissemination structure only poses a threat to those who cannot access it and so cannot benefit from it.

In their collaborative work, *Capital Market Revolution*, Patrick Young and Thomas Theys are of the opinion that 'the old hegemony of existing institutional investors, exchanges, and brokers is doomed to collapse under the "New Reality." Just as the clerics lost power after Gutenburg, the information revolution undermines the power of established financial institutions.'[23] It is true that the demise of the London International Financial Futures and Options Exchange's (LIFFE) domination of the Bunds (German bonds) market was due to the inability of its members in agreeing to embrace the new technology ahead of the competition. LIFFE's willingness to change just about every facet of its organisation and operation after the event illustrates that they came to their senses a bit late in the day. The driving force behind that change was the inroads made into the London market's volumes by the electronic Deutsche Terminbörse (DTB) operating out of Frankfurt, which merged with the Swiss Options and Financial Futures Exchange (SOFFEX) to create the European Exchange (EUREX). It is in the area of securities trading, settlement and custody that technology has had the most impact in transforming the way in which fund managers behave.

Although the internet revolution is in its infancy, most people recognise its potential for lasting change. Worldwide computer power has been growing at the rate of 35% a year over the last decade. A third of households in countries belonging to the OECD (Organisation for Economic Cooperation and Development) have a personal computer. The share of IT in the US economy doubled from 4.2% in 1977 to 8.2% in 1998. While there is a lag between innovation and its implementation in generating growth, as was the case with the industrial usage of electricity (when productivity soared to 3.8% between 1917 and 1927), there is data to suggest that average annual productivity growth in the US has risen to about 2.5% since mid-1995; this is from 1.5% in the early 1990s and from an average of 1.2% between 1970 and 1990. More recent data suggests that average productivity growth in 1999 and 2000 in the US was 2.6%. Assuming that some of that growth was indeed cyclical and in light of the lower spending on IT, America's long-term rate of productivity growth is now estimated at 2%,[24] which is still a marked improvement on the rate of growth achieved in the previous two decades.

The US spends significantly more on technology as a proportion of their national wealth than all European countries, with the exception of Sweden, and double that of some of the larger European markets such as Germany and France. While European companies have been slow to take advantage of the benefits of technology, consumers will continue to play a crucial role in the rapid adoption of technology in

Table 1.8 *Internet usage across the developed world*[a]

Country	Percentage of population
US	37
Canada	36
Scandinavia	33
Australia	31
UK	15
Germany	10
Japan	10
France	8

[a] Source: Schroders, June 2000

Europe (Table 1.8). Deregulation of the telecommunications sector in Europe has helped in driving prices lower and increasing access to the internet. As the battle moves from personal computers to mobile telephony and the internet, Europe is well placed to challenge the traditional dominance of the US in the technology sector.[25] However, despite this growth potential, across Europe few companies have made all the changes necessary to meet the demands of transacting business on the internet. According to research conducted by Schroder's technology team, fewer than 31% of small and medium-sized European companies rate themselves web-enabled and a further 30% claim not to be using the internet as effectively as they should within their organisations. However, the world's largest and most successful companies have employed their financial strength in becoming web-enabled. Also, the traditional distinctions between new and old economy are gradually disappearing.

The gap that the availability or otherwise of access to such rapidly evolving technology can create globally is going to have a far more profound effect on our lives than we are able to envision today. Technological change and financial liberalisation result in a disproportionately fast increase in the number of households at the extremely rich end, without shrinking the distribution at the poor end.[26]

By 1993 an American on the average income of the poorest 10% of the population was better off than two-thirds of the world's people.[27] Thus, the anticipated trickle-down effect of free market economics has not been seen to be working. Considering the US has transformed itself into the most technologically advanced economy of the world as well as its most competitive, credit is due to its government and its policies. But even in the world's richest and most efficient economy, the gap between the poor and the rich has widened over the last couple of decades.

According to one study by William R. Cline at the Institute for International Economics, technological change was estimated to be five times more potent in widening inequality in America between 1973 and 1993 than, for example, global trade, including FDI. Trade accounted for only 6% of the unequalising forces. Other studies confirm that globalisation, trade and economic integration, etc., exerted a far milder influence on wage inequality than technology.[28] Thus, a case can be made that the gains of free market for goods and capital tend to be concentrated in the top levels of income distributions. One of the reasons could be that this group has greater control over issues such as pricing, access to capital and technology. In a truly efficient market system, such anomalies cannot exist for any long period of time. However, even in the US, they have persisted. One of the striking conclusions of William Cline's study was the high 'equalising' impact of education and training, including retraining, when individuals are forced to change jobs as a result of economic growth. Such public investment in increasing the stock of skilled labour has not yet been endorsed in any meaningful way.

Although the contribution of the new technology towards generating wealth in the US has been significant, its real contribution to the global economy will only increase as more and more of the world's people have access to it as much as to the market process. Governments and other publicly funded bodies have an important role in ensuring a more equitable access to the benefits of free markets and technological innovation. Compared with a decade ago, governments around the world are now receiving higher tax revenues as a percentage of GDP, so they do have money for public investment in education, technology and training. Providing access to better education would be the simplest way of starting to address global disparities. A recent OECD report concluded that the 29 OECD countries were moving towards a 'knowledge-based economy' in which the production, diffusion and use of information have become the key components of corporate competitiveness and economic performance.

More than 60% of the jobs created in the EU during the past five years were either in high-skilled, non-manual occupations or in the high-technology sector. Between 1995 and 2000, 1.5 million high-tech jobs were created and a further 5.5 million in high education sectors, representing a significant growth in professionals, technicians, managers and senior officials. These new jobs were predominantly in healthcare, education and social work, general business and computer and related services.[29] The demand for computer scientists, economists, statisticians and financial engineers is high. This level of activity cannot be sustained without higher investment in schools, colleges, hospitals and other basic infrastructure such as transport and communication technologies. But what of those countries in the least developed parts of the world, where the market process is distorted by factors that impede economic growth, such as gross fiscal mismanagement by governments, corruption, lack of access to education, health or housing by the poor? While the market dynamics has been effective in stopping private sector companies from running the world for profit, it has not been that successful in curbing public sector mismanagement or corruption.

During the transitional period, the introduction of new technologies can have a negative effect on employment levels, unless human resource development is kept abreast of the process of technological change. Even in Japan, the world's second largest economy, restructuring the corporate sector has been a major challenge to the country's culture of lifetime employment, and thus difficult politically as it involves a significantly higher level of unemployment. The current level of unemployment in Japan has overtaken unemployment in the US at 5.0% of GDP; it is the highest level in Japan since 1953. This has also been the curse of liberalisation in countries such as Russia, China and India, where adequate social security measures do not exist. Developing countries face the challenge of keeping pace with global technological trends while addressing the problems of rising unemployment, retraining the workforce and providing support while this transition takes place. The onus is on governments to address such issues.

As governments struggle to reduce their fiscal deficits, the per capita income growth in many developing economies has steadily declined over the past decade as individuals strive to cope with the new economic disorder. According to studies conducted by Yuri Dikhanov and Michael Ward of the World Bank, world income distribution became more unequal during 1988–93, the period under observation. The income of the poorest decile declined by 27.3%, while that of the richest decile increased by 8.3%.[30] As globalisation impacts more on the trade of goods and services and influences growth and development prospects around the world, the role of free trade and free markets in the global allocation of capital is set to rise. However, with growing evidence that global inequality is on the rise, what stake do developing countries have in adhering to free market principles, particularly when the beneficiaries of such a process, namely the US and Europe, have become more inward-looking by seeking to protect their gains via trade pacts and other such measures that do not support free market policies? Greater trade openness within the US and Europe would benefit the poorer nations of the world.

In terms of geography or the size of their population, the developing countries are huge, but in economic terms they remain small. The exports of all the world's poor and middle-income countries – including giants such as China, India, Brazil and Mexico, big oil exporters such as Saudi Arabia, and large-scale manufacturers such as South Korea, Taiwan and Malaysia – represent about 5% of global output. This is equivalent to the GDP of Britain. Thus, a concerted export drive by those parts of the developing world not already engaged in the effort would put no strain on the global trading system.[31] While world trade is dominated by the developed world, when one looks at economic growth the picture is startlingly different. Some of the fastest-growing economies of the world during 1990–98 were also efficient exporters (Table 1.9).

However, the stock markets in these countries have not necessarily rewarded their investors accordingly. The market infrastructure was simply not in place in some of these countries to reflect the productivity of the economy. Also, the rate of economic growth has not

Table 1.9 *The fastest-growing economies of the world: percentage average annual increase in real GDP for 1990-98[a]*

Country	1990-98
China	11.2
Singapore	8.5
Vietnam	8.4
Sudan	8.0
Chile	7.9
Ireland	7.7
Lebanon	7.7
Malaysia	7.4
Uganda	7.3
Lesotho	7.2

[a] Source: The Economist

always coincided with the rate of technological investments made in these countries. With the exception of Singapore, Ireland and Malaysia, technology has not really played a large part in that success, although trade has made a difference.

The main consequence of a global environment is that the ability to keep up with international patterns of technological change has become more important to the survival of industrial firms than it was in more protected economies. This makes it difficult for latecomers to follow successfully the path of export orientation because access to 'high technology' has become an important factor in determining competitiveness. Product life cycles are becoming shorter as the pace of global technological change quickens. Production techniques are also restructuring the international division of labour and replacing raw materials by man-made substitutes. In a global market evolving a new concept of industrial competitiveness, developing countries continually have to respond to these challenges. They realise that their traditional advantages, with respect to natural resources and cheap labour, are no longer the key ingredients for achieving international competitiveness.

It has taken a prolonged crisis in a developed economy such as Japan's for management to examine something as basic as return on investment. It is only recently that the ice began to thaw in corporate Japan. Renault's acquisition of a 36.8% stake in Nissan in 1999 is just one example of a high-profile acquisition of Japanese assets by overseas investors. Renault has the right to increase its stake in Nissan to 44%, and Nissan also has the right to buy Renault shares, but both parties are content with their strategic alliance at the moment. Nissan's loss of ¥684 billion ($6.1 billion) during the financial year ending March 2000 was turned into a profit of ¥331 billion the following year. The successful alliance between Nissan and Renault may have paved the way for other such alliances in the painful restructuring that Japan has to undergo. NEC, the electronics giant, is now talking about shareholder value, free cash flow and return on equity. Japan's financial markets have only recently become nearly as free of regulation as the markets of New York and London. Even Europe's largest companies started paying attention to shareholder value and adopting international governance standards as they aspired to extend their businesses globally.

Restructuring in the US during the early 1990s involved a high level of investment in technology, which contributed to their recent productivity growth. The US has also been more open to inward foreign investment. It was the presence of the Japanese, for example, that enhanced productivity in the automobile sector in the US. By increasing labour mobility and equipping workers for change, American companies benefited from restructuring. Those countries that achieved the highest gains for their workers are those that decided early on in the cycle of growth to take advantage of international opportunities and to rely more on market forces rather than on their governments for their resource allocation. But in those countries where the infrastructure for such action was severely limited, companies suffered great disadvantages as governments played a significant role. However, the expected benefits may also be harder to reap in a fiercely competitive global marketplace.

THE CHANGING PROFILE OF FUND MANAGEMENT

The three main pillars or the core competencies of the fund management industry can be broadly classified as:

- Analysis and research
- Trading, settlement and custody
- Distribution and servicing

These three areas require completely different sets of skill, which often do not thrive together. More importantly, the costs involved in investing in technology to keep abreast of developments can be prohibitive, particularly for medium to small firms. As a result, outsourcing has become a powerful strategic weapon in the highly competitive world of finance. The investment management industry has seen outsourcing of custody, cash management, unit holder registration, investment administration and various other functions. In 1997 some 50% of fund managers used independent custodians, by 1999 this figure had risen to 71%. Outsourced activities now account for 10% of managers' costs.[32] Large firms, however, have a different set of challenges to manage vis-à-vis the use of technology.

The major contribution of technology to the asset management industry has been in enabling management to focus on their core competency while outsourcing other aspects of their business. As trading, settlement and custody along with sales and distribution are volume-driven and benefit from economies of scale, these functions are set to benefit the most from IT. Even the research and analytical function within fund management, which is driven by timely and superior analysis of a wide range of information, has gained from the new technology. 'The information-aggregation function of markets is almost certainly better at the dawn of the 21 century than in prior times.'[33] In *Free to Choose*, published in 1980, Milton Friedman argued that advances in technology and organised market have increased the speed with which information is reflected in prices.[34]

The increasing use of derivatives today has eclipsed trading volumes in underlying assets, thereby enabling securities markets in aggregating information regarding its participants. According to research conducted by Greenwich Associates, the percentage of US investors who value equity derivatives as a hedging tool jumped from 60% in 2000 to 75% in 2001. This is a key indicator of how market volatility has made equity derivatives more attractive to investors. Investors used equity derivatives for buying put protection (55%) and synthetic shorts (46%). Those using equity derivatives for extracting cash rose from 18% in 2000 to 26% in 2001. Derivatives users are interested in investing as well, in particular in covered call writing. The percentage of those investing in equity derivatives for that reason rose from 33% in 2000 to 40% in 2001. Derivatives have become 'an attractive surrogate' for straight equity investing because it requires less capital and provides more leverage for investors.[35]

Historically, good investment advice was essentially 'insider information' that enabled its recipient to better manipulate the market. Even today a negative report by an analyst on a company's prospective earnings has an impact on its share price. However, investment outperformance today is not driven by insider information (there are punitive laws against that), although personal contact and 'relationship management' continue to be important. The wide use of computers and global communication technology has translated over the years to an increased use of quantitative techniques in the management of assets. The increasingly abstract nature of investing, the rise in the use of derivatives, futures, options, insurance contracts, indexation, market-neutral or simple programme trading strategies are all part of this development. While the application of derivative instruments within asset management has been limited in the past, such an approach in the management of risk is set to change.

One of the factors influencing the growth of the credit derivatives market, for example, is the blurring between the role of commercial and investment banks. The convergence of banks and insurance companies has also spurred the creation of exotic investment products in the alternative risk market. Usually highly rated companies raise working capital by selling commercial paper, and as an insurance policy, they secure back-up credit lines from banks. Thus, the crucial weapon in the commercial bank's arsenal is their ability to offer huge lines of credit. These promises of credit operate essentially as options, similar to the ones traded in the derivatives market. Given the shortage of suppliers, commercial banks have been able to charge more for such lines of credit.

However, in their effort to break into investment banking, many commercial banks are promising cheap credit to their clients provided they get the bulk of the corporate business. For Philip Purcell, chairman and chief executive of Morgan Stanley, what we are seeing is 'a credit derivatives market developing, so the credit risk gets put in the right hands.' He sees the day when all credit promises trade at market prices and investors, such as pension funds without tax bills to pay, hold most of these loans. 'You can make a very strong argument that the interest-income part of the loan is best off in the hands of a non-tax-paying entity so the return goes straight to the beneficiaries.'[36] As pension funds and other institutional investors are the recipients of such products, their influence on shaping this market is considerable.

The rise of hedge funds or absolute return strategies in fund management is also transforming the industry. During 2000 the board of the California Public Employees' Retirement Scheme (CalPERS), the largest pension pool in the US, committed $1 billion to hedge funds, signalling a major shift in the institutional market's understanding of the process and its applications in overall performance. For Paul Platkin of General Motors Asset Management, 'We all grew up as believers of the efficient market, so it was a significant bridge to cross for us, to believe in these absolute return strategies that are all about alpha and get their returns from exploiting market inefficiencies.'[37] It is no coincidence that the rise of absolute return strategies caught the imagination of both buyers and sellers at the end of a long bull market in equities. Many of these strategies use a multi-asset, multi-manager approach to asset allocation, thereby enabling the investor to have better diversification and lower risk.

Investment firms, including hedge funds, are essentially a network of individuals who excel at asset allocation, sector research, stock selection; thereby adding 'alpha' to an investment portfolio. This small, highly interactive group of fund managers can prosper by distributing their products through branded channels at low cost, thereby altering the existing profile of investment products. Although research by blue-chip, investment firms is available on the internet, most active fund managers still conduct their own research and evolve a house style, which is essentially a way of branding their investment product. Thus, we have various manager styles – value, growth, thematic, large cap, small cap, sector-based funds, hedge funds, venture capital. Often there is blurring at the margins, when value and growth within large-cap and small-cap sectors become increasingly difficult to distinguish. What investors are striving to exploit are market inefficiencies. Thus, within the hedge fund sector there are several styles and strategies ranging from convertible arbitrage to distressed securities. In reality there are as many styles as hedge fund products. However, if hedge funds wish to attract institutional clients, they too will need to demonstrate greater adherence to their individual investment process. Again, it boils down to a question of identifying core competency and finding a niche in the market for selling that skill.

The explosion of information that needs to be analysed by any serious investor cannot be overemphasised. A staggering amount of information – macroeconomic, sector and stock-specific – has to be fed into today's investment models. The importance of companies such as I/B/E/S, which collates the consensus forecasts of brokers' research on individual companies or the proliferation of credit rating agencies worldwide, implies that fund managers increasingly need to keep abreast of market developments. They also need to devise optimisation models that will process this new information faster but also in the very individual way they want it to be analysed. It is how information is interpreted and acted upon that will distinguish the survivors from the dinosaurs. In spite of disasters, such as Long-Term Capital Management, institutional investors are increasingly deploying technologically driven solutions to their investment processes. Although the skill factor is heavily emphasised, there is virtually no major manager that does not use a significantly high level of quantitative analysis of fundamental data in its investment research process today.

There is considerable opportunity for firms to assist with application integration within fund management companies which have a series of functions – from research, stock selection, order management, trade support, settlement, trade reconciliation and cash management. Some of the systems that fulfil these functions are off-the-shelf and others are home-grown. There is scope for developing a seamless method of data exchange within the firm. Software vendors can add a lot of value by providing such integrated systems.

And this applies to all the activities down the value-added chain – fundamental research, asset allocation, risk analysis and implementation, portfolio construction, trading, performance measurement and attribution, accounting, settlement and processing. In fact, the client servicing function largely consists of ensuring these processes work smoothly for the institutional investor.

Thus, outsourcing is not a magic bullet. Large investment firms can better manage their resources by buying software solutions or having software developed by speciality firms. The other option is consortium-type arrangements that mimic the cost savings one gets through mergers without merging. The consortium comprising the sponsors of the Global Straight Through Processing Association, for example, has 85 members headquartered in 12 countries with the express objective of reducing the high rates of failure in cross-border securities processing. While the revolution in the distribution of investment services is still in its infancy, major fund management houses are already outsourcing various aspects of their back-office functions.

With the greater use of derivatives and quantitatively driven investment styles, the edifice of the asset management industry is under greater pressure, as the current fee structure will come under greater scrutiny, particularly in the retail sector. Investors increasingly link fees to performance. In the institutional sector there is little evidence of direct competition on the basis of fees alone, although there is scope for higher competition from passive managers. International comparisons tend to rate the UK reasonably on the prices charged by fund managers. According to Frank Russell Company, for a £100 million mandate in equities and a similar-sized mandate in fixed interest, the median charges for equities are 40 basis points per annum in the UK compared to 44 in Australia, 42 in the US and 24 in Canada. In the fixed-interest sector, the median fee in the US at 26 basis points per annum is the highest, followed by 19 in Australia and 18 in both the UK and Canada.[38]

According to the Myners Report, there are no grounds for major competition concerns in the fund management market, for the following reasons:[39]

- The level of concentration which existed when balanced management was the norm, has begun to break down.

- Fees for fund management in the UK do not appear to be especially high relative to those in other countries.
- Switching between firms is relatively simple and frequent.
- New firms have been successfully able to enter the market in recent years.

It is true that the fund management market in the UK has come a long way since the mid-1990s, but it is still in the critical stage of what can be called 'the chewing the cud' stage of restructuring. The success of firms such as Deutsche, Fidelity, Capital International, First Quadrant and JP Morgan suggests that the nature of the UK asset management market is changing. The rise of private equity/ venture capital managers along with hedge fund managers suggests that the market concentration is giving way to greater choice of management styles as well as asset classes. But the experience of smaller companies, apart from hedge funds, generally suggests that the market for innovation and new products is still in its infancy.

Advances in technology have altered completely the way in which asset managers deliver their products to clients. Web-based distribution has reduced costs and improved service via superior knowledge of the customer. Research is delivered to the fund manager as well as to their clients via email or posted on relevant websites. In spite of its tendency to 'commoditise' the investment product, the new technology favours customisation. The net beneficiary of this technological revolution is the private client or the individual investor, hitherto the poor cousins of institutional investors in terms of service such as research, real-time data and prices. Today pools of liquidity in cyberspace allow shares to be traded outside the restrictions imposed by traditional markets.

Firms such as Barclays Global Investors have launched iShares or exchange-traded funds worldwide, for both institutional and individual investors. Fund supermarkets today represent the greatest advance in innovative ways in which individuals can access a wide range of investment groups and their products. Cofunds was set up by four of the UK's leading unit trust management groups – Gartmore, Jupiter, M&G and Threadneedle – with each owning 25% of the new entity. Fidelity's Funds Network is a similar concept except that it is owned by Fidelity. Both offer access to all of the main fund managers, except that Cofunds does not offer Fidelity funds and Fidelity's Funds Network does not offer those of the four owners of Cofunds. The unit trust sector in the UK has registered an average growth rate of over 40% per annum since 1995. The new electronic bond trading platforms are expected to transform fixed-income trading over the next few years by increasing efficiency via lower costs and greater transparency. Creation of new indexes, like the tech-MARK 100, provides investment opportunities for the retail player. Venture capitalists are also able to directly access capital from the private investor. With lower costs and a better range of products available to the retail investor across Europe, including the UK, the retail sector has been one of the major beneficiaries of the technological revolution.

The availability of timely information implies that the opportunity for individual enterprise is huge. But the proliferation of investment products is something that individual investors may simply not have the time, the inclination or the ability to master. Considering that the professionals have failed to 'beat the market' or to foster private enterprise, what evidence is there to suggest that the individual investor or the sole trader will be more able to combine all these objectives and achieve a superior asset allocation strategy? Individual investors may lack the skill of professionals, but they are very clear in terms of their objective; most prefer absolute returns to relative ones. Thus, there will be a greater focus on performance. In a global context, branded distributors are more likely to offer investment products from diverse 'unbranded sources' with a consistently superior performance record. How these distribution structures will evolve also depends on the regulatory framework that governments are able to put in place to monitor these developments and provide investors with a basic level of protection. Keeping a fine balance between investor choice and market competition, and offering basic investor protection will be the sort of challenge that regulators have to face.

Estimates suggested that over a quarter of all retail trades in 1998 in the US were conducted online. This figure rose sharply over the following year and appears to have fallen back to about one-third of all trades today. In the UK, online investing rose from barely 1% of deals in 1999 to 21% a year later and accounts for one-quarter of all trades currently, down from 29% in first quarter 2001. The past two years have been extremely testing times for most equity investors; those who invested in the NASDAQ market and in the other newer exchanges in Europe, for example the Neuer Markt, have suffered extraordinary losses. However, most long-term equity investors have also made substantial capital gains over the past decade. Those who managed to switch to bonds and cash investments before the market peaked in March 2000 would have done very well, although they would indeed be very difficult to find. While trading frequency may have declined among private investors, the cult of equity investing remains strong. There is little evidence to suggest they have been diversifying their investments into gilts, bonds or even foreign shares.[40]

As the internet empowers individuals to manage their assets online and governments withdraw gradually from providing reliable social security and pensions, are we en route to a more equitable society or are we laying the foundations for a society driven by greed and fear? Will the new technology shape a new meritocracy backed by private capital investment and directed by innovative individuals or lead to further divisions between the haves and the have-nots? Research suggests that the gap will widen further unless urgent action is taken by individuals in influencing governments to legislate change. There is a lot of talk about access and opportunity for all. But in reality the right to work and receive a fair wage for one's work, food, shelter and healthcare are not considered to be basic human rights at all. The UN's International Covenant on Civil and Political Rights lists rights such as the right to vote, the right not to be tortured, the right to free speech and these rights find wide support in real laws and both national and international level. However, the International Covenant on Economic, Social and Cultural Rights, including rights such as the right to health, food, employment and cultural identity, are systematically violated all over the world, although the extent of such violations vary considerably.

Even *The Economist* is of the opinion that 'governments may intentionally torture their citizens; they do not usually intentionally inflict on them poverty and ill health. The moral imperative to stop poverty or disease is therefore not as convincing as the moral imperative to stop torture.'[41] The major shortcoming of market economics is the assumption that all individuals are equally equipped to participate in the market process. That is simply not true. To be poor all one's life and have no meaningful way of redressing that condition due to lack of education and health facilities, for example, is as good as being marginalised by one's government. However, at the same time, simply providing low-grade primary education is not only a waste of revenue but is of little use to the supposed beneficiary of that wealth redistribution.

Admittedly, it is a lot cheaper to guarantee civil and political rights and enormously more expensive for governments to guarantee economic and social rights. These rights are therefore considered to be undefinable and hence undeliverable. Even in the most developed economies, such rights are not considered inalienable. America has not yet ratified the International Covenant on Economic, Social and Cultural Rights, as US citizens would then sue their government for the enforcement of such rights. The hope is that as developed countries start demanding such rights for others in less developed countries around the world, they might realise that such social activism begins at home.

There is a long way to go before we get there. Institutional investors are still coping with basic corporate governance issues, which are on the rise; from the environment to child labour, companies are being called to account by their shareholders, particularly minority shareholders. Socially responsible investment (SRI) is now a requirement of UK occupational pension funds; their boards of trustees are expected to indicate their SRI policy in their statement of investment principles (SIP). The major obstacle to such policy-making is that governments, companies and other organisations have no means of measuring variables such as the cost to the environment, health and the full range of human development issues.

The fact that we do not know how to measure something usually means that we are unable to create an efficient market for it. As markets are best indicators of the value of an asset, if one cannot trade it then the market process is really not very useful in that area of human activity. Thus, we pay millions to investment bankers but a pittance to teachers, nurses and social workers, among others, because no effort has been made by governments, statisticians, economists or analysts to value their input in market terms and reward individuals accordingly. Our unwillingness to do so has led to considerable devaluation of individuals who devote them-selves to these enterprises that remain essential to delivering what we refer to as public services. In such a social system it would be rational to expect that the best brains in the country would auto-matically gravitate away from such services, particularly when society and media revere a celebrity culture dominated by rich individuals.

EFFICIENT MARKET THEORY: MYTH OR REALITY?

The efficient market hypothesis (EMH) has far-reaching implications for the future of markets as it is premised on the assumption that the optimal creation of wealth is based on the efficient allocation of capital. If the market can be relied upon to mirror economic signals, then it can also transmit useful signals to both suppliers and users of capital; the suppliers build up their investment portfolios and the users establish criteria for the disposal of funds. Efficient markets are more likely to deliver effective investment decisions, thereby enabling capital to flow towards strategies that can deliver superior risk-adjusted returns.

Markets came into existence to enable individuals or companies to raise capital for their ventures. Equity markets are for risk-takers; the pricing mechanism incorporates the risk premium demanded by investors. While we analyse in some detail various theoretical aspects of the EMH in Chapter 2, in reality at any moment the price of a company's share indicates the point of equilibrium between demand and supply, not necessarily a fair or right price. In fact, there is no such thing. It can safely be said that the market is perpetually moving towards a fair price, reflecting the uncertainty surrounding the demand curves of other investors. In the long term, the market tends to reward a company's profitability and productivity profile, thereby taking into account the company's ability to generate cash flow, economic value added, etc.; but in the short term, aberrations do occur, sometimes over long periods.

On 5 December 1996 Alan Greenspan, chairman of the Federal Reserve Bank, used the term 'irrational exuberance' to described the behaviour of the US stock market. But by 1998, as any open-minded rational thinker would, he was willing to consider the prospect of a 'new paradigm', acknowledging that the traditional methods of monetary policy decision-making perhaps needed to be re-examined in the context of such unprecedented global circumstances. It was not until March 2000 that the market's self-adjusting mechanism kicked in. And two years later it is still not clear whether the market is 'fairly' valued as companies in various sectors continue to issue profit warnings. Thus, manias, panics, bubbles and crashes are all part of the market process. With the increased volatility in capital markets, there is greater concern not only about the nature of global capitalism, but also of the efficacy of markets in determining an optimal asset allocation strategy. Even some of its major beneficiaries, such as George Soros, have expressed grave doubts about capitalism and its impact on society.[42]

The decline in the market valuations of small-cap companies on a global basis has raised serious questions about the market and its role in fostering enterprise and innovation. While investing in private equity/venture capital funds was all the rage a few years ago, the bursting of the TMT (technology, media and telecommunications) bubble helped in bringing down valuations in the sector of the economy where the highest level of investments were being directed. Thus, many of the private equity funds launched since 1998 are now struggling with major losses on their original investments. Inevitably, the banking sector got caught up in this bubble, and once again Mr Greenspan had warned of such a danger growing within the banking sector. The lesson to be learnt from the bursting of this latest asset bubble is that no sector or asset class can be truly immune from such formidable market forces. Markets have a tendency to overreact to events as human beings do. So in the aftermath of severe market corrections, there are usually plenty of opportunities to get back into these relatively unfashionable investments for those who have the available funds and the conviction of their analysis.

While the concept of private equity investing remains critical to the economic prospect of any country and plays a vital role in nurturing enterprise, the fate of small companies once they are listed in the market is equally important. The problems in the smaller companies sector have prompted reaction from most analysts who are concerned about the functioning of the capital market. One of the major reasons for going public by any company is the ability to raise capital, in the form of equity or debt, at competitive rates. Thus, market capitalisation matters as far as corporate borrowing is concerned from banks and other financial institutions, which is backed by collateral. Loan conditions (such as interest rates and the size and duration of loans) depend on the net worth of companies. With asset price declines and market uncertainty, credit availability diminishes while the real cost of borrowing rises.

Market conditions have also favoured investments in private equity in the large-cap sector, leaving companies in the small to medium range with a competitive disadvantage in raising capital for their investments. The market is by no means responsible for nurturing companies from their conception as an idea to their virtual death or takeover. But when the market tends to reward companies with a larger capitalisation as opposed to those with a smaller capitalisation, there has been a rush to merge and enlarge one's capitalisation to exploit the market process. In industries such as telecommunications, oil, finance and pharmaceuticals, globalisation has accelerated this consolidation as companies increasingly compete on a worldwide basis. To maximise their global potential, companies in these sectors have found it desirable to merge and redefine themselves as global players. This increasingly appears to be the trend in most industrial sectors, be they in manufacturing or the services sector.

However, purely from an investment perspective, as Vodafone grew from a relatively small company to the second largest company in the FTSE All Share index, its return on equity (ROE) and overall profitability ratios declined. Thus, its growth was not achieved via genuine value addition in its internal utilisation of capital, but through external acquisitions via its ability, or more accurately the ability of its brokers, to place its shares with investors and its bankers' willingness to finance such deals. The recent acquisition of BT's interests in the US by the Vodafone group has further deteriorated its ROE profile. If market capitalisation were linked to a company's productivity ratios such as ROE or return on capital employed (ROCE), reflecting managers' ability to add value per unit of capital invested, then the value of Vodafone shares would have declined significantly, not risen. The rate of share price rise for Vodafone declined a few years ago, but due to its active M&A activity, the group's market capitalisation soared. In fact, there is little evidence of any consistent relationship between corporate profit and its market value.

As the Vodafone group's weighting in the FTSE 100 and All Share indexes rose, indexed managers who passively replicate these indexes invested in the stock, regardless of its high valuation. The active managers, already under pressure due to poor performance, found it more prudent to track the index than to back their judgement, particularly when market distortions have been known to extend for years, during which fund managers could lose their mandates on account of poor performance alone. Portfolio managers are not rewarded by their clients or their employers for their ability to judge the intrinsic or fair value of stocks over a long-term investment horizon. If they attempt to do so, they usually lose their fund management mandates and eventually their job. At the same time, active managers bear the crucial responsibility in maintaining market efficiency.

While the asset management industry is under severe threat of commoditisation, as is evident from the rise in indexed managers, the deeper reason for superior financial analysis is competitiveness. The big question is, What is the total cost of the lack of independent analysis? You can measure return, but after the event it is very difficult to measure the risk advice. Poor analysis impacts not just investment returns but also corporate performance and eventually the nature of the society that we create. How exactly is that to be measured or how do you measure the consequences of investment decisions not taken, as we are unable to measure advice based on a probabilistic basis? It is much easier to measure the return on your portfolio and compare it to the index return or that of its peer group.

Thus, while the notion of a market-driven economy is a valuable one, it is also clear that market distortions exist and sometimes persist for long periods of time, even among the developed markets in the world. Consider the Japanese market, not to mention emerging markets, where the notion of an efficient market, at least as far as domestic stock markets are concerned, simply does not exist. The Japanese market experienced an asset bubble lasting for over five years since 1985, and the market has not been able to recover since its peak in 1990 simply because the investment decision-making process as dictated by the market can often be a complex one. Japan is a good example of what an inefficient market can deliver. In order to bring about fundamental change, the entire structure of industry and society needs changing. That process is painful and requires building a broad consensus that accepts the changes involved; change is least disruptive when it comes from within.

The market does not protect the investor, regardless of the fact that price is largely determined by the marginal investor. The marginal first-time, long-term investor in the Japanese market in the late 1980s and early in 1990 would have been crucified as a result of that miscalculation. While each investor bears the responsibility of shaping the nature of the market, those investors with the largest funds under management are more likely to have a deeper market impact. 'Most investors also seem to view the stock market as a force of nature unto itself. They do not fully realize that they themselves, as a group, determine the level of the market. And they underestimate how similar to their own thinking is that of other investors.'[43]

This instinct to herd together is a survival skill and has been witnessed more among sophisticated players such as institutional investors, who own more of the bulk of assets managed on a global scale. The way in which these assets are invested matter not only because they represent the savings of millions of ordinary people, but also because the investment decisions taken by these institutions have long-term implications on the economic welfare of all concerned. Not only do these institutions play a pivotal role in the efficient capital allocation in the economy, which in turn has a profound impact on productivity and growth, but they also determine collectively the nature of the market they operate in. According to Robert Shiller:

> How we value the stock market now and in the future influences major economic and social policy decisions that affect not only investors but also society at large, even the world. If we exaggerate the present and future value of the stock market, than as a society we may invest too much in business start-ups and expansions, and too little in infrastructure, education, and

other forms of human capital. If we think the market is worth more than it really is, we may become complacent in funding our pension plans, in maintaining our savings rate, in legislating an improved Social Security system, and in providing other forms of social insurance. We might also lose the opportunity to use our expanding financial technology to devise new solutions to the genuine risks – to our homes, cities, and livelihoods – that we face.[44]

However, do periods of market overvaluation or undervaluation mean that the market is irrational? For Mark Rubinstein, Paul Stephens Professor of Applied Investment Analysis at the University of California, Berkeley, 'Rationality means "know thyself" but not necessarily knowing others.'[45] This argues in favour of each investor setting a specific or customised benchmark as opposed to second-guessing the peer group. Rubinstein argues that in a 'maximally rational' market, investors would trade infrequently and make intensive use of indexed funds. Markets can be rational even if all investors do not behave rationally. So, in a 'rational' market (not a maximally rational one), investors trade excessively and fail to diversify adequately. Even 'minimally rational markets' fail to supply opportunities for abnormal profits:

> For example, if you tell me markets are irrational because prices are too volatile to fundamentals or that closed-end funds sell at discounts, there may be no way I can use that information to make profits. If you tell me such-and-such stock is overpriced but there are significant obstacles to short selling or significant costs to trading the stock, again, I may not be able to do much about the opportunity.
>
> In these cases, I say that although markets are not perfectly rational, they are at least, 'minimally rational'; that is, although prices are not set as if all investors are rational, nevertheless, no abnormal profit opportunities exist for the investors who are rational. If markets are only minimally rational, investors will be more easily misled into thinking they can beat the market, and it then becomes even more important for money managers to give sound advice.[46]

Thus, occasionally a small group of irrational investors have the power to influence asset prices and the large body of investors are simply not equipped to benefit from such opportunities. Such deviations from market rationality are relatively unimportant and infrequent in the scope of the totality of market transactions. The inability of investors largely due to regulatory constraints to make use of all available market information may result in a minimally rational market. Hedge fund managers, not similarly constrained, are in a better position to exploit such short-term market inefficiencies. A large body of investors, being naturally overconfident, influence market prices in important ways. However, if markets are rational, then irrational investors are largely shielded except from the damage they do themselves via overtrading, low diversification or paying a high fee for poor advice.

According to David Dreman, the famous 'contrarian' investor,[47] Rubinstein fails to effectively counter the argument that Shiller has advanced for many years that 'stock price volatility is out of all proportion to any plausible volatility in such fundamentals as earnings prospects.'[48] Others such as Paul Samuelson, the father of modern mathematical economics and professor emeritus at the Massachusetts Institute of Technology, are of the opinion that the stock market shows 'micro efficiency' but not 'macro efficiency'. In a letter to Robert Shiller and John Campbell, Samuelson wrote:

> Modern markets show considerable *micro* efficiency (for the reason that the minority who spot aberrations from micro efficiency can make money from those occurrences and, in doing so, they tend to wipe out any persistent inefficiencies). In no contradiction to the previous sentence, I had hypothesized considerable macro inefficiencies, in the sense of long waves in the time series of aggregate indexes of security prices below and above the various definitions of fundamental values.[49]

Thus, according to this view, as markets are micro-efficient, it is advisable to hold a widely diversified portfolio. For others, however, investor reluctance to take short positions (in terms of short selling, etc.) allow overpricing in individual stocks, as was the case with dotcom stocks in the late 1990s. The pricing of fad stocks is left to the only people who still trade in them, the very investors who are most susceptible to fads. For these stocks, prices loose their moorings and ultimately yield poor returns for the investor. This leads Robert Shiller to the conclusion that markets are not only macro-inefficient but also micro-inefficient to a substantial degree.

Investors (institutional or retail) have a significant role to play in the competitive strength of any economy. In the UK, due to the size of assets under management and their importance to the stock market, institutional investors have played an important factor in the economy. The existence of a large pool of capital forms the basis for the provision of specialised fund management services, research, derivatives trading and other market-related activities, which help to keep the market optimally efficient and competitive. The value added to the UK economy from fund management alone was approximately £3.8 billion in 1998.[50]

CONCLUSION

This book aims to explain issues that impact on investments, be they at the institutional or retail level. Chapter 2 deals with the theoretical assumptions involved in the efficient market hypothesis and its applications in portfolio management. Chapter 3 analyses the rise of indexation and its implication for investors and markets. In Chapter 4 the vital role of the traditional 'active managers' is discussed, particularly in their contribution to fostering an efficient market. While indexation is all about capturing beta, or what is essentially the market, Chapter 5 examines the role that absolute return strategies play in delivering alpha. In exploiting market inefficiencies, hedge fund managers help to restore market efficiency, but SRI does not come into that calculation. In Chapter 6 we examine the role of investments in private equity and venture capital in nurturing innovation and enterprise. Like hedged strategies, private equity investments are seen as an alternative investment class. As the scope of alternative investments is vast – real estate, art, antiques, wine, commodities, precious metals, etc. – this study confines itself to equity and related investments.

Chapter 7 is devoted to the new growth area in asset management, socially responsible investment (SRI). It analyses to what extent investment behaviour is going to be regulated by SRI and what can be achieved in the field of corporate governance and SRI, not just in a national context but in a global one. Chapter 8 deals with the future of capital markets and the responsibility that investors bear in shaping it. With the rise in competition, distribution of investment products and client servicing have gained significance over the past years. While it is not relevant to predict the future of the asset management industry, an understanding of the major drivers of change may help some investors in their long-term asset allocation.

This study offers an overview of the changing face of the asset management industry. As more and more individuals get involved in managing their own investments, the relevance of markets in the management of savings also becomes very important, not just to individual's own retirement and pension arrangements but also to the sectors of the economy where these investments are directed. There has long been a tradition of attaching an aura or mystique to wealth and to its more successful managers. The celebrity culture so popular today is an extension of that attitude. While the world's richest people tend to be reclusive and secretive in their lifestyles, the rise of TMT has ensured that we increasingly get a slice of that thrown into our ordinary lives, whether we want it or not. However, in attempting to understand the fundamental issues in the creation of wealth and its preservation, we can all participate and benefit from our own wealth creation and management potential and opportunities.

Apart from the obvious factors such as globalisation, technology and demographics that have influenced market and corporate behaviour, one of the unknown factors is the role of governments, regulators and individuals. With the rise in the power of MNCs and institutional investors, it remains to be seen how far governments will intervene in regulating the financial services sector or how far they will address competition issues globally. Many voters feel disenfranchised today due to the convergence of economic policies between the major political parties in countries worldwide. This marginalisation of politicians, and indirectly of their voters, in the boards of major MNCs and PLCs has been an additional source of tension between capital and labour in many countries. It remains to be seen how far individuals, on a global basis, will succeed in making their governments accountable in delivering better support in making markets work more efficiently; for example, in terms of providing universal education and health, investing in technology and infrastructure and setting up adequate regulatory structures for markets.

National governments and regulatory bodies are often paralysed into inaction when faced with issues beyond their jurisdiction. The problems that investors face in the context of the euro-zone are a simple example of the sort of barriers that need to be overcome, be they regulatory, technological, cultural or language-related. Thus, greater government cooperation in dealing with these issues has to be effective. While the internet seems to have achieved the impossible in its truly global reach, it also comes with a price, namely the empowerment of criminal activists such as paedophiles and other financial terrorists in organising themselves globally. The global consensus demonstrated as a result of the events of 11 September 2001 to address terrorism illustrates that such a coalition is possible. However, it needs to be stressed that the scale of the disaster made such action possible.

The study also aims to address issues with reference to the concept of the market and its implications in the distribution of wealth and other development issues. In a global world, global solutions are required to address many of the problems that investors already face in their decision-making. However, such global non-commercial organisations still do not exist, organisations to deal with environmental issues, for example, including natural disasters. And when they do exist, their impact on global issues is marginal. With the rise in globalisation, there has been an equal and opposite rise in economic, religious and racial fundamentalism in most parts of the world. This rise of intolerance and indifference to the grand diversity of human races and cultures reflects not just the shortcomings of how we manage our natural resources, but also the nature of markets and societies which have come to shape us. Together we help in defining markets and create the sort of world we would choose to live in. The sooner we recognise that we have a stake in building the future and the sooner we take responsibility in establishing an efficient market process, the better for us it will be, not just as passive investors but as shareholders in a global economy.

CHAPTER 2

The Alpha and Beta of Investing

INTRODUCTION

In the world of the efficient market hypothesis (EMH), the market is perceived to be in a state of equilibrium, reflecting at any point in time the sum of all the individual trades executed by the market participants. Thus, the market price reflects the consensus opinion of all the market participants. In the real world, market participants do not have an equitable share in the outcome of their decision-making. If an individual sells or buys a security, it is unlikely to have any significant impact on the price of that security. However, if the same security is sold or bought in the market by the likes of Fidelity, Merrill Lynch or Deutsche Bank, it is more likely to have a big impact on the price. And if most of the major investment institutions think similarly, their combined financial clout will have an even more staggering price effect. Thus, the market decisions of those managing the most money have the largest influence on prices. And this is true of any market, not just the stock market.

As most developed stock markets have a large number of players and most of these players have access to the same information, their consensus opinion of risk and return is largely reflected in the market price. If this were not the case, it would create an imbalance in the pricing of securities. In developed and efficient markets, price distortions are unlikely to last for any length of time. If poor analysis of information results in overoptimistic assessment of the future prospects of a company by a one group of analysts or investors, then 'buying' by that group will drive up the price of that stock. For the price to rise, demand usually must exceed supply. The reverse occurs if the value is perceived to be unreasonably high and investors start 'selling', bringing the price down. Therefore, any substantial variation of prices from that estimated by the professional investment community will unleash counterbalancing market orders.

In the world of security analysis and investment management, individual perception of risk and reward vary considerably. One analyst's estimate of risk and return for a certain security is likely to differ from those of others, as such projections involve subjective estimates dealing with the future, which in itself is uncertain. Besides, every analyst's estimate changes in time as new information is released or obtained. Security markets are exciting precisely because they pose a continual challenge. Whether individual participants are able to profit from the market's vagaries depends on several factors. The market does not reward all the participants equitably. Due to the large number of variable factors and participants, who in many ways comprise what we call the market, any measure of the relationship between risk and return resembles a movable feast or famine.

Better access to technology and increased competition have also meant that analysts' forecasts have tended towards a higher degree of convergence than in the past. There are many reasons for that: there is greater transparency and frequency in the issuance of companies' reports and accounts; thanks to laws on insider trading, companies provide information to their analysts simultaneously as it is disseminated electronically to the rest of the world. Besides, analysts' forecasts with their financial models are more easily accessible by investors. If an analyst has a view which differs considerably from the consensus, that analyst has a lot of explaining to do and may even be considered a source of risk, for both the buyer and the seller of such information. The clout of the higher echelons of companies in terms of market capitalisation is such that an analyst making a forecast that defies the consensus is likely to do so at the risk of losing their job. Between 1995 and 2000 the ratio of buy to sell recommendations by analysts rose faster than at any other time in the history of corporate research. This herd mentality among analysts is similar to the herd mentality among fund managers in their asset allocation decisions. As a result, performance among analysts and managers tends to be 'median' and market efficiency can get compromised unless short sales among managers are also prevalent, which is not the case.

However, quantifying risk and return constitutes the crucial task of any investment strategy. Risk and return are so interlinked that it would be naive to analyse them in isolation. As pointed out by William Sharpe, 'In an efficient capital market there will be likely relationships between risk and return; investment analysis should begin by considering such relationships, then proceed to assess the possible extent of deviations in particular cases.'[1] At the same time, risk has entered our common parlance to such an extent that their alliance needs to be understood better. Due to the difficulty in quantifying each part of this self-adjusting equation, investors often accommodate a high level of risk in their investment decisions or forego a higher level of return for the same risk. It is not possible, for example, to compare with any certainty the performance of one particular investment fund except perhaps for indexed funds with that of the market, as the risks involved are not fully comparable. The task of financial analysis lies in identifying and evaluating the major factors that contribute to the risk, which determines the level of expected return. More importantly, it is up to the investor to use this information in arriving at the desired investment decision as risk essentially lies in the conceptualisation of it in the mind of the investor.

RISK AND RETURN IN PORTFOLIO MANAGEMENT

Investing in the stock market is considered risky precisely because there is usually a range of possible outcomes. In financial jargon, this spread of uncertainty is described as the *standard deviation* or *variance*.[2] Thus, *deviation* is the difference between the actual return and the expected return. Expressed mathematically, it is actual return minus the expected return. If the expected return of a security over a one-year holding period is X, assuming that event Y were to transpire, but the actual return is Z; then deviation would be calculated as $Z - X$. It can represent positive or negative values but a weighted average will equal zero (with probabilities as weights).

The risk of investing in any stock involves two different types of risk: there is a risk that is unique to the stock and there is a market risk, which relates to the valuation of the particular market. Investors can easily eliminate stock-specific risk by investing in a diversified portfolio. Fifty years ago in 1952, Harry Markowitz demonstrated how an investor could reduce the standard deviation of returns by investing in a diversified portfolio of stocks whose price movements were not correlated. But eliminating market risk is altogether a different issue. International diversification for the US investor was proposed as a method of reducing market risk over the long term. Thus, all the risk of a fully diversified portfolio is expressed as the market risk. And an individual stock's contribution to the market risk of such a fully diversified portfolio is indicated by its sensitivity to market variations. This sensitivity is measured as the stock's *beta*. In the traditional world of portfolio management, investors are not rewarded for taking stock-specific risk, only market risk.

The reason behind such an approach is that no analyst or investor could be expected realistically to be able to take into account every conceivable contingency, analyse its probability of occurrence, as well as its impact on each investment candidate and estimate the likely degrees of correlation for all combination of securities. Besides, the general principle that higher risk should bring higher expected return is not specific enough to enable an investor to judge how great a reward is necessary to compensate for the added risk. An intelligent investor needs to simplify and focus on the essentials, even develop models of markets, securities, portfolios, to understand the process involved. With the arrival of superintelligent computers and the phenomenal rise in their computational power, analysts are actually in a far more powerful position to analyse and thus take better stock-specific risk. This is reflected in the rise in quantitative management techniques, not simply in the industry as a whole but also in the more active segment of the market, such as with absolute return strategies and other derivative-based investment strategies as with capital-protected products.

The notion that there exists a relationship between expected return and risk is widely known as the Capital Asset Pricing Model (CAPM). Although the CAPM has now been superseded by more sophisticated models, it remains the foundation for various practices and applications in the investment industry. Thus, it is worth having some understanding of the basic premise of the model. In the mid-1960s three economists, William F. Sharpe, John Lintner and Jack L. Treynor, developed the CAPM, which states that in a competitive market the expected risk premium varies in direct proportion to beta. In assessing risk in the pricing of securities, investors consider more than the expected return and the variance of the individual stock. They also take into account the interrelationships between the returns on different stocks in their portfolios.

In 1990 Sharpe's role in developing the CAPM was recognized by the Nobel Prize Committee. Sharpe shared the Nobel Memorial Prize in Economic Sciences that year with Harry Markowitz and Merton Miller, the University of Chicago economist. A professor of finance at the Stanford University Graduate School of Business since 1970, Sharpe has crafted several financial tools that portfolio managers regularly use to quantify investment risk, including returns-based style analysis, which assists investors in determining whether a portfolio manager is sticking to his/her stated investment objective. The Sharpe ratio, for example, evaluates the level of risk a fund accepts versus the return it delivers.

Any measure of risk takes into account both the probability of an outcome as well as its magnitude. In more sophisticated models, one measures the probability of a range of outcomes. However, the overall risk of a portfolio is not determined by the total risk or the standard deviation of the constituent securities in isolation, but is dependent on their covariance,[3] or the extent to which individual securities respond to events together. When two securities' returns are perfectly negatively correlated, then it is possible to combine them in such proportions that all risk is eliminated. This is the principle behind all hedging strategies. Portfolio diversification can ensure risk reduction if the security components are uncorrelated.

For the sake of simplicity, the original CAPM made various assumptions:

- Investors base their portfolio investment decisions on the Markowitz expected return and standard deviation criteria.
- This assumes that the probability distributions for portfolio returns are all normally distributed. Stated simply, it means that

given two portfolios with the same variance, investors will prefer the one with the higher expected rate of return. Or, given two portfolios with the same expected return, investors will prefer the one with lower variance. The only abiding investment concerns are risk and return. There are no other investment restrictions or considerations.

- All investors agree on a stipulated time period as their investment horizon, e.g. one month or one year.
- All investors have equal access to the same information.
- All investors have the ability to analyse, assimilate and act upon it similarly. Thus, there is universal agreement in the analysis of securities and in the construction of portfolios.
- There are no transaction costs.
- Investments are infinitely divisible. All assets are marketable.
- Every investor is able to borrow or lend any amount of money at the Treasury bill rate. Unlimited short sales are allowed.
- Taxation has no effect on investment policy.
- There is no inflation or inflation has no role in the formulation of investment policy.
- Capital markets are in equilibrium and there are no market imperfections.

The limitations inherent in each of these assumptions are together transferred to the CAPM as markets do not operate in this ideal world. In the real world there is a cost attached to accessing information, and investors do not have equal access to information. Nor do they have equal ability to analyse the information and arrive at the same conclusion. Investors do not and cannot lend or borrow, without any restrictions, at the risk-free rate. Needless to mention that brokers, analysts, custodians, etc., have to be paid. Besides, taxation can significantly influence one's investment decision and so can inflationary expectations. Most investors do not gear or sell short. Even efficient markets are not always in equilibrium as information and liquidity flows are virtually global and instability in capital markets regularly spreads across the world. However, the final test of any model is not how reasonable or real its assumptions are but how well the model explains reality. As it happens, the model does provide some startling conclusions about the relationship between risk and return.

THE CAPITAL MARKET LINE

All efficient investment strategies start from the premise that they include only the market portfolio with borrowing or lending. It is also evident that securities can be combined in such proportions that a portfolio of securities is less risky than the risk inherent in investing in any one or even a group of its component stocks. The market portfolio represents the most efficient of investable portfolios. However, investors are not obliged to take on any risk. To put it differently, investors are rewarded according to their decisions to add or reduce the level of risk in their portfolios. Investors have the option to invest in a risk-free asset like a Treasury bill or a bond whose payment is guaranteed at the end of a fixed term. Thus, in the conceptual world of the CAPM, the relationship between risk and return for efficient investment strategies can be depicted graphically along the capital market line (CML).

In Figure 2.1 point *M* represents the market portfolio and point *R* the risk-free interest rate from investments in Treasury bills. As investment strategy is controlled solely by risk and return, all preferred investment decisions will plot along the CML, which in Figure 2.1 is *RML*, representing various combinations of risk and return by mixing the market portfolio with borrowing or lending.

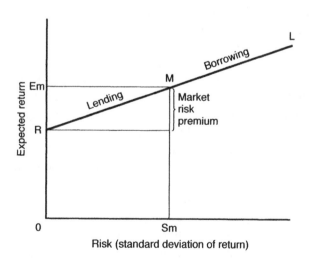

Figure 2.1. *The Capital Market Line*

Thus, the line of equilibrium in the capital market lies between the two risk-return points. One is the reward for waiting, or the risk-free interest rate point *R*. The other is the reward for risk taken as represented by the CML. Thus, the capital market is a place where time and risk can be traded and their prices determined via demand and supply. The risk-free interest rate is the price of time and the slope of the CML the market price of risk.

A steep CML indicates that the market is charging a high price for risk and a flatter line suggests that the market is willing to take on the risk at a relatively lower rate of return. The slope of the line *RML* can be seen as the reward per unit of risk, which is equal to the difference between the expected return on the market portfolio and that of the risk-free security $(E_m - R_f)$ divided by the difference in their risks $(S_m - 0)$. Thus, the equation for the CML is

$$\text{CML} = \frac{E_m - R_f}{S_m - 0}$$

where E_m is the expected return on the market portfolio, R_f is the risk-free rate and S_m is the standard deviation of return on the market portfolio.

The CML establishes a relationship between expected return and standard deviation of return for efficient portfolios. Thus, all investment decisions other than those using the market portfolio and borrowing or lending would lie below or very close to the CML. It implies that any investor can devise a desirable investment strategy without having to pay for the services of analysts, portfolio managers or investment advisers. The activities of professional analysts help to make an efficient market, and their total value to investors and the economy is considerable, but the marginal value of additional analysis to any individual investor can be small. Thus, any investor can avail themselves of all relevant financial information and work out an optimal investment strategy depending on their individual requirements.

Individual securities will normally plot below or above the line. In any event, a single-security portfolio is most certainly an inefficient portfolio even though it plots above the CML. An investor with a higher risk tolerance may choose to do so but should not expect to be rewarded for that decision. In the realm of the CAPM, all investment decisions result in investment holdings that will plot along the CML. An investor with a taste for higher levels of risk would be invested in a borrowing portfolio but not in a single-stock portfolio. As all investors are expected to hold combinations of the market portfolio and a risk-free security, it is also known as the *two mutual fund theorem*. The rationale of investing in indexed funds springs from such a premise. The CAPM does not aim to explain the relationship between the expected returns of individual securities and their total risks or standard deviations of return. An individual security's risk is of less importance than its contribution to the total risk of a portfolio. To understand more about securities' expected return, we must consider the changes in the risk and return of an efficient portfolio.

THE PRINCIPLE OF PORTFOLIO OPTIMALITY

Most investors need to know the effect on the risk and return of their portfolio before making a decision to change their existing holdings. The expected return of the portfolio is a weighted average of the expected returns of the component securities. And the marginal contribution of a security to the expected return of any portfolio equals its expected return and its proportionate share of the portfolio. But the same is not true as far as the risk of the portfolio is concerned, for that depends on the covariance between the return of the security and the return of the portfolio.

The effect of any change in the holdings of a security on the risk of a portfolio depends on the characteristics of both the security and the portfolio. Thus, changes in a holding of GlaxoSmithKline plc will have a different impact on the risk-return profile of a portfolio of pharmaceutical stocks than on the risk-return profile of a portfolio of European stocks, a technology fund or a global portfolio. Marginal expected return and marginal variance indicate the changes on a portfolio's characteristics as a result of changes in the holdings of any security. In the real world of portfolio management, changes are extremely complex, usually involving simultaneous buy and sell decisions for different sets of securities.

Given estimates of expected returns, risks and correlations of securities, an analysis of portfolio optimality would involve computing the marginal expected return and marginal variance for each security. Suppose a portfolio consists of securities *A* and *B* with the marginal expected returns of 18% and 14%, respectively, and marginal variance of 300, then the return of the portfolio can be improved upon without any change in its existing risk profile by holding the entire portfolio in security A as there is no advantage in holding B with the same risk profile but offering a lower return.

In an optimal portfolio, all securities with a given marginal variance should have the same expected return. Stated differently, if securities in a portfolio have the same marginal variance but different expected returns, such a portfolio is not optimal. Since investors are assumed to be risk averse and inclined towards higher returns for the same level of risk, it follows that a security that adds to variance or risk should also add to expected return. It follows that in an optimal portfolio, all securities will plot on an upward sloping straight line with expected return plotted on the vertical axis and marginal variance on the horizontal axis (Figure 2.2).

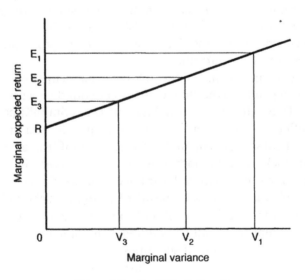

Figure 2.2. *Portfolio Optimality*

THE MARKET RISK PREMIUM

One of the main applications of the CAPM is to determine the rate of return required for any prescribed level of risk. The difference between the return on the market portfolio and the risk-free interest rate is called the *market risk premium*. In the 1960s, for example, the risk premium for the US market ranged from 7% to 10%. Thus, investors expected risky investments, like equities, to yield anywhere between 7% and 10% more than risk-free securities. Even if one were to assume that the risk premium on the US market has declined substantially, to say 3–4%, then taking into account the current US 3-month Treasury bill's yield of around 2.2%, US equities would be expected to provide a rate of return of 5.2–6.2%.

Taking into account the rate at which companies have been issuing profit warnings and announcing reductions in the workforce, such returns are unlikely to materialise in the short term. Currently the real rate of interest in the US is down to zero. This is clearly a short-term measure, albeit a necessary one, in light of 11 September 2001. In fact, since March 2000, annual returns on equity investments have been negative in the US and in Europe. As stock markets form a new baseline and companies face a year of reckoning, a recovery in earnings is currently being engineered. Since markets tend to discount earnings in advance, then in terms of market returns, 2002 could prove to be better than 2000 and 2001.

Valuating equities is a complex business, but it is universally agreed that market price is an indication of future prospects such as earnings growth. The 1990s boom in the US stock market and the growth in the mutual fund industry indicated that the risk premium on Wall Street had steadily declined. Over the past 50 years or so, the trend line of growth in earnings per share for US equities has been 6% per annum although it has been higher at well over 10% annually over the past decade. However, to justify a high valuation for the US stock market, it would mean that investors were assuming an even higher rate of growth in earnings for the next decade with no real evidence of that in sight within the US at the present time.

One also has to assume that the US economy has been able to smooth out its economic cycle so that investors no longer view equities as a riskier asset class than bonds. Both assumptions being what they are, it is reasonable to conclude that the 'market risk premium' asserts itself as escalating expected returns increasingly become unsustainable. With a lower level of inflation, the market risk premium has indeed been adjusted downwards. Risk is variable for each investor, so it is usually expressed in relative terms. When one refers to a security's beta value, the beta value is relative to the market portfolio. The covariance of a security vis-à-vis the portfolio is stated in the same unit as the variance of the portfolio. The measure of a security's relative marginal variance is referred to its beta relative to the portfolio. This relationship is expressed as follows:

$$\beta_{xp} = C_{xp}/V_{xp}$$

where β_{xp} = security x's beta value relative to portfolio p, C_{xp} = the covariance between the return on security x and the return on portfolio p, V_{xp} = the variance of portfolio p. The covariance of a risk-free security with a portfolio is zero. Thus, $\beta_{xp} = 0$ if security x is risk-free.

The beta value of a portfolio is a weighted average of the beta values of the component securities, using the actual proportions invested as weights. In an optimal portfolio, all securities must lie along an upward-sloping straight line on a graph that plots expected returns on the vertical axis and the beta relative to the market portfolio on the horizontal axis. This straight line is also known as the security market line, which passes through the market portfolio with an expected return of E_m (Figure 2.3). An insured bank account paying a known rate of interest is risk-free, so it has a beta of zero. But an investment in a fully diversified portfolio of stocks has a beta of 1. In return for bearing the risk of investing in common stock, the investor would normally expect a higher rate of return than the fixed and safe rate of bank interest.

The relationship between beta and shares can be compared to duration and bonds. The measurement of exposure to movements in underlying markets is necessary for portfolio risk estimation. Most portfolio managers would be able to get the details of expected volatility on the market portfolio or its proxy like the FTSE All Share index or the S&P 500, which is then multiplied by the average beta of the portfolio to arrive at the volatility of the particular portfolio.

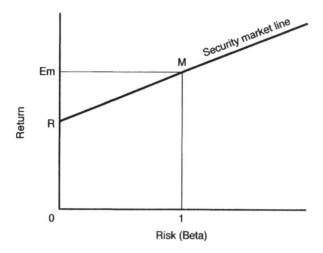

Figure 2.3. *Risk and Return*

When calculating a security's beta, an analyst needs to take into account various *scenarios* of the state of the market, economy, politics, etc., that might impact on that security's return. Having fed into the computer model these varying scenarios, the analyst then needs to allocate probability weightings to be able to work out the returns associated with the security and that of the market. Suppose five different equally plausible scenarios are identified with a return on the security and a return on the market given for each scenario, then the expected return on the security is simply an average of the given estimated returns. A similar calculation is arrived at for the market portfolio. The overall risk of a portfolio is not determined by the total risk or the standard deviation of the constituent securities in isolation but is dependent on their *covariance*, or the extent to which individual securities respond to events together. The covariance is a weighted average of the products of the deviations of the returns from their expected values, using the probabilities of the deviations as weights. The beta value is covariance divided by the variance of the security.[4]

It is possible to estimate beta values without having to go into detailed forecasts for securities by arriving at betas based on past values. A security's historic beta is derived by establishing its actual return versus that of the market. Historic betas are often adjusted or used as guides to the valuation of future betas. However, as the fortunes of companies change over time, using historical betas to estimate betas over some future time period may be quite misleading. A security's beta value measures the expected change in its return for a perventage change in the return on the market portfolio.

Thus, securities with beta values less than 1, e.g. most utility stocks, are also called *defensive*. When markets go up, the prices of defensive stocks tend to rise at a slower rate than the average security. On the other hand, they tend to fall at a slower rate when markets decline. If the beta of a security is 0.5, then a 1% increase or decrease in the expected market return is likely to produce a 0.5% increase or decrease in the expected return of the security. Firms with beta values greater than 1, e.g. airline companies, are termed *aggressive* as they tend to outperform bull markets. But they plummet faster than the average stock in bear markets. Betas of utility stocks tend to be low, as the environments in which they operate are controlled by government regulations so that the spread between revenue and cost is less prone to changes in economic activity.

Although the value of beta is expressed in terms of changes in market price and dividend payments over a short period, it fundamentally reflects the relationships among expectations about the values of economic variables over a longer time frame. The beta of a firm is thus an indicator of the sensitivity of the underlying assets' prospects, at least investors' assessment of such prospects, to those of the economy as a whole. Remember that because high-beta stocks are expected to deliver higher returns does not mean that they always do so. If they did deliver consistently higher returns, they would not be considered more risky. They are considered risky precisely because from time to time they produce lower than expected returns, although over a longer period of time they are expected to deliver higher returns. The key insight of the CAPM is that higher expected returns go with the greater risk of doing badly in bad times. Beta is a measure of that. Securities or asset classes with high betas tend to do worse in bad times than those with low betas.

Any security's risk can also be divided into market risk and non-market risk. The total variance of a security can be segregated into the portion related to market moves, called market risk or systematic risk, and the portion not related to such moves which are more stock-specific, called non-market risk or unsystematic risk. To calculate a security's market risk in variance terms, the variance of the market portfolio is multiplied by the square of the security's beta. The non-market risk is simply the difference between the total risk, expressed as the total variance of the security, and the market risk. Non-market risk, or stock-specific risk, can be reduced through diversification, whereas market-related risk is not as easily diversifiable. Investing in overseas markets is the necessary diversification option.

The original CAPM did not have such diversification in mind, although today such an option clearly exists. However, the measurement of beta can be complicated by such factors. In theory, beta measures a security's sensitivity to a widely diversified market portfolio including stocks, bonds, real estate and other assets. Most empirical studies have used a broad-based index of widely traded stocks, as adequate data on other securities have been unavailable. A security's beta relative to, say, the New York Stock Exchange 'market portfolio' would differ considerably from that measured relative to the Frank Russell 3000 index portfolio, let alone an international market portfolio, such as the MSCI World index. The CAPM also assumes a capitalisation-weighted index as opposed to a GDP-weighted index, for example. In a global portfolio, currency issues surface. Despite these problems, the concept of beta is useful as it is instructive to see how stocks with different historic beta values have performed over time. Studies indicate there is a positive relationship between beta values and long-term returns.

The overall risk profile of a portfolio is arrived at by calculating the beta value for the portfolio, which is the weighted average of the beta values of its component securities. But such a relationship does not exist for non-market risk. On the other hand, the non-market risk of a portfolio may be considerably less than the non-market risk of any of its component securities, owing to the power of diversification. At the portfolio level, it is likely the market risk will substantially outweigh the non-market risk. The value of understanding and differentiating between market risk and non-market risk arises from the fact that market risk is related to the risk of the market portfolio and to the beta of the security or portfolio: the higher the beta, the greater the market risk, hence the need for compensating returns.

Thus, high betas are associated with higher returns. The product of these two relationships is that securities or portfolios with greater market risk should also have greater expected returns. Non-market risk is not reflected in beta. Thus, there is no explanation in the CAPM why securities or portfolios with greater non-market risk should yield higher expected returns. The CAPM therefore asserts that market risk is rewarded but non-market risk is not. As non-market risk can be reduced considerably by diversification, there is no reward for taking such risks. In brief, it is more difficult to override errors in asset allocation via stock selection. The potential for risk reduction is greater with a wider range of possible investment choices. But risk cannot be totally eliminated; non-market risk can be reduced by diversification, but market risk will remain. For a portfolio manager, strategic asset allocation adds more value than stock selection.

Total risk = Market risk (systematic risk or non − diversifiable risk) + non − market risk (unsystematic risk or diversifiable risk)

The principle of portfolio diversification represents how total risk is lowered as securities are added to a portfolio. Non-market risk or stock-specific risk can be virtually eliminated in portfolios of let's say 50 securities drawn from industries which are not closely related in their economic activities; for example, pharmaceuticals, utilities, airlines and oil exploration. However sector-specific they may be, portfolios such as an infrastructure fund are more likely to hold securities in related sectors than in a general portfolio. Diversified portfolios thereby tend to move in line with the market. In fact, market indexes like the Dow Jones Industrial Average (DJIA) of 30 stocks, the S&P 500 or the FTSE 100 are essentially diversified portfolios. We shall explore in greater detail the problems arising out of holding a so-called market or indexed portfolio in Chapter 3.

According to the CAPM, investors should hold only diversified portfolios to minimise risk, because non-market or unsystematic risk can be eliminated through diversification. It does not pay to take non-market risk, as it does not increase a security's expected return. The model provides a convenient measure of market or systematic risk in the form of beta, which gauges the tendency of a security's return to move in tandem with that of the market.

Interpreting the correlation between changes in the market price of stocks and the index can be encapsulated as follows:

$$R_i = \alpha_i + \beta_i R_m$$

where R_i = return on security i, α_i = the component of security i's return that is independent of the market, R_m = the rate of return on the market index, β_i = the beta of security i. This equation simply breaks down the return on a stock into its component risks. However, the component of a security's return that is independent of the market can be further broken down into a set of variables. Thus, a company's beta value, as a measure of risk, implies that it changes over time as the company's prospects alter with changes in capital structure, interest rates and other random variables that affect the company's future earnings. Studies have been made to examine the relationship between seven firm variables and the company's beta value. These variables included dividend payout, asset growth, leverage, liquidity, asset size, earnings variability and earnings beta. For example, a high dividend payout is indicative of confidence on the part of management, which would suggest a low beta, whereas firms with high growth expectations would be considered more risky. As betas are calculated with a random error, the larger the error over a certain period, the less predictive its power if used as a guide over another period. Fluctuations in the betas of individual securities during two different periods are likely to be higher than those of the portfolio. Thus, errors in the calculation of a portfolio's beta are likely to be lower than the errors for individual stocks.

Betas also provide investors with a guide to the sort of returns that are associated in the marketplace with a certain level of risk. Thus, the CAPM can also be used to find the discount rate for a new capital investment. If, for example, the beta of company Z is 1 and its expected return is 15%, then the cost of capital for a further investment in the same business is 15%. In practice, choosing a discount rate for corporate financiers is usually more complicated. However, the basic concept of expected return for a certain level of risk is a useful tool in asset management as the risk premium demanded by investors is proportional to beta.

Thus, an investor can always obtain an expected risk premium that is a product of beta and the difference between the market return and risk-free return, by holding a mixture of the market portfolio and a risk-free loan. In an efficient market, nobody needs to hold a stock that offers an expected risk premium of less than that level. If firm Z cannot expect to earn 15% rate of return on its investment then, in theory at least, funds should be returned to shareholders who can earn equivalent returns on marketable securities of the same risk level. As the CAPM relies on various ad hoc estimates of expected return on the market and beta values, it is not as widespread in industry as in investment management. However, the model does provide vital clues to ways in which returns are determined in the securities market.

THE EFFICIENT PORTFOLIO

In the theoretical world of the CAPM, all market participants would inevitably arrive at sets of 'efficient portfolios'. However, everyone would by definition also have the same combination of securities in their efficient portfolio. It is already established that diversification can reduce the overall risk of a portfolio. Thus, by investing in different securities in different proportions, one can obtain a wide selection of risk and expected return. In Figure 2.4 each cross repre-

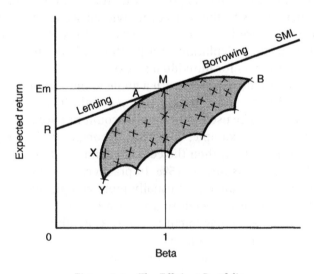

Figure 2.4. *The Efficient Portfolio*

sents a combination of expected return and risk, or standard deviation of return, from investing in any single security. The shaded area demonstrates the possible combinations of expected return and standard deviation of investments in a mixture of securities. The line *AB* represents the *efficient portfolio,* a term coined by Markowitz. Point *B* represents a higher return compared to point *A*. Thus, depending on one's appetite for risk, the portfolio indicates an appropriate level of reward.

Efficient portfolios are arrived at by a standard quadratic program, which is based on the expected return and the standard deviation for each stock as well as the correlation between the stocks in the portfolio. Thus, an efficient portfolio has less risk than any other portfolio with comparable expected return, and more return than any other with comparable risk. It is evident that when an investor lends a portion of their money, the investment profile of that investor is somewhere between *A* and *M*. But if the investor can borrow money at the risk-free rate, then investment possibilities lie beyond point *M*. The diagram also illustrates that, depending on the investor's risk tolerance, the highest expected return can be obtained by a combination of the market portfolio *M* and lending or borrowing. But there is no justification ever for holding portfolio *X* or *Y*.

Thus, an investor's job lies in establishing that optimal relationship between risk and return. Only if an investor assumes they have better information than their rivals will they want the optimal portfolio to include large investments in stocks they consider to be undervalued and will they sell those that are overvalued. In a competitive market, such a situation is unlikely to arise over a long period of time. Besides, in a regulated market, any investor dealing on the strength of 'inside information' is likely to be prosecuted. Hence the market portfolio or an indexed portfolio is as efficient an investment vehicle as any investor can get.

This led Tobin to what is known as the separation theorem; it states that an investor's choice of the level of risk is independent of the problem of deriving the optimal portfolio of risky securities. As the market portfolio represents the optimal portfolio of risky securities, all investors in choosing an efficient portfolio are necessarily directed to it. The risk level associated with this market portfolio may be too high or too low for an individual investor. Thus, the investor can hold a lending portfolio if they prefer lower risk and accept a lower expected return than the market. Alternatively, the investor can hold a borrowing portfolio if they wish to gear up to a higher level of risk and return. This decision to hold a lending or borrowing portfolio is a financial decision determined by the investor's risk level and has little to do with the composition of the market portfolio. However, if there's only one portfolio to choose from plus borrowing and lending, it has got to be the market as, net of costs, the returns for the average active manager are destined to be worse. Assuming markets are efficient, investors buy the market and then use borrowing and lending to the extent they can. The basic philosophy of the CAPM carries through in more complex settings, although the results are not always quite as simple.

If the market outlook appears to be favourable, then with no constraints on borrowing or lending, investors can gear up their portfolios by any preferred combination of risky securities. The opposite would be true if the outlook for the stock market were perceived to be unfavourable. However, the conclusion is that every efficient portfolio would have a very similar combination of securities for the same level of risk and return. It also implies that if company Z is not included in this model universe, then investment advisers will make a recommendation to sell that holding. Prices will thus fall until analysts find the new valuation attractive enough to start recommending investors to buy Z at the lower price offering better value.

The opposite would also transpire if everybody concluded that security A should constitute 10% of all efficient portfolios. Buy orders would flood in and drive the price of A to levels that would ultimately be considered unattractive. But that may take time as a higher valuation alone may not be sufficient reason to trigger a sell recommendation because as long as A constitutes 10% of the efficient market portfolio, not holding 10% of A may result in an inefficient portfolio. At some point, however, analysts will start to recommend reducing holdings in A as it becomes grossly overvalued.

It is inevitable then that in order to secure equilibrium in the pricing of any security, the demand for and supply of that security should be matched over a period. In a state of equilibrium, prices remain unchanged. However, in a changing world, the fortunes of firms change over time, ushering in factors that trigger price changes. It is the same for the market. Markets too can reach varying levels of disequilibrium due to a variety of reasons. Market equilibrium can be reached when the combination of risky securities contains every such security, each in proportion to its outstanding market value. Such a combination of securities is called the *market portfolio*; it includes all possible combinations of investments from bonds, stocks, property, gold, art, wine and other such candidates. In fact, in an increasingly global world, the market portfolio should include the global market.

But in the original CAPM of mid-1960s America, global investing was in its infancy. Efficient investment strategies included any combination of the US 'market portfolio' like the S&P 500 stock index, the Wiltshire 5000 index, the Russell 3000 index or the DJIA of 30 stocks, and borrowing/lending at the Treasury bill rate. In the UK, according to the CAPM, investors could park all their funds in UK government bonds, gilts, high-yielding deposit accounts with a AAA rated savings bank or even in AAA money market funds. Investors will only choose the market portfolio if in their opinion it would offer a higher return than more secure investment alternatives.

THE SECURITY MARKET LINE

The key implication of this analysis is that every security, and by definition every portfolio, must plot on the security market line (SML). As the SML represents the line of equilibrium between risk and return, it also helps to indicate the level of expected return for securities or portfolios with different beta values. The CAPM enables an investor to understand the relationship between risk and return and is an aid to constructing efficient portfolios. The investor often has no option but to take security prices, their prospects and relationships, as they exist under given market conditions. But the investor is not under any obligation to hold any of those securities or any amount of those securities unless they contribute towards his/her optimal portfolio. Thus, the investor is a passive price-taker but an active quantity-adjuster; security holdings can be adjusted until their risk or marginal variance is balanced with their expected returns. If the total amount of any security collectively sought differs significantly from the amount available or normally traded, a price adjustment follows to balance out demand and supply establishing equilibrium.

The SML thus emphasises an equilibrium theory of expected returns, a theory which offers an explanation of the relationship between the expected return of a security and its attributes. Thus

$$E_{ei} = f(a_{i1}, \ a_{i2}, \ ...)$$

where E_{ei} = the equilibrium expected return of security i, $f(...)$ = a function of or is related to, a_{i1} = attribute 1 of security i, a_{i2} = attribute 2 of security i. According to the original CAPM, only one attribute is relevant and that is the beta relative to the market portfolio. So the relationship can be restated as

$$E_{ei} = f(\beta_i)$$

where β_i is the beta of security i relative to the market portfolio.

The equilibrium expected return of a security is a function of its beta value relative to the market portfolio. As the market portfolio and the risk-free security plot on the SML, the relationship can be written in terms of the expected returns on these investments:

$$E_{ei} = R_f + (E_m - R_f)\beta_i$$

The equation clearly states that the equilibrium expected return of a security is determined by the risk-free rate of return and the beta value of the security relative to the market portfolio. Thus, the CAPM can be a powerful predictive tool and, if correct, it can be of enormous value to any investor. More importantly, the cost of such analysis is virtually free.

As asset prices adjust until every security plots on the SML, if any security plots off the SML then the situation is one of disequilibrium. The job of security analysts and fund managers is to spot securities that appear to be mispriced as that will be the simplest way of adding value to their portfolios. Thus, according to the CAPM, a security is underpriced if its expected return is greater than the appropriate expected return for securities with comparable relevant attributes, and overpriced if its expected return is less than the appropriate expected return for securities with comparable relevant attributes. The whole issue of relevant attributes and appropriate expected returns can be explained in an equilibrium theory of expected returns.

The extent to which any security is in disequilibrium, or is mispriced, is measured by its *alpha* value. The alpha value of a security is the difference between its expected return and its equilibrium expected return:

$$\alpha_i = E_i - E_{ei}$$

In the CAPM, a security's alpha is measured by the distance it plots above or below the SML. As a general rule, a security is underpriced if its alpha value is positive and overpriced if it is negative. A security is correctly priced if its alpha value is zero; in equilibrium all securities are correctly priced and all alpha values are zero. Since the expected return of a portfolio is simply a weighted average of the expected return of its component securities, the alpha value of a portfolio is also a weighted average of the alpha values of the component securities. Thus, 'investment managers who try to "beat the market" hope to construct portfolios with positive alphas. Those who do not try to beat the market expect to construct portfolios with zero alphas. Those who try but make incorrect judgements may erroneously choose portfolios with negative alphas.'[5] Figure 2.5 illustrates the concept of alpha values.

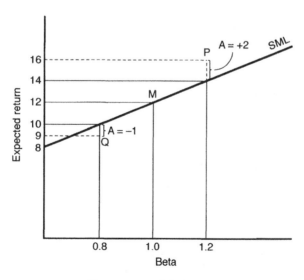

Figure 2.5. *Alpha Values*

The expected return in this case on the market portfolio is 12% and the risk-free interest rate is 8%, determining the location of the SML. Let's assume security *P* has a beta value of 1.2 and an expected return of 16%. The SML indicates that correctly priced securities with betas of 1.2 have an expected return rate of 14%. Security *P* therefore offers an extra return of 2% and its alpha value is + 2%. For security *Q*, with a beta of 0.8 and an expected return of 9%, the SML suggests that an appropriate expected return should be 10%. Thus, security *Q* offers 1% less in expected return and its alpha value is − 1%. Portfolios that outperform the stock market will tend to have securities that lie above the SML, and portfolios that underperform will hold securities that fall below the SML. As the expected return of any portfolio is the weighted average of the expected return of its component securities, the alpha value of a portfolio is the weighted average of the alpha values of the component holdings.

The challenge for an analyst or 'active' portfolio manager is to use their predictive skills so that stock holdings lie along the SML, if not above it. Thus, according to the CAPM, as the systematic return of a security is correlated with the market return, it may be expressed as a factor (beta) of the market return. A security's beta therefore indicates the expected responsiveness of that security's return to changes in the market level. The alpha value gives the expected return of the stock when the market return is zero and it represents the average value over time of the unsystematic return of the security. While active managers aim to enhance the alpha value of their portfolios, it is among hedge fund managers that the importance of alpha is singularly recognised.

CONCLUSION

It is often true that the simplest ideas are also the most difficult to test. It is the ultimate test of any model whether it fits the facts, and in dealing with expected returns instead of actual returns, the CAPM does make the task complicated. Studies conducted by Black, Jensen and Scholes in 1972 and Fama and Macbeth in 1973 did confirm that the actual returns on their portfolios plotted along the SML. Overall, their results did support the conclusions of the CAPM. Whether expected returns would have plotted exactly on the SML cannot be tested empirically. Besides, the key concept of the market portfolio in principle should comprise all risky investments in the international economic system – stocks, bonds, commodities, real estate, art, wine, etc. Most market indexes contain only a sample of common stocks. Even global indexes offered by Morgan Stanley Capital International, for example, contain mostly common stocks and reflect 80% of the relevant country's total market capitalisation, an improvement on the 60% in the past. Betas are calculated by using the stock market indexes. Thus, by definition, they are limited in their coverage.

Richard Roll pointed out in 1976 that because the market portfolio can never properly be identified and researchers have to use a proxy for the market, such as the DJIA or the S&P 500, the benchmark used for risk measurement is not entirely reliable. If one were able to calculate betas using the full market portfolio of all risky assets, it remains unproven what one might arrive at in terms of expected returns. However, Roll's critique of the CAPM does not invalidate the model. Despite the imperfections of the CAPM, provided the chosen market index consists of a high proportion of the total market value of securities, it would appear to provide reasonably reliable beta values for investment decisions and performance measurement. Thus, the basic conclusions of the CAPM remain valid. Studies have confirmed, for example, that professionally managed funds are unable systematically to outperform the market in the long run.

The CAPM has also been accused of not fully explaining why returns on small-cap stocks or firms with low market capitalisations in the US (where extensive studies have been conducted) have been significantly higher than predicted by the model. Thus, between 1926 and 1981, returns on stocks listed on the New York Stock Exchange that were in the bottom quintile in terms of market capitalisation were on average 6.7% higher per annum than the return of Standard & Poor's Composite index. Surely the higher risk premium attached to small caps, or highly illiquid securities, may have something to do with their outperformance. While studies of global liquidity flows are a part of any institutional investor's tool these days, there is still no good explanation for the relationship between the market capitalisation of companies, liquidity and expected returns, although all these factors clearly influence the pricing of stocks. If it is proven that factors other than beta command a premium in portfolio investment and analysis, then the CAPM will be displaced by the new model.

However, the validity and the role of the CAPM are widely recognised. As the model is concerned with the pricing of stocks in efficient markets, it has important applications in the realm of portfolio management. Few would quarrel with its basic concept that investors require extra return for taking on additional risk. Equity returns have generally been higher than returns on risk-free investments like US Treasury bills, UK gilts or other fixed-interest vehicles. The CAPM captures the relationship between risk and return, as investors appear to be concerned with those risks they cannot eliminate via diversification. Investors aim to enhance the expected return on their portfolios while trying to reduce the standard deviation of that return. The CAPM concludes that each security's expected risk premium should increase proportionately to its beta. Thus, the choice of a portfolio's risk is likely to have a much greater impact on its return than the manager's ability to pick stocks. Besides, investors cannot expect to be rewarded for risks that can be diversified.

While several alternative theories have been put forward, like the arbitrage pricing theory, the jury is still out whether in time new theories and models of risk and return will eventually provide a superior explanation of their inalienable relationship. Despite its acknowledged shortcomings, none of the alternative models is as widely used as the standard version of the CAPM. Even the 'extended' capital asset pricing models, in which expected return is a function of beta, taxes, liquidity, dividend yield and other factors, does not annul the basic premise that there is no rational reason to expect reward just for bearing diversifiable risk. What Sharpe introduced to investing in the CAPM is the ability to quantify risk and illustrate how covariance of returns is more important in that calculation.

Investor's compartmentalised approach in dealing with risk often leads to sub-optimal solutions because they don't take covariance into account. 'Correlation is important. You want to think about how things move together,' Sharpe pointed out like an artist in an interview in 1998. Even in a global context where stock prices increasingly move together, the basic concept of the CAPM serves as a useful tool in asset allocation. Security prices change significantly in response to unanticipated changes in prospects for future profits.

Unexpected changes in risk premium, as a result of any number of factors such as unanticipated inflation rates or industrial production figures, all impact on prices of common stocks. However, at its most basic level, the CAPM can provide essential clues towards determining our asset allocation strategy.

CHAPTER 3

Indexation

INTRODUCTION

Improved and wider technological applications have made the dissemination of information easier and faster, making it difficult for financial analysts to beat the market. As price is determined by demand and supply, secondary markets remain essentially a zero-sum game. Decades ago, William F. Sharpe established conclusively that it is mathematically impossible for the average active manager to beat the market over a long period of time. A closer examination of the record of the median performance of active managers over the last 20 years offers no evidence that active managers of equity portfolios have outperformed the relevant market index. Collectively, active managers have not been able to sell at the top or to invest back at the bottom of markets. In fact, the greater risk has been in being out of the market than being fully indexed in it. Although a few active managers have managed to beat the market over long periods, it is difficult to identify them before the event.

In the UK it was not until the late 1980s that indexation secured acceptance among fund managers. The second half of the 1990s witnessed a steady rise in the use of quantitative management techniques, manifested mostly in the form of indexation, which included enhanced indexed strategies. Presently, an estimated 22% of the UK equity market is indexed, held mostly by institutional investors (Table 3.1). Other estimates indicate a higher level of indexation in the UK market. As Barclays Global Investor's global chief investment officer for index investments, Andrew Skirton, pointed out, 'The bigger question is why it has taken so long?'[1] Even in the US,

75

Table 3.1 *Percentage of institutional assets indexed in Europe*[a]

	1998	2000
UK	16	22
Netherlands	5	9
Ireland	2	7
Switzerland	3	5
Spain	0	3
Germany	0	2
Denmark	0	2
France	0	1
Finland	0	1
Norway	0	1
Sweden	0	0
Portugal	0	0
Italy	0	0

[a] Source: William M. Mercer

where the use of indexation originated in the early 1970s, institutional acceptance was rather slow; assets in index funds totalled $12.7 billion in 1980 compared to some $1.4 trillion in 1998. Worldwide, assets managed by leading indexed managers increased from $1.8 trillion in December 1998 to $2.3 trillion by December 2000.

Like many other financial innovations that originated in the US, the concept of indexation pioneered a revolution transforming the investment industry with the introduction of the first S&P 500 index fund in 1973 by the Wells Fargo Bank. In 1976 Vanguard's founder, John C. Bogle, launched the first indexed mutual fund. Indexation gained intellectual support from academics who were advancing theories of portfolio diversification, which enabled investors to quantify risk and think of the relationship between risk and return. With the development of option pricing models, quantitative active investing also got a significant boost. Thus, indexation and quantitative management strategies emerged from the same principles of investing that were being developed within academic research in the 1970s in the US. Since then, indexed management has grown in acceptance, particularly throughout the US.

Barclays Global Investors' (BGI), one of the largest index managers worldwide, was formed in October 1996 as a result of the merger between BZW Investment Management and Wells Fargo Nikko Investment Advisors (Table 3.2). BGI's assets under management grew from £226.5 billion in December 1996 to £536.4 billion by the end of December 2000, registering strong growth in both its index and active investment management business over that period. On 30 June 2001, BGI's total assets under management stood at £548.5 billion, with £424 billion of it being in indexed products. For State Street Global Advisers (SSGA), funds under management swelled from $160 billion in 1994 to $711 billion at the end of 2000. In 1999 alone, SSGA added some $174 billion worldwide, with market appreciation accounting for half of that growth. Funds under management more than doubled for most fund managers during 1994–99; the market simply took you there, if you had an indexed strategy in place.

Active managers heavily lost business to the indexed managers over this period. It was the poor performance of the traditional balanced managers that drove business into indexed strategies. In the UK this coincided with the introduction of the Pensions Act 1995, which focussed the mind of trustees on issues such as the minimum funding requirement (MFR) and the risk profile of their schemes. The

Table 3.2 *The 10 largest indexed managers in the world: assets ($bn) as at 30 June 2001*[a]

	Worldwide	US-based
Barclays Global Investors	790.6	496.2
State Street Global	610.7	524.7
Vanguard Group	233.6	225.4
Deutsche Asset Management	132.0	124.5
TIA-CREF	92.8	92.8
Mellon Capital	82.4	80.0
Fidelity	71.8	65.7
Northern Trust Global	64.1	64.1
JP Morgan	55.4	44.2
Dimensional Fund Advisors	33.6	33.0

[a] Source: *Pensions Investments*, September 2001

importance of strategic asset allocation among trustees increased as a result. The ability of 'balanced' fund managers to consistently add value in strategic asset allocation was seriously questioned. Even within stock selection, it became evident that no single fund manager could be expected to assemble market-beating expertise in all sectors of all markets.

Several factors conspired in the indexation revolution. Skilful quantitative active management and the utilisation of derivative instruments helped combine active management with the benefits of passive management, thereby offering investors the advantage of security selection (alpha) while retaining the performance from underlying asset classes (beta). The rise in the use of derivative instruments in the management of risk in fund management intro-duced a dimension to the investment process as never before. Long and short positions of equal beta are systematically combined to eliminate systemic risk. The resulting market-neutral portfolio, with the residual firm-specific risk, can be controlled further through an optimisation process. Portable alpha strategies employ the best financial engineering tools available to fund managers in their management of risk and return. Beta, in the form of indexation, can be cheaply acquired. The UK lagged in the use of technology in asset management and was slow in embracing quantitative management techniques, including indexation. But when it did get around to doing so, it caught up very fast with the US.

Active and passive/indexed strategies are often represented as polar opposites but when we examine the key characteristics, they complement each other. The important attributes are highlighted in Table 3.3.

While the classic indexed fund simply seeks to match the index, many indexed managers offer enhanced index funds, which aim to outperform the index. For the 10 years ending in 1998, the index (S&P 500) actually outperformed the average active manager in the US by 3.5 percentage points, and did better than more than nine out of 10 active managers. Over the past 30 years, a $10,000 investment in the index would have grown to $311,000 (after expenses); in the average general equity fund, the same investment would have grown to $171,950.[2] In theory active and passive management are worlds apart; in practice they influence each other significantly. For exam-

Table 3.3 *Active and indexed fund management: a comparison*[a]

	Active	Indexed
Objectives	Beat the index Beat the peer group	Match the index
Mandate	Discretionary Accept diversifiable risk	Rules-based Avoid diversifiable risk
Approach	Stock or sector selection Market timing Buy and sell	Index tracking Buy and hold
Scope	Asset allocation Asset selection Need not be fully invested Ability to gear	Fully invested in index assets
Depth of coverage	All assets All markets	Greater focus on equities Greater focus on developed markets
Analytical technique	Qualitative 'Art'	Quantitative 'Science'

[a] Source: BGI and PwC, *25 years of indexing: an analysis of the costs and benefits, 1997*

ple, in theory most active managers have considerable discretion in their investment activity. However, in reality pension fund sponsors limit this discretion in order to prevent what is commonly known as 'style drift' or small-cap managers investing in large caps and vice versa. An increasing number of active managers make use of highly quantitative techniques in picking stocks. But in paying close attention to benchmark indexes, they remain 'closet trackers' in their unwillingness to take on additional risk by deviating greatly from the benchmark.

It is the systematic application across a large universe of stocks using computer-readable data sets rather than individually gathered corporate reports, broker's research and stock exchange filings that distinguish traditional active strategies from quantitative strategies. One could understandably argue that the limitation of such an approach may lie in the market coverage of the data sets or even in the efficacy of its analysis and interpretation. Otherwise, in endeavouring to reduce or eliminate subjective assessments of selected companies, quantitative strategies are better able to harness alpha. Nevertheless, there is no substitute for the human skill factor; even intelligent computers can only process the data that is fed to them.

INDEXATION AND LEGISLATION

Despite regulatory involvement with Robert Maxwell's group of companies, the disappearance of more than £400 million from the Maxwell pension funds severely tested people's confidence in the supervision of occupational pension schemes. The Pension Act 1995 aimed to restore public confidence by improving the security of occupational pension schemes. As more individuals were faced with the responsibility of having to provide for their own retirement rather than depend on the state, the regulation of this sector became vital to the common welfare. Unfortunately the mis-selling of personal pensions and endowment policies along with the gross mismanagement at Equitable Life, which left most of its policyholders in the lurch, has not inspired confidence in the adequate regulation of the pensions industry in the UK.

The Goode Committee, under the chairmanship of Professor Goode, was appointed in July 1992 to conduct a comprehensive review of the law relating to occupational pensions. The Pensions Bill reinforced trust law as the basis for pension law; brought the management of all schemes up to the level of best practice; gave scheme members more influence in the running of their schemes by giving them the right to select at least one-third of the trustees; emphasised the fact that the trustees are responsible for running schemes properly and gave them the tools they needed to do so; introduced a statutory solvency requirement to maintain the adequacy of pension fund assets and set up a compensation scheme, thereby establishing an occupational pensions regulator with robust and wide-ranging powers.[3]

While it is widely recognised that technology and globalisation accelerated the use of indexation, demographics and legislation clearly conspired in its favour. The Pensions Act of 1995 was introduced to ensure that corporate pension funds remain adequately funded to meet their liabilities. Thus, they were required to maintain a minimum level of funding, which was ensured by an annual minimum funding valuation test with pensioner liabilities being valued against a basket of gilt yields, index-linked yields and UK quoted equities, depending on the nature of the liabilities. While corporate pension fund managers are not obliged to invest in these assets, it is the simplest way to reduce volatility when measured against the funding standard. At the time the MFR was devised, there was a greater degree of consensus over actuarial assumptions. However, the period following that has been one of rapid and turbulent change, when such a consensus has no longer been available.

The National Association of Pension Funds (NAPF) estimates that of the pension assets totalling some £850 billion, 15% is invested in gilts, and the demand for gilts is set to rise as pension funds mature. However, there is no matching supply of the same from the government, as public borrowing requirements are at their historic lows. As gilt yields fall, the value of pension liabilities rises and the funding position deteriorates. The response of trustees to a reduced cushion of surplus in the fund is often to adopt a more cautious investment strategy, which implies more bonds. This additional demand for bonds has not being matched by additional supply from the government. On the contrary, according to several experts, the gilt market is expected to shrink in the coming years. While the MFR was meant to be a public good, as are lower government debt, inflation and interest rates, the combination created an unsustainable market situation for pension funds and the insurance sector.

The recent decline in yields has not only affected the MFR funding position of UK pension funds, but also the solvency ratios of UK life insurance companies. Developments in demographics, leading to an increasing maturity of pension assets; a balanced government budget, thanks to the decline in inflation and a relatively buoyant economy boosting revenues; changes in the Advanced Corporation Tax and the guaranteed annuity issue with life insurance companies; the unwinding of various hedge fund positions during 1998–99; all these factors came together in a severe supply/demand imbalance in the gilts market, resulting in the gilt yield inversion, thanks to the premium being paid for such a scarce commodity. With global equity markets weakening and investment institutions looking to buy more gilts and bonds, it created a considerable imbalance in the supply/demand position.

The introduction of the MFR had a definite impact on pension funds' investment strategies. Trustees typically resorted to using an asset liability model and then appointing one or more fund managers to manage these assets according to the specified benchmark. The fund manager is therefore responsible for stock selection and perhaps for any tactical asset allocation, leaving the strategic asset allocation to the trustees. This encouraged a shift towards a combination of any of the following structures: single manager, multi-manager multi-asset, specialist and core–satellite (Table 3.4). Whatever managerial structure the trustees settled for, it would inevitably consist of a core of gilts, fixed-income and indexed equity components. Such a requirement spurred the growth of indexation as more and more schemes opted for the specialist and core–satellite structures.

Table 3.4 *Manager structures by benchmark: total sample 224 funds (£316.5bn)*[a]

Manager structure	Benchmark used
Single manager	
39 funds	Peer group (31 funds, £50.2bn)
£60.2bn	Customised (8 funds, £10.0bn)
Multi-manager multi-asset	
69 funds	Peer group (61 funds, £28.2bn)
£30.6bn	Customised (8 funds, £2.4bn)
Specialist	
44 funds	Peer group (18 funds, £12.9bn)
£82.1bn	Customised (26 funds, £69.2bn)
Core–satellite	
72 funds	Peer group (45 funds, £66.0bn)
£143.5bn	Customised (27 funds, £77.5bn)

[a] Source: The WM Company, data as at end 2000

The bulk of tax-exempt pension assets under index management in the US are also invested in domestic equities. Plan sponsors adopted an eclectic approach by borrowing the alpha generation process of active managers, which was grafted on to the bedrock of risk control, diversification and the low cost of a passive, indexed core. According to Alan Brown, chief investment officer of SSGA, 'Once you adopt such an approach, what indexation does is to enable you to focus more clearly on your risk budget or where exactly you want to employ your active risk; obviously where you can get the best reward or where the highest information ratio is available.'[4] In a world where clients are looking for certainty, indexation struck a chord during the years when the stock market performance was strong.

A STRATEGY THAT HAS ARRIVED

Now that over half the pension funds in the UK are using customised benchmarks, based on indexes other than a peer group comparator, plan sponsors are increasingly setting clear investment objectives reflecting their fund's liability or risk profile. However, even those who do use peer group benchmarks rarely do so without a study of their scheme's liabilities. It can be argued that this group of trustees use their peer group's benchmark as a default guide when their studies suggest that the peer group allocation is broadly appropriate. Besides, the other consideration is cost. Small funds with similar liability profiles may find it cheaper to use a peer group benchmark. However, as peer group benchmarks create herding incentives for asset allocation, they need to be avoided whenever possible.

It is true that the majority of trustees have had no professional qualifications in finance or investment and have no in-house professionals to assist them in their difficult decision-making process. But with the passage of time, trustees in the UK are slowly gaining experience. It is not surprising they have not been in a position to exercise genuine power in making efficient decisions for the funds entrusted to them. The review of institutional investment in the UK, conducted by Paul Myners of Gartmore Investment Management and sponsored by HM Treasury, concluded that the MFR 'distorts investment and fails to protect scheme members.'[5] The subsequent abolition of the MFR by the Chancellor of the Exchequer is aimed at encouraging a more efficient allocation of capital in the economy. The death of the MFR is unlikely to be mourned. Most industry participants believe that greater transparency, annual statements and vigilance by trustees, scheme actuaries and members should ensure schemes are not seriously underfunded. In a recent report by Bacon & Woodrow, 17 FTSE companies' sponsored schemes are said to be underfunded, with Vodafone emerging as having the worst underfunding among the FTSE 100 companies.[6]

It can be argued that trustees in the UK have a steep learning curve ahead. According to some experts in the industry, it is the plan sponsors over the past 20 years who have done a good job in the US rather than the fund managers. The plan sponsors chose to have a higher exposure to equity in their portfolios and implemented their strategies in a way that ensured they had a beta of something close to one or to their benchmark. They expected their fund managers to deliver some positive alpha. In reality, active managers delivered negative alpha, but the plan sponsors benefited from the risk premium attached to equities, thanks to a roaring bull market. But in a world of significantly lower inflation, that risk premium may not be available for plan sponsors to fall back on. The rise in total return strategies, such as the use of hedge funds or capital-guaranteed products, reflects investor's need to acquire a beta of zero while importing positive alpha into their portfolios.

The proportion of pension funds in the UK with tailored benchmarks has definitely gone up. The big difference between the UK and the US is the way in which pension plans are governed. In the US, professional staff are responsible for taking investment decisions; in the UK, lay management are left in charge of the same decisions. It is not surprising that many have found the more complex, fund-specific approaches to investing more difficult to grasp and respond to in a meaningful way. However, with the maturity of schemes varying widely and pension fund consultants becoming more active in promoting specialist and core–satellite structures, trustees are becoming more aware of complicated investment issues. According to Anthony Watson of Hermes Pensions Management:

> If you were a trustee you would ask, What is my risk-free rate of return? As to why more funds do not have more customised

benchmarks. In order to do that, you need judgement. If trustees think they are just there to act as a policeman, to ensure there is no hanky-panky, then who is going to make the judgement call? The problem can be that nobody is prepared to take the risk in making those judgements. The differential between trustee and manager sophistication is the same as it was several years ago. If Schroder, Mercury, Gartmore among others have lost money over the last several years, it is because their judgements have been poor, not because they have been balanced managers.[7]

Manager selection among trustees has been known to be arbitrary and can suffer from short-term influences. According to CAPS, 23% of pension funds chose a new manager in 2000, withdrawing a mandate from an existing manager or opened a specific contract; this figure has gone up from 16% in 1999 and 14% in 1998.[8] Taking into account the high cost of switching managers (although appointing new ones is not as expensive and may even help to drive down costs) along with the difficulty of selecting the best managers just as they are entering a positive phase on their performance curve, manager selection can be fraught with challenges. If trustees get it wrong, it damages overall pension fund performance and encourages fund managers to be risk averse. Not acting in a timely manner also leads to poor performance and manager complacency. According to Tim Gardener, 'the average tenure of a manager is about 5 years. I would plan for a 5-year holding period, but it could be a lot longer. Sometimes, fund managers need to be sacked by several clients to force the manager into making the necessary internal changes.'[9]

One of the advantages of indexation, apart from reducing diversifiable risk, is avoiding the risk of selecting poor quality managers. As the industry was in the throes of a major restructuring, asset manager volatility was high, spurred by takeovers and mergers. The situation was also compounded by increased volatility in markets. Such an environment was not conducive to enterprise and risk-taking. The drive to merge and acquire in the investment industry is part of a bigger global trend and it is one that is mostly likely to continue. For William Cotter: 'In a period of transition, it is not uncommon for trustees and their consultants to put managers on a "watch list" – so that they can monitor the impact that change is having on the way their portfolio is managed. In my experience, they often have concerns about the firm's ability to retain key staff, sometimes not unfounded.'[10]

As many American asset management companies have become more active in the UK market, it is not surprising that with a significantly higher IT spend totalling between one-quarter to one-third of their overall expenditure, they have been more successful in winning quantitative mandates. American asset managers with quantitative management styles such as SSGA and BGI have been more successful in winning mandates in the UK, along with local indexed managers such as Legal & General (L&G), substantially adding to their assets under management. The rising exposure to indexed strategies in the UK has been helped by the poor performance record of the so-called balanced managers. According to Tony Watson:

> The reasons behind the rise in the application of quantitative management techniques among fund managers are the failure of typical judgemental techniques to beat the index whenever indexation is the risk-free alternative, coupled with the availability and the ease with which great amounts of data can be manipulated and analysed. On the risk side, people are interested in controlling the risk of under-performance, which has also led to the rise of the use of quantitative techniques.[11]

There is little evidence that active managers consistently do better than the market, apart from changing their asset allocation, perhaps by holding more bonds. There are real problems with big pension funds in applying active management in terms of market impact. Thus, if the benchmark is the FTSE All Share index, which has some 757 stocks in it, active managers hold no more than 100–150 of these companies. And that is a huge risk as far as knowing enough about the prospects for the companies invested in, compared to the ones not held. Indexation offers an attractive option when used as a component of a mix of techniques ranging from a core indexed portfolio to market-neutral strategies, total return strategies along with a private equity exposure.

The convergence of rising stock markets, increasing commoditisation of investment products due to the prevalence of the new technology, the inability of active fund managers to beat a bull market, the entry of new providers of retail indexed products by the likes of Richard Branson, all contributed to the rising popularity of indexation. Although growth in indexed strategies has not been strong since mid-2000, the fall in market valuations with increased volatility has spurred the rise of quantitative, market-neutral techniques. It resulted in the growth of the hedge fund sector with other fixed-income products, including the more exotic capital-protected products and high-yielding emerging market debt funds. Many managers and investors tend to interpret the core–satellite approach, or even the specialist approach, as one where an indexed equity portfolio is applied alongside an active portfolio. William Cotter of Bank of Ireland Asset Management, for example, views it as an opportunity for his own firm:

> Going forward, I think many plan sponsors will be more bench-mark-driven for the main body of their portfolio and this will benefit index managers and others whose style is benchmark-driven. However, they will also seek out complementary managers, who by their nature will be unconstrained and will have the capacity to add significant value in performance terms.

> From our perspective, we recognise that our strength is primarily our stock selection skill. We're happy for others (consultants) to perform asset allocation; we then add value through specialist mandates. We don't disregard benchmarks, but we do think that constraining managers to tracking error limits can lead to 'bunching' and closet index matching.[12]

With the abolition of the MFR and in a world of low inflation, a high exposure to equities may not prove to be the best investment strategy for mature pension funds. As the new technology intensifies competition, investors are more likely to opt for a lower-cost core (indexed equity or bonds) and a performance-related satellite (active alpha or total return) investment strategy. An ageing population and lower inflation rate may also force pension fund managers to increase their investments in bonds or fixed-income products compared to equities. UK institutions have traditionally manifested

a greater appetite for risk in their preference for quoted equity investments when compared to their continental peers. It is not clear
whether their 'preference for certain kinds of risks over others reflects
sub-optimal decision-making.'[13]

In light of the fact that many of the new approaches to portfolio
management mirror the evolution of methods in corporate finance,
in the words of Andrew Skirton:

> It is actually quite shocking that a lot of the companies that
> investment management firms seek to evaluate have changed
> their production processes radically over the last 15 years. Yet
> the investment management firms that seek to make judge-
> ments about them have really had processes in place that have
> not changed over a long period of time. They have been more
> artistic in nature and not very scientific, nor quantitative in
> their approach. A number of asset management firms have
> ended up taking inappropriate, ill-informed risk, but have
> not been appropriately compensated for that risk. They have
> not been able to evaluate investment opportunities consis-
> tently by taking into account relevant data, which has been
> widely available.[14]

What Skirton is referring to is the high level of inadvertent or
unintended risks inherent in active portfolios, risks that could easily
drown the source of alpha, thereby reversing the intended outcome,
i.e. leaving the manager with a high risk and a negative alpha. Risk-
adjusted performance is something that UK plan sponsors are gradually becoming more conscious of. Accounting for risk in performance analysis has been a contentious issue. The problem with
using conventional measures of performance, such as gross or total
returns, is that they do not include risk in the return data. They ignore
the fact that higher performance may have resulted from the investor
also taking a significantly higher level of risk.

If costs are computed into the equation, the loss made by investors
can be significant. As a group, the loss runs into billions of dollars.
According to research conducted by BGI and PricewaterhouseCoopers, the annual savings to US institutional tax-exempt domestic
equity investors from choosing indexed rather than active external
management had risen to almost $14 billion a year by 1997. Under a

slightly different scenario, the estimated saving was even larger at $18 billion a year.[15] While one might question the assumptions on which the cost-benefit model was based and arrive at lower or even higher figures by changing the assumptions, the fact remains that indexation is the cheaper option. Investors prefer performance-related fees, although the retail investor has no leverage in securing them. While greater competition may have delivered lower costs, the high fees and poor performance could have annulled that to a great extent for many investors. Thus, indexation offers an ideal solution.

LOWERING COSTS ENHANCES RETURNS

With the greater use of derivatives and quantitatively driven investment styles, the traditional edifice of the asset management industry is under threat. Portfolio turnover among active managers is generally higher than for indexers; average stock turnover for active funds is around 100% compared to 10% for indexed funds. Thus, costs associated with trading are also lower among indexed funds. Major indexers can control these costs even further by 'crossing' their trades rather than taking them to the market, thereby reducing market impact. Market impact refers to the effect that buying or selling a stock has on its price. Although there is no consensus in the industry as to how exactly to measure it, most fund managers follow some internally established guidelines when placing an order in the market. Dealer, or bid-offer, spreads are further costs when buying or selling shares that can erode performance. The other area where the active manager incurs costs is in research and analysis or in advisory fees.

Studies within the US indicated that for the US large-cap market, the cost differential between active and indexed equity fund management was about 45 basis points for a medium-sized mandate in 1997; and the range of costs was five times as great for an active portfolio as for an indexed portfolio. The average expense ratio (expenses as a ratio of the fund's average net assets) of an actively managed portfolio was 0.6% higher than that for an indexed portfolio over the period 1988–97 for the institutional sector, and 0.8% higher for the retail sector. Within the UK, reliable cost data for the institutional sector was not available, but retail data from Micropal provided further confirmation of the cost advantage of indexing. Initial fees were 2.2% lower for FTSE 100 tracker funds, and annual fees were also 0.3% lower.[16]

Even within the indexed sector, how much can managers charge when investors are able to buy cheap, liquid and transparently priced alternatives on the derivatives markets? Vanguard's index fund (based on the S&P 500) has an expense ratio of around 18 basis points compared to L&G's 55 basis points. While the Vanguard funds are much larger and benefit from various efficiencies of scale (they account for some 60% of the US indexed funds market), it indicates that the cost structure in the UK could come under additional pressure. It is the high fee structure that is responsible for attracting the likes of Vanguard into a lucrative market in Europe.

Technology has also enabled fund managers to measure the costs of implementing the strategies they devise, allowing them to concentrate their business with those brokers that achieve the best combinations of price and transaction cost. In their decision-making process, quantitative managers are better able to take into account costs, market timing and impact, volatility of the underlying asset classes. In his report, Paul Myners points out that 'the sum which pension funds pay in commissions to investment houses, stockbrokers and so on, for providing dealing and research may well be similar in size to the fees which they pay for active fund management.'[17] Yet the disclosure of brokers' commissions is far from transparent.

Myners' recommendation that fund managers should absorb these costs, treating brokers' commissions as a cost integral to their own business, may disturb the status quo. A more transparent costing structure – from management fees, brokers' commissions to administration and custody, etc. – can benefit the industry. But not all fund managers support Myners' recommendation on greater transparency of fees and other costs. Trustees, consultants and scheme members could benefit from knowing how much it costs to run their schemes beyond the headline fees. These significantly extra charges include custody and commission costs, along with other hidden costs such as below market interest rates on cash holdings as well as market impact costs on equity trades. Most of these costs can be measured, but it is not yet clear what the government's set of principles would be in response to the Myners Report. As broker commissions can be broken down into the bid-offer spread, local taxes and the market price impact, it remains to be seen if removal of broker commissions will help investors or simply widen the bid-offer spreads and heighten market impact. Fees and hidden costs are a predictable component of long-term performance and investors can only take these matters into account if that information is available and easy to understand.

According to Tim Gardener, Myners was absolutely right: 'What goes on at the moment is scandalous, demonstrably open to a huge amount of abuse. It is not clear how clients are served in the present system. It will be a tremendous benefit to clients if something can be done to make sure that the current system in which the fund manager uses someone else's money to buy services for his benefit is abolished altogether.'[18] Lack of such information currently leads to inefficient investment decisions. Bad portfolio construction results in higher levels of risk and poor use of information in return forecasts. 'When we make investment decisions, we take into account the return on the stock with an awareness of the cost of the transaction and a good understanding of the risk within the portfolio,'[19] confirmed BGI's Skirton. The total return and the impact of the return on the overall portfolio risk need to be understood. Implementation costs usually lead performance to fall short of the return expectations created by research.

> Indexed strategies offer a very low cost exposure to markets in a diversified way, hence they are very efficient. They are low cost because investment management fees are low and also, very few transactions are required to keep the investments in line with the index. Thus, trading costs are low. Index funds allow investors to acquire assets in a shape that is often assumed in their asset liability studies The performance you can get from indexed funds, after fees, compares favourably in the short run with active managers and extremely favourably in the long run with active managers. That's been experienced in developed and in developing markets around the world. As a core component of a pension fund, indexation has been very attractive to clients looking to get the right balance between an indexed core and an active component. It is a very efficient way of controlling risk in building an investment portfolio.[20]

Higher trading costs basically lead to underperformance. Effective trading strategies help to lower costs, strategies such as using a block desk, crossing networks, limit or market agency orders, or other computer-based services offered by brokers who are able to release portions of the order to the market in such a way that the trade is as close as possible to the volume weighted average price for the day. While direct costs such as brokerage commissions and bid-offer spreads are measurable, indirect costs such as market impact or opportunity cost are more difficult to measure. However, an attempt at measuring trading costs after the event can help to reduce future costs. Analysis of data on realised costs can help in cost rationalisation. 'The way we trade will change radically as well,' adds Skirton. 'We see increasing use of crossing networks. We did a joint venture with Merrill Lynch Investment Management to establish the first investment manager owned equity-crossing network. So, in the quest for lower trading costs, technology will help.'[21] In BGI's experience, the use of optimisers that allow trading costs to be incorporated into the model can lead to a considerable reduction in trading costs, sometimes as high as 30%.

In the trading and reporting areas of the asset management business, the industry is in a complete replacement environment as trading moves to accommodate T + 1 in the US. Trade information from the marketplace will have to migrate from a largely end-of-day batch process to a real-time process so that information feeds into the clearing system at the moment of trade execution. One of the critical issues in T + 1 will be irrevocability of settlement. Apart from participants having to confirm what they are expecting to settle on any particular day, it makes it difficult to unwind any transactions. The cost of mistakes can be high, but the long-term advantages are many. Here are some of the benefits of T + 1 according to Deborah Lamb, CEO of Investment Industry Consultants: [22]

- Reduced hands-on involvement in trade settlement provides more time for client relationship management.
- It provides for real-time trade status, reduced error risk, the ability to monitor portfolios intra-day, and more effective codes and standards of practice.

- Technically, achieving T + 1 will force interoperability through better software and dataware programs.
- Monetarily, a T + 1 environment will provide the platform for reduced credit and settlement risk, reduced online software and failed trade costs, and lower overall administrative and operating costs, including headcount.
- All of this translates into increased firm profit margins. The T + 1 path may be resource-intensive, but the rewards will be plentiful and long-lasting.

Straight-through processing (STP) was conceived as the most efficient process delivering economies of scale, offering superior risk control, eliminating manual intervention in a free-flowing global marketplace that operates round the clock. The move towards global STP is necessary as larger volumes of trade imply higher costs and operational risk. Thus, from making investment decisions, precompliance checking, and trading, to accounting, settling and reporting, the whole process is expected to move smoothly and be as close as possible in real time, i.e. in different time zones. This seamless industry-wide ownership and liability process will require major reform in settlement, impact how financial service firms structure their operational and trading systems, and most importantly, how the entire industry will communicate with others in a real-time global STP environment. For Deborah Lamb, 'institutional managers have treated trade settlement problems as individual, isolated administrative exceptions rather than as industry-wide concerns. Accurate and speedy information transfer is critical in the shortened settlement life cycle and, unlike the T + 3 transformation, will necessitate coordinated manager and vendor efforts to create programs capable of achieving real-time end-to-end solutions and compatible communications and reporting automation.'[23]

The sell side appears to have incurred most of the financial costs in this technological transformation as investment managers lag in taking a proactive role in the T + 1 initiative in the US. SSGA has developed in-house products such as Quadrant, which allows asset managers to flow trades to them, and via them to the appropriate custodian through their SWIFT interface. With a rise in outsourcing, Global Securities Services aim to capture every stage of the transaction cycle, from the investment decision to the settlement of the trade. 'We are all going to have to install new generation technology to keep pace with all these changes; it is not an option but a question of survival,' confirms SSGA's Brown:

> We need to be able to accommodate local practices (for example, Japanese accounting systems in Japanese) but otherwise all our systems are becoming more global. All the data is in one central place anyway. It is a question of packaging that data for the particular market. With the internet, individual customisation will increase even more rapidly. Clients also want the information more and more near real time, which means that as an organisation we have to move from batch processing towards a more continuous production process. It is a major operational burden, as technological cycles are rapidly getting shorter.[24]

However, increasing deployment of technology within the industry is not merely a question of fashion. What is driving this change is the need to manage efficiently one's operational risk, reduce costs and deliver superior client service. Similarly, the best fund managers today depend on quantitative techniques to identify investment opportunities; they deploy technology to acquire and distil information rapidly, reliably and accurately. It is leveraging the investment insight of the professionals by using technology and that is indeed a very positive trend. The really big rise in quantitative asset management has clearly been in indexation. Active quantitative strategies have also benefited, but the major growth has come from indexation. As more and more traditionally active managers are using quantitative strategies in their investment decision-making, the distinction between active and passive strategies is getting blurred as skill and judgement come into play in all efficient strategies.

RISK AND BENCHMARK SELECTION

In the benchmarked world of professional investing, risk has shifted from the asset managers to the trustees or the plan sponsors. What is more relevant among pension fund managers today is the recognition of the importance of benchmark orientation. The function of the customised benchmark is not only to assess how a manager has performed relative to the index, but the selection of the benchmark becomes a critical investment decision for the pension fund. To that end, plan sponsors need to be innovative in their indexed strategy:

> Choosing the benchmark is the single most important investment decision to be made. Whether customised or peer group, it is a matter of judgement. Hence that judgement like any other can be flawed. Risk is that the benchmark does not deliver the pot of money that the trustees need to make the liability payments. Even though the liabilities are known, companies have chosen to match these by equities rather than matching with bonds or index-linked investments.[25]

The Myners Report is of the opinion that risk controls for active managers in the UK are increasingly set in ways 'which give them little choice but to cling closely to stock market indices, making meaningful active management near-impossible.'[26] It is the abdication of this core responsibility in choosing a fund-specific benchmark by trustees that is examined in some detail in the Myners Report:

> The peer group benchmark has a further distorting effect, tending to produce investment decisions – in particular asset allocation – based on what other funds are doing. This is not in the best interest of pension funds and their members. A pension fund should set its asset allocation because it believes, on the evidence available, that a particular allocation will best enable it to meet its liabilities at its projected rate of contribution, not because other pension funds have a similar allocation.[27]

It is true that creating a customised benchmark is indeed an extremely complex process and in general trustees are not well equipped to address such matters. A large number of investment consultants use what is commonly known as the stochastic asset liability model when choosing a benchmark. As is often the case with any model, the outcome is determined largely by the data that is fed into the model. Asset liability modelling is particularly challenging as there are many assumptions about long-term interest rates and other economic indicators such as inflation and growth as well as data on asset classes, all of which require long historic, time series data. Given the structural changes that have taken place in financial markets over the past three decades – including privatisations, deregulation, radical shifts in ownership of assets, etc. – historical data fails to be a good indicator of the future.

Besides, the asset liability model is highly quantitative in its orientation. Thus, the understanding, assessment and quantification of risk are not simple when those responsible for making vital decisions are not fully cognizant of the implications of their decision. On the contrary, it could be positively detrimental to the outcome. Even those with a high level of knowledge and skill in such matters have made serious miscalculations; the fates of Baring, Long-Term Capital Management and Equitable Life are a salutary warning to all who fail to hedge the potential risk inherent in their investment decisions. If trustees in the UK as a group have not made a bigger mess as yet, perhaps it is because legislation and their relative lack of expertise have protected them from taking bigger risks. Research suggests that among schemes using an asset liability model, trustees were involved in the setting of these underlying assumptions in only 30% of cases.[28]

The other major factor in such decision-making is that, by definition, it excludes any asset class that is new and does not have historic time series data; or precisely those areas of economic activity in the marketplace where inefficiencies occur and hence there exists a chance of capturing alpha, if you have the skill for doing so. The FTSE All Share, while capturing over 98% of the nation's listed companies, does not reflect the total productive activity in the economy. It excludes the venture capital market, for example, along with the other major unlisted sector, the public sector. Plan sponsors fail to include private equity due to its perceived higher risk profile and lack of long-term data, although returns from private equity investments have been superior to the listed share market. Thus, many pension funds in the UK have sacrificed unwittingly the higher alpha available from private equity funds. Note that many of the local authority pension funds in the UK have 'an allocation to private equity, with some of them targeting such investments in order to try to help their local economy.' It is also worth mentioning that the level of index tracking in local authority funds was 'lower than for pension funds'.[29]

The availability and the investability of indexes on a global basis remain the key to indexation's future. Most hedge fund managers use quantitative techniques to identify inefficiently priced assets for their tactical asset allocation. It is also true that the portfolio construction techniques used by quantitative managers is more rigorous in the areas of risk control and diversification. Quantitative modelling enables the construction of portfolios with a desired set of investment attributes, while maintaining a target level of predicted tracking error relative to the chosen benchmark. Studies indicate that those indexes with a larger tracking error coupled with a capitalisation bias due to the limited number of stocks can cause a significant over- or underperformance over time. Sometimes performance can differ markedly; the year 1998 saw the biggest gap between growth and value, large-cap and small-cap indexes in the US as in the UK. Even over longer investment periods, choice of benchmark makes a major difference to performance.

Understanding the composition of an index can make a crucial difference to performance. For example, in March 2001 over 68% of the FTSE World Europe index consisted of financials (28.7%), non-cyclical consumer goods and services (28.6%) and resources (11%). The subsectors that dominated this series were banks, telecommunications, oil and gas, and pharmaceuticals. Overall market impact was greatly influenced by the behaviour of these sectors, as evidenced in the correction in the bubble valuation of not just the IT sector (6% of index) but also the highly geared telecom sector. The telecom sector was heavily weighted in Vodafone, Telefónica de Espana, Telecom Italia and Telecom Ital Mobile. The level of concentration in the IT sector was worse due to the domination of Nokia and Ericsson. If an index is being used primarily for diversification, then its constituents need to indicate that. As indexed mandates avoid diversifiable risk, choice of index is vital when risk diversification is an important element in the investment.

Managing benchmark risk is an essential aspect of asset allocation. Particularly when plan sponsors also set limits to the fund manager's stock selection decision, which may inadvertently distort the original allocation decision. Besides, with the increasing arbitrariness of M&A activity and irrational valuations attached to some companies and sectors, the stocks that get included in an index negate the

97

rationale of indexing. Vodafone-Mannesmann is a case in point. Had Mannesmann taken over Vodafone, which was an equally plausible scenario, then indexed managers would have had to sell their holdings in Vodafone as it would no longer have been part of the FTSE index. Thus, one dangerous feature of indexing is that the fund manager automatically raises the portfolio weighting of stocks to reflect the market portfolio when more attractive investment opportunities lie outside that specific index, for example, in real estate, emerging markets or bonds. However, that does not mean indexation is somehow an inefficient strategy; all it means is that the choice of index matters.

The rise in stock-specific risk in benchmarks over the last few years does raise the issue of benchmark risk, which can be addressed by hedging those companies in the index that constitute such risk, in which case the cost of hedging should be added to the overall cost of running an indexed portfolio. There has also been a shift towards higher investment in overseas equities due to a narrowing of the UK market in terms of exposure to stock and sector. Global diversification is partly a response to alleviate this concentration in the market. It was aided by the abolition of the advanced corporation tax in 1997, which resulted in the withdrawal of the tax advantage available to UK pension funds for investing in domestic equities.

If the whole purpose of investing in the FTSE All Share index is diversification and risk reduction, then the concentrated composition of the index defeats that objective. The top 10 stocks account for some 54% of the FTSE 100 and 45% of the FTSE All Share, and are dominated by banks, oil and pharmaceutical companies. The FTSE 250 accounts for less than 13% of the FTSE All Share. The FTSE 350 represents over 96% of the FTSE All Share. It is not surprising that market analysis is focused on these 350 companies. This high level of stock-specific risk in a widely used index does not bode well for anybody – not the market, not the indexers, not the active managers who are measured against it. The 766 companies in the FTSE All Share index in March 2001 represented over 98% of all the listed companies in the UK market with some 1,190 companies in the Fledgling and AIM index accounting for the rest. Considering the main reason for getting a listing for a small-cap firm is the ability to raise capital, then such a scenario discourages new firms from getting a listing in the first place and the London Stock Exchange becomes an elite club for the top 350 companies in the UK.

The creation of Euroland, the trend towards globalisation and industry consolidation, and the rise in technological applications have jointly contributed to the increased relevance of stock market indexes within the fund management industry as investors embrace a more regional approach when investing in Europe. Many of Europe's largest funds have also moved from their home country bias to restructuring their portfolios on a euro/non-euro or pan-European basis. Considering that indexes now define markets and fund managers are required to follow the changes made by index providers, the whole issue of narrow benchmarks and attendant investment risk has gained in importance. This reversal of roles, where indexes define the market rather than the other way round, is an interesting development. As long as index providers are aware of their role and responsibility in defining the market, they do make a distinct contribution to market efficiency.

The explosion of available indexes – by providers such as FTSE International, Morgan Stanley Capital International (MSCI), Standard & Poor's (S&P), Dow Jones and Frank Russell – indicates the intense battle for market share in Europe, the new growth frontier. Greater competition encouraged MSCI to expand its country coverage from 60% to 85% of market capitalisation. The introduction of free-float adjustments in the calculation of indexes by both FTSE and MSCI is also a welcome development. The Salomon Smith Barney index series was already free-float adjusted and the Dow Jones STOXX made the transition a year ago. What the free-float adjustment means is that a company's market capitalisation will reflect the total amount of shares that are available for investment, thereby excluding corporate cross-holdings, government holdings, founders' share ownership and any foreign ownership restrictions. As a result, the US and the UK will see the largest increase in country weights at the expense of Japan, France, Germany, Italy and emerging markets. The industry group that will gain the most is technology hardware and equipment, whereas telecommunication services will lose out as many of the large companies in the sector have lower average free-float of shares compared to other sectors.

Considering the benchmark index is used for performance measurement, analysing and structuring asset allocation decisions, identifying and managing portfolio risk as well as for a range of stock, sector and country analysis functions, its importance to a portfolio cannot be overemphasised. The benchmark index determines the universe within which the asset manager invests. Investing in a truly representative index is a low-risk way of spreading equity exposure over the market. The derivatives index forms the basis of derivative contracts, which are used for hedging and risk management purposes. Despite the vital role played by the benchmark, the process associated with the selection of a benchmark was fairly unscientific and random. According to Chris Sutton of Barclays Global Investors, 'The factors behind selection of indices by investors are dictated more by cultural influences and branding than by the technical attributes on offer.'[30] As most investors remain relatively unaware of what the indexes really measure, it is not surprising that UK investors remain FTSE-oriented while euro-zone investors show a strong preference for the MSCI indexes. The indexes that have picked up most support over the past few years are the Dow Jones STOXX indexes, although their broad Europe counterparts are less widely used. The 2001 Thomson Extel Pan-European Survey indicated that MSCI continued to be the most widely used index in benchmarking and tracking by investment professionals, winning twice as many votes as their nearest competitor.

Index providers today must be capable of building a variety of benchmarks to meet their clients' specific investment needs, assemble the most comprehensive data and information consistent on a global basis, deliver data in the most flexible manner and license products so clients can offer products to their customers. With growing investor awareness and sophistication, those benchmarks that are perceived to offer the greatest transparency, accuracy and liquidity are most likely to win market share. In the end, a broad variety of attributes create the superior index; they include completeness, investability, relatively low turnover of index constituents, consistent index construction across all countries and industries, historical return information, broad acceptance by investors and resulting investment critical mass, quality of benchmark research and maintenance and real-time availability.[31] While the index providers battle it out for the largest share of the market, investors are left to cope with assessing risk, performance and the matching of their asset liability profile.

As multinational companies become larger through mergers and acquisitions, the representation of smaller, local companies in various indexes have shrunk. With greater investor sophistication in Europe, it is most likely there will be demand for greater differentiation in styles and market cap as in the Russell indexes available for the US. The UK market has changed significantly over the past decade and index providers are still catching up with these massive changes. The listing of foreign companies on the London Stock Exchange, the purchase of shares in large-cap companies by overseas investors, both portfolio and direct, the late introduction of rebalancing in the weights of shares in the FTSE indexes, all contributed to price escalation as indexation caught the imagination of investors. While passive managers have the bulk of their assets invested in the FTSE All Share, the lack of trading in small-cap shares by passive managers contributed to the poor liquidity and the lack of interest by active institutional investors.

Faced with such unprecedented convergence of events, active managers turned closet indexers, concentrating their holdings in 'momentum' stocks or 'index' stocks. In the process, they enhanced the overall risk of their portfolios and contributed actively in distorting the efficient market process. Most investors agree that trustees do not empower active managers to genuinely add value as they are constrained by how much they can diverge from their given benchmark. Thus, active managers end up with holding companies they do not particularly view as positive candidates for investment simply because they cannot afford to deviate too much from any given index they are being measured against. The active managers, who are meant to be the price setters, turn into closet indexers as they surf passively on asset bubbles.

IS THERE A DOWNSIDE TO INDEXATION?

Institutional investors generally use indexes for benchmarking and the key to any external benchmark is that it represents the total investment opportunity. However, as the late John Morrell of John Morrell &

Associates reminded us, 'Indices have been conscripted in recent years into a role for which they were not originally intended.'[32] Index providers make better profit margins out of the trading in derivatives contracts based on their indexes. As many of the new benchmarks are targeted at derivative contracts, they have tended to be narrow, such as the DJ STOXX 50 or EURO STOXX 50, the FTSE Eurotop 100 or the MSCI Euro & Pan-Euro indexes. However, as pure benchmarks they are not truly representative of the whole market. But all these index providers also offer fairly broad indexes.

Despite the explosion of benchmarks, both new and old, 'it is interesting that as yet no one has actually brought out a benchmark that truly represents the investment opportunities on a pan-European basis' says Suzanne Mitchell, performance measurement manager at Russell/Mellon Analytical Services. There is as yet no equivalent in Europe of the broad set of Russell 3000 indexes for the US market, for example. For Suzanne Mitchell: 'The Salomon Smith Barney (SSB) benchmarks, both Europe and Eurozone, are probably the best ones, in their very broad pan-European coverage. The SSB Europe index, for example, includes over 1,850 companies which extend over 15 countries, 35 sectors/industry groups and target 100% market capitalisation coverage of companies with float over $100 million.'[33] None of the other indexes offer such a broad level of coverage.

Monitoring the benchmark is vital, particularly when it alters dramatically over long periods of time. From the FTSE to the Nikkei, users need to be conscious of benchmark risk. Just because an index exists, there is no reason to invest in it. If one is index-oriented, then it makes sense to use a widely diversified index that captures a high level of productive activity in the global economy. A move towards an era of greater customisation of benchmarks and towards more total market capitalisation indexes will be necessary. When analysing benchmarks, one usually looks at listed corporations, although governments and other factors of production also contribute to the total economic activity of any country. It has been the practice to concentrate on listed firms when creating benchmarks, although unlisted firms are also generators of wealth. Governments and other publicly owned factors of production are perceived to be distributors of wealth and so are not included in any investable index.

Opportunity cost is not captured by narrow benchmarks. If the benchmark is truly representative of investment opportunities, then it should reflect just that. By using a narrow benchmark, a lot of the investment opportunity can lie outside that benchmark; in which case, doing the most detailed analysis of the benchmark versus the portfolio is still not reflecting a true picture of where the investment returns are going to come from. The IT investment frenzy in 1999 was narrowly based and if you did hold a widely diversified global portfolio, you would have still missed out on spectacular returns in that sector. However, unless you had the sense to sell at the right moment, you would be sitting on huge losses today had you invested in the IT sector. Thus, broadly based benchmarks work best over longer investment cycles. With the rise in indexation, passive managers have been investing in companies at prices set by active managers. But when active managers behave as closet indexers, the basic concept of the market mechanism gets distorted. With short selling not widely prevalent among long-only managers, closet indexing due to the current management structures within the pension fund sector is the greatest threat to the market. It is desirable for investors, institutional or retail, to use a greater diversity of asset allocation and stock selection styles.

Although index funds may benefit a wide range of investors, their widespread use is indeed a threat to efficient capital markets. The primary and highest function of any capital market is to allocate capital to its best and most efficient use. Although there is no immediate threat of such an eventuality, and active managers along with hedge fund managers are thriving today, one could argue that if the majority of investors become passive price takers, capital markets will fail to function effectively, and capitalism itself will fail to deliver. While acknowledging that the median active managers in the US as in the UK have underperformed the passive index consistently over the past two decades, passive allocation of assets is only a viable strategy when it is supported by a dominant active sector. Thus, active managers provide the basis for an efficient market where indexation can succeed. When indexation takes over, it creates inefficiencies which are then arbitraged away by active managers, thereby restoring market efficiency. The problem arises when active managers turn closet indexers.

Benchmark risk is what asset managers have to watch out for. The previous practice of ignoring the free-float of shares in a company caused major distortion in its pricing, which was determined by the marginal buyer of the stock. Thus, it was possible for firms to offer a small free-float of shares while enjoying a large market capitalisation, which helped enhance its fund-raising profile. And if a stock has a large market capitalisation, it puts pressure on investors to include it in their portfolios, thereby distorting the pricing structure even further. With changes in the free-float rules in the London Stock Exchange and the transparency of the major indexes, some of the sources of such market distortion have been overcome; albeit recently. It is a very welcome development.

There persists a popular misconception that index funds cause the stocks of large companies to appreciate while depressing the price of smaller companies. That is obviously not the cause of the nature of market distortion we are referring to. On the contrary, the self-rebalancing attribute of indexation implies that such funds only trade when the underlying index includes or deletes issues. The problem arises when the index adds companies whose market capitalisation is not backed by underlying earnings and deletes companies whose market capitalisation does not adequately reflect underlying earnings. While an active manager has an opportunity to exploit such market inefficiencies, this option is not available to the passive manager. BGI's Andrew Skirton maintains that 'the market has proven regularly to be right in judging substantial change. One of the advantages of an indexed strategy is the self-balancing mechanism in taking into account succeeding companies and we think the market's judgement in the long-term will be proven to be correct.' He admits:

> It is active managers that are setting the prices for these stocks. Index investors just end up owning them. We do not chase prices. Our portfolio is automatically rebalanced to reflect market changes and the correct weighting in the index. If the company appears from nowhere and goes to becoming one or two percent of the index, that is what is reflected in our portfolios. It is marginal turnover in the securities that is setting the price; it has little to do with indexed investors. We are buyers/sellers of the whole market and not of individual stocks.[34]

Anthony Watson of Hermes has a similar explanation with reference to indexation and market efficiency. The onus is clearly placed on active managers in setting the price as owners of select stocks, though admittedly most active managers would hold no more than 200 companies in their portfolio. Contrary to popular opinion, it is the indexers who own more companies in the FTSE All Share index than the active managers:

> It is not as if index managers are setting the price of those stocks without any earnings attached to them. It is the active managers who are in the driving seat and passive managers are probably getting unwittingly sucked into investments that have no earnings. The whole point about indexation is a belief that markets are efficient! Here one should hold no strong views about any individual stocks, such as Vodafone, BP-Amoco or Glaxo, until it becomes fairly obvious that such a share gets to such a high market weighting in the index that there are concerns about lack of sufficient diversification. At that point there has to be a trade-off between a belief in indexation (and market efficiency) and concern about whether the scheme is overexposed to any single asset. But you also see many highly rated IT companies exiting the FTSE 100 share index, which of course makes not a jot of difference to us as we are benchmarked against the All Share. If Baltimore Technologies goes from the 100 to the 250, it is not a big thing for us. Also, when companies move from the bottom up or enter at the bottom, it does not have a real impact on us.[35]

However, if the whole market went indexed (i.e. when active managers also behave like closet indexers), then you no longer have an efficient market. Active managers provide the research and the trading activity, which forms the basis for indexation. If indexation were to rise beyond a certain level of market share, it would lead to market distortions and destroy the efficient market process. During 2000 many IT firms entered the FTSE 100 index, but most of these companies were not generating any earnings. However, indexed managers would have automatically acquired those stocks. Then during 2001 most of these companies fell out of the same index, and once again, passive investors would have acted accordingly. 'Regarding the efficient allocation of assets, as we all know markets are not exactly efficient,' agrees Alan Brown. 'Hence that is a real concern. Active fund managers were buying those stocks because it was more risky not to own them. Hence, we view the recent correction in the TMT sector as being healthy.' Alan Brown maintains that 'all we are doing is passively implementing the active stock selection strategy of the index committee; and although we may be acting in a passive form, the client in choosing a benchmark is making an active decision.'[36] The choice of the benchmark is therefore critical. So is giving active managers the mandate to back their conviction.

The major constraint in using an index as a benchmark, particularly within traditional active investment strategies, is that the manager's total expertise is rarely utilised. Hedge fund strategies are better able to make use of their total investment recommendations, particularly those stocks with both negative expectation and conviction, by short-selling them. In having to track an index, active managers have traditionally resorted to underweighting a stock they did not like. Here are the views of one major active investment manager in the UK, who did not wish to be identified:

> The starting point for portfolio construction is the focus list, which is used as a building block for all portfolios. The focus list contains stock ideas and analyst recommendations. Stocks are rated as positive, neutral or negative, reflecting where the portfolio constructors will want to be over- or underweight. The next stage of the process is to construct platform models, i.e. positive conviction in the focus list would lead to overweighting a stock on a platform model. Negative conviction in the focus list will therefore lead to an underweight position on a platform model. If a view on a stock within the focus list changes, the platform model weighting will be altered to reflect the new view. There are typically three platform models: alpha, alpha plus and high alpha. All client portfolios are derived from these platform models and clients will sit under the platform most appropriate to their risk/return appetite.

By definition, a portfolio of stocks with positive alpha will outperform the market. If such a portfolio fails to outperform, then it reflects the manager's lack of skill in identifying alpha. If a manager has a negative conviction about a stock, in a truly active style it will not be included in any portfolio. And that is where active managers genuinely add value to their clients' portfolios and to the market as a whole, and hopefully they send a signal to the company if something other than its price is also not right. Being underweight in a stock with negative conviction just because it has a large weighting in the index violates the basic idea of an active investment strategy. For Paul Myners:

> As an investment strategy, passive investing seeks to free-ride off the more or less efficient capital allocation of active managers. As such, it could in principle lead to odd pricing effects. However, it would not be legitimate to argue on that basis that institutions should not use it. Their concern is not with the efficiency of the capital markets as a whole, except insofar as this may affect the interests of their beneficiaries. Passive investing is a legitimate strategy for an investor who values its tangible cost advantages over the possibility of achieving additional return through superior stock selection.
>
> The greater one's belief in the efficiency of the market concerned, the more convincing this argument is likely to be. Indeed, a rational investor might expect to invest passively in some markets but not others, on the basis that they believed that one market, because of poor liquidity, lack of information and similar factors, held opportunities for active investment to add value, whereas other markets, with high liquidity and good information, did not.
>
> The decision about whether to have active or passive management is a strategic one, which investors must take asset class by asset class.[37]

The efficiency of the capital markets as a whole is directly linked to the self-interest of individuals today, regardless of who is going to provide for their pension – the state, employers, individuals themselves or a combination of these sources. Indexation as an investment strategy has considerable merit and appeal. Unfortunately, it has its limitation and remains flawed in its current incarnation. However, there is no reason why we will be unable to develop more meaningful benchmarks that will prove more conducive to optimal investment decisions.

CONCLUSION

While most indexed strategies actively replicate a given broad market capitalisation based index (which does not reflect future earnings expectation), it would be equally plausible for plan sponsors to require, for example, the FTSE All Share to be indexed on a formula reflecting firms' operating earning and operating margin along with the free-float of shares. Some may argue that such an index is backward-looking as it is based on historic earnings while markets are forward-looking, in which case the index can be tilted to reflect the consensus I/B/E/S forecasts. At least that will incorporate the active research element that is currently ignored in indexed strategies, although indexers will argue that the market price reflects such research and incorporates analysts' views in the daily movements.

However, under such a scenario, analysts will need to be truly independent and perhaps not work on the sell side or for investment banks and their corporate finance department, but for institutions that only provide research. Currently, investment analysts are employed either by the buy side (the fund managers) or the sell side (investment banks). There are a few independent research companies but their market impact is not comparable to the collective impact of the analysts within the industry. Buy-side investment analysts' forecasts are not publicly available although it can be argued their clients benefit from such research. The I/B/E/S forecasts consists of only the forecasts of the analysts on the sell side. Thus, buy-side analysts use sell-side analysts as a useful investment tool. Sell-side analysts provide essential information that is market-related. These analysts also know the industry better and the buy-side values this in-depth knowledge of companies. The I/B/E/S consensus forecasts provide the buy-side analysts with their sources of alpha. There are perhaps more buy-side analysts and buy-side analysts are theoretically more independent than their sell-side counterparts. But sell-side research is distributed among the buy-side analysts and their fund managers, and the market influence of sell-side analysts is decidedly more significant.

The merits of indexation will emerge as the composition of the benchmark is taken more seriously and more research is put into its creation. Indexers have become conscious of the dangers of using narrow benchmarks. As Alan Brown points out:

> I think we will be moving into an era of more customisation of benchmarks and towards more total market capitalisation indices. MSCI, for example, currently provides only 60% of each country's market cap. But if you start from 90% of the world's capitalisation, then you can reduce it to a home country bias and play around with the index in a way that reduces stock-specific risk or even sector concentration. At the moment, the benchmarks do not lend themselves to being 'sliced and diced' in the same way, which prevents one from being more creative in benchmark selection.[38]

The key to ensuring a superior indexed strategy is to use as wide a benchmark as possible. In the UK, over 90% of all indexed investment made by firms such as BGI, SSGA or L&G are in the FTSE All Share index. One of the major arguments in support of indexation is the benefit of diversification of risk by owning what is essentially the market. However, with the MFR-inspired 'home bias' among pension funds, with trustees investing the bulk of their assets in the UK market and only 20-25% in international equity markets, tracking will inevitably reflect the stock-specific risk inherent in the relevant market index. Such a bias might be justifiable if the equity universe were sufficiently diversified in terms of stock-specific and sector risk; in reality, finding an adequate benchmark remains the most important decision for any investor, not just an indexer.

Despite its limitations, indexation has major advantages and shows no signs of losing its popularity among pension fund managers. Among the top 10 managers who won the most mandates and assets in 2000 on a global basis, the top two were indexed managers who also have demonstrable strengths in constructing active portfolios, based on their quantitative research and trading capabilities (Table 3.5).

Table 3.5 *The top 10 global equity managers with the highest wins in 2000*[a]

	Total value (£bn)	Average size (£bn)
Barclays Global Investors	18.1	1.10
State Street Global Advisers	15.7	1.60
Merrill Lynch Investment Managers	9.8	1.40
Alliance Capital	6.2	1.20
Mellon	2.9	1.45
Putnam Investments	1.4	0.18
Northern Trust Global Investors	1.4	0.20
Capital International	1.3	0.14
Strong Capital Management	1.3	1.30
Bank of Ireland Asset Management	1.2	0.06

[a] Source: FT Mandate Research

As benchmarks are here to stay and constitute a vital part of the investment process, the way they are managed and the cost involved in that process need to be transparent as well. Obviously, most managers prefer to work with benchmarks with certain characteristics but both FTSE and MSCI have those characteristics. For Dimitris Melas, global head of research at HSBC Asset Management:

> What we require are transparency, low turnover and liquidity. Otherwise, we don't really favour one benchmark over the other. We manage money across a wide range of benchmarks including FTSE, MSCI, IFC, TOPIX or the Hang Seng. Once we are happy with our client's reasons for a benchmark, it is simply a matter of adhering to our guidelines.

> MSCI manage their benchmark in an interesting way. While they don't charge for their benchmark per se, when a client measures us against their benchmark and we have to get it for our investment and performance measurement purpose, we have to pay them for that access.[39]

It is time that the users of such indexes, i.e. the trustees who eventually pay for the existence of such service providers, considered ways of having greater input in the creation of eligible benchmarks instead of passively using the ones created by others for possibly different purposes. Customisation of benchmarks reflecting the individual scheme's liability profile has been considered to be the right approach in addressing the asset allocation anomaly. Fund managers rightly take proprietorial pride in their in-house research as it is integral to their branding exercise. Thus, if their analysts do a good job, it is reflected in their consistency in beating the market. However, as markets drive the asset allocation process to such a huge extent in the modern economy, not using the input of the buy-side research is a great loss as well. Buy-side research is utilised in the asset allocation decisions of the fund managers, i.e. primarily in stock selection. The reality is that strategic asset allocation is driven by the trustees of pension funds, and fund managers simply do the best they are allowed to within a defined benchmark.

Fund managers are not able to back their conviction via short sales, for example. Besides, there are other factors that inhibit the independence not just of the sell-side analysts but also the buy-side analysts.[40] As there are several alternative sources of analysis, such as the rating agencies for the bond markets, at the country and corporate levels, there are no major independent equity research firms that purely offer research services to a range of users from trustees to fund managers. There are some notable independent asset managers operating in Europe today, such as Capital International, Fidelity and SIM, who have invested heavily in research. Fidelity and Capital have a long history of independent research, but there are not many pure asset managers in the industry. While asset managers, investment bankers and consultants regularly commission research reports from outside sources, the lack of firms that provide purely unbiased research is ample evidence of the fact that there is no such thing, as no one is prepared to pay for it.

Asset managers in the UK believe that moving to a fee-based approach for research would mean that brokers would become more like consultants, and smaller companies that provide research might well be squeezed out of the marketplace. In a discussion hosted by the UK Society of Investment Professionals (UKSIP) in response to the Myners Report and specifically with reference to the issue of broker research and commissions, it was pointed out that research by smaller companies often provides more intellectual creativity than research by larger ones. There was also the fear that research may become more focused to individual requirements as opposed to the current practice, whereby once research is written, it gets disseminated to all managers, irrespective of its relevance. As asset managers currently use consensus broker forecasts as a means of measuring their own in-house views, it is perhaps understandable that they are reluctant to see that system disappear.[41] However, the price of such a practice has been high.

Breaking down the various costs associated with fund management, including the cost of research and trading, will help investors in the long term. While the value of independent research is recognised, no effort has been made by the industry to use it on a scale that will truly add value to the investment process, for example, an I/B/E/S type consensus forecast that includes all the information available to the market, not just the sell-side view. It is simply assumed that the market price reflects all information, and this belief is reinforced by developments in communication technology. In fact, the CAPM is based on such a belief. However, as all 'intelligent investors' will acknowledge, there is an inherent contradiction in such thinking. For a truly efficient market process, the market needs to be deep and wide and its participants should be well equipped, skilled and free enough to exercise their full range of views. While in theory that is meant to be the case, in reality huge barriers continue to exist. It cannot be denied that some progress has been made over the past decade, but there is a long way to go before the market achieves a higher level of efficiency in most parts of the developed world. However, investors do not have to believe in total market efficiency to believe in indexation. Arguments have been made that even in the more inefficient emerging markets, indexation has proven to be a cost-effective strategy.

Active portfolio managers do not subscribe to the view that markets are efficient, as that would challenge their very existence along with their rationale for charging relatively high fees to their clients. In the words of Paul Samuelson:

> There are very few people or organizations who have any presumptive edge over a low-cost, no-load set of indices, particularly on a risk-corrected basis. However, this message can never be sold on Wall Street because it's in effect telling most people to drop dead.[42]

The whole concept of sharing any of their in-house research and analysis would also be anathema to the fund management community as it would go against their belief in their unique ability to add intrinsic value. However, the truth is that the top 10 holdings of many active managers in any country or sector portfolio are likely to be similar; the weightings will vary somewhat but not dramatically. If research is indeed the production machine that drives the active sector of the asset management business and identifying market anomalies results in superior performance, then it would be more appropriate if manager fees were linked directly to their performance, as is the case with hedge fund managers.

However, investors in active funds do not always realise that the odds are stacked against them. Over the past two decades, only some 13.25% of surviving mutual funds in the US have beaten the cumulative returns of the S&P 500 index. This dismal performance has turned passive investing into the ascendant philosophy of money management with 25% of all US pension funds' investments being indexed.[43] While academics and indexed managers are more willing to concede that markets no longer appear to be as efficient as they were once thought to be, it does not alter the fact that the number of market-beating fund managers are small, as is the likelihood of investors having access to their skill in a cost-efficient way. Unfortunately, hedge fund managers have been among the worst offenders; investors have found it quite difficult to find cost-effective hedge fund managers. Investors are constantly being reminded of the need for careful selection and monitoring of hedge fund managers. But when the prospect for doing that is proving difficult with traditional managers, where investors have access to a lot of information, finding a hedge fund manager with a good long-term track record who will also accept you as an investor can be compared to searching for a needle in haystack. In the final analysis, indexers consistently win out in terms of cost and performance.

CHAPTER 4

Active Management

INTRODUCTION

In his book *The Midas Touch*, John Train describes the strategies that make Warren Buffett the world's most successful investor alive today: 'He [Buffett] does not try to be a futurologist. He looks for the impregnable business franchise, rather than the prospect of dramatic new developments. He is not the person you would go to for a prediction on the changes in the shape of the world in the year 2020, or the outlook for fiber optics or beta blockers.'[1] Another of the world's great investors alive today, Bill Gates, also attempted to create just such an 'impregnable business franchise', except that his Windows franchise has now been invaded by the new technology, particularly the internet. As both Buffett and Gates are among the world's richest individuals and the internet has helped create more millionaires in our time, even in developing countries such as India, China and Russia, perhaps its 'public good' characteristics have been exaggerated somewhat. The fact remains that if you had invested your savings early in the cycle with either of these great investors, you would have done well for yourself. The world's best investors excel in identifying companies with strong business franchises.

If asked what are the most significant issues confronting the investment community today, investors refer to globalisation, demographics, technology, regulation, analyst independence, market efficiency or the lack of it, corporate governance, disparity in the distribution of wealth, climate change, etc. Although the concept of the new economy has been overthrown, many believe that the future is also about greater global connectivity and mobility, as

115

many of the issues confronting us today can best be addressed on a global scale. The new technology is also recognised as playing a role in this development. The reality is that technology is replicable and thus needs to innovate itself just to stand still. This is reflected in the price of computers and other electronic goods that keep falling while each new model comes with a superior technology. Also, you no longer need Windows or even a PC to access the internet; you can do so via your TV screen or your mobile phone. Payphones provide internet access among other facilities. In Bill Gates' famous words, 'the internet changes everything', including his own monopoly of accessing it.

Thus, the new technology is intrinsically antithetical to the concept of a strong business franchise with high profit margins. And so are markets. Businesses usually collapse or are taken over if they fail to make a profit. Hence it would be naive and unrealistic to expect businesses to be focused on anything other than profits. However, what stops businesses from running the world for profit are not governments, but markets. Undeniably, governments have the power although they fail to use it wisely. Sometimes, out of conviction, politicians decide to help companies reshape the world for private profit. Often, anti-market thinking leads them to help big business. And sometimes, when companies set out to buy the policies they want, they find in governments a willing seller. However, it is markets that keep the spoils of corruption small.[2] Markets and technology together form a pretty formidable coalition against 'strong business franchises'. Besides, the job of investors has become harder than ever before as most of them are looking for similar companies. Their own actions usually arbitrage away the market value of such companies fairly swiftly.

The intense technological competition that is still to come from Asia (and the list of countries has grown since the 1980s from Japan and Korea as the world's best replicators to include Taiwan, Singapore, Malaysia, India and China) will ensure the commoditisation or, as one head of an American investment firm in London put it, the 'casiofication' of the world will continue. It is not surprising that technology stocks did not feature prominently among Mr Buffett's investments. In the brave new technological world, holding on to impregnable business franchises is not going to be easy as technological penetration of the so-called old economy continues at a steady pace. This technological upgrading of industry and society is nothing new. However, the importance of markets in our world and the application of technology in the market process are relatively new.

The dramatic rise in the availability of investment vehicles within the sector during 1999–2000 was a clear indication that the technology market cycle was peaking. Less than five years ago there were just a few specialist technology unit trusts or open-ended investment companies (OEICs) in the UK. The proliferation of such funds, not to mention more targeted themes like European technology, UK technology, global titans, internet funds and biotechnology funds, to name a few, indicated that the market was witnessing a top-of-the-cycle fad. While the marketing people seized the moment, in a rapidly changing world dominated by technology, the role of analysts and fund managers has become more demanding than usual.

'Investment managers find it as difficult to time the market as to select underpriced securities. Such is the lot of a participant in a highly efficient market.'[3] When William F. Sharpe wrote this in his seminal work, *Investments*, first printed in 1978, he was referring to the lot of fund managers in the US. Since then, portfolio theory and management have evolved considerably, yet the handicap of any financial analyst or asset manager has remained unchanged. If anything, it got worse. As communication technology makes it easier to access information, the job of the analyst becomes more challenging, not less. They inhabit the world that Lewis Carroll described so accurately in *Through the Looking Glass*, where it takes all the running you can do to keep in the same place. If you want to get somewhere else, you must run at least twice as fast as that!

Most fund managers acknowledge their unique skill in asset allocation and stock selection. But when it comes to sustainable long-term performance, the gains made from exploiting market inefficiencies are elusive indeed. The performance of active money managers during the years of the stock market's most recent 'irrational exuberance', is a stark reminder of how things go awry in inefficient markets. This does not imply that just because one is bound to get the wrong answer from time to time, the research and analysis contribute no added value. As we know, scientific progress has been based on mistakes alone. It is our mistakes that provide us with the insight into the right path. In the new millennium, the harnessing of knowledge to commercial uses is set to become the driving force for economic growth. In the realm of fund management, knowledge is paramount; analysts and fund managers hold the key to assimilating the information flow within the organisation and in harvesting its commercial value. So how does the organisation protect and retain the intellectual property it has developed? More importantly, how do investment managers distinguish themselves from their peers? Thanks to technology and market forces, intellectual property and branding, once unique selling points, are increasingly threatened by commoditisation

In response to such a challenge at the initial stages of the techno-logical revolution, the market witnessed the traditional retreat to quality and greater concentration in a few brand names. In time, changes in the distribution of investment products will enable rela-tively unknown firms with good performance records to be able to sell their expertise via branded channels. The same technology will also have the power to deliver greater consumer choice by delivering new enterprises to the market, along with their new ideas. Good equity managers will certainly thrive, but the internet will lead to a more sophisticated investor base and could lead to more direct investments in the market. In the words of William Cotter: 'We are likely to see growth towards multi-product providers, who have brand recognition and whom customers find accessible. But this will not, in my view, be at the expense of good niche firms. Ours is a talent business and investors recognise this. That's why there is always scope for small start-ups that can demonstrate that they have something of value to offer.'[4]

COMPUTING POWER: HANDMAIDEN OF INVESTMENT SUCCESS

'At a time when electronic computers have been rapidly gaining acceptance within industry, the City has been noticeably slow to adapt these machines to the various facets of its own work, and it is only during the last year or so that the possibilities for using them in relation to investment analysis, in particular, have been investigated. Nevertheless, a certain amount of useful work is now being undertaken and, of more importance, some of the potentialities for the future are becoming apparent.' With these words, Graham Bease began an article, published in the *Investment Analyst* in November 1961. He was the investment officer at the BOAC/BEA pensions fund. Bease's conclusion was equally valid: 'Sceptics will suggest that attempts to introduce computers into investment analysis oversimplify the problems facing investors and that no substitute is available for flair, judgement and sense of timing.' He acknowledged the importance of these qualities unreservedly, but pointed out that the use of quantitative analysis could 'perhaps make a small contribution towards raising the standard of investment management.'[5] The more things change, the more they stay the same.

The new technology's ability to disseminate knowledge globally implies that any competitive strategy based on unlimited access to that same pool of knowledge is also under threat. Globalisation, like the new technology, is a double-edged sword. For Laurence Fink, chief executive officer of BlackRock: 'Globalization does not mean more opportunity. By contrast, it means better information and fewer opportunities. You need a system to access this information and a process to synthesize it and translate it into a cohesive global perspective and investment strategy.'[6] Fund managers are organising themselves in precisely such a way. The challenge lies in managing the explosion of information, generated internally and externally, in an efficient way. For Stuart O'Gorman, head of technology at Henderson Global Investors: 'Additional investment tools are unfortunately a zero sum game for the financial community – if somebody outperforms then someone else logically has to under-perform by just as much. There are probably limited productivity improvements that could be achieved by new products in the fund management side – reliability increases are probably the way productivity could be improved most. But in the past IT departments haven't focused much on this aspect of productivity.'[7]

'We are thrown back on the almost unlimited ability of modern software to absorb information at an atomised level and to process it into patterns of interest for decision making and analysis,'[8] affirms Professor Daniel Hodson, Mercers' School Memorial Professor of

Commerce. While economic models are static, economic activity is not. Traditional models thus fail to interpret market trends until it appears in the data, when it is often too late for the potential user of that information. The implications of the growing access to vastly increased computing power aligned with the use of non-linear applications are indeed profound within asset management. From enhanced indexers to hedge fund managers, the use of technology in quantitative analysis forms the basis of major investment decisions and trading strategies. As one prime broker pointed out, 'We are just a technology company that happens to do prime brokerage.' That analogy can be extended to any number of examples; Fidelity or BGI are technology companies that do fund management.

What analysts and fund managers want is a system that seamlessly integrates multiple databases, enabling them to transform information into actionable intelligence. Even within the research function, including asset allocation and stock selection, which is *the* area in asset management where the skill factor is critical, the new technology has made a real contribution. What most active, equity asset managers aim to do is to reflect the stock-picking skills of their analysts, based worldwide, in their asset allocation decision. As Jill Dodds, director of equities at UBS Asset Management pointed out: 'If our analysts' price intrinsic value approach leads to estimates in a certain company, sector or region that are above consensus, then we must use that information to our advantage. The portfolio constructors are able to make their own sector bets, taking into account the alphas of stocks in various sectors. If we can detect a catalyst for that alpha being realised, then that obviously triggers a buy signal. What we strive to do is to communicate that within the firm in the most efficient way.'[9]

The renowned stock-pickers of the investment firmament actively deploy standard quantitative, technologically driven solutions to their individually designed investment process. According to Simon J. Fraser, chief investment officer for Fidelity Investments in London:

We use quantitative analysis to digest internal data from a modelling point of view. Thus, instead of focusing on one stock, let's say stock X because our estimates are above consensus, and so we must buy X, what we do is a lot more analysis by consolidating all our estimates in that country or sector; and if they are on average above consensus, then that filters into the asset allocation model. That is how we drive our asset allocation decision. We also use it for risk modelling. But ultimately all analysis boils down to accessing data on a daily basis because a model is only as good as the data you put in.[10]

While investment brokers have established individual websites encapsulating all-in-one research applications delivering totally new functionality to investment managers anywhere in the world, asset managers are striving to do the same for their internal analysts, along with the external sell-side analysts, among other research available within the industry. The process is far more complicated on the buy side as an asset manager not only needs to integrate available information on any company generated by its internal analysts based around the world, but it also needs to provide a platform for those analysts to incorporate into their assessment the views of other external, sell-side analysts. Thus, if one analyst on the buy side covers let's say 20 companies in one or two related sectors, then that analyst has to be aware of the views of all the major sell-side analysts involved. Suppose there are 10 major sell-side analysts covering each of the 20 companies that the buy-side analyst is responsible for, then the buy-side analyst has to monitor about 200 analysts' views along with the views of the finance directors of those companies and any other sector specialists and individual research firms operating in that sector.

Managing that flow of information is a greater challenge for the buy-side analyst, particularly when the analyst is often out of the office interviewing senior management of companies in which the firm already has investments or which it sees as potential investment candidates. The analyst has to filter any change in his/her view and convey that information as clearly as possible, often in a quantifiable manner, to fund managers who are often based in different time zones. In short, asset managers need technological systems that are capable of seamlessly integrating any type of data, in any format, from practically anywhere in the world. As a high element of 'judgement' is involved in this process, a certain level of prioritising the new information is also required. Even companies with enormous IT budgets acknowledge the problems involved in achieving just that. At Fidelity, when a research analyst publishes a note, it is available on their intranet to the internal fund managers on a worldwide basis. 'It also alerts them to any new developments. Amalgamating email with voice-mail has proven immensely useful. We live in an age of information overload. So, what we try to do is to enable fund managers to cut through that overload so that they can access what is most useful to them.'[11]

To achieve that seamless quality, asset managers have moved into browser-based technology so that all systems are internet-compatible. Whether products and services are obtained or delivered via the internet depends on the client's level of comfort and the technological processes involved. Increasingly, investment decisions by active managers are predicated not just on research anomalies, but also on trading choices as firms operate globally and individual stockholdings impact on what stocks and how much of it investor firms want to own. 'That's our biggest problem,' confirms Simon Fraser. 'We need to know, for example, all our holdings in any single company as it impacts on our investment decision. You might have a huge risk, if you don't have that information in front of you. We have our own internal limits and external regulatory limits apply as well. So, that information is critical to our investment strategy.'[12]

Active managers are skilled stock-pickers who endeavour to enhance their interpretation of the data relating to companies, sectors and countries via superior technology. 'We use technology as a tool for the fund manager, not as something that can replace them. If we find out a very mechanical, scientific or technological way of picking stocks that seems to be successful, then we immediately question it because it will work until it doesn't work. We do not attach too much weight on any one approach, as we are all too conscious of the fact that technology cannot replace judgement,' confirms Fidelity's Fraser. 'We don't use something like BARRA that tells you what to buy, but we might use BARRA as it comes up with suggestions versus our risk profile,'[13] he adds. A very similar position is maintained by Jill Dodds: 'We might use BARRA to test the risk in our portfolios but the best software you can have is the human brain.'[14] For Alan Brown, 'the debate between active quantitative strategies and traditional strategies is getting a bit sterile. We do not have the monopoly on arithmetic. Besides, in the quantitative-strategies we use, active judgement comes into play. It is not a black and white area; there are shades of grey. The spectrum of quantitative management runs from true passive indexation to active enhanced index strategies.'[15] Thus, fund managers of all persuasions, including indexed managers, emphasise the individual skill factor.

In light of increased market volatility and the problems associated with forecasting long-term inflation and interest rates, leading to various seminal problems in the UK pension and insurance sector, such a conclusion is a stark reminder that the margin for human error is high. There is indeed no substitute for the human brain. Most of the financial crises encountered in history, be they macro or micro, illustrate that human error was the single most important contributory factor. Examples of macro crises are the Asian crisis in 1997 and the Russian default in 1998; the Russian default triggered the problems at Long-Term Capital Management. Examples of micro crises are the events leading to the takeover of Baring and the uncertainty surrounding the future of Equitable Life. Computers are programmed to do what they are instructed to do. A certain level of 'intelligence' is inherent in the latest computers, but we have not yet created a 'Frankenstein' computer, hence it remains the stuff of science fiction and horror movies. Market or corporate failures occur when warning signals are ignored, usually over a long period of time. In the end, some external or internal shock precipitates a crisis. While traditional forecasting has relied more on linear techniques, the future will probably make better use of non-linear techniques that try to learn from the data itself instead of imposing a certain preconceived and perhaps limited pattern on it. Once again, computers will enable and empower the 'skilled' practitioner, not replace them.

TECHNOLOGY: APPLICATION VERSUS VALUATION

One of the more obvious ways in which technology has influenced fund managers is expressed in their asset allocation decision, which has become more global in orientation. There may be disagreements about the level of productivity increase influencing the long-term growth potential of the US economy, but the fact remains that the contribution of technology has altered the way in which we calculate factors of production. Even in the UK, a major structural change is evident, although it is not directly related to technology spending per se. In the UK, inflation is at its lowest in 30 years and so are long-term interest rates, government borrowing and unemployment. While some of this has been secured at the cost of investments in infrastructure, education and health services, better overall management is at the core of this achievement. A buoyant global economy and rising world trade underpinned such growth, although analysts remain uncertain of the future prospects because the global picture is dominated by developments in the US, where the role of technology in sustaining productivity and growth was most notably witnessed.

For the same reason, it is feared that with slowing US investment and consumption, a global recession is inevitable. The front cover of the 25 August 2001 issue of *The Economist* proposed '2001 things to do in a recession'. The editorial stated:

> For the seventh time this year, America's Federal Reserve has cut interest rates, this time by a quarter-point to 3.5 percent, leaving the federal-funds rate a full three percentage points lower than at the start of 2001. Americans hope that Alan Greenspan, the Fed's chairman, is doing enough to prevent a recession. But for some it is too late. The sharp slowdown in America has already caused a recession, maybe not at home, but in Mexico, Singapore, Taiwan and elsewhere. In more and more countries around the world output is now stalling, if not falling. Total world output probably fell in the second quarter for the first time in two decades.[16]

Long before the slowdown in the US, the world economy was in difficulties. Japan has been sick for almost a decade and Europe preoccupied with the creation of Euroland and all the problems associated with such a process. Emerging markets have been in deep trouble since the tequila crisis of 1994. The process of economic liberalisation that exhibited such promise in the early 1990s in various emerging markets stalled or even reversed in some cases in the second half of the decade. It was the strength of the US economy, in terms of investment and consumption, that kept the rest of the world going. Global demand for the dollar due to higher inward investment in the US, mostly from Europe, contributed to the strength of the currency. A strong dollar helped US imports and the high US current account deficit financed the growth in the global economy. A slowing US economy during 2001 threatened to unravel many of these links.

The outlook for the US economy was further distorted by events of 11 September 2001. Real interest rates in the US have now been reduced to zero with a view to stimulating the economy. A concerted reduction in interest rates around the world, including the major economies of Europe, UK and Japan, after the attack on the World Trade Centre and the Pentagon by terrorists on 11 September 2001, illustrates the global concern about recession. However, the global economic outlook was poor to start with. After the attack on the US, it has shaken consumer confidence and affected some sectors of the economy, such as the airline industry, more than others. As job losses continue in various companies worldwide, it is difficult not to see the opportunistic nature of many of these decisions. In most cases they would have happened regardless of the unprecedented terrorist attack on the US.

The technological revolution that transformed America barely got started in Europe, not to mention the developing world. The reason it never got going was the general perception that a downward correction in the price attached to technology was imminent. We had an unsustainable situation where the price of accessing the so-called new technology was declining, yet the market kept on marking up the price of the same technology companies. Globalisation encouraged the view that as technology and finance enable US firms to increase their penetration of global markets, the virtuous cycle of investing in technology is not worth curbing as a result of a market bubble. According to various experts, on the central issue of productivity, the evidence indicated that the productivity pickup was 'structural not cyclical'. However, after technology spending had risen at a breathtaking rate in the previous several years, a slowdown was inevitable. Technology managed to deliver non-inflationary growth through higher productivity gains between 1996 and 2000. But even technology is not immune to cycles. Asset inflation is a market virus that can damage even the most benign of developments.

The present slowdown in technology investing does not alter the fact that a high level of investment in technology was an important factor in the remarkable revival in US productivity. While the cyclical adjustment was necessary and overdue, for those who argue that somehow the US economy is on the brink of a 1929-type recession are ignoring the fact that both the US economy and the world economy have changed beyond recognition since the 1930s. It is true that economies are more integrated through trade and investment, and with collapsing demand and investment in the US, and with no compensating growth in demand from either Europe or the Far East, world growth is bound to slow down. That was already the case and also the reason behind the easing of monetary policy in the US. In fact, it is the European Central Bank that failed to act more responsibly, and Japan offers a useful lesson to other countries on how not to handle the bursting of an investment bubble.

The rise in telecommunications, media and technology as a proportion of various indexes worldwide confirms the increasing importance of technology in the global economy. Although the 'bubble' level of technology-related investment in the US is clearly over and late-cycle investments have suffered huge losses, the rest of the world has been lagging behind in getting e-enabled. If Europe and Japan were to restructure their economies and invest in technology, the global economy could benefit from a higher level of connectivity. The upside to the slowdown in technology investing is that demand is now lagging supply, putting downward pressure on margins. Although that may rattle stock markets and bring down prices, it is a boon to the real economy, where lower prices boost consumer spending, help generate innovation and bring new products to the market.

The stock market began to differentiate the qualitative strengths of the players in the technology sector rather late in the investment cycle. The inefficient producers within the inflated sector will perish, if they have not already, but the more efficient ones are likely to benefit from higher demand as it begins to recover. In the cyber world, instead of creating excess capacity, e-commerce companies expand markets by creating new products and improving the supply of traditional products at lower prices. Traditional analysts with their long-established analytical methods may find that forecasting has become more complex. The innovative ways of pricing dotcom companies (e.g. using option pricing strategies), introduced to the market when the TMT (technology, media and telecommunications) boom was at its peak, have now been discredited but the new technological revolution has affected the way analysts conduct their research. 'We go a lot more to trade fairs than to individual companies because you learn more that way. For example, if you take a Nokia phone apart, we are probably investing in each of the companies that are making the parts, be they in Japan or the US. All our analysts are examining how technology is affecting businesses globally,'[17] clarifies Simon Fraser.

Even those highly sceptical of the new technology recognise its contribution to the global economy. But when it comes to evaluating firms, as Nick Ferguson of Schroder Ventures reminds us, 'There is no such thing as the new economy, there is only new technology.'[18] Both capital and human resource allocation to the sector rose to match the investment exposure by asset managers. For many investment firms, organising their research effort in the most efficient manner is simply a question of good practice. Schroder Investment Mangement, among other asset managers, set up a global technology team in London to coordinate 'the team process and provide thematic support to regional analysts, as well as to manage some technology sector focused portfolios.'[19] At HSBC it is similarly a question of enhancing the investment process:

> Technology comprises the largest sector in the various indices, and from our perspective, it is neither advantageous nor disadvantageous to our activity. We are not a hedge fund manager; our investment exposure is linked to the benchmark. The impact on our asset allocation decision is significant. We have established an independent, specialist global technology team consisting of the technology analysts based in their local markets so that they can share their knowledge within the team and better communicate developments within their markets. So we do recognise that technology is evolving almost as a separate asset class from a global perspective.

We are also moving to establish similar teams in various other sectors such as financials, pharmaceuticals, perhaps resources, although there are sectors that do not so easily lend themselves to a global approach. This is a reflection of the fact that we are flexible in our approach. While a decade ago country factors were dominant, today Europe has gone pan-European and in some sectors the industry factor is rising. As we go forward, the regional factors and industrial factors may come to dominate. We are enhancing the investment process accordingly.[20]

It is possible that in terms of human resource allocation, there was a higher level of inventory than is viable. As Jill Dodds predicted in April 2000, 'There are far too many analysts covering internet stocks that are going to go bust.'[21] Many investors lost small fortunes in the inevitable bust that followed the technology boom as a high proportion of listed dotcom companies exhausted their cash pile in marketing and investing in enhanced technology to support the marketing effort, which in total accounted for over half the costs of such firms. Most of these companies did not have any sustainable cash flow, but that hard fact appears to have been overlooked by many seasoned investors. Thus, while the internet was creating greater transparency for its users, accountants and analysts faced the dilemma of valuing companies without any tangible cash flow. The collapse of Boo.com, the online sportswear retailer, among other spectacular failures in that sector, testifies that selling goods via the internet has its price, both for management and investors. Even in the US, the Mecca of internet shopping, such activity fell by over one-third in first quarter 2001 and has been declining ever since. The round of redundancies in corporate America during 2001 also supports such data. Evidence suggests that matters got significantly worse during fourth quarter 2001.

However, the wealth that has been created as a result of the technological boom of recent years cannot be denied. According to a report from Cap Gemini Ernst & Young and Merrill Lynch, the wealth of dollar millionaires, i.e. those with over $1 million to invest, rose by 6% to a staggering $27 trillion in 2000 despite crumbling stock markets around the world. The number of millionaires grew by 2.9% to 7.2 million, but 80,000 'minute millionaires' appeared and then disappeared with the dotcom boom and bust.[22] It is true that 'the new economy and the internet gold rush are not the same thing, despite these concepts being used interchangeably by many commentators.'[23] There is a huge difference between investing directly in the new technology to improve business efficiency and investing in the shares of technology-related companies with grossly inflated valuations.

While the rules of picking winning stocks are being redefined continually, the basic issue of technological innovation and upgrade for business efficiency is not a matter of choice. According to Simon Fraser: 'We increasingly reinvest our profits back into the business generally, but particularly in technology because that's the only way we are going to make the most out of it and stay ahead of the competition. If anything, we overinvest in technology. The rationale is that unless you invest in ten projects, you are not going to find the five that pay off.'[24] The really exciting thing is that the benefits of the application of the new technology are only just being appreciated and the infrastructure is being put in place for the opportunity to use this information. Superior methods of accessing and processing information are what this technological revolution is all about. 'From an investment perspective, information gathering on potential investment opportunities is becoming easier and quicker, thanks to email, company websites and aggregators of other economic and company-specific data,'[25] affirmed Nicola Ralston.

This need to adapt to the new technology has been complicated by the increased merger and acquisition activity in the industry. Not only do fund managers need access to financial information worldwide as and when they need it, but the software systems used in their various offices often do not interface with each other, although they do connect to the internet. Companies are therefore building their own proprietary, intranet applications to address their information management and integration needs as much as installing extranet solutions. 'We have to invest in new-generation technology as it is no longer an option but a question of survival,' confirmed Mark Boylan, chairman of UBS Asset Management in London, as the firm integrates various parts of its merged businesses into a global operation. 'We have a number of technological platforms with some interconnectivity between them. This is the result of the amalgamation of a number of large organisations, each with their own systems, which are working towards communality in their entirety,'[26] confirmed Boylan. European asset managers, who have gone global, such as Deutsche, Axa, Alliance or Credit Suisse also illustrate this trend as they settle down to chewing the IT cud and digesting disparate parts of their operations into a seamless unity.

It is not only Europeans who are actively establishing a global presence, Americans had an earlier start in achieving that ambition. Simon Fraser of Fidelity affirms a high commitment to technology: 'We have been investing more than normal over the past few years to replace and rebuild our global technology platforms. This is all part of our globalisation of the investment management group. We now have three distinct groups – including traders, analysts and fund managers – based in Boston, London, Tokyo and Hong Kong. What we have done is developed technological platforms for each of these groups. So, we have a global trading platform with its own dedicated systems team to support it. The same goes for global research and investment management. Each of these groups has distinct functions and systems. We have rebuilt the back end of the systems so that we can recreate some local adaptation on the front end, which was a real challenge for us.'[27]

The industry is replete with examples of such technological transformations. Although fund managers need to accommodate local practices (e.g. Japanese accounting systems in Japanese and in the various languages in the financial centres in Europe), technical systems are increasingly becoming globally interlinked and playing a significant role in the process of establishing global standards of best practice. And that's where the internet has a crucial role to play. While the internet may not have 'changed everything' for fund managers, information and communication technology has revolutionised the communication paradigm. Even the humble email has been an invention par excellence due to its ability to communicate across time zones, and amalgamating email with voicemail is a giant step forward for fund managers. Even Jill Dodds, a sceptic of the technology mania, acknowledges that 'one of the greatest technological inventions is the email. Its contribution to our industry, in terms of speed and the organisational aspects of the business, is highly significant.'[28]

The asset management industry in the UK has been slow to respond to opportunities in e-business. But change is on its way and most major companies are deploying significant resources into technology. It is therefore only a matter of time before critical mass is achieved, which will trigger a major transformation in the way the investment business moves forward. However, the process is far from static, as technological cycles have also become shorter. If you have a three-year development plan, by the time you get there the technology could be out of date. As David Roche explains: 'Take the web – bandwidth, processing power and memory improvements spark increased demand which in turn generate technological improvements in everything from software and computers to routers, chips and storage. That creates fresh demand for the products and the cycle starts again – but in a form of condensed super-history compared with other technology cycles.'[29]

The problem of technological applications in the fund management sector in the UK, according to several industry experts, can be reduced to the issue of cost. The investor is still not prepared to pay for it. 'Nobody has yet put up their hand to say they are going to pay for it. Like a lot of things in the UK, it boils down to who is going to pay for it rather than thinking about the long-term implications of it,' says Simon Fraser. 'Even a year ago, the internet was perceived as having a huge deflationary effect because if you charged $25.00 a trade, then someone else would charge $20.00 and that was coming straight out of your bottom line. But a year later, volumes have tripled and 80–85% of trading is being done on the net. Thus, productivity of the group has gone up. As there is greater cynicism about technology in the UK, it will be harder to go from the 50% to the 90% level on average as the investor attitude is to speak to your stockbroker or financial adviser.'[30] As we well know, changing investor attitudes is a slow process.

'The most important lesson I have learned in my 30 years in the investment business is that things take time,' affirms Ole Jacobsen, head of Nordea Group's investment management division. 'Two examples of that are the development of the Asian economies and the development of the New Economy of the information age.' He views the changing tide of the market over the past couple of years with equanimity as there are many people in the industry who have never experienced a bear market. From that perspective alone, many investors have a lot to learn. 'One of the advantages of the New Economy is that success is not necessarily related to where you are located; it is related to the competence level you create in your organization. Only the best is good enough in the global market-place.' And that level of competence is created within strong teams by sharing information, which creates more value to an organisation than fostering individual stars. 'To me, stars are related to the Old Economy. ... All that really matters is the value you create for an organization; that is a very important part of the New Economy.'[31]

ENHANCING THE SKILL FACTOR: TRANSFORMING INFORMATION INTO ALPHA

As knowledge is power, the new technology's ability to disseminate information globally implies that the new breed of analysts and fund managers increasingly face the responsibility of responding to markets on a rolling 24-hour, real-time basis. As a result, both product and service cycles have become shorter. Just as technology has helped companies in lowering inventory cycles, the speed at which information needs to be analysed or customers expect to be attended to has also been reduced sharply. This has given rise to a greater degree of specialisation, and with specialisation has come greater competition. The need to remain at the top of the league table in one's specialised field implies continual access to information, incisive and speedy analysis of data, and the transmission of that analysis, if relevant, to the end-user. In a world of information overload, the role of the analyst is to ensure that fund managers are not inundated with irrelevant information but receive distilled intelligence. Thus, IT has been both the cause of this information revolution as well as its solution.

The arrival of the new technology has inevitably spawned considerable opportunity for associated firms to assist with application integration within fund management companies as the combined IT spend of the industry is a multibillion dollar business. The acquisition of Primark, owners of I/B/E/S International, Datastream and Extel by the Thomson Corporation, sponsors of Thomson Financial and First Call, indicates that data management today is big business. The merged entity is now a leading global e-information and solutions company. Other leading providers of integrated data and information include firms such as FactSet, Bloomberg, Morningstar and Multex.-com, which are focused on developing customised, internet/browser-based, efficient solutions for the institutional investor and the retail investor. Internal IT departments of large asset management firms are under increasing pressure to deliver more solutions using better technology in shorter time frames.

Intense competition has led to the evolution of a multiplicity of service providers such as Bloomberg Professional Service, providing news, data, analytics, straight-through processing, and electronic trading tools on a single integrated platform for investment professionals. Various non-core activities are being routinely outsourced to enable asset managers to focus on their core competencies. 'The costs of maintaining what are essentially commodity services in-house are increasing and the market is now being driven by economies of scale. For companies whose core competencies are not IT orientated, outsourcing is a very viable option. We currently outsource our support and maintenance legacy applications to a company based in India,' confirmed Nicola Ralston. 'Going forwards, we expect to witness a rise in the outsourcing of administrative functions in the industry as a whole.'[32] This focus on core competencies inevitably results from greater competition in the industry and the need to deliver customised services to clients.

While in the past, an analyst was an aggregator of data; today I/B/E/S Active Express enables analysts to spend their time more efficiently in analysing that information. Active Express is a fully integrated equity workstation that takes I/B/E/S earnings estimates with real-time notes, broker research and company fundamentals and links them with the internal research data generated by in-house analysts of firms. Set up in 1971, I/B/E/S has grown from its small base and today covers over 18,000 companies in 60 countries monitored by 850 brokers worldwide. Analysts today cover much more than just earnings per share or cash flow forecasts, and I/B/E/S is often the only source for all available forecast data in one platform, including historical data, which makes it ideal for quantitative analysis, forecasting and historical back-testing. Historical data goes back to 1976 for the US and to 1987 for the rest of the world.

It covers some 30,000 companies and is extremely useful for testing investment theories in various market conditions. I/B/E/S Global Aggregates looks at forecast data on country, sector and industry levels and is a powerful global asset allocation tool.

The data items provided by I/B/E/S that are continually updated include revenue, EBITDA, EBIT, profit before tax, operating net income, net income, price targets, return on equity, book value, net asset value, dividends, cash flow and recommendations. This data is clean, standardised for purposes of global comparison and is available via 50 electronic sources, including its flagship I/B/E/S Active Express, the I/B/E/S FTP site, the internet and other redistributors and data integrators such as FactSet, Bloomberg, Bridge, Data Downlink and FAME. It is not often that a data provider gets the endorsement of a Nobel laureate of the stature of William Sharpe, who acknowledged the contribution of the service to the investment industry, 'While I/B/E/S is not the only company collecting earnings expectations data... it was the first and remains the leader in the field.'[33] I/B/E/S services not only active managers who compete with each other in beating the consensus. Over 90% of the quantitative market is serviced by I/B/E/S as quantitative tools are being widely applied by both active and passive managers.

Most companies use the technology behind Active Express to fully integrate I/B/E/S data with their own proprietary databases or access the data via the internet and other redistributors and data integrators. Now part of Thomson Financial's Research and Analytics Group, I/B/E/S provides its customers with cost-effective, internet-based solutions available in the marketplace. A team of IT experts often work with the asset managers, research staff and traders in identifying specific customer needs and then individualise access to such information, providing them with the means of analysing it any way they want to. Flexibility in manipulating data is the key attribute for any successful data provider. FactSet's proprietary software tools, for example, permit its clients to manipulate and analyse data and present it in an infinite variety of formats, including their own custom-designed reports.

Established in 1978, FactSet is a major supplier of online, integrated, financial and economic information to the investment management industry. It offers over 100 databases and sources of information, including I/B/E/S, Reuters and Bloomberg. By tapping into FactSet's vast trove of current and historic data covering 100,000 global securities, investment professionals can do basic screening analysis or produce a portfolio attribution report for a client meeting. Applications for the investment professional include Universal Screening, Company Explorer, Market/Economic Analytics, Quant Suite, Portfolio Manager's Workstation and Supercharged Spreadsheets. FactSet provides a complete solution, including design, development, hosting, maintenance and support. It has survived on the leading edge of technology by continually refining and expanding its proprietary software offerings.

Within asset management companies, analysts use the FactSet research system not only to assess fundamental ratios of stocks held (such as price/earnings, debt/equity, price/cash flow) for key platform models but also to screen stocks for the purpose of generating ideas. Many of the following indicators are assessed in seeking to identify potential unexpected earnings growth: ranges in broker forecasts, consensus revision trends, increases in volatility, strong or accelerating growth trends. FactSet's Quant Suite is an innovative set of applications designed to meet the special needs of quantitative analysts. These applications, Alpha Testing, Backtesting, and Portfolio Optimizer, leverage FactSet's strongest skill sets – database integration and computing power – to make quantitative research more manageable. According to Peter Hopkins, head of quantitative research at Baring Asset Management: 'With FactSet, you can access and manipulate a vast quantity of data and use it in a way that enhances your decision-making. Companies offering such innovative solutions have helped fund managers access strategic information to enhance investment return, generate sales and build closer client relationships.'[34]

From research, trading and sales to client servicing, there is demand for more and more straight-through processing to ensure transparency and better risk-control mechanisms. Not only do investment analysts have access to data globally, so do their clients who have access to information on their portfolios. Pension fund trustees now have the ability to access their own portfolio information via their fund manager's website. The internet delivers greater transparency to the relationship without additional cost in terms of time or human resources. The transparency of the net, though a great threat to those involved in the analysis of information, is the key to success in other areas of investment activity such as client servicing and management.

Multex.com adopted internet-based protocols in 1996 and started distributing research for all of the top brokerage houses in the US, Europe and Asia. Through partnerships with Bloomberg, Reuters and Dow Jones and through financial web portals including AOL, Yahoo and CBS MarketWatch, Multex.com's financial information services are available on major portals and financial websites, giving them a strong distribution franchise. Focused on financial content, connectivity, commerce and community, Multex.com offers products and services across multiple business groups. Using the internet, and through customised intranets, it provides up-to-date investment research, earnings estimates, company data and other financial services. It delivers information in a wide variety of formats, including data files, HTML reports and web hosting. The most commonly used investment platforms include its own, MultexNET and FactSet.

Multex.com's Market Guide, for example, specialises in the compilation, integration, display and delivery of descriptive and analytic information on more than 15,000 publicly traded corporations. Its Global Estimates provides real-time consensus and detailed forecasts of earnings, cash flow, profitability and other key data for virtually every public company in the world. In addition, Multex Express enables fund managers and other financial institutions to distribute their proprietary financial research as well as other corporate documents to their employees and other selected customers such as trustees of pension funds. Multex IR provides comprehensive shareholder analysis and market intelligence; it is designed to help investor relations professionals but it can also help investors in communicating with the company jointly on socially responsible investment issues.

While a lot of the software used in devising investment strategies remains home-grown, the proprietary software that many of these firms use is devised by firms such as I/B/E/S, FactSet, BARRA, Bridge, Northfields, Quantec, Riskmetrics and Lattice. Started by Professor Barr Rosenberg in 1973, BARRA pioneered the commercial development of multifactor risk models, and made these models widely available to money managers by selling software subscriptions. Thus, firms with no internal expertise in quantitative management techniques availed themselves of some of the latest tools by subscribing to BARRA analytics. While the use of BARRA analytics to the construction of efficient portfolios is still in its youth in the European marketplace, the emerging field of anomalies research suggests that a number of investment ideas might be used to capture incremental returns. Leading investment managers operate from a leading-edge technology platform. What matters is astute management of technology as a powerful tool for cost control and risk management, as much as for communication and analysis. Harnessing technological innovations to such ends is gaining momentum.

All major asset managers use an extensive range of software for every aspect of the investment process, from fundamental research, quantitative analysis and risk analysis to portfolio construction, performance measurement and attribution analysis. Thus, asset managers have developed internal information platforms containing a wide array of analytical processes based on different types of software provided by external vendors. Schroder Investment Management were generous enough to share the extent of their technological applications within the firm:

> We place great emphasis on ensuring our staff has sufficient time to focus on their core competencies. To support this, we have made substantial investment in improving our systems, software and administration.
>
> Thus, as far as fundamental research is concerned, we have developed a Global Research Investment Database (GRiD) with Multex.com. This is an intranet-based database containing research, models and stock analysis. It has the following capabilities:
>
> - Access to external broker research alongside our internally generated research
> - Easy access to our own analysts' latest recommendations and thoughts
> - The ability to hold all internally generated research and meeting minutes

- Links to the Reuters news service
- The ability to obtain stock quotes
- An internal discussion forum
- Sector, country and regional focus lists of stocks

This information platform therefore contains different kinds of information on different types of software.

We also have a proprietary company valuation and forecasting model, based in Excel, which individual analysts use, as well as a number of standard research documents in Word and Outlook.

With reference to risk analysis and quantitative analysis, we use different systems depending upon our specific requirements. Thus, predicted risk figures for equity and fixed-income funds (e.g. beta, tracking error) are almost always derived from the BARRA model. However, to improve accuracy, we sometimes adjust these numbers for model portfolios using in-house tools in order to take into account current market conditions. We would usually use Wilshire to back-test a given investment strategy, but when more statistical-based calculations are required we would either use RATS or S-Plus (two statistically based programming languages). These last packages are particularly powerful for calculations on large data sets.

For stock-level attribution we use FactSet and/or Wilshire depending on the equity desk in question.

For style analysis, we have developed our own tool in-house, which we call the Stock Book. This analyses a fund's exposure to eight predefined characteristics, monitors the return to those characteristics and also recommends style tilts (based on an underlying business cycle model). The software combines the statistical power of RATS with an Access database. We are currently turning the Stock Book into a full risk model that may eventually replace BARRA.

We have access to Eviews and Microfit for regressions (as well as RATS and S-Plus for cross-sectional estimation).

In terms of performance measurement and attribution analysis, we use CAPS IMS32. Additionally, we have a number of in-house Visual Basic and Access applications. We also use WM Spectrum for those client's that are audited/ verified by WM. However, all reporting is via CAPS IMS32. We also use CAPS IMS32 for attribution analysis. However, for a number of port-folios we also use Frank Russell's RPA (Russell Performance Attribution) application.

Within portfolio construction, to assist managers in operating within the portfolio guidelines, we have introduced a mandate checking system which alerts a fund manager, at the point of making a trade, to the many constraints (such as banned stocks) placed on the client's portfolio. This standard feature of our checking and control procedure ensures that the regional specialist fund managers are signalled automatically prior to transaction concerning the client's guidelines for investment. When constructing portfolios, both in asset allocation and stock selection, fund managers and analysts refer to a number of computer-based information systems, which show absolute and relative positions against the benchmark such as the FMPD valuation system (which allows automated downloading of performance and fees data).

In addition to the above we also utilise the following software; Client Information Base, which facilitates easy information flows between fund managers and support staff. We also have a number of investment information tools, including an asset allocation system, which are in use.[35]

The level of technological sophistication that now exists within asset management in the UK was not prevalent, for example, in 1995. While the stock market valuations of technology-related companies have been decimated, the penetration of technology into all aspects of industry and society has continued, albeit at a slower pace. The market correction may even help raise the economic value added (EVA) of some of these companies. At the end of the day, businesses make money for their shareholders or partners when they earn more than they spend. Or, to put it differently, the cost of borrowing money is lower than the cost of running the business. The advent of the so-called new economy could not have altered that basic reality, i.e. that no business can run successfully over any length of time if costs exceed revenues. Even asset management firms collapse when they run their business similarly.

The authorised vendors of FTSE European indexes include other services and information providers such as ADP Financial Information (UK) Services Ltd, ADVFN.com, AXL Performance Solutions Ltd, BARRA, BBC Ceefax, Bloomberg Systems, Bridge Information Systems Inc., BSkyB, CMA, Cellnet, Charles Stanley & Co., Commodity Market Services, CQG International Ltd, Datastream International Ltd, Donaldson Lufkin Jenrette, Dow Jones Telerate Inc., Easdaq, Electronic Share Information Ltd, Erinne Srl, FactSet, FAINEX Intl, FIDES Information Services, FINNINFO, Finsight Limited, Firstquote, Freequotes, FT Information, Futuresource, Futurespager, GL Consultants SA, Hutchinson Telecommunications (Australia) Ltd, IFX, ILX, Infosis, Instinet Corporation, Micropal, Natwest Stockbrokers, Olympic Worldlink, Portfin.com. Prestel On-Line, QUICK Corporation, Reuters, Riskmetrics, S&P Comstock Ltd, SDIB de Valores de Madrid, Share Sentry, ShareLink, Six AB, Skydata, Sprintel, Sunergy Software Ltd, Telekurs AG, Thus Plc, Teletext, Tenfore Systems Ltd, The Share Centre, TIJD/Beursmedia, Tokyo Broadcasting Systems, Track Data Corporation, Trademade International Ltd, Valuelink Information Services Ltd, VWD-Vereinigte Wirtschaftsdienste GMBH, Wilshire, and Yahoo. The majority of these companies did not exist a decade ago and will not exist in ten years' time, as greater consolidation in the sector takes hold.

THE ROLE OF ANALYSIS

There is no doubt that in the second half of the 1990s any investment strategy geared to a fundamental measure of company valuation based on objective data was doomed to fail. Indexation indeed proved to be the safer investment strategy as it suited the 'irrational exuberance' of the market during that period. Did that justify the action of some active managers who abdicated their responsibility, their beliefs and skills and chameleon-like transformed themselves into closet indexers? Market inefficiencies get arbitraged away due to the collective action of active managers, analysts and traders. Fund managers are paid to take risks based on their extensive knowledge of the market. And in markets as in real life, professionals do get it wrong from time to time. Or, to put it differently, no single investment style fits the market mood at all times. So, if a fund manager of conviction is true to a single investment style, the chances are that every few years, performance will be in the bottom quartile. But in a world driven by quarterly and annual performance reviews, large tracking error with poor return is not a viable survival strategy.

Many fund managers with a value bias, albeit with a growth overlay, were unable to participate in the market's overall high valuation, particularly in the TMT sector during 1998–2000. Unfortunately, as their overall investment performance was also linked to benchmarks, there was a tendency to stick close to the stipulated benchmark even when managers had a clear view on several of the individual stocks in the benchmark. Some of these views were unfortunately not sufficiently supported by hard facts and others not by action. Thanks to the 'irrational exuberance' of markets, many research teams took shelter in quantitative analysis, which could amalgamate a host of investment styles while providing objectivity and discipline. The investment bank Credit Suisse First Boston (CSFB), for example, came out with *The Euro Q-Book*, which aims to provide investors with a quantitative evaluation of the largest 250 companies in Europe based on three broad drivers of share price performance: value, growth and sentiment.[36] After years of indifferent performance, many quantitative managers were forced to examine their value models by adding growth or momentum factors to it, which dominated share price behaviour during 1995–2000. Managing change and the evolution of analytical constructs is one of the growing challenges for analysts today.

What plan sponsors are increasingly trying to create is a style-neutral investment strategy. The rise in the multi-manager, multi-asset, multi-style approach to wealth management partly explains the response of the investment advisory community to the market's irrational pricing mechanism. The need for risk-adjusted returns and low tracking error has helped the case for quantitative orientation among asset managers, who have strengthened their in-house risk measurement and research teams to reflect this trend and increasingly describe their investment style to their clients as one based on capturing alpha in their portfolios. This search for and the rise of alpha is the key to a whole host of investment styles from absolute return strategies to the traditional relative return, active investment approach. Dimitris Melas, head of research at HSBC Asset Management, describes their investment style in the following words:

> We are neither value nor growth managers. We respond to different stages of the business cycle and determine where we want to be. We do not favour value versus growth all the time. So, while the benchmark is determined by the client, our advice in setting this benchmark is usually sought by the client. But once it is set, that is what we adhere to be measured against. Indexation is not going to disappear nor is it going to rise exorbitantly from current levels. So we believe that, going forward, an active process has much to offer investors.[37]

An attempt at analysing and formulating a view of the world is decidedly better than following the herd. It is true that for small pension funds or for many retail investors, the cost (including the cost of investing the time to do the research and the risk of getting it wrong) of such analysis can be exorbitant. Thus, like index managers, this category of investors may find it more efficient to follow the leaders in the field, or failing that, the median peer group. Sometimes, even to arrive at such a conclusion, a basic level of competence and ability to make an investment case is required.

> For the investment analyst, every judgement about the price of a security involves a view about the future, and whether this is consciously admitted or not each man's assumptions are part of his own private economic forecast. These notions are seldom rationalised, most of us absorbing a climate of opinion from the flow of articles in the financial press. Yet every serious contributor, looking forward at some aspect of the economy, has his own underlying set of assumptions about the economy as a whole.[38]

So wrote James Morrell in 1962. In the same article, he also wrote: 'The present uncertainties concerning entry to the Common Market are sufficient warning of the difficulties in estimating the likely timing of changes in course for the economy. At the best of times one cannot see very far ahead and for the moment it is nearly impossible to see beyond the end of 1963.' He concluded that section with the following warning: 'Wall Street has given us a particularly useful indicator of approaching recession in the United States throughout the post-War period and this should also be consulted in appraising British prospects in the short run.'[39] In over 30 years of progress, the hurdles that forecasting encounters have not been reduced; the stakes have got higher.

There exists a perennial conflict between the role of analysts, active fund managers and proprietary traders, who as a group are constantly striving to add value to their investment decisions by identifying mispriced opportunities in markets, with that of the concept of an efficient market. The EMH assumes that markets reflect equilibrium in the pricing of stocks, and that no individual or a group of individuals or institutions are equipped to predict future prices with any accuracy over a long period of time. At the same time, most market participants, including passive indexers, do not subscribe to that premise, otherwise all analysis would indeed be redundant. Most market players believe there is value to be added via genuinely independent analysis. The analyst's job is to identify stocks or sectors that are wrongly priced. In fact, analysts and fund managers collectively play the role of keeping markets efficient by investing in the discovery of pricing anomalies. By their buy/sell decisions, they are able to contribute towards an efficient market process.

As the eyes and ears of the marketplace, the competitive analysis of these participants ensures that all relevant information is reflected in the price. The reason markets are efficient is simply because analysts, fund managers, brokers and other market participants collectively make it so. While each group acts to protect its own self-interest, their competitive collective action cancels out any serious aberrations. The problem arises when some of these groups become too powerful or they create mini cartels and thus distort the pricing mechanism. The creation of the mega-multinational firms over the past few years has led to such fears. Thus, we have a scenario where analysts, fund managers, brokers and bankers, equipped with technology, can either be a force for good collectively in ensuring that markets are run efficiently or they end up as rogue traders, price-fixers or even passive price-takers, thereby distorting markets.

Most of the major asset managers today rely on their internal resources in terms of value-added analysis. Active investors buy a stock when its forecast growth is likely to exceed expectations or be sustained beyond consensus expectations, and sell when they believe growth may prove disappointing, relative to consensus expectations, thereby endorsing the view that stock prices already reflect consensus market-implied earnings growth rates. The research process identifies companies that are likely to deliver alpha. This research effort is repeated within every major asset management firm. No study has been made of the combined cost of research in the investment process on a global basis. However, it will easily add up to billions of dollars and significantly more if the cost of the sell-side research is taken into account. Unfortunately, this massive investment in value addition to the investment process by the industry is not reflected in the performance figures of the active asset managers. Many indexed managers argue that the excessive cost of research is not reflected in the performance of the average active manager. Instead, it is passed on to the consumer.

Any analyst will tell you that sales growth and net profit margin improvement are the key drivers of earnings growth. Furthermore, sales growth and net margins depend upon the industry in which a company operates and the franchise of the company within its industry. Focusing on proprietary analysis of industry and sustainable competitive advantages has become essential to the process of identifying companies with such strong franchises. Warren Buffett has been doing just that for his clients for well over half a century. The problem is that both globalisation and technology are putting tremendous pressure on margins. Thus, holding on to franchises has become more difficult than ever before. The fundamental issue is detecting early enough the turning points within sectors or in companies. These turning points are triggers for a buy or sell decision. Thus, the valuation of stocks is essentially what company research is all about. Sell disciplines are considered of vital importance to the investment process and can depend upon changes in company management, profit warning, market valuation or the overall prospect for the sector.

Asset managers' investment philosophy, research process and portfolio construction techniques are usually based on a longer-term appraisal of stocks, although some may endeavour to take advantage of short-term price movements in executing their investment strategy. In general, their expertise does not lie in trading stocks. Even when they buy stocks, they buy over a long period of time, taking into account the market impact of their own activity. Similarly, they have to be careful of market impact when selling stocks. It can be argued that those asset managers with superior sell disciplines are the ones that ultimately take their position among the top-quartile performers in the industry. It also distinguishes asset managers from investment bankers whose mindset is altogether different. They may know a company inside out, but their skill lies not in the valuation of stocks. That is the area in which the best asset managers truly excel.

Fund managers and insurance firms also specialise in combining risks in such a way that the total risk profile of the portfolio is different than its individual components. Thus, the risks and rewards of securities are best considered within a portfolio context rather than in isolation. Whether or not a security is suitable for a particular investor should not be determined by evaluating the characteristics of the security alone. Investment professionals need to consider securities' characteristics within the context of the client's portfolio, taking into full account the client's investment objectives and constraints. Including a new 'risky' asset in a portfolio may actually reduce the portfolio's overall risk without impacting its returns, if adding the security increases the portfolio's diversification. Thus, individual stock recommendations do not have the same impact on institutional portfolio managers as they may have on individual investors, who may not have the expertise or the tools for in-depth portfolio analysis.

Dissatisfaction with analysts follows a market correction as night follows day. Conflicts of interest are nothing new. Nor do they stop at the tension between independent research and the corporate finance department. Brokerages without corporate finance departments still have an interest in persuading investors to trade. Yet the market for equity research still functions reasonably efficiently. Individual analysts' reputations are important. Professional investors can take care of themselves, by ignoring tainted research and brokers with poor internal controls, buying research from independent research houses, or by increasing their own internal research resources.

The overwhelming – and illogical – preponderance of analysts' buy recommendations is only really a problem to the extent that retail investors take them at face value. That largely explains the noises coming from the Securities and Exchange Commission. Which, together with looming congressional inquiries, means it would make a lot of sense for the Wall Street banks to agree a code of best conduct to minimise conflicts and promote disclosure. Beyond that, caveat emptor remains as important a principle when buying research as when buying stocks.[40]

If one is to understand why sell-side analysts have such a difficult time writing 'sell' recommendations, it may be worth thinking of the constraints under which they operate. When making a buy or a sell recommendation, analysts on the sell side are often disenfranchised by a conflicting set of demands. If company X is a major client of the investment firm Z, whose analyst is writing the report, then a negative report or a recommendation to sell X has a range of implications, not just for the investor Y, who owns the stock and is a recipient of the report (and ostensibly the beneficiary of the report), but also for company X, whose share price will be impacted by the report and the relationship between the investment firm Z and its client X. Often the reason that the analyst is able to come up with such a recommendation is because they have better access to X, thanks to the special relationship between X and Z. The reality is that for such a report to be issued, it would first have to be discussed internally whether such a course of action benefits the investment firm overall. If the net benefit is perceived to be positive, then the report will be given the green light for circulation.

It is perhaps understandable why buy recommendations are easier to make than sell recommendations. While it makes life easier for analysts in a raging bull market to issue a spate of buy recommendations, it makes it equally difficult for them in a bear market, particularly when reputations are at stake. However, the lack of independent analysis is also costly, not only for investors who base their decision on such analysis but ultimately for the companies themselves. An efficient market helps in the efficient allocation of capital for all kinds of investors, including corporations. If investors lose their trust in such a process, not only will it affect their investment decisions, it will also add to the costs of establishing the fair value of their investments.

This tendency among analysts to recommend buys in a bull market and sells in a bear market is compared by one investor to the behaviour of banks that lend you an umbrella when the sun is shining brightly and then want it back the moment it starts to rain. Economists have also been known to behave in such a manner, their response being likened to 'a thermostat gone berserk, turning on the air conditioning when temperatures drop to the freezing point and switching on the heat when the mercury climbs.'[41] While there is some merit in going with the flow and knowing that the market trend is your friend, you have to be a pretty good judge of the market to get off and back on at the right turning points. For most investors it is an impossible task, thanks to what statisticians refer to as the *random walk* of the market price of shares.

Size or the market capitalisation of firms also matters where analysis is concerned; there is better value addition to be had from the underresearched small-cap sector. Some of the world's best investors have been good at picking fledgling companies before they turned into giants and subsequently lost their ability to generate a consistently higher return on capital. As the price impact of a sell recommendation on a small-cap firm can be magnified due to lack of liquidity among other factors, the relationship between the smaller-cap firm and its investment banker is based on a greater understanding of market reality. While large-cap firms have a greater role in influencing the decision of their bankers, such an option may not always exist for the smaller firm. Large-cap firms have been known to cut off the supply of information to analysts who do not write a favourable report. A study by Reuters indicated that companies retaliate against analysts who issue 'negative' recommendations. Retaliations include denying analysts direct access to company

147

executives and to company-sponsored events, or bringing lawsuits against analysts personally, thereby creating a climate of fear that does not foster independence and objectivity.[42] There is a significantly higher level of risk for the analyst writing a sell recommendation than a buy recommendation.

It is now widely recognised that sell-side analysts operate under a conflicting set of institutional demands. According to Arthur Zeikel, former chairman of Merrill Lynch Asset Management and current governor of the Association for Investment Management and Research (AIMR) and chair of the AIMR task force on selective disclosure and analyst independence:

> The audience for a sell recommendation is primarily limited to people who own the stock. Second, researching a 'sell' takes away from finding a buy recommendation, which requires the same amount of work, has a larger potential audience, is probably more crucial, and... speaking in generalities... is more fruitful for the analyst. Third, you alienate a lot of people... it alienates the corporate executive, who may be an investment banking client; it alienates the investment banker who's the relationship manager; it alienates the portfolio managers out in the real world who own the stock; it alienates the employees of the company, who may already have a morale problem. So, even when analysts can't recommend a stock, many feel it's better to use a variety of words that indicate a less-than-complete enthusiasm for today's price.[43]

Thus, with regard to analytical objectivity on the sell side, there has been growing concern that analysts' independence was being seriously compromised. In a speech in October 1999 the US Securities and Exchange Commission (SEC) chairman, Arthur Levitt, noted a 'web of dysfunctional relationships' between Wall Street and corporate America that encouraged analysts to rely heavily on company guidance for their earnings estimates. Analysts, he noted, were 'all too often falling off the tightrope on the side of protecting the business relationship at the cost of fair analysis.'[44] As expressed by Thomas A. Bowman, CFA, AIMR President and CEO, in his testimony to the US House of Representatives Committee on Financial Services,

Capital Markets, Insurance, and Government Sponsored Enterprises Subcommittee on the issue of analyst independence:

> It is important to recognize that the conflicts that sell-side analysts face are not new. But the pressures on the analyst have escalated in an environment where penny changes in earnings-per-share forecasts make dramatic differences in share price, where profits from investment-banking activities outpace profits from brokerage and research, where the demographics of the investors who use and rely on sell-side research have shifted, and where investment research and recommendations are now prime-time news.

> The particular conflict posed by analysts' involvement in their firms' investment-banking activities has been the focus of recent media attention. But this is by no means the only conflict that we must address if we are to provide an environment that allows analysts to operate without undue or excessive pressures to bias their reports and recommendations. Pressure to prepare 'positive' reports and make 'buy' recommendations may also come from corporate issuers and institutional clients who may have their own vested interests in maintaining or inflating stock prices. An investment professional's personal investments and trading pose another conflict ... Human factors also affect the content and quality of a research report or investment recommendation. Analysts are not infallible, after all, even when independent and objective.[45]

Bowman also encouraged the subcommittee to allow the profession to develop its own response to the problem rather than address it via any legislative action. One focus of the subcommittee hearing was the recently released Securities Industry Association (SIA) 'best practices' guidelines on analyst conduct, which have been endorsed by 14 of the largest investment banking firms representing some 95% of the securities underwriting business. These guidelines are voluntary. According to Tom Bowman, 'Most, if not all, of what is in the SIA "best practices" has been part of the AIMR *Code of Ethics and Standards of Professional Conduct* for over 30 years.' Thus, the AIMR Research Objectivity Standards can provide a solution if embraced and adopted by those who have a stake in preserving the integrity of research and the professionals who conduct it.[46] While Wall Street analysts, or analysts working for large sell-side firms, are a minority of AIMR members and investment professionals in general, the reputation of the whole profession has been called into question as a result of their irresponsible action. An estimated 90% of AIMR members work on the buy side.

If public confidence in the stock market has not been dented by the poor performance of analysts because the market has repeatedly bailed them all out in a bull market, the situation could change in a bear market. Investment professionals are expected to be bullish about the long-term outlook for the market, about the importance of not being unsettled by short-term trends and the advantages of holding on to a long-term strategy. This is also the conventional wisdom shared by their clients. After all, these market analysts are often employed by firms, such as investment management, brokerage or underwriting firms, with an interest in the market remaining high.[47] In a world dominated by the media and with an increasing number of individuals making their own investment decisions, there is greater need for investor education and market transparency. While investors need to be more aware of market-moving information, they must also recognise that the information available in the media is not individually tailored to their personal risk-return profile. It is the responsibility of the media to ensure that appropriate disclosure to investors of relevant conflicts of interest by their sources and those they interview be made in no uncertain terms.

> Increasingly, private investors are demanding and accessing research reports and recommendations through their brokers, the media, and the Internet. Although a typical research report is many pages in length, these intermediaries often condense the report to its 'bottom line' – an earnings forecast or a buy, hold, or sell recommendation. Although this makes a good sound bite, and we can't keep people from trading on headlines, investors need to be informed, and should understand that headline ratings or recommendations do not provide sufficient information to justify buying or selling a security.

Investment research is multi-faceted and investment decision-making can be complex. Research results that are over-simplified not only lose their value, but they also may have a detrimental impact on the investment decision-making of those who rely on them. Brokerage firms, the media, and other investor-information providers should review and revise, if necessary, the form and content of their communications. At a minimum, they should urge investors to become familiar with entire reports before assessing, either on their own or with a professional advisor, whether the recommendation is appropriate to their particular situations, investment objectives, and constraints before taking any investment action.[48]

Recent changes proposed to the National Association of Securities Dealers Regulation (NASDR) in the US would require analysts and other brokerage employees to disclose potential conflicts of interest during public appearances, including TV or radio interviews, seminars and interactive electronic forums. The rule proposes that for recommendations made in public appearances and in written materials, the associated person or firm would be required to make the following disclosures:[49]

- The analyst responsible for the recommendation has a personal financial interest in the recommended security
- The member firm owns 5% or more of the outstanding shares of any class of security of the recommended issuer
- The member firm has received compensation from the issuer of the security for investment banking services
- And that these disclosers appearing in advertisements and sales literature be specific and prominent, not consisting of boilerplate at the end of a research report or in a footnote

The SEC has issued an investor alert addressing the potential conflict of interest that analysts may face and provides tips for researching investments. If the US SEC feels the need for alerting investors not to rely exclusively on analyst recommendations, it is perhaps understandable that in less developed markets there is an even greater need for investor protection. In the US, the SEC has adopted another rule that requires brokers and dealers to submit, on request, information on customer and firm securities trading. This will enable the SEC to better analyse transaction information and help the SEC in its enforcement investigations and trading reconstructions.[50] In a country where freedom of information is accepted as the norm, investor access to information is far superior than in other countries, including the UK, where individuals simply do not have similar access.

The situation is quite complicated in Europe, where the transition towards a more open market is a recent development. European firms demand a special relationship with investment bankers even in the trading of shares, let alone in analysing them. It was reported, for example, that Deutsche Telecom (DT) promised future business to six chosen investment banks if they agreed not to trade large blocks of its shares held by big investors, in an attempt to prevent a sharp fall (a 20% fall within a week in mid-August 2001 and almost 80% decline since its peak in March 2000) in its price prompting a tidal wave of sell orders. While DT did not offer roles in specific transactions, it made it clear to the six banks that they would be the firm's preferred partners in future equity and debt offerings. DT threatened to exclude Deutsche Bank from future business after the bank sold some €1.04 billion (£630 million, $949 million) of DT shares for one big investor. According to Ron Sommer, DT's chief executive, Deutsche Bank's action was 'a serious professional mistake' and blamed that action for the subsequent sharp decline in DT's share price. At the same time, Deutsche Banks' action came within days of its telecommunication analyst reiterating a buy recommendation on DT shares.[51]

Taking into account the dire state of the telecommunication sector, it is not surprising that the placement of a large tranche of DT shares had a heightened market impact. The shares sold by Deutsche Bank were reported to have come from an affiliate of Hutchinson Whampoa, which became a large DT shareholder when DT acquired VoiceStream of the US. Others that also ended up as large shareholders, as a result of the VoiceStream deal, include Telephone & Data Systems, Goldman Sachs and Sonera of Finland. They accounted for an additional 520 million DT shares. What DT wished to secure from its agreement with the banks was that they would refrain from putting any pressure on an already depressed DT share price ahead of the expected flowback of shares from VoiceStream investors in the US who are prohibited from holding foreign shares. What is also worrying for DT is that it was Germany's biggest privatisation, and DT shares are the most widely held by first-time private investors. For a country that is making a transition from its traditional business model based on the relationship between corporations and their bankers to a market-oriented equity culture, such a shift has its pitfalls. Investors have still to learn that prices of shares can go down as well as up.

If Europe has been rather slow to respond to market transparency, freedom of information and issues associated with investor protection, it is because the financial market has operated under a completely different ethos. It was not until 1995 that insider trading was made illegal in Germany. Even in the UK, legislation focusing on market manipulation made insider trading a criminal offence via the Companies Act 1980. By comparison, anti-manipulation legislation in the US was introduced in the form of the American Securities Exchange Act 1934, which was enacted in the wake of the Wall Street crash. It was not until 1973 in the UK that the Stock Exchange and Takeover Panel issued a joint statement in favour of criminal sanctions against insider dealers, although the Prevention of Fraud (Investments) Act 1958 made it an offence to make false or misleading statements for the purpose of inducing investments.

In light of the forthcoming pension reform in Germany, modelled after the US 401(k) plans, when individuals will be able to actively plan their retirement, necessary changes in legislation to protect investors are now gathering momentum. The regulatory authorities support initiatives to ensure full and fair disclosure of information needed for investment decision-making, investor protection, and market integrity. The Forum of European Securities Commissions' (FESCO) consultative paper *Standards and Rules for Harmonizing Core Conduct of Business Rules for Investor Protection* is evidence of such a movement. This initiative is a critical step towards an efficient, single European financial market. Only if investors believe that the information available to them is fair, accurate, timely and transparent can financial markets be truly efficient. FESCO must attempt to balance the investment professionals' need for harmonised and reasonable rules against the need for investor protections.

While FESCO is planning to issue a second consultation paper on core business rules for investor protections, Germany is proposing to introduce a voluntary code of ethics for analysts and their respective firms as well as for business journalists. This new self-regulatory code would require banks to disclose their commercial interest with the company concerned within the last three years. It would allow investment banking firms to deal in shares they also research, only if they can demonstrate the existence of adequate Chinese walls between their brokerage and sell-side business units. The code would also prohibit analysts and journalists from making personal investments in the companies they follow and would bar analysts from participating in oversubscribed initial public offerings (IPOs) if their firm is part of the issuance consortium.[52] The effective regulation of financial markets is fundamental to their efficient functioning. But Europe has a long way to go in creating a free and efficient market. Even in more developed markets, such as the US or UK, market distortions abound.

One of the obvious 'intellectual' problems with an analyst's report when making a buy recommendation is that the analyst will almost always endeavour to demonstrate that the company's earnings' prospect is positive or better than what the market expected; the implication being that the market has not yet priced that information into the stock price. Often the rise in expectation of improved earning is on the back of higher profit margin realised by the firm, perhaps due to lower costs. On the back cover of *Forbes Global* magazine, 28 May 2001, Oracle proudly advertised, 'In a quarter when the economy slowed we increased profits and improved margins.' Not that such performance had anything to do with its share price during the same period. As such bravado is clearly unsustainable, within a month Oracle had changed its advertising campaign to showing how cheap it was versus IBM in terms of its software costs to the consumer.[53] From any company's viewpoint, rising earnings and margins cannot be sustained ad infinitum. Research suggests that, for individual firms, profitability (profits divided by assets) is mean-reverting at the rate of 38% per annum.[54]

Markets tend to discount earnings in advance. That is why share prices decline soon after companies announce results in line with market expectations. The market thrives on surprises. To engineer a positive market response, firms often resort to delivering news that is better than the market expected. It is inevitable that rising market expectation can be met by firms only up to a point. Beyond that, it is a matter of financial engineering and speculation. The value addition of research to the investment industry has been low because analysts have not been able to produce independent research. Thus, the cost of research to the industry has been high. For many active asset managers, the main contribution of broker research lies in arriving at a consensus view and then using that view as a basis for adding alpha. Even asset managers with strong in-house capabilities like to measure their own views against the consensus; they therefore wish to retain access to a range of external research. According to Peter Chambers, chief investment officer of Gartmore Investment Management:

> We consider broker analysts a valuable (but not the primary) source of information on sectors and stocks. Broker-side analysts are not normally a good source of ideas, although there are two major indications of unexpected earnings growth available from this source: (1) when a broker changes a long-standing view and (2) broker forecasts. Seventy percent of our research is conducted internally and this includes frequent company visits. Commissioned work is an important aspect of research conducted externally. We also use broker research to help understand consensus views on sectors and stocks. This helps the search for areas of potential earnings surprise.[55]

Such a view is supported by most other fund managers. However, if analysts are constrained from providing independent research, then the value addition of the consensus forecasts to the buy side also disappears. While professional investment firms are committed to doing their in-house research because that serves as a branding exercise for their products, the information is rarely made available to all their clients. Most retail investors, for example, are not privy to the investment views of Fidelity, although its website does provide a lot of information for its retail clients and is thought of as one of the best in the industry. Does that make the investment behaviour of retail investors irrational? Many would argue that their logic is consistent with the 'free-rider' argument. That is, if millions of researchers and investors are studying stock prices and confirming their apparent value, why waste one's time in trying to figure out reasonable prices? One might as well take the free ride at the expense of these other diligent investors who have investigated stock prices and do what they're doing, i.e. buy stocks in a bull market and sell them in a bear market! But unknown to most investors is the troubling lack of credibility in the quality of research being done on the stock market, to say nothing of the clarity and accuracy with which it is communicated to the public. Certainly some researchers are thinking more realistically about the market's prospects and reaching better-informed positions on its future, but these are not the names that grab the headlines and thus influence public attitudes.[56]

On 10 July 2001 AIMR made public its issues paper on analyst independence. It was suggested that investment banking firms must take care to implement policies and procedures that minimise, effectively manage and adequately disclose any conflicts to investors. Effectively managing conflicts would require firms to do five things:[57]

- Foster a corporate culture that fully supports independence and objectivity, and protects analysts from undue pressure from investment banking colleagues
- Establish or reinforce separate and distinct reporting structures for their research and investment banking activities so that investment banking never has the ability or the authority to approve, modify or reject a research report or investment recommendation
- Establish clear policies for personal investment and trading to ensure that the interests of investors are always placed before analysts' own
- Implement compensation arrangements that do not link analysts' compensation directly to their work on investment banking assignments or to the success of investment banking activities
- Make disclosures of conflicts that are prominent and specific, rather than marginal and 'boilerplate'

The AIMR Code of Ethics and Standards of Professional Conduct already recognises the potential for, and the appearance of, conflicts of interest with respect to members' personal securities holdings and transactions. It also sets out clearly the standards of behaviour under such circumstances. However, recent media attention and the subsequent action by some firms to ban personal investments by analysts in the companies they follow, raise issues about whether these conflicts can indeed be managed in an effective way. In theory there is nothing unethical about analysts investing in their own ideas; it would indeed be absurd if they didn't. What is relevant is that they put the interests of their clients, the interests of the firm and the interests of the profession above their own.[58] Information about firms' policies and procedures as well as information about analysts' holdings in the stocks they cover or which the firm covers, as long as this information is in the public domain, clients and other regulatory bodies are able to access it if they need to.

Buy-side clients of investment banking firms may also have a stake in sell-side research, and brokers may be under pressure to issue positive reports on the largest holdings of their major clients. Stock price volatility in response to rating changes can damage the performance of portfolios with a large exposure to those companies that get downgraded by analysts. Considering portfolio performance determines fund manager compensation, buy-side investors can also have enough influence on analysts and their recommendations. This was clearly the view of Tom Bowman:

> Institutional clients may also pressure analysts to issue positive reports. In the short-term, stock prices are often very sensitive to rating changes. Portfolios with significant positions in a particular security may be adversely affected by a rating downgrade. Poor portfolio performance may have a subsequent negative impact on the portfolio manager's performance evaluation and compensation. Consequently, some portfolio managers support sell-side ratings inflation and may retaliate against analysts they perceive as 'negative' by shifting brokerage to another firm or by reporting those analysts to the company in question, thus launching the corporate retaliation mentioned earlier.[59]

The conflicts sell-side analysts face are widely recognised and professional investors are fully aware of the limitations of their investment recommendations. However, the conflicts inherent in buy-side research are subtle and certainly not in the public domain. As research has gone global, investment managers strive continually to assess the prospects of the major contenders for the investment of their assets under management. There has been a move towards model portfolio structures as managers adopt a global approach to their businesses. Having to justify to their clients any significant deviation in performance for a similar mandate would not fall within the criteria of good business practice. Thus, while portfolio construction centres around producing maximum return per unit of risk, platform models are created from which all similar client portfolios are derived, ensuring a team approach to portfolio construction with all members of the team contributing to stock selection and country allocation, where appropriate. A team approach to portfolio construction enables all clients' portfolios to benefit from the skills and expertise of all members of the team. It also ensures consistency and risk control across the portfolios.

> We are moving towards a model portfolio structure for different kinds of mandates which would reflect the major investment categories such as in the UK for small-caps, FTSE 100, MSCI, high-risk and low-risk, etc. The major objective of the asset allocation process is the ranking of the asset classes over a six-month period. Once that decision is made, we determine the allocation within the asset class and in the final stage the portfolio managers create the portfolio for their clients reflecting both the client's mandate and the conclusions of the strategic committee. We do give our portfolio managers sufficient latitude in their stock selection strategy but if two clients have exactly the same mandate, they are also most likely to hold similar portfolios.[60]

Although firms claim to have a quantitative investment process, there exists a strong home bias among managers. It is true that, historically, legislation obliged investors to hold the bulk of their investments in the domestic market. The creation of the euro-zone ensured that the home bias for that group of investors was enlarged significantly. However, an analysis of the median asset allocation of pension funds in the UK, the US, Europe and Japan indicates that the home bias factor has a definite impact on the performance of funds. The situation is significantly worse in developing countries, where most pension assets are not only locked in the domestic market but also obliged to invest heavily in government securities. Thus, governments in these countries have been systematically plundering the savings of people without any compensation for that loss. One of the challenges for fund managers in asset allocation is to correct this propensity towards a home bias.

Analysis of companies and sectors on a truly global basis is a relatively recent phenomenon. Asset allocation is still largely driven on a country basis rather than on a sector basis. Research by investment firms and research teams has made an attempt to move away from country-based teams to sector-based teams. In many cases there is an overlay of research expertise between sector and country, and client-servicing expertise is based on a matrix of products and type of clients: corporate, institutional, retail. The largest fund managers emphasise their research capability by having analysts based on the ground. According to HSBC's Dimitris Melas: 'A larger firm will have the capability of employing people on the ground and that should lead to better performance. So, instead of covering Japan from London, you have people based in Japan, completely at home in the local market and culture, who can add value as they have better access to the local management of companies. Thus, from a top-down approach, the asset allocation is not distorted by local sensitivities.'[61]

In reality the existence of large teams, spread over the world, has its own set of management issues at stake. It cannot be denied that information gathering is most likely to be superior when you have good analysts based locally. The challenge for the firm then lies in filtering through the range of investment opinion emanated internally from different parts of the globe within the organisation and then reflecting that adequately in the asset allocation decision. Otherwise, the expertise of the analysts is not being utilised by the firm. At the same time, the individual temperament of the analyst has a part to play in their recommendation. There may be a range of expectations and outcomes. And it largely depends on the analyst's skill in reflecting that accurately in the report. This deviation of actual return from expected return needs a complex appraisal mechanism to be of any use to the firm. The problem is inevitably exaggerated in the small-cap sector or in areas of the market that are not well researched, such as in emerging markets. As local expertise is inevitably hired locally, finding locals who think globally is not easy.

However sophisticated the stock selection and asset allocation may be, in a management structure where the different parts of the same entity compete with each other for funds, as funds under management also determines unrelated factors such as compensation packages, etc., there is scope for conflicts of interests and human error. Some companies appear to be more successful in managing these structures by giving their analysts greater scope in managing their own specialist investment portfolios within larger core portfolios. The need to create composite portfolios or model portfolios arises purely from a marketing perspective, because two clients of the firm with exactly the same guidelines and mandates would expect similar returns. Performance might vary marginally depending on the timing of cash flow. But the measurement of performance would be adjusted for such movements.

Other assets managers such as Bank of Ireland Asset Management (BIAM), who adopt a more theme-based approach to stock selection, address these issues by creating what is essentially a single investment product, a global equity portfolio with the best 100–120 stocks at any point in the investment cycle. As a result, the firm tends to concentrate on larger-cap companies globally where research is readily available. All the analysts/fund managers for BIAM are based in a single room in their head office in Dublin and are collectively responsible for all the stocks that go into the global equity portfolio. There is no incentive to recommend a stock in Europe as opposed to one in the US or Japan, because the bonus structure for the team generating investment ideas is based on the performance of the global portfolio.

As with most management structures, there are limitations – it would not work if the number of analysts grew beyond a small manageable, interactive group. Also, the firm would not be able to sell emerging-market products, for example, or even a portfolio of stocks invested in Japan, if the global portfolio did not have sufficient stocks also invested in Japan. The advantage, unique to Ireland, is that there are only a few investment companies in Dublin. Leaving one fund manager in Dublin to work for another is a highly sensitive issue, as opposed to the situation in London, where the industry's staff turnover is high. Dublin has a unique business franchise in the fund management sector and BIAM should prove to be a good investment candidate on that franchise alone. There is value added in the investment as a potential candidate for a takeover or merger. Ireland's strong links with the US market are an additional strength.

Another example of a similar franchise is Nordea Investment Management (NIM) in Denmark. When it was created in early 2000, with the merger of four Scandinavian banks, no senior-level executives left the company. 'From the beginning we accepted that we were focusing on the competence level and not on hierarchy or titles,' affirms Ole Jacobson. Both asset managers have been nurtured by the extraordinary personality and vision of their reigning heads, William Cotter at BIAM and Ole Jacobson at NIM. It will be worth watching whether the departure of these individuals will unravel the teams they have assembled. Creating teams is not easy in the world of asset managers, where egos prevail and the true spirit of enquiry is often lacking. Like BIAM, NIM has a highly acclaimed thematic investment process. According to Ole Jacobson: 'On the equities side we are focusing on the structural changes going on in the economy, such as demographics, globalization, and information technology. We look to invest in companies that will benefit from those changes. I don't think we are either a value or a growth investor. I think our investment process is a third way of adding value. That is why it is so interesting; we are a little different in our philosophy compared to our competitors.'[62]

The need to capture the outperformance potential of stocks, enjoying unexpected earnings growth, has meant that there is greater convergence among active managers in their investment approach. The pressure to deliver through different stages of the economic cycle also means that the research process fundamentally leads them towards companies that enjoy strong or improving franchises. Managers also have to ensure that investment style is not affected by volume of assets under management. Two essentials are ensuring flexibility for liquidity is built into the investment process, and encouraging the pooling of assets for effective management of smaller portfolios. Model portfolios ensure adherence to a defined investment profile and philosophy. The team-based culture and the use of model portfolios facilitate an increase in assets under management without jeopardising the integrity of an investment philosophy.

The tendency of market participants in following the 'current'

161

investing fad is not new. As David Dreman indicated in 1982, and in spite of the move towards quantitative analysis among institutional investors, there has been no change in the psychological principles of investing: 'Living through a number of these cycles, I became increasingly convinced that the investment methods in which we are all schooled are not sufficient by themselves to make us consistent winners. Without a grasp of systematic ways to protect ourselves against psychological overreactions, chances are we will continue to make the same or similar mistakes time and again.'[63] As EMH theories flourished, so did findings based on cognitive psychology and financial statistics. While David Dreman's investment methods were based on 'contrarian principles' or principles that go against the flow of popular market opinion, the important point to emerge from his method is that the whole point of analysis is to challenge the status quo, not for its own sake but for the sake of capital preservation. To evolve any investment method that captures risk-adjusted returns is the ultimate aim of all market analysis. Due to our limited ability at configural or interactive reasoning and the vast amount of information that analysts or fund managers are required to analyse, errors are common. However, reasonably good earnings estimates are vital to markets: 'Stock prices are strongly dependent on earnings changes, both absolute and relative to analysts' estimates.... It is clear that an accurate earnings estimate is of enormous value in stock selection.'[64]

Ideas generation therefore remains the key element of an active manager's investment process. The main differentiator of this process is the way in which active managers focus on indications of unexpected earnings growth, thereby creating a strong link between their investment philosophy and process. According to Peter Chambers of Gartmore, there are four main triggers of idea generation, each associated with several indicators of unexpected earnings growth potential:[65]

> Company contact is our primary source of information and ideas with over 900 one-on-one contacts every year. In terms of idea generation, we use company meetings to identify shifts in competitive advantage and niches experiencing strong or accelerated growth, both of which are indicators of potential

unexpected earnings growth. The media is a secondary source. It is important that our analysts are well read in each area of expertise. Analysts subscribe to both newspapers and journals and use the internet proactively. When using the media to generate ideas, we focus on the following indicators of unexpected earnings growth:

- Technological innovators
- Management changes
- General trends and implications
- Industry consolidation
- Regulatory changes

The asset manager's goal in meeting with company management and third-party sources is part of the process associated with generating new ideas which help set the investment agenda and arrive at new insights that may give them an advantage relative to the competition. It also helps to highlight any exposure of the firm to errors in growth estimates, overseas earnings potential or balance sheet weakness. In the world of EMH, such an assumption is not admitted; although in the realm of active fund management, in-house research forms the basis of competitive advantage and branding. Whatever jargon is used to describe their investment process, most active investors are looking for ways to sharpen their perspective on the potential for unexpected earnings growth of current holdings and candidates for investment. Most also subscribe to the view that a combination of growth in market share and improvement in net profit margin sustains earnings growth.

However, margins are determined by global factors and the franchise of a company within its industry. Therefore, research focuses on industry analysis and franchise assessment. The franchise of a company is defined as the dynamic system of resources that enables the company to sustain and increase its competitive position within its markets. However, franchise strength is far from static. According to Peter Chambers: 'Gartmore's aim is to identify areas where companies' competitive positions are improving or deteriorating, and which particular companies control crucial resources as they determine pricing or bargaining power and ultimately profit growth. These resources are difficult to replicate, its replacement value is high; it is not mobile and it is durable. Companies controlling such crucial competitive resources are more capable of generating earnings growth in excess of consensus expectations.'[66]

Investing in strong franchises is how Warren Buffett began his long investment career. However, almost 50 years later, with an increasing army of asset managers adopting this strategy, the returns from such an approach are likely to diminish. Coca-Cola is no longer the great investment it was. The other factor is that with rising globalisation, companies are finding it harder to hold on to their franchises. In the world of stock market investing and in the corporate sector, there is a slow erosion of the value attached to natural franchises. Even in closed economies such as China and India, which instinctively veered towards protecting such franchises within their national boundaries, their uniqueness has virtually disappeared due to lack of external competitiveness.

Fifty years ago the national tobacco companies in China and India had a distinct franchise. However, the lack of shareholder awareness, thanks to the inability of the private sector to compete globally, meant that the value attached to these companies did not rise as fast as that of Philip Morris. The fact that the courts in the US can bankrupt tobacco firms, while in the developing world such legislative power is lacking, is a different issue altogether. Although half of Philip Morris's revenue is derived from non-tobacco operations, the risk of the firm's earnings being affected by legislation is a significant factor. Ethical concerns are additional non-financial factors that need to be taken into account when analysing expected price returns of tobacco firms, although the rise in socially responsible investing is not confined to the tobacco sector alone.

Gauging the ability of a company to finance its future growth is an important part of stock analysis. Understanding the company's ability to generate internal cash flow and the appropriateness of its capital structure, given the risks and rewards inherent in the business, are all part of this process. Many firms use the Holt cash flow return on investment (CFROI) approach to assess the creation of shareholder value by comparing CFROI to the company's cost of capital. The focus on cash rather than accounting profits and the measurement of returns relative to the opportunity cost of capital provides important insights into the company's investment. The industry and franchise assessments provide an estimate of the earnings outlook for a company. The proprietary earnings per share forecast arising from this analysis is then used in a number of valuation methodologies to establish whether the current share price has discounted such a view. The setting of price targets is an important aspect of analysis as the magnitude of upside or downside to the notional fair value is a key driver of all stock recommendations.

The asset allocation process of many fund managers is driven by earnings and interest rate trends. Valuation is used as a guide to how far expected movements in these primary variables are anticipated to generate changes in market prices. Corporate earnings are regarded as a key determinant of equity market performance. Analysts would compare their own views on earnings prospects with the estimate of the market consensus. Markets which have the prospect of sustained upward revisions in earnings expectations usually offer the prospect of higher returns than markets where earnings uncertainty or disappointments are more probable. Interest rate trends are a key influence on market performance. Falling interest rates increase expected equity returns by lowering the rate at which future profits are discounted, and by boosting expectations of future corporate earnings growth. However, falling interest rates do not always trigger a market rise. US interest rates declined ten times in 2001 without eliciting such a response.

Considering how important it is for global managers to carry out bottom-up research and to identify stock-specific risk, the requirement for companies to account for all their financial assets and liabilities, including derivatives, on their balance sheets will be a vital step forward. The concept of showing everything on the balance sheet at fair value is still not fully realised in Europe. Even Japan has introduced changes in accounting rules whereby historical book prices are substituted by current market valuation, thereby preventing any misleading accounting practices. Corporate accounting rules have also changed in such a manner that the financial situation of a company's pension plan directly affects the company's earnings in the UK. Such a level of transparency is not yet common practice in Europe. The retail investor often has the least access to information regarding their own investments. Very few pension funds send an annual report and accounts to their individual members.

Perhaps the most challenging aspect of analysis in the future will be assessing non-financial risks associated with companies and markets. With the current fashion for quantitative analysis, the whole gamut of research revolves around the company's balance sheet. Firms do not account for non-financial risks and are not obliged to include those in their balance sheet or notes. While most firms are insured against various forms of claims against them, even insurance companies are only prepared to insure for risks they can measure. Genuine risks, such as pollution of the environment, the use of child labour, abuse of human rights and corporate manslaughter, fall outside the domain of investment research. Analysts might take into account factors such as the competence and integrity of the management, but they are neither clearly defined nor properly quantifiable. It is much easier to demonstrate an increase in shareholder value, as it is highly price sensitive.

ASSET ALLOCATION: GLOBAL VERSUS LOCAL

In a global world, national indexes become less relevant as currency risk can be hedged. Many investors recognise that the investment environment has changed and identifying investments on a sector basis provides a valuable tool in asset allocation. The cutting edge of the corporate world has led the way in sectors such as telecommunications and IT, automotives, pharmaceuticals, financial services and oil. As capital and information begin to flow seamlessly between countries, spurring industrial consolidation, it is increasingly clear that the industry within which a company operates has become an important factor in determining share price behaviour. Corporate consolidation has also led to a rise in sector and stock-specific risk in various indexes such as the FTSE 100, creating a greater need among UK investors for better global diversification. Thus, investing in companies on a sector or thematic basis reflecting the global economic cycle is also on the rise among investment managers.

A natural corollary to globalisation, as was the case with the creation of the euro-zone, is the rise in the use of sector-based indexes or investing in growth sectors of the global economy rather than in country-based indexes. Most active stock selection techniques already focus on companies within a global context. However, very few investors worldwide do invest in a truly global context. Pension funds may be global but they are locked into domestic markets through some form of legislation; this has helped to create a superior level of expertise in the domestic market but it has proven a barrier to investing on a global scale. Developing global expertise involves cost, time and effort. The corporate sector has been better able to invest in such research and development as it needs to take a long-term view of investment simply because people, plants and machinery are not as mobile as capital. While fund managers in the US and Europe are more guilty of a home bias in the developed world, their home markets are also hugely diversified. That cannot be said of UK investors. There is no reason to believe that with the rise in the retail sector, investor behaviour will become more globally oriented.

As the world's major companies today invest globally, many fund managers argue that by investing in these companies they buy exposure into parts of the world that are costly to access, such as emerging markets. The top five FTSE companies – BP, Vodafone, GlaxoSmithKline, HSBC and AstraZeneca – have widely diversified streams of income. But with recent declining return from global equities and the superior performance of emerging-market debt securities, pension fund managers and their consultants are re-examining their exposure to a wide range of alternative assets, albeit on a selective basis. As pension fund trustees and their advisers assess the merit of assets at the strategic allocation level, it is important that they keep an open mind and do not exclude any asset class or include others just because it is fashionable. As Tim Gardener explained:

> At any point in time there is a set of asset classes which satisfies a set of criteria that it is suitable for pension fund investment. So, for example, works of art do not satisfy that criteria. We start from the basis of bonds and equities; we are not in the business of introducing esoteric asset classes to make this year's model look different to last year's. We are happy to stick to bonds and equities in the future, if we can't find alternative

167

asset classes that suit our investment criteria. We position ourselves to give best advice on the asset allocation process.

Doing a good job means always being aware of new opportunities but never putting them on for want of fashion. About three years ago, we concluded that the next ten years were unlikely to be as profitable as the last ten for pension funds. Most pension funds are funded on the basis of achieving future investment returns, which were rather optimistic in our view. We coined a phrase 'the search for excess return'. What we initiated was a study to ask ourselves what asset classes were out there which offered the potential for excess return. It would obviously have risk but the incremental risk would not be great.

So we went to our clients and said that, going forward, they have a choice, i.e. carry on being conventional and invest in bonds and equities as in the past. Returns will be decent but they will not generate a high level of surplus. But if they agreed that returns will be hard to come by, then we suggested they come with us on a journey and that involves investing in corporate bonds, real estate (including property development), private equity, hedge funds, emerging markets' debt and equity. The main criteria for the asset class being: Is it going to deliver excess return over the alternative asset class? Is the risk acceptable? Does it have any characteristics which make the risk more one-dimensional, the obvious one being liquidity? That is how we approach the whole issue of developing expertise in the alternative investment sector.[67]

Thus, definition of investment objective is critical to any investor's asset allocation process. The problem with investing in companies with a global diversified source of revenue reflected in indexes such as the FTSE Multinational index can be that such a portfolio may not necessarily capture the dynamics of global trade or economic productivity, if one is a growth-oriented investor. When companies merge, they do not necessarily enhance productivity, except of course via cost-cutting, which takes a few years to filter through. Most investors recognise that, in a global world, the rational approach to investing is to capture as far as possible the dynamism of global economic activity. The problem arises when there is no opportunity of doing that; thus bringing us to the question of investor objective and market efficiency.

One way of dealing with economic bubbles, it has been suggested, is by expanding trade. The creation of the euro-zone was based on such a concept, although it was also seen as creating the largest trade block, which in its turn accelerated the creation of other trade areas that have stood in the path of freer global trade. Alan Greenspan, in his testimony before the US Senate Finance Committee on 4 April 2001 reiterated his view that expansion of trade is a panacea for global economic slowdown, 'There is no question in my mind that, as the economy slows, we of necessity must accelerate our endeavours towards free trade.'[68] Similar concerns were echoed by Mike Moore, the director-general of the World Trade Organisation, for whom the growing regionalisation of international trading relations as witnessed in the planned Free Trade Area of the Americas or the European Union's proposed enlargement mean exclusion for the least developed nations of the world.[69]

While Greenspan acknowledges concerns over the impact of freer trade, he is even more worried about the consequences of import restraints on US living standards. After all, his primary job is to manage the US economy, not the global economy or the US stock market. But as more and more individual savings get invested in the stock market, the future of the US economy and that of its investors get more aligned. Since 11 September 2001 the state of the US economy has become critical to the rest of the world, as stock market falls across the world have wiped out savings and investments indiscriminately. People no longer feel as wealthy or as secure as they did before. It has been argued that as long as the US remains a strong and competitive economy, then stock market distortions will take care of themselves without causing undue damage to the real economy. If that were indeed the case, then the whole notion of market economics, on which so much depends, would simply be a big hoax. And developing countries' hopes of gaining access to developed markets would be only an illusion. Just as global trade underpins the prospects for global economic growth - and many observers recognise the need for expanding trade and enabling the developing countries to enlarge their share of exports – global portfolio investing could equally benefit from enlarging its coverage of markets and companies. Institutional investors are in the strongest position to take advantage of this opportunity.

The creation of global multinational indexes attempts to address the issue of providing a benchmark, but more for large-cap oriented investors, as opposed to local small-cap, value or growth investors. But investment consultants such as Frank Russell do not recommend fragmentation of benchmarks into multinationals and locals as it distorts the overall market and places an additional asset allocation burden on plan sponsors. Also, not all sectors lend themselves to a global brief. Besides, an investor who had indeed held the MSCI World index, for example, would most certainly have missed out on the spectacular returns made in the TMT sector in the second half of the 1990s, but equally been less exposed to the bust that followed. Holding more diversified portfolios is recommended on grounds of risk reduction, although there will be periods when it fails to deliver. The solution is an overall reduction in the level of exposure to the equity market (Chapter 2) with or without the use of absolute return strategies (Chapter 5). Large institutional investors do not always have the ability to make radical changes in asset allocation. However, increasing their exposure to less risky securities such as fixed-return investments, as opposed to equities, would have been an option. However, there is no evidence in the UK that they did so. Overall exposure to equities remained high (Table 4.1).

It was widely recognised that the TMT asset bubble posed a threat to the market, and indirectly to the growth of the global economy with the rise of the dependency of growth attached to that sector. The Federal Reserve chairman, Alan Greenspan, warned investors of the market's 'irrational exuberance' as long ago as 1996. However, the rising investment by venture capital funds in the dotcom sector provided the liquidity to feed the asset bubble. While massive investment in the technology sector delivered lower inflation to the real economy, it engineered a stock market frenzy that defied all traditional methods of valuing investments. It even created the illusion that technology had created a new paradigm, a new way of measuring reality. However, the reality was that during this period, the average price of stocks in the Russell 3000 index did not rise.

Small-caps, value and domestic or local companies did not fare well in such a euphoric market environment.

Japan experienced a similar asset bubble between 1985 and 1990, when inflation was nil, the yen was strong and liquidity in the domestic market was high. There is no asset bubble in Japan today, but even after a decade of poor corporate and economic showing, Japan boasts the largest current account surplus in the world and the US boasts the largest deficit. Also, after a decade, many Japanese companies remain expensive. If Japan has not recovered from the market excesses of the 1980s, it is largely due to the lack of restructuring in its corporate sector. The greater flexibility of the US economy and the willingness of its central bankers to react to a slowdown will engineer a recovery. However, the lack of restructuring in both the euro-zone and Japan continues to pose a threat to regional and global growth. In 1988 Japan constituted 44% of the MSCI World index compared to 29% for the US and 21% for Europe, including the UK. By 1998 Japan had fallen to 10% of MSCI World while the US had risen to 51% and Europe stood at 34%. At the end of September 2001, the market capitalisation of Japan remained at 10%, the US was at 53% and Europe represented 32% of the MSCI World index.

One of the salient effects of the introduction of the minimum funding requirement (MFR), resulted in trustees investing the bulk of their pension assets in the UK. Such a home bias would have been justified if the equity universe were sufficiently diversified, as is the case with the US. However, the recent trend towards mergers and takeovers has resulted in a high level of stock and sector concentration in both the UK and US indexes. On 31 December 1999 some 50% of the FTSE 100 was represented by the top 20 stocks compared to 38% at the end of December 1995. By March 2001 the top 20 stocks in the FTSE 100 represented 67% of the index, with the top 10 accounting for 54%. With the overall equity component rising, many pension funds could have held significantly more of these 10 stocks in their portfolios than in the rest of the world.

With just half of UK pension funds using tailored benchmarks based on indexes other than a peer group index, a clustering around the median allocation of the peer group defeated the rationale behind active management. Thus, fund managers could have held significantly more of BP-Amoco or Vodafone than the entire US market.

Table 4.1 *Changes in discretionary portfolio asset distribution (in balanced funds): numeric average figures expressed as percentages[a]*

Sector	2Q 99	3Q 99	4Q 99	1Q 00	2Q 00	3Q 00	4Q 00	1Q 01	2Q 01
UK equities	54.8	53.9	55.2	54.5	52.8	53.8	53.8	53.5	53.4
Overseas equities	17.6	18.7	21.5	22.1	23.1	22.3	21.8	21.7	23.2
US equities	1.9	1.6	1.6	1.8	2.1	2.5	2.6	2.6	3.7
European equities	9.9	9.9	11.0	10.9	11.8	11.4	11.8	11.2	10.9
Japanese equities	2.7	3.9	4.7	5.0	4.9	4.5	3.8	3.9	4.2
Pacific ex Japan equities	2.2	2.4	2.9	3.0	2.9	2.8	2.7	3.0	3.2
Pacific equity units	0.0	0.0	0.0	0.0	0.0	0.0	0.0	0.0	0.0
Canadian equities	0.0	0.0	0.0	0.0	0.0	0.0	0.0	0.0	0.0
Emerging market equities	0.9	0.9	1.3	1.4	1.4	1.1	0.9	1.0	1.2
Overseas equity units	0.0	0.0	0.0	0.0	0.0	0.0	0.0	0.0	0.0
UK bonds	9.0	8.9	7.8	7.8	7.8	7.4	7.8	8.0	7.3
Overseas bonds	7.7	7.8	6.9	7.1	7.4	7.7	8.2	8.5	8.1
Global index-linked	–	–	–	–	–	–	–	–	–
UK index-linked gilts	0.3	0.3	0.2	0.2	0.3	0.2	0.2	0.1	0.2
Overseas index-linked	0.6	0.6	0.6	0.6	0.5	0.6	0.5	0.5	0.3
UK cash balances	7.0	6.6	4.9	4.6	5.2	5.0	4.6	4.6	4.2
Overseas cash balances	0.4	0.4	0.4	0.5	0.4	0.4	0.4	0.3	0.5

Table 4.1 (*continued*)

Sector	2Q 99	3Q 99	4Q 99	1Q 00	2Q 00	3Q 00	4Q 00	1Q 01	2Q 01
Currency hedging	0.0	0.0	0.0	0.0	0.0	0.0	0.0	0.0	0.0
Other assets	0.1	0.1	0.1	0.1	0.1	0.1	0.1	0.1	0.1
Total fund ex property	*97.5*	*97.3*	*97.6*	*97.5*	*97.6*	*97.5*	*97.4*	*97.3*	*97.3*
Total property	2.5	2.7	2.4	2.5	2.4	2.5	2.6	2.7	2.7
UK property unit trusts	2.2	2.4	2.2	2.3	2.2	2.2	2.4	2.4	2.4
UK direct property	0.3	0.3	0.2	0.2	0.2	0.3	0.2	0.3	0.3
Overseas property	0.0	0.0	0.0	0.0	0.0	0.0	0.0	0.0	0.0
Total fund	100.0	100.0	100.0	100.0	100.0	100.0	100.0	100.0	100.0

[a] Source: Combined Actuarial Performance Services Limited, UK

Changes in discretionary portfolio asset distribution over several quarters illustrate this point. Exposure to US equities remained below 2% until second quarter 2000, while investments in Japanese equity was twice as large. If active managers in the UK genuinely believed the US market to be overvalued, they should have reduced their exposure to a risky asset class and not increased it when they did. Those managers of conviction who did precisely that lost their mandates to others of lesser conviction.

Overall equity allocation at the peak of the global market cycle also remained uncomfortably and unjustifiably high. Some trustees ended up with higher levels of risk relative to the true cost of funding for benefits, which they could have otherwise avoided. It was therefore irrational to increase US equity exposure from third quarter 2000 onwards. Based on information provided by the Combined Actuarial Performance Service (CAPS) as at 30 June 2001, US equities lost 8.6% over the past 12 months. The highest return by US equity was over a five-year period, delivering 16.8% return per annum. However, the average pension fund exposure to the US market was very low during that whole period. As we know, trustees play a crucial role in asset allocation, and as pension fund assets account for a large proportion of institutional assets, their collective decision is important in influencing the market. Thus, their efficient asset allocation decision is fundamental to the security of our pension funds.

STYLE INVESTING

In terms of market sophistication, the US has taken the lead in developing innovative investment strategies. With greater investor sophistication in Europe, it is inevitable there will be demand for greater differentiation in investment styles – value/growth and large-cap/small-cap – as the Russell indexes make available for the US market. However, the distinction between value and growth has blurred significantly. The principles of value investing, initially defined by Benjamin Graham in *The Intelligent Investor*, remain secure. So do T. Rowe Price's principles of growth investing. What smart investors try to do today is combine the merits of the two – growth at the right price (GARP). Growth is simply the calculation used to determine value. While the debate between the relative merits of growth and value investing remains unresolved, many plan sponsors are now taking a slightly different perspective on the issue.

There is a growing realisation that there is little advantage in having two different styles in the same area, e.g. growth and value in US equities. Both sets of managers have too much business risk to ignore the other's universe entirely, so there are many mutual shareholdings. According to Alastair Ross Goobey of Hermes:

> Much more interesting for the plan sponsor is risk stratification – i.e. indexation, low-risk active manager, higher-risk active manager, private equity and small-caps and alternative investment strategies – without dictating whether it is value or growth. You can then allocate your risk budget more efficiently. So, you can allocate increasingly smaller amounts at the higher end of the active sector. But there is a greater concentration on allocation of funds to fund managers that can demonstrate a track record in adhering to a certain risk profile and not changing their investment strategy. Plan sponsors wish to make their own asset allocation and not be thwarted by their fund managers. Otherwise, it could lead to a mismatch in asset allocation between plan sponsor and the various fund managers. We have also adopted such a layering in our asset allocation.[70]

Plan sponsors want even greater control not simply in determining the allocation of assets but also in ensuring there is no replication or contradiction in the strategies used by the managers they appoint. As risk management becomes increasingly important to trustees, asset managers are under greater pressure to demonstrate adherence to the investment strategy they claim to implement. As long as the market continues to reward different groups of investors differently, asset managers will continue to have to define their investment strategy accordingly. For all investors, focusing on getting the long-term investment strategy right can prove to be as rewarding as capturing short-term market moves. For example, 1998 saw the biggest gap between growth and value, small-cap and large-cap companies, while returns were reversed in 2000. Thus, within a period of three years, the market rewarded different groups of investors very differently. For long-term investors to be able to capture such short-term

175

trends requires a combination of asset allocation strategies, both strategic and tactical.

A look at recent returns in the US reflects the extent to which the market rewarded different groups of investors (Table 4.2).

Table 4.2 *US equity index returns[a]*

	2000	YTD[b]	1 year[c]	3 year[c]	5 year[c]	10 year[c]
All US stocks						
Russell 3000 index	-7.5	-6.1	-13.9	4.3	13.8	15.0
Russell 3000 growth	-22.4	-13.3	-35.3	0.7	11.2	13.4
Russell 3000 value	8.0	-0.3	11.6	5.4	14.7	15.7
Large US stocks						
Russell top 200 index	-12.1	-8.7	-19.4	3.2	14.7	15.1
Russell top 200 growth	-24.5	-14.5	-37.1	-0.5	12.6	14.0
Russell top 200 value	2.3	-3.2	5.1	5.1	15.5	15.6
Midcap US stocks						
Russell midcap Index	8.3	-2.0	1.0	8.2	14.2	15.8
Russell midcap growth	-11.8	-13.0	-31.5	7.0	12.3	14.3
Russell midcap value	19.2	3.3	23.9	6.4	14.2	16.0
Small US stocks						
Russell 2500 index	4.3	3.8	2.4	8.5	12.6	15.2
Russell 2500 growth	-16.1	-2.9	-24.0	7.3	8.9	12.8
Russell 2500 value	20.8	7.8	25.2	7.1	14.4	16.3

[a] Source: Frank Russell Company
[b] As at 30 June 2001
[c] Annualised total returns for quarter ending 30 June 2001

The performance looked quite different just two years ago. Over longer investment periods, the disparity between growth and value, large-cap and small-cap tends to get arbitraged away by the market. But even over a 10-year period ending in June 1999, for example, growth was at a premium to value. While in 2001 the reverse was the case. The disparity in the overall index return was less pronounced. As the effect of compounding on total returns is powerful, selecting the right investment strategy appears to be as critical as market timing. Conventional wisdom has it that over the long term, say over 20 years, returns in value or growth investing tend to be similar. An examination of the data in the US reveals that it may not always be the case.

For example, if one had invested $100,000 on 1 January 1979 in the Russell 1000 growth index, it would have increased to $2,473,378 by 1 January 1999; if invested in the value index, it would have grown to $2,499,000. So returns were fairly similar over that period. Interestingly enough, during the next two and a half years, returns diverged considerably. By 1 January 2000 the same investments, if left untouched, would have grown to $3,293,526 with the growth index and $2,682,633 with the value index, a difference of 22.7% in one year. This trend was reversed the next year and that reversal extended through 2001. By 30 June 2001 the investment in the growth index would have become $2,191,147 but the investment in the value index would have been $2,834,589.

However, if one had invested the same $100,000 on 1 January 1980, then by 1 January 2000 it would have increased to $2,658,067 in the growth index and $2,225,376 in the value index. So returns were far from similar over that 20-year period for value and growth investors; growth exceeded value by some 19.4%. It was not until November 2000 that value started to outperform growth and that outperformance lasted through most of 2001. At the end of August 2001, the same investments would have declined to $1,583,204 with the growth index but risen to $2,252,426 with the value index, an excess of more than 42%. Over even longer investment cycles, returns from small caps have been superior. Between 1926 and 1998, for example, small-cap stocks in the US returned 12.4% per annum. At the end of 1998, the total return of the S&P 500 index averaged 11.2% a year for the 73-year period beginning in 1926. Over the same period, government bonds averaged 5.3% and Treasury bills 3.8%. However, there is no guarantee that over the next 70 years small caps will outperform large caps.

Over the last five years, larger companies have been better able to make progress in cost control as well as in their ability to manage technological innovation. Large caps were also in a better position to exert oligopolistic pricing policies, which were simply not available to smaller companies. Stock market returns thus varied considerably

177

depending on which sector of the market one was invested in. The market rewarded companies that were able to generate growth in a relatively difficult global environment. Also, the emergence of a low-inflation environment led investors to attach a premium rating to companies that could deliver growth. In a growth environment the market tends to reward value; the reverse is the case when growth is more difficult to come by.

In the UK, since the mid-1980s, the performance of small caps has been poor. The year 1998 saw the largest variation of returns between large caps and small caps; the FTSE 100 index recorded a total return of 17.5% compared to the 4.2% of the FTSE 250 (a proxy for medium-sized companies). Between 1995 and 2000, for example, the FTSE 100's growth index outperformed its value counterpart by 5.5%. At the end of 1998, the FTSE 100 represented over 80% of the total market as opposed to 74% in 1997. The FTSE 100 currently represents 96.6% of the FTSE All Share. Small-cap companies have remained massively undervalued by markets, thereby crucifying the performance of investors who found better value in small-cap companies. The FTSE Small Cap index represented 8% of the market in 1997 compared to just 3% today. Typically over a year, an average of 35 companies exit the FTSE Small Cap index due to M&A activity or delistings. The result has been a steady erosion of the index with no means of replacing companies in the index except at the annual review.

In 1986 Professors Dimson and Marsh of the London Business School produced their famous report on the 'smaller companies effect'.[71] Their research showed that, between 1955 and 1986, smaller companies outperformed by 6% per annum. This report was interpreted at that time by the City as a strong buy signal; in retrospect it marked the top of the market for the sector and actually indicated a sell. Until their turnaround in 1999, small caps in the UK have under-performed the market since 1986. There are three reasons for this poor performance. First, the mid-1980s marked the top of the investment cycle for that sector, attracting a lot of poor quality companies to the market when smaller companies were all the rage. Second, the latter half of the 1990s witnessed the 'irrational exuberance' of the major Anglo-Saxon markets, led by Wall Street, and large-cap companies, which with their global reach fitted the mood of that investment cycle better than smaller companies. The third reason is that small caps are cyclical investments, and therefore these shares performed poorly when the UK economy slowed in 1988.

As much of the world's economy has been in trouble, larger companies have been able to make progress in both cost control and the ability to manage change by being able to exert superior pricing pressure and cut costs via mergers. Smaller companies did not have any of these options open to them. As large companies have become larger through mergers and acquisitions, the representation of smaller companies in the index has shrunk. It stands to reason that the 100 largest companies in the UK do not have the monopoly on enterpreneurial flair and commercial skills. According to many investors, smaller companies are capable of producing good profits and dividend growth, their bosses are far more aware of shareholder value, and one can buy the smaller companies index for a significant discount to the overall market. The question then arises for investors, How do you realise that discount if the market fails to see what you see?

Outside the FTSE All Share index there are approximately 1,175 listed companies in the FTSE Fledgling and Alternative Investment Market (AIM) indexes, which are capitalised at just £26 million. Many of these companies, regardless of their growth profile, fail to interest active fund managers on account of their size and attendant market liquidity. According to Brian Woods-Scawen, chairman of accountants PricewaterhouseCoopers in the Midlands (UK), the equity market has failed smaller companies, 'It is almost impossible to have a new issue for a smaller company, however powerful the growth prospects and however strong the management... there is a major disconnect between the stock market and the regional economy.'[72] The problems in the smaller companies sector have prompted reaction from most analysts.

According to many experts, it has become not just an issue of investment performance but one which raises questions about the proper functioning of the UK capital market as a whole. If one of the functions of the market is to facilitate economic activity by enabling companies across the board to access capital, then the experience of small-cap firms and their investors has not been rewarding. Also, within the small-cap sector, there is a high dispersion of earnings expectations. Those companies demonstrating organic growth, and relatively immune to changes in GDP, command high ratings and have little problem in raising additional capital. But there are a larger number of companies whose growth prospects are closely linked to underlying factors such as the level of interest rates or the level of sterling or the state of the manufacturing sector within the economy. These companies have little option but to try to maintain margins by mergers and acquisitions, yet they do not find it easy to raise capital. Nor do they find it easy to restructure their businesses.

There is a third group of companies that deliver no organic growth, but suffer from overcapacity and pricing pressure. These companies are the worst affected as they are the sort of companies that only venture capitalists might be interested in as they would be in a better position to ascertain the risks and restructure both management and the business. Thus, if you are a small company generating poor returns, remaining listed fails to make sense as capital-raising via share issue is ruled out. Thus, many small to medium-sized companies that were of little interest to large institutional investors and suffered a lack of share liquidity and many operating in unfashionable sectors or experiencing problems but having potential through restructuring decided to go private again in order to get some venture capital backing and the mentoring that goes with it to turn around their fortunes. This was also the time when private equity investing was all the rage.

The persistent underperformance of smaller quoted companies in the UK raised concern among policy-makers and business organisations. To access the life cycle of a typical UK small-cap company, Professor Mario Levis at City University Business School examined the interquintile movement of companies in terms of their size during the period 1984–88, when the Hoare Govett Small Companies index outperformed the FT All Share index by an average of 7.2% per annum. Professor Levis confirmed that 'even at the best of times the performance of small companies is driven by a relatively small number of such companies with exceptional performance.'[73] Thus, small companies behave no differently than larger ones. The majority of the small-cap universe was static, composed of companies that migrated to this group as a result of bad performance or companies almost permanently in this position following years of indifferent performance. According to various experts, these problems can be attributed to the poor competitiveness of small-cap companies. A high mortality rate among small firms is certainly a universal phenomenon as they are more likely to be inefficient producers with high financial leverage and limited access to capital markets, particularly during periods of tight credit conditions. While small caps may regain their flavour at some point in the market cycle, global economic uncertainty and slowdown do not augur well for the sector.

The distinction between value and growth investing can be complicated as managers are often not very transparent in their investment process. A rigid and inflexible style can also hamper performance. Value and growth stocks are to be found in both the large-cap and the small-cap universe. Although traditionally growth has been associated with small-caps, that idea was seriously challenged during the 1990s. What both group of managers have in common is that they all aim to include stocks with higher alphas in their portfolios. This is emphasised by Peter Hopkins, head of the quantitative research team at Baring Asset Management:

We do not necessarily define ourselves as value managers, although value is one component of our overall investment strategy. The only way that active managers can beat indexers is if they, i.e. the active managers, are able to capture the alpha through their research. Technology is deployed by both classes of investors. We take a market overview by examining country, regional and industry trends at a macro level. Thus, these macroeconomic views serve as a top-down guide to asset allocation. But along with quantitative research, which tends to rely on historical information, we conduct extensive fundamental research which is driven by subjective forecasts and the stock-picking skills of our analysts in terms of their ability to make above average decisions on any company or industry they follow in terms of cash flow, competitive advantages – or the micro approach. They would prepare stock lists in their areas of specialisation, which would then feed into the global model. Portfolio construction is then determined by risk control based on strategic, thematic issues reflecting the client's mandate.[74]

Thus, what both value and growth managers want tends to converge in the concept of GARP or growth at the right price. Nicola Ralston, for example, did not refer to SIM's investment style as 'value' but 'search for growth at a reasonable price'.[75] When an investor speaks of identifying value, the reference is to the discovery of companies with growth prospects that have not been discounted by the market, not a company without any prospect of growth, for such a company would actually decline in value. Investing in a company with a higher growth rate albeit with a higher valuation is better than investing in a company with a lower rate of growth and a lower rating.

For example, if stock *A* has a price/earnings ratio (P/E) of 15 and is growing at 10% and stock *B* has a P/E of 20 but is growing at 20%, then better value lies in investing in stock *B*. Let's say that *A* is priced at 100. With a P/E of 15, its earnings per share (EPS) is 6.7 and with a growth rate of 10%, this EPS will rise to 7.3. At the end of the year, the stock price will be 110. Stock *B* is also priced at 100. But with a PE of 20, its current EPS is 5 and with a growth rate of 20%, its EPS will rise to 6. At the end of the year, *B* will be valued at 120. If this process is compounded the following year, then the prices of *A* and *B* will be 121 and 144. It is clear why holding *B* is better value than holding a cheaper stock such as *A*. However, markets also take into account other factors such as dividends, track record of management, etc.; stock *A* might have a history of higher dividend yield compared to *B*, along with a better management record. Seasoned investors are more likely to focus on the more established companies with a track record of earnings growth rather than on start-ups where earnings expectations are highly volatile. Thus, price is a reflection of the aggregate valuation of a company's prospects by the market.

There are three things an investor wishes to identify:

- Companies already growing at the same rate as the other companies in the sector but which are rated at a lower value by the market for no good reason. These stocks will have a lower P/E compared to the average for the sector. The other way is to divide the P/E by the expected rate of growth. For most value companies it will be less than 1.

- The analyst has reason to believe that a company's growth expectation is not reflected in the consensus forecasts. A low P/E ratio does not automatically mean that a stock is cheap. It only means the earnings expectation for the company is low. Stocks with low P/Es have been known to get cheaper. When the analyst is fairly confident that the market is mispricing a security due to lack of information, then investing in such a company makes commercial sense.
- The analyst expects the sector as a whole to undergo a rerating due to earnings revisions, as was the case with the oil sector during 2000. The opposite can also happen when sectors undergo a derating, recently the case with the TMT sector.

Investment managers strive to arrive at an optimal asset allocation that determines the split between equities, bonds, cash and any other asset class. As equities have comprised the largest component of the asset mix, the secondary allocation between broad regions of the US, continental Europe, the UK, the Pacific and emerging markets have been equally relevant. Often trustees have made these decisions for their pension funds with advice from their consultants and actuaries, leaving the fund managers to get on with investing within the style parameters agreed upon. As the strategic asset allocation is made at the pension fund level, the role of fund managers is restricted to their excellence in stock selection. Even that process is largely defined by benchmarks and tracking error, etc., making it impossible for fund managers to deviate from their benchmark. Thus, the starting point of the asset allocation process for the individual fund manager may lie in stock selection. But for the pension fund, the strategic asset allocation dictates the funds' risk profile. Stock selection is a secondary activity for the pension fund sector.

The nature of stock selection is very similar in the retail market. Even among active fund managers, at the retail level, deviation from benchmark is determined by the risk profile of the fund. Thus, for example, Fidelity's MoneyBuilder Growth Fund is considered a conservative portfolio as it invests primarily in the larger UK stocks; over 65% of the fund was invested in FTSE 100 companies as at 30

June 2001. According to its manager, Tim McCarron, who is also responsible for other funds: 'I am relatively conservative in the way I structure the portfolios, and sector allocations typically diverge by no more than ±5% of the benchmark index allocation. Individual company allocations tend not to exceed ±3% of the benchmark index.'[76] Fidelity's Special Situations fund, for example, does not invest similarly, but it is considered a riskier investment because the portfolio is biased towards shares of medium-sized and smaller companies. It is 'a pure stock picking fund and is not managed relative to its benchmark. Sector exposures result from stock selection and not from macro-economic considerations. Consequently, they are relatively volatile investments.'[77]

CONCLUSION

Success in the management of assets comes not only from branding power and cost control, but also from the ability to deliver consistent, top-quartile investment performance. While there is a high level of concentration of assets within the industry, wealth management is a cottage industry where small groups of investment managers thrive in an independent and enterprising environment. The performance of these small but successful teams can be accessed by clients through an extensive network of consultants and advisers. With the rise in the retail sector, absolute returns and long-term fund performance will rise in importance as the key to success in asset gathering.

At the institutional level, however, performance is important but so are other factors. For Dimitris Melas, head of research at HSBC Asset Management, performance is not the only factor in determining the success of a fund manager:

> The key to continued success for any asset management firm is retaining and growing funds under management. If we have stellar performance, we do not actually gain much competitive advantage as, for example, having above consistent average performance. In fact, if we did very well one year, clients will wonder what will happen the next year and we might even lose assets as the perception rises that we have undertaken a higher

level of risk to achieve that extra return. So, while good performance is essential, it is not the sole factor for success in our industry. There are four elements to ensuring the continued retention and growth in assets under management. They are a clearly defined investment philosophy, an appropriate process, the right people to capture the philosophy and deliver the process and good products that meet client needs.[78]

Like bankers, fund managers have good reason to fear being seen as unconventional or original. It is consistency not flamboyance which secures flow of new business, and the safest way to win a place among the top 10 fund managers is to copy what the other nine are doing. 'You might think that the job of the institutional investor is to forecast which of the assets will perform best in the future rather than simply reflect the past,' says Alastair Ross Goobey. 'But the pressures investment managers are subject to makes them relatively cowardly when it comes to taking an independent stance.'[79] Dominic Hobson describes this herd mentality among fund managers in the following words: 'Owners but not controllers, abstracted rather than involved, it seems the modern fund manager is also bovine. They all want the same things.'[80]

The debate surrounding the relative importance of investment performance and the effective communication of investment process, etc., to clients will evolve over time. However, they are both important to each other. It will be an uphill struggle for the marketing department to sell poor investment performance; similarly, excellent investment process and performance can be undermined without effective communication. In many ways, with the rise of the retail sector, communication and trust are as important drivers in business development as consistent top-quartile performance. However, as most retail clients have little direct contact or feedback from the fund managers they invest in, they are more inclined to take their investments away from a poorly performing manager than engaging with the fund manager to find out why that was the case. Sometimes such a decision may even prove to be very expensive to the investor, unaware of fund managers' performance cycles.

Like stock markets and companies, fund managers also go through periods of poor performance, and sometimes they can last for years before things change. A retail investor does not have access to the specialised information given to institutional investors, mainly via their consultants. Considering that the average professional gets it wrong most of the time, there is no reason to conclude that individuals will be any better at choosing the right asset allocation or fund manager for most of the time. Longer investment horizons do help in compensating for short-term market movements and poor investor decisions by both professional investors and the less experienced. The dispersion of returns associated with skill-based strategies tends to be higher than with market-based strategies. Thus, a wide dispersion of returns means that the worst-performing fund will do significantly worse than the best-performing fund. To an investor with no edge, such as the retail investor, this can certainly be a risk. But to an active and skilled investor, this competitive edge offers an opportunity.

CHAPTER 5

Absolute Return Strategies

INTRODUCTION

Alternative investment strategies are primarily designed to generate alpha by hedging the market risk, the credit and the interest rate risk as well as the liquidity risk that drive returns in more traditional, long-only strategies. Institutional investors, under increasing pressure to maintain their rapidly eroding margins, are examining absolute return strategies in their search for non-correlated diversification and risk-adjusted performance. Access to modern investment techniques and markets also enables them to charge higher fees. Hedge funds, as they are more commonly known, have little correlation with traditional asset classes, largely due to the dynamic trading strategies used in exploiting inefficiencies in global capital markets. They are also not constrained in their investment strategies by benchmarks. In attempting to meet increased demand, hedge funds are becoming more institutional and global in their orientation. And in doing so, they have also to deal with more traditional issues such as transparency, performance measurement, cost competitiveness and regulation.

The hedge fund sector is in the throes of transformation, not only as a result of the fallout from the LTCM debacle of August 1998, which focused investor attention on the risks associated with such vehicles. The asset management industry itself is undergoing a massive restructuring with the rise of indexed products and the use of technology for distribution. We have seen a radical shift among investors today wanting parts of their assets managed passively (which delivers the risk-free rate of return plus beta at very low cost) and a rising interest in absolute return strategies (which delivers the risk-free rate plus alpha, usually at a higher cost). Just as international equity and private equity have found a place in institutional portfolios, absolute return strategies are beginning to find favour among institutional investors, although investor understanding of the various strategies involved remains an issue. The lack of long-term performance data, transparency and the higher cost of executing complex investment strategies is also a deterrent.

The announcement by the California Public Employees' Retirement Scheme (CalPERS) on 31 August 1999 stating that it would invest $11.25 billion in 'hybrid' investments legitimised alternative investments as an asset class for a wide range of institutions seeking a new way of protecting their capital gains. Subsequent announcements by various other funds such as the Netherlands' Algemeen Burgerlijk Pensioenfonds in May 2001 to invest up to €2 billion over the next few years provides a further vote of confidence in the sector. Contrary to popular opinion, hedge funds are not a new invention; they have been around for well over 50 years. Besides, private foundations and endowments in the US have made substantial investments in hedge funds for several years. Public pension funds, on the other hand, have been rather cautious due to their concerns about risk. Thanks to developments in technology and financial innovativeness, hedge fund managers today have at their disposal superior methods of risk management than in the past.

Investors are prepared to pay a performance fee where returns are risk-adjusted rather than what they consider a high, fixed cost for relative returns. When the incentives for both the manager and the investor are more closely aligned as with hedge funds, it reduces the conflict between the two and encourages superior attention to the management of assets. All active managers, without exception, emphasise the skill factor, as that is the sole justification for higher fees. The lucrative incentives in the hedge fund industry are considered one of the main drivers of higher returns, as it tends to attract managers with superior skill. However, hedge fund managers enhance market efficiency, particularly when traditional active managers bound by direct or indirect regulation turn into closet indexers.

To reduce tracking error, most traditional managers hold securities into which they have no particular insight. Hedge fund managers, on the other hand, invest with much greater conviction. When short selling is restricted, as is the case with traditional managers, and investor opinion is diverse then market prices tend to get distorted and the CAPM and arbitrage pricing theory fails to hold. Without complete freedom to exercise one's market views. i.e. sell short, the pessimism of some investors will fail to reflect in security prices and so market prices will no longer be efficient, although the market itself may not be irrational. Investment strategies that generate alpha are normally skill-based strategies. However, if the flexibility of the manager is reduced, so is the ability to generate alpha.

Whether hedge funds are able to deliver consistent, superior risk-adjusted performance depends largely on the skill of the individual manager. Just as trackers are dependent on active managers in setting the price of individual stocks, hedge fund managers (particularly the short-only specialists) are defined by the availability of derivative instruments and the liquidity of the underlying assets they invest in. Active managers provide the research and trading activity that secure the basis for indexation as much as for certain types of hedged strategies. All indexed strategies believe in efficient markets just as all active managers swear by the individual skill factor and by implication the ability of investors to exploit market inefficiency. Skill-based strategies thus offer a source of return not defined by the CAPM. In the realm of CAPM, markets are assumed to be efficient. Therefore, increasing one's return is directly linked to taking undue and diversifiable risk. But in the realm of hedge fund investing, the relationship between risk and return is not inversely proportional.

In actively deploying technology in the management of risk, hedge funds potentially have the edge over traditional managers. While the same technology is available to all investors, due to the nature of hedge fund investing, and depending on the skill of the manager concerned, hedge funds have the unique ability to rise in value when the value of their underlying investment falls. Interest in hedge funds soared when the major stock markets peaked in March

2000. Investors realised they need exposure to investment strategies that have a low correlation to market movements. Non-directional strategies are able to exploit short-term market inefficiencies while hedging the exposure to the market. While other strategies have a higher market exposure and thus have a strong directional bias, due to their ability to sell short, gear and engage in innovative trading strategies, many hedge funds have an advantage over traditional, long-only portfolios. In his study published in the *Financial Analysts Journal*, Bing Liang found that during the 1990s, hedge funds offered a risk-return trade-off superior to the S&P 500, although the index achieved a higher total return. The Sharpe ratio of hedge funds was higher due to their ability to use 'cross-style diversification, dynamic hedging, cross-border investing, and a variety of non-traditional financial instruments.'[1]

A long-only manager is limited to generating alpha by buying (over- or underweighting) or not buying stock. But an equity market-neutral manager can double alpha by both buying and selling stock. The skill factor of the manager is crucial as realising the alpha of an investment idea via derivatives trading can be lost due to high gearing, bad market timing/judgement and size of portfolio or a combination of any of these factors. Are hedge funds at risk of being cannibalised by active, long-only managers? The range of investment disciplines offered by hedge funds is so diverse that traditional, active long-only managers may find it less efficient to grow that expertise in-house, due to differences in pricing the product and in its distribution. At the same time, as the hedge fund sector gains acceptance and moves away from the margins of the investment industry into a more mainstream asset class, it will lose some of its distinguishing characteristics manifest today. It is conceivable that the big divide between active management and hedge fund management will narrow in time.

Thus, to what extent the hedge fund industry can be 'institutionalised' will depend on the various factors that are already driving significant change in the asset management industry today. In many ways, the long-term investment horizon of pension funds is ideal for hedge fund managers. At the same time, the low returns currently available in the market imply that pension fund managers could benefit from the expertise of hedged strategies. Both groups need to adapt to establish a mutually beneficial alliance, although there are many barriers that seem insurmountable at the moment, with lack of transparency and risk management being the more obvious ones. For most hedge fund managers, the extent to which the sector will lend itself to 'institutionalisation' will be determined by the extent to which institutions are prepared to be imaginative in their approach and consider changing the current constraints on their fund managers. Pension fund managers may not demand detailed position disclosures by their hedge fund managers, but any sensible investor will want information about processes, policies and practices. Hedge funds could certainly use the stability of long-term funding that pension funds can provide. However, some hedge fund managers do not see the gap between institutional management and hedge funds narrowing:

> I would fall back on the Socratic idea that we have two sides to our character – the creative and the analytical. The creative tends towards anarchy but the problem with reason and order is that it tends towards conformity, which fosters mediocrity and inhuman practices. The truth is, as things become more complex, they demand answers. But in fact, it is very foolish to attempt to explain them, because you have to introduce practices that result in the destruction of the creative aspect of yourself. In any decent organisation, you need very creative thinkers. But institutions today do not have that flexibility.[2]

Most companies succeed by keeping an eye on the bottom line. If profitability could be enhanced by a more creative corporate culture, then organisations would have no difficulty in changing their style. As the fees that accrue from most active strategies, including hedge funds, tend to be attractive, there is every incentive for institutions to set up their own hedge fund operations to benefit from the growth in that sector of the market. Increased market volatility over time has also alerted investors to the significant uses of hedged strategies and the potential differences in returns available between absolute return and relative return managers. In fact, the institutionalisation of hedge funds will ensure greater discipline in manager adherence to defined styles as well as better regulation and performance measurement. To what extent trustees of pension funds have any flexibility in terms of their regulatory responsibilities, that is another matter. But demand for and interest in hedge funds is on the rise, albeit from a very low base.

In September 2000, Deutsche Asset Management (DeAM) launched Xavex, a fund specifically structured for the German market, and the firm had no difficulty in raising over $1 billion within days. The European hedge fund industry is dominated by private banks (especially in Geneva and Zurich), the fund of funds industry, and to a lesser degree, family offices. Changes in Swiss pension fund regulation enabled them to take more risk as long as they adhered to the prudent man rule.[3] While a few years ago there were very few products for the retail investor, today the market offers a greater choice for all kinds of investors. In the US, however, hedge fund companies are barred from marketing their products and services to individual investors. In the most highly regulated investment market in the world, hedge funds are obliged to turn away all but 'accredited investors', which designation applies to investors with $1 million in investable assets and an income of $200,000 for two consecutive years. Hedge funds in the US are debarred from posting their performance figures on their websites as this could be misconstrued as solicitation for funds.

The reason for caution or protection from regulatory authorities stems from the fact that evaluating the risks associated with hedge funds is not an easy task for the lay investor, which is true. Ironically, in regulating mutual funds and pension funds for the benefit of ordinary shareholders, managers of such funds are also excluded from the sort of market opportunities available to hedge funds. Alternative investment strategies entail non-traditional risks based on leverage, credit, liquidity, financing (margin calls and buy-back), back-office settlement and custody, capacity, growth, change of investment style or turnover of key staff. Change in any of these areas can significantly impact the fund's strategy, more so than in traditional, long-only investment strategies. The evolution of structured products, such as capital-protected products (CPPs), is aimed at overcoming some of these underlying risks to the investor. The growth in that market is testimony to the demand for absolute return products by individual investors.

It is estimated that historically some 75% of the net assets in the industry came from high net worth investors,[4] but today institutional investment in hedge funds is growing steadily. In the US, institutional investors account for one-third of new money flowing into hedge funds, with university foundations and endowments being the most aggressive allocators. Pension funds under pressure to diversify their holdings across a wider range of asset classes are allocating capital to hedge funds, as are overfunded pensions seeking to preserve wealth by lowering their risk profile.[5] Traditional institutional investment firms now offer hedge fund products wrapped around their in-house 'star' managers. This is driven by their need to retain key fund managers as much as to maintain their margins in an increasingly competitive business. Not only have asset managers benefited from the higher fees accruing to hedge funds, investment banks have realised that their income from stock lending and a host of other services provided to the hedge fund sector is as lucrative as that derived from the traditional managers. As new and innovative products are introduced to the market, the hedge fund industry is bound to adapt itself to such competition. However, hedge funds remain an attractive investment proposition due to their unusual characteristics as enlisted in Table 5.1.

DEFINING HEDGE FUNDS

Diversity, difference or heterogeneity is the salient feature of hedge funds. The term covers a wide variety of styles consisting of non-directional (or market-neutral) strategies and directional strategies, which include global macro and emerging markets to event-driven investments in deeply discounted, non-performing Japanese/Asian bank loans and other distressed securities. In fact, the increasing diversity of corporate finance type hedge funds ensures that, as an asset class, there will be growing demand for them, thanks to the rise in distressed assets and bad debts around the world. It was widely reported, for example, that John Duffield, chairman of New Star Asset Management and ex-chairman of Jupiter International Group (JIG), made two-fifths of JIG's worldwide profits of £172 million in 1999 in his Thai property investment rather than his conventional high-profile UK asset management operation. Accord-

Table 5.1 *Trends in hedge fund characteristics between 1995 and 2000*[a]

	Percentage answering yes	
	1995	2000
Fund manager is a US registered investment advisor	54	68
Fund has a hurdle rate[b]	17	18
Fund has a high water mark[c]	64	87
Manager has $0.5m of his own money in fund	78	79
Performance and accounts are externally audited	97	96
Is diversified	57	52
Can short-sell	76	84
Can use leverage	72	72
Uses derivatives	77	71
Can access hot issues[d]	25	54

[a] Source: Van Money Manager Research
[b] Hurdle rate: the return above which a hedge fund manager begins to charge performance/incentive fees. If a fund has a hurdle rate of 10% and the fund's return is 20%, then the fund will take performance fees on 10% of the return above the hurdle rate
[c] High water mark refers to the agreement that the fund accrues fees only on profits over and above the original investment. Thus, if $1m is invested in a hedge fund and that declines over the year by 50%, leaving $0.5m, then the manager will not receive any performance fees for that year. In year 2 the fund does very well and doubles, bringing the original investment back to $1m. If a fund has a high water mark, it will not take incentive fees on the return in year 2 either as the investment has not grown. The fund will only charge performance fees when the investment grows above the initial investment of $1m
[d] A newly issued stock that is in great demand and thus appreciates rapidly in its value. Special distribution rules apply to the distribution of hot issues

ing to Fitch IBCA, bankruptcies reached a record $23.3 billion during second quarter 2001, with a first half total of $45.5 billion for 2001, triple that for the first half of 2000.

Event-driven strategies concentrate on companies that are subject to restructuring, takeovers, mergers, liquidations, bankruptcies or other special corporate situations. Typically, these strategies rely on fundamental research as much as on the assessment of legal and structural issues surrounding the event as the strategy is geared towards the deal being accepted by both regulators and shareholders. Sometimes the manager takes an active role in determining the event's outcome. At other times, global macro funds are able to influence the desired outcome due to their sheer size and flexibility. Macro hedge funds had a significant short position in pound sterling in 1992, which eventually precipitated the withdrawal of the UK from the European Monetary System. It is difficult to establish whether hedge fund activity caused the devaluation of sterling as it coincided with strong capital outflows from the UK. However, hedge fund managers, such as George Soros, enriched themselves conspicuously as a result.

During the Mexican crisis, when the peso was devalued by some 40% in December 1994, hedge funds fared significantly better than traditional mutual funds invested in the region. The IMF concluded that Mexican residents, not foreign investors, played the leading role in the 1994 crisis. The unwinding of the leveraged 'carry trades' resulted in the Asian currency crisis of 1997, in which hedge funds played a significant role with other larger market participants. Carry trades allowed Thai corporations and banks to borrow in foreign currencies, which had a lower interest rate than in the domestic currency. Thus, borrowing was cheaper as long as the currency did not devalue. Also, by following a fixed exchange rate policy, the Thai Central Bank was effectively paying the risk premium to foreign investors to fund the domestic investment needs. In the end, such a policy became unsustainable when in July 1997 foreign investors decided to unwind their carry trades in Thailand. It is difficult to conclude that hedge funds caused the unwinding of these positions, as the economic conditions were ripe for such an accident to happen.

Hedge funds were severely affected by the economic crises of 1998 when Russia defaulted on its debt. More funds died that year than in any other year during the 1990s; 179 funds died in 1998 while 202 were born, the lowest number of births since 1993.[6] The year 1998 also produced the highest volatility in hedge fund returns during the decade. As the Russian crisis spread to other markets, there was a flight to safety and investors bought heavily into US Treasury securities and other forms of government debt, thereby widening the credit spreads between high-quality debt instruments and risky ones. Liquidity risk premium also soared for corporate bonds, mort-

195

gage-backed securities and other illiquid securities. Hedge funds, such as LTCM, that were betting on the convergence in yield spreads before the crises obviously got their analysis wrong and were forced to liquidate their positions, deleverage their portfolios or simply go out of business. The credit squeeze that followed the 1998 crises had a shattering impact on global macro funds and fixed-income arbitrage funds.

Due to the very specific nature of hedge funds, there are as many definitions of hedge funds as there are hedge funds. Broadly speaking, these are private partnerships where the manager has a significant personal stake in the fund and is free to operate in markets, utilising whatever strategy that is deemed appropriate, including gearing and selling short. For tax and regulatory purposes, hedge funds often find themselves an offshore domicile. Hedged investments come in many guises and many of the strategies involved have little correlation to each other. Understandably, a portfolio of non-correlated investments has many advantages over a traditional one. Non-correlated investments have become a fast-expanding investment genre as they offer strategies by which investors can effectively insulate their portfolios from undue risk and optimise returns from conventional asset classes.

In broad terms, hedge funds can be classified into categories that give an indication of market exposure. The classification used in Table 5.2 was provided by UBS Warburg. Other classification systems use directional and non-directional instead of relative value, event-

Table 5.2 *Hedge fund style classification*[a]

Relative value	Event-driven	Opportunistic
Convertible arbitrage	Risk arbitrage	Global macro
Fixed-income arbitrage	Distressed securities	Short-sellers
Equity market neutral		Long region, Industry or style
		Emerging markets
		Long/short equity
————————————	Increasing market exposure	——————→

[a] Source: UBS Warburg

driven and opportunistic. The main consideration is to what extent a strategy is correlated to the market, as volatility is primarily a function of beta. A high exposure to the underlying asset class results in higher volatility, and risk-adjusted returns tend to be lower in such strategies than in those with lower market exposure. Dispersion of returns is also higher in strategies more exposed to market movements.

Categorising hedge funds is difficult as many strategies straddle across different styles (Table 5.3). The hybrid nature of the asset class makes it impossible to fit it neatly into a box. However, broadly speaking, long/short equity is the largest style with 30% of the market share, based on the number of funds as well as assets under management. But the managers in this group are far from homogeneous with styles varying from market-neutral to short and long biases. Although global macro funds represented 15% of assets, they have been shrinking as an asset class during the 1990s, declining from just over half the assets under management in 1990. The fund-of-funds sector was around 14% of the total number of funds in

Table **5.3** *Distribution by style as of 1998*[a]

	Funds (%)	Assets under management (%)
Long/short equity	30.6	29.8
Managed futures	18.6	15.9
Fund of funds	14.1	NA[b]
Event-driven	11.9	16.6
Emerging markets	5.6	3.5
Fixed-income arbitrage	5.1	7.7
Global macro	4.0	14.9
Equity market neutral	3.8	3.9
Convertible arbitrage	3.5	4.4
Equity trading	1.1	2.4
Dedicated short bias	0.5	0.4
Other	1.2	0.5

[a] Source: TASS Investment Research Limited
[b] As funds of funds invest in other funds, the percentage of all hedge funds under management has not been given, to avoid double counting

1998, but this sector is anticipated to increase rapidly as investors prefer a diversified exposure to hedge funds than carry the risks associated with single funds or styles. Identifying hedge fund winners is not only costly and time-consuming, but statistically the chances of getting it right remain rather low.

Estimates of the size of the hedge fund industry deviate considerably. According to the *Report of the President's Working Group on Financial Markets*, April 1999, the hedge fund universe as of mid-1998 consisted of 2,500–3,500 funds, managing $200–300 billion, with approximately $800–1,000 billion in total assets. Compared with other US financial institutions, the estimated $1 trillion in assets under hedge fund management is relatively small compared to assets with commercial banks ($4.1 trillion), mutual funds ($5 trillion), private pension funds ($4.3 trillion), state and local retirement funds ($2.3 trillion) and insurance companies ($3.7 trillion).[7] With the growing popularity of the sector, the average size of hedge funds is also decreasing as new funds enter the lucrative market. As of 1999 some 83% of all funds under management were allocated to funds below $100 million and 52% to funds smaller than $25 million.

In a report issued by TASS Investment Research in September 2000, $60 billion of new assets flowed into hedge funds since January 1994. Total assets for the 2,200 funds covered by TASS had grown by an additional $100 billion of performance appreciation between January 1994 and June 2000. With a fourfold increase in assets to $205 billion during this period, the report illustrated that not only did investors have an increasing appetite for diverse types of equity exposure but investors also withdrew money from funds dedicated to global macro strategies. The data confirmed a consistently increasing appetite for equity market-neutral styles as overall market volatility rose. And while investors resisted adding assets to distressed funds, they rewarded the merger arbitrage players, although it would appear that investors could have better timed their investments into convertible arbitrage. Total assets under management in the hedge fund sector, according to this report, were estimated to be between $350 billion and $400 billion. Some $50 billion is estimated to be in private managed accounts within hedge funds and a further $100 billion is estimated to be under management with funds that do not report to TASS or any other information service.[8]

The 104 hedge funds that started in Europe in 2000 raised $7.3 billion of assets, which is more than double the money raised by new funds in 1999, according to EuroHedge, the trade publication for the European hedge fund industry. In 1999 a total of 77 hedge funds started in Europe and raised $3.5 billion. One of the key characteristics of the growth in assets in 2000 was the emergence of European arbitrage managers, which raised $3.2 billion compared with only $913 million in 1999. Almost $2 billion was raised by merger/event-driven arbitrage funds. Start-up equity hedge managers raised $3.6 billion in 2000, compared to $2 billion in 1999 and European long/short managers raised $2.5 billion in 2000. In the first half of 2001 a total of 62 new hedge funds were started in Europe, raising a total of $2.2 billion of assets. This compares with 41 start-ups in the first half of 2000, raising $3.5 billion. Thus, although the number of new funds increased in the first half of 2001, their average size at inception declined. According to EuroHedge, there is evidence of strong asset flows into existing funds, although many have also 'closed' their funds to new investors. The dominant investment style among the new hedge funds started in 2001 has been in European long/short equity, which has attracted $1 billion in new money. The arbitragers who were successful in their fund-raising in 2000 were less conspicuous in the first half of 2001, with $357.4 million of new funds.

PERFORMANCE OF HEGDE FUNDS

Due to the private nature of hedge funds, there is a lack of long-term data on returns and inadequate information on investment process. Thus, for example, the CSFB/Tremont hedge fund indexes are only available from January 1994. Information on returns, risks, fee structures, investment process, etc., of hedge funds are not in the public domain as they are non-regulated partnerships or offshore corporations that are not required to disclose such information. The data vendors in the industry include Hedge Fund Research (HFR), Managed Account Reports (MAR), TASS Management Limited and Van Hedge Fund Advisors. None of these data providers publish directories of individual hedge funds or their performance record. Most of the hedge funds submit their data to these providers on a voluntary basis, although most would have audited accounts. The use of benchmarks varies enormously among the hedge fund investing community. If investors wish to use a capitalisation-weighted benchmark, they opt for the TASS database and its CSFB/Tremont hedge fund index; there are nine subfund indexes, representing each of the major categories of funds (see Table 5.6).

Having acquired the alternative investment fund databases and related intellectual property from MAR, Zurich Capital Markets (ZCM) anticipates that the Zurich hedge fund indexes will become a market standard for the industry. As with traditional markets, investors require performance indexes, which accurately reflect the performance of individual strategies. The Zurich hedge fund indexes aim to help investors differentiate between the hedge fund managers' individual skill or alpha, and the market factors, which systematically drive returns, such as changes in credit spreads, or market volatility. As with traditional investment strategies and the use of benchmarks, the availability of benchmarks within the hedge funds sector that are transparent, liquid and consistent would be an aid to investors, many of whom believe that hedge funds should be benchmarked against each other by strategy rather than pooled together.

Institutional investors would welcome greater transparency in the data. However, that appears to be unobtainable at present. If the investor wishes to use an equally weighted index, then there are some offered by MAR, HFR and Van Money Manager Research. Weighting by capitalisation is an important measure as the size of the funds vis-à-vis their performance does matter. Investors need to know how every dollar invested has performed, and that is difficult to do without a capitalisation-weighted benchmark. The TASS database, launched since January 1994, is widely recognised as among the most accurate and comprehensive hedge fund databases available today. Its CSFB/Tremont hedge fund index is currently the industry's only asset-weighted hedge fund index and remains the leading benchmark for alternative investment products.

Investors need to treat the performance data with some caution as 'survivorship bias' impacts average returns and volatility ratios in hedge funds. Due to the non-regulatory nature of the industry, poorly performing funds do not submit their data and may disappear from the data altogether. The calculation of total fund returns get distorted as a result; in fact, they generate an upward bias in the returns of the surviving funds. The survivorship bias tends to differ from database to database and researcher to researcher. Thus, for example, Fung and Hsieh documented an annual survivorship bias of 1.5% in their research whereas Brown, Goetzmann and Ibbotson reported an annual survivorship bias of 3% for offshore funds. Others, such as Ackermann *et al.* found that it was smaller – an average of 0.16% per year.[9]

According to data by Van Money Manager Research, hedge funds as an asset class in the US strongly outperformed both mutual funds and many broad market indicators; not only did they give better return but they also delivered lower risk. Certain hedge fund styles demonstrated superior returns while others suffered (Table 5.4).

The Van Hedge Fund Index, produced monthly, originally represented the industry's first benchmarking information based on a very large and representative sample. The index shows returns monthly, by sector and style, for US hedge funds and offshore funds separately, and also combined as a global index. The company's database, which is used in the construction of the index, covers over 3,400 hedge funds

Table 5.4 *US hedge fund performance for certain strategies (1 January 1988 to 31 December 2000)*[a]

	Net compound annual return (%)	Sharpe ratio	Correlation to S&P 500	Beta
Aggressive growth	23.3	1.01	0.8	1.06
Distressed securities	18.8	1.22	0.3	0.24
Market timing	22.8	1.38	0.6	0.60
Opportunistic	24.8	1.45	0.6	0.63
Financial sector	23.0	1.45	0.4	0.40
VAN US hedge fund index	19.4	1.54	0.7	0.51
S&P 500	16.7	0.90	1.0	1.00
MSCI world equity index	9.1	0.34	0.8	0.95
Average equity mutual fund	13.3	0.64	0.9	0.98

[a] Source: Van Money Manager Research

Table 5.5 *Performance comparison: US hedge funds and mutual funds (five-year net compound annual returns, first quarter 1996 to fourth quarter 2000)*[a]

	Hedge funds (%)	Mutual funds (%)
Top 10	53.6	36.0
Top 10%	37.5	21.9
Top 25%	29.9	18.5
Bottom 25%	4.0	2.4
Bottom 10%	-1.5	-0.5
Bottom 20	-7.7	-19.8

[a] Source: Van Money Manager Research

(2,000 US and 1,400 offshore) and these funds represent about $182 billion of assets. The Van Global Hedge Fund index, as at July 2001, delivered a net compound annual return of 17.0% between 1996 and 2000 compared to 18.3% for the S&P 500. Over this period, 'aggressive growth' strategies delivered the highest return of 25.9% annually while the 'short selling' strategy delivered the worst returns, −4.4%.

According to Van Money Manager Research, the average hedge fund also outperformed the average mutual fund with the best-performing hedge fund significantly outperforming the best-performing mutual fund (Table 5.5). In a study covering five years between first quarter 1996 and fourth quarter 2000 inclusive, returns of the highest-returning hedge funds exceeded those of the highest-returning equity mutual funds by 11.4% to 17.6%, depending on the investment style of the manager.

Data by TASS research, the CSFB/Tremont hedge fund indexes, over a shorter time period provide another comparison where hedge funds found it difficult to outperform the market and those with a dedicated short bias fared the worst (Table 5.6). As with any other investment strategy, the choice of manager and the timing of the investment are critical. Remember that the term 'absolute return strategy' can be a bit of a misnomer, as it does not always deliver absolute returns. In order to secure a guaranteed protection on capital, the investor will need to buy products which have an element of capital protection attached to them. Capital-protected products are discussed later in the chapter.

Table 5.6 *Performance comparison*[a,b]

	3 year Aug 98 to Jul 01		5 year Aug 96 to Jul 01		Since Jan 94 to Jul 01[d]	
	Return	Volatility[c]	Return	Volatility	Return	Volatility
Equity market neutral	14.48	2.47	14.53	3.16	11.84	3.36
Long/short equity	14.13	16.62	17.94	14.05	14.10	12.33
Convertible arbitrage	12.95	6.42	13.20	5.15	11.03	4.95
Event-driven	8.43	8.59	12.31	7.24	12.05	6.39
Hedge fund index	5.95	10.44	13.66	9.84	11.98	9.59
Managed futures	5.82	11.81	6.66	11.20	4.83	11.35
Fixed-income arbitrage	4.67	5.53	6.17	4.67	6.85	4.21
Global macro	2.32	13.00	15.97	13.76	14.04	13.80
Emerging markets	0.10	21.85	4.05	19.93	4.18	19.85
Dedicated short bias	-1.36	24.07	-1.96	21.04	-0.29	18.95

[a] Source: TASS Investment Research
[b] Annualised returns in percentage terms
[c] Volatility is annualised monthly standard deviation expressed as a percentage
[d] CSFB/Tremont indices were created in January 1994

As with traditional investment products and styles, hedge fund performance varies widely, depending on the period under review. Thus, for the five-year period ending May 2001, the S&P 500 returned an annual 15%. Nine of the ten weight-averaged classes of hedge funds monitored by CSFB/Tremont delivered sub-S&P returns, after fees. Over a 10-year period, the performance was even worse. According to MAR, of its 14 major hedge fund categories only one, Global Established Markets, managed to beat the S&P's 18% per annum return from 1990 through the end of June 2000, and it did so by a rounding margin.

Research conducted by UBS Warburg confirmed that between January 1990 and April 2000: [10]

- Long/short equity hedge funds had the highest absolute returns
- Equity market-neutral and convertible arbitrage were the least volatile
- Risk arbitrage and equity market neutral had the highest risk-adjusted returns based on Sharpe ratio and also the smallest 'worst one-year return'
- Short-sellers performed poorly in the period analysed
- Emerging market hedge fund returns were high but achieved with great volatility

An analysis of the correlation to capital markets by the different hedge fund strategies indicated that: [11]

- Short-sellers have the lowest correlation to equity markets as well as to other strategies
- Fixed-income arbitrage and equity market neutral also had low correlation to equities as well as to other hedge fund strategies
- Long/short equity has the highest correlation to the equity market, indicating the long bias of the strategy
- Returns in risk arbitrage were negatively correlated with returns in fixed-income arbitrage

Growth in the hedge fund sector globally has been driven largely by private clients or individuals and US institutions. Both of these groups are expected to continue to allocate capital to hedge funds, which is being augmented by investment from some European institutions. In Europe, according to a survey on the hedge fund industry conducted by Golin/Harris Ludgate, 64% of institutions responding to the survey either had investments in the sector or planned to invest in the foreseeable future, up from 56% in 2000. Hedge fund usage had doubled since 2000 with 36% of European institutions investing in the asset class compared to 17% a year ago. Existing exposure to hedge funds in the institutional sector was highest in Switzerland (60%), France (53%) and the UK (43%) and least popular with institutions in the Netherlands (10%), Germany (13%) and Scandinavia (20%). The largest markets for growth in hedge funds in Europe are Scandinavia, where some 70% of institutions intend to invest. The most popular types of hedge were internally managed funds and fund of funds. Average asset allocation to hedge funds across Europe was 2.3%. The most commonly used strategies were market neutral and equity long/short.[12]

RISK ALLOCATION: THE CORE–SATELLITE APPROACH

The widespread use of derivatives offer the sophisticated investor efficient exposure to markets. Derivatives also require very little cash to maintain a desired market exposure. They also allow the separation between alpha and beta. A combination of these traits in derivatives enable investors to allocate capital first to the high-alpha strategies and limit the use of scarce capital to strategies that do not generate alpha with a derivatives overlay. Once the use of such derivatives becomes widely understood, two kinds of investment structures are likely to gain momentum:[13]

- The core–satellite approach in which the core of the portfolio is managed passively and the rest actively; this already exists in the pension fund community
- The portable alpha concept where the capital market exposure is bought with swaps and the capital is invested in skill-based strategies; hedge funds are expected to play a key role in the search for alpha

As most reasonable-sized pension funds in the UK now use specific or customised benchmarks, many more are looking at specialist or core-satellite structures in their portfolios. It enables them to allocate their risk more efficiently. For Alastair Ross Goobey: 'Much more interesting is risk stratification, i.e. indexation, low-risk active manager, higher-risk active manager, private equity and small caps and alternative investment strategies. You can then allocate your risk budget more efficiently.'[14] This shift in approach in pension fund management in the UK has coincided with the rise of alternative investment strategies, thanks to the bull market in equities during the 1990s.

The greater application of quantitative strategies has also helped the hedge fund sector, although not all absolute return strategies are quantitatively driven. However, with the rising use of quantitative techniques in traditional long-only techniques, the role of technology in the complex trading strategies used by hedge fund managers cannot be ignored. Market-neutral strategies, for example, aim to have no exposure to any sector. If the long portfolio consists of 10% in technology stocks, then the short portfolio will also have a similar exposure to the sector, reducing the net exposure to zero. This strategy then frees the investment manager to decide how exactly to 'spend' the active risk. Whether the exposure to technology should be 5% or 15% is then determined by optimising the expected returns on individual stocks against their risks. This process is quantitatively determined.

In the UK there is a small but growing group of trustees and consultants who are comfortable with the investment logic of hedge funds. They understand that market-neutral, long/short portfolios are more efficiently constructed, offer a source of return that is uncorrelated with markets, and through performance fees, align the interests of both manager and investor. However, the majority are not comfortable making an allocation, although they are not prohibited from doing so. Their main concern is in understanding the nature of the risk involved in such vehicles, including the role of leverage, understanding the fee structure, lack of transparency, low liquidity and possible capacity constraints. As the pension fund industry itself moves into a more transparent environment, where fees are clearly enunciated for them by their managers, net risk-adjusted returns will outweigh other considerations. As the impact of consultants on the pension fund industry is significant, some investors believe that hedge fund managers should be lobbying pension fund consultants as well as institutional investors. For Kevin Coldiron, head of BGI's market-neutral strategy in London:

My belief is that investor reluctance reflects concerns about the liquidity, safe keeping and transparency currently involved in hedge fund investments. These things are improving but until hedged funds are genuinely comparable to traditional investments on these measures, many trustees will remain hesitant. Perhaps a more succinct way to put it is: there are certainly trustees prepared to take the investment risk of hedge funds, but very few are as yet prepared to take the operational risk.

The situation with consultants is similar to that of trustees: they understand the investment logic behind hedge funds but are cautious about the operational risk. I think they are playing quite a productive role at present. They are doing a good job at making a high-level case for market-neutral investment in order to educate trustees. At the same time, they are putting pressure on the hedge fund managers to address the operational concerns.[15]

BGI uses quantitative processes to capture as much information in the real portfolios as possible: 'We quantify the risks we are taking and use our technology to hedge out exposures we do not want and isolate the risks we are willing to take. We have been applying these capabilities to long-only active equity portfolios for 15 years. These long-only strategies operate in virtually all the developed world equity markets and have produced consistent risk-adjusted outperformance over long periods of time – something few managers can genuinely claim to have achieved.'[16] While BGI's quantitative capabilities have proven successful in the long-only world, it believes they can work even better when used to run long/short strategies as gearing can magnify the effect. According to Richard Grinold and Ronald Kahn, managing directors at BGI: 'The long-only constraint induces biases (particularly toward small stocks), limits the manager's ability to act on upside information by not allowing short positions that could finance long positions, and reduces the efficiency of traditional (high-risk) long-only strategies.'[17]

Asset managers with a quantitative discipline automatically rank all companies in the market, which means they have clear views on which stocks to buy and which to short. The potential for more efficient use of information, particularly downside information, is available to long/short strategies as opposed to long-only strategies. Being quantitative helps to understand, measure and hedge unwanted exposures.

> An enhanced index fund (or an active portfolio) can be thought of as a combination of an index portfolio and a long/short portfolio. The long/short portfolio consists of overweight and underweight bets the fund manager is making against the index. For investors looking for a moderate, risk-adjusted outperformance this structure works well. What a hedge fund does is hive off the long/short portfolio into a separate fund. This gives investors the freedom to choose an allocation to the long/short strategy that suits their particular risk budget.[18]

Despite being very different beasts, index funds and hedge funds actually have a symbiotic relationship. They are both very efficient ways of taking certain kinds of risks, and those risks are complementary. Index funds are cost-effective, reliable tools for taking market, industry or style risk. Hedge funds are the most efficient way to take active or manager skill risk. Blending index and hedge funds along with other asset classes such as corporate bonds can be a very effective way of building an efficient portfolio. As more investors adopt this approach, it should directly benefit hedge funds, although a majority of investors see potential for conflicts when running both long-only and hedge processes in-house. Investors in Switzerland, Scandinavia and the UK are more sceptical about the dangers of this situation, whereas French and Italian investors appear to be more relaxed about it, although in Italy mixing long and hedge fund operations within the same institution is against market rules.[19]

According to Crispin Odey, chairman of Odey Asset Management:

> The key difference between long and short investing is that the long-only investor traditionally has not worried about volatility. Short selling is a discipline that traditional managers do not make use of. What happens on the long side is that they spend a long time evaluating the companies that might go into their portfolio. But once a stock goes into a portfolio, there is a

denial from then on about selling it. In the hedge fund sector, we are not paid to hold any company. We are very price sensitive. Also, we have the balance sheet and can turn the volume on in gearing up the portfolio if the situation warrants it. So, one can make supernormal profits, albeit not for very long. Gearing should be used very sparingly and usually very early into a new cycle.[20]

Although short selling is not commonly used in traditional investment strategies, they still depend heavily on a disciplined approach to analysing share value. Stocks are bought only when they are perceived to be cheap and sold when they cease to be cheap. The business behind the price is irrelevant. The question of going into a denial about selling any stock simply does not arise in the classic value style of investing. While certain investments do remain as core holdings over long periods of time, the sensitivity to value and thus to price is the only criterion for a truly disciplined long-only investor.

Leverage, on the other hand, is an important issue to investors. It is defined in balance sheet terms as the ratio of total assets to equity capital or net worth. In risk terms, it is a measure of risk relative to capital. As hedge funds vary enormously in their use of leverage, an understanding of the nature of this leverage is important in gauging the risk involved. Although trading desks of investment banks may take similar leverage to hedge funds, they may find themselves in a more vulnerable position if the full value of their illiquid positions cannot be realised in a difficult market condition.

Based on Van Money Manager Research, some 68% of hedge funds used leverage as of December 2000 (Table 5.7). However, only 24% had balance sheet leverage ratios exceeding 2:1. Although the use of derivatives and the use leverage are often thought of as the same thing, derivatives and leverage are actually quite different instruments and deliver results accordingly. Almost one-third of hedge fund managers do not use any leverage. Some 57% of market-neutral arbitragers were leveraged above the 2:1 level. Investors in distressed securities, value investors, aggressive growth and emerging market investors did not resort to a high level of leverage, although the majority used some leverage to boost returns.

Table 5.7 *Global hedge funds: use of leverage (as of December 2000)*[a]

	Don't use leverage (%)	Use leverage (%) Low (< 2:1)	High (> 2:1)	Total
Aggressive growth	29.3	56.3	14.4	70.7
Distressed securities	50.9	45.6	3.5	49.1
Emerging markets	36.5	49.2	14.4	63.6
Fund of funds	35.6	47.9	16.5	64.4
Income	49.2	28.6	22.2	50.8
Macro	10.0	48.0	42.0	90.0
Market neutral: arbitrage	20.7	22.0	57.3	79.3
Market neutral: securities hedging	35.5	25.6	38.8	64.4
Market timing	42.1	22.4	35.5	57.9
Opportunistic	27.3	44.9	27.8	72.7
Several strategies	34.9	36.5	28.6	65.1
Short selling	30.3	45.5	24.2	69.7
Special situations	28.2	55.6	16.1	71.7
Value	31.6	55.5	12.9	68.4
Total sample	31.6	44.8	23.6	68.4

[a] Source: Van Money Manager Research

LIMITS TO GROWTH: LIQUIDITY IS THE KEY

Interest in hedge funds is primarily driven by investor need for uncorrelated strategies that deliver superior risk-adjusted return. The benefits of diversification by pension fund managers have also been reaped by the private equity sector. While private equity managers have enjoyed a bonanza never experienced before in their history, hedge fund managers are bound by the nature of their investment methodology. At the 2000 Hedge Fund Symposium in London, Louis Moore Bacon indicated five warning signs for investors to watch out for when investing in hedge funds. They are size, leverage, transparency, funding and hubris. Size matters in hedge funds as it becomes increasingly difficult to generate alpha as the fund grows beyond an optimal point. It is comparable to companies that keep on issuing shares and then find it harder to keep up with the return on equity (ROE). Leverage and liquidity are linked as a fund's risk is geared to its open positions. Most of these factors also apply to traditional long-only or private equity investors.

The interdependency of the different participants in the market cannot be ignored, and the market is a zero-sum game. Thus, if you short-sell a stock with low turnover or liquidity, you could be seriously penalised by the market if your decision proves to be incorrect. If you buy shares that decline 20%, you have the opportunity to average down if you have sufficient cash flow and you still believe in your original investment decision. However, averaging down at the long end does not always work, as every trader is painfully aware, including the so-called long-term investor. But if you sell a stock that you do not own and it goes up, you have a different kind of a problem altogether – your short position increases in size. To continue to take advantage of that position, the short-seller has to increase that exposure without creating an uncomfortable concentration in a single stock that could still appreciate in price. In certain market conditions, short-sellers face a squeeze and security borrowers have problems with small, less liquid stocks, which are precisely the kind of stocks that present interesting short-sale opportunities. The problem can be equally severe in larger companies. Management of risk is the major difference between hedge funds and traditional active management (where stock-picking is the key). This difficulty is clearly demonstrated in the poor performance of short-selling strategies.

'Hedge fund managers pride themselves on their ability to control risk and you can only control risk by being able to trade out of positions you've got. So, the fact is that the hedge fund community can only be as great as the daily liquidity of the marketplace, which is less than 1% of the total market capitalisation,' explained Crispin Odey. With reference to the process of hedge fund investing itself, he is of the opinion:

> If you are looking at the history of hedge funds, they tend to peak at the end of long bull markets, i.e. it is driven by people who have made a lot of money and are very scared of losing it as they fully understand that pricing is always at the margin. Thus, going back to the point that liquidity is only 1% of the market capitalisation, but that has an influence on the pricing of the 99% that is not traded. When it comes to the question of how big can short-only hedge funds get? The answer is they can't get too big. Otherwise, you end up becoming self-destructive.[21]

Nicola Meaden, chairman and chief executive officer of Tremont TASS (Europe) Limited, concurs: 'Liquidity is crucial to most hedge fund strategies. If you don't have liquidity, you can't execute your exit strategy. The third quarter of 1998 was a classic example of that liquidity crunch.'[22] All of the strategies used in hedging depend on available liquidity, particularly when selling in a crisis. That is basically what caused the crisis in 1998 when global financial uncertainty led to a flight to quality and the market in some illiquid areas dried up. Thus, the size of the hedge fund industry will always be capped to the available market liquidity. With some relative value strategies, there exists a natural capacity constraint determined by the number of opportunities in the market and the amount of capital chasing these deals.

'Capacity is a major concern for many of the market neutral strategies: there is a serious limit to how much can be effectively managed,' pointed out Bruce Ruehl, Tremont Advisers' managing director and chief investment strategist. Assets have flowed into this investment category virtually steadily since 1994. One of the big questions is, Can market-neutral strategies handle the demand as many of the managers have significant capacity constraints? Investors in this category are seeking equity exposure without having any directional market exposure. Convertible arbitrage, on the other hand, is the most cyclical of all the categories within the hedge fund sector.[23] Although the European long/short hedge fund sector has grown rapidly over the last five years, it is still small compared to the overall long-only investment in pan-European stock by asset managers worldwide.

For Crispin Odey personally, the transformation from a long-only manager to a hedge fund manager was a baptism of fire:

> When I started as a hedge fund manager in 1992, I did not have a clue about hedge funds. I was a good long-only manager who was used as the eyes and ears of the hedge fund community in New York. I thought I was going to get some funds from UK pension fund managers but it was all too new in this market to set up without institutional backing. The US hedge fund industry picked me up and while they saw what I did, I did not see what they did. I could not see the way in which they ran a balance sheet. I was far too leveraged in 1994. I did not know how fast liquidity could turn in a bear market that would prevent you from getting out of the market that was plummeting. I would have had to take some very big losses in order to get out; an overall bigger loss than I was prepared to countenance. When you have 90% redemptions, you cannot have any strategy. Undoubtedly, after 1994 I became a hedge fund manager. All the classic concerns of any hedge fund manager also became my concerns, i.e. liquidity, willingness to change your mind and take positions that were quite contrary to your macro view, balancing fundamentals with technical analysis because it is dangerous to go against the market.[24]

Lack of liquidity and the investment expertise in the hedge fund sector along with lack of transparency and regulatory hurdles have stood in the way of pension fund managers in making an allocation to such an investment strategy. Market-neutral strategies have had a major impact on pension fund managers in Europe. According to some studies, both conservative and aggressive portfolios demonstrate a significantly higher probability of outperforming their benchmarks using allocations to absolute return strategies of up to 16%. Deutsche Asset Management (DeAM), for example, use a proprietary optimisation technique, the probabilistic efficient frontier, with mean–variance calculations in identifying an appropriate allocation for hedge funds, i.e. the allocation that will offer maximum return for a given level of risk. Such studies largely reflect growing institutional interest in hedge funds.

However, if pension funds in North America and Europe were to allocate anywhere between 5% and 15% of their portfolios to the hedge fund sector, there would not be the capacity to manage them efficiently. There is a consensus among institutional managers that inflow thresholds are essential for hedge funds in order to maintain flexibility and manageability. There are fears that the quality of hedge fund managers would be diluted by the sudden growth in the industry, leading to poor performance. Besides, greater competition among managers is widely seen as reducing the inefficiencies in the market, which are likely to affect some strategies more than others.[25] 'There is not enough hedge fund capacity – anywhere – to absorb even a fraction of these projected flows,'[26] confirms Kevin Coldiron. Capacity is the biggest issue in the industry. For Nicola Meaden, 'talk about fees, regulation, transparency, liquidity, etc., are irrelevant if there is not enough good capacity to handle the anticipated demand from the institutional market. I don't think the industry is nearly as open in making this issue known to the institutional market. If the institutions do decide to make an allocation to hedge funds, the capacity is simply not there.'[27]

Those investors who are either unwilling or unable to make an allocation to alternative investments might find themselves locked out of hedge funds with longer track records that will be closed for capacity reasons. In fact, many of the new and larger hedge funds, such as Vinik Asset Management with $4.2 billion under management, closed their funds in 2000. The founding fathers of the hedge fund industry, George Soros and Julian Robertson, closed their hedge fund investment business in 2000 as well. If the majority of skilled managers are at or near capacity, latecomers run the risk of only being able to choose from managers who may not be able to deliver added value. But that is true of any late-cycle investment. With average institutional exposure to hedge funds being low, the market has a steep learning curve ahead of it.

Tim Gardener of William M. Mercer considers an investment exposure of less than 5% to alternative investments as less than optimal, considering the time and effort that goes into the decision-making process. For him, exposure to hedge funds currently should be zero, 'not because it is a bad thing but due to the amount of money that is going into the sector. One asks oneself, whether it is the next disaster waiting to happen, except for the market-neutral strategies. As the existing exposure of pension funds to hedge funds and private equity is low, it will rise. But pension funds also have a history of getting into new investment areas rather late in the investment cycle, as was the case with property in the 1970s. There are hedge funds that are good investments even today. But such is the weight of money today that I see a bubble developing in the hedge fund sector.'[28]

Many active, long-only managers also refrain from asset gathering when market conditions are difficult or when they do not see value in the marketplace. Warren Buffett has been known to refund his client's monies due to lack of appropriate investment opportunities. The obstacle to good performance within a large fund is well established. Most large companies too find it difficult to retain profit margins and deliver consistent return on equity. Thus, it is unbelievable that LTCM at its peak in 1997 commanded funds worth $129 billion and a derivatives portfolio with a notional value of $1.25 trillion. Intellectual capital was not lacking either. Its founding partners included John Meriwether, the former Salomon Brothers vice-chairman, along with Robert Merton and Myron Scholes, both Nobel laureates who between them, and with Fischer Black, invented modern finance with their theory on option pricing.

Yet by September 1998, LTCM had lost 90% of its value and the US Federal Reserve coordinated a bailout of LTCM by 14 of the world's largest and most prestigious investment banks. Only 11 reporting hedge fund families, including LTCM, had total assets exceeding $10 billion at the end of 1997. While LTCM was far from representative of its sector, it tainted the industry and left many investors bruised. By November 1998, after the intervention by the US Federal Reserve, including the lowering of interest rates, LTCM had made a profit and returned $2.6 billion of the $3.63 billion the group had injected into the fund. The fund's founder was even approved by the 14 institutions to launch a new hedge fund.

Thanks to a culture of risk-taking in the US, there began a growing legion of institutional investors experimenting with hedge fund investments in 1999 and 2000. In the UK and to a greater extent in Europe and Japan, the trend is firmly positive. Hedge funds have also seen strong growth due to the large retail element in the pension fund sector. It has grown from around 600 hedge funds in 1990 worth some $38 billion to some 3,500–4,000 funds currently with assets worth over $400 billion. In Europe, apart from the UK and Holland, where the pension fund sector is still largely dominated by the public sector, the hedge fund sector is much smaller. Apart from the structure of the industry with a bias towards bank loans/bonds (in Europe) and equities (in the UK), the availability of derivative instruments will eventually decide the size of the hedge fund sector in the future.

European long/short hedge fund assets have grown in size from some $7 billion to $39 billion over the past five years. Long/short equity represents half of all assets in the industry. Short-only strategies account for less than 1% of total assets. And it is true the market impact of such a strategy can be significant. Capacity is clearly one of the biggest issues facing the industry. And that covers not only market capacity to absorb the assets without affecting the performance, but also the availability of the requisite skill sets, not just in investing but in fund administration including trading, settlement, custody and related activity. An efficient back office is critical to the success of hedge funds. The full-service prime brokers currently provide this service and firms such as Morgan Stanley and Goldman Sachs have the largest market share of the international marketplace. Others such as Deutsche, CSFB, Lehman and Barclays Capital are all seriously trying to expand their prime brokerage business and it is one of the most active areas of development within investment banking.

Currently, there are a handful of prime brokers dominating the hedge fund sector. How this trend will evolve in shaping the market is not clear. But what may become the deciding factor in this arena will be the cost of financing. If a bank can borrow at LIBOR flat or minus, it can pass that cost advantage on to its clients and boost the in-house hedge fund business. In fact the growth of capital-protected products in Europe is an indication that better use of the bank's balance sheet has already begun in a serious way. Success of prime brokerage is also linked to a high level of investment in systems. That also entails high commitment at the firm's most senior level. Prime brokers also have valuable market and risk-related information. Better commercial use of that information by their clients would also be an option. The growth in prime brokerage reflects the growth in the hedge fund sector. In fact, it also raises various other issues in terms of research and trading facilities available to clients of investment banks, as issues surrounding the independence of broker research and measuring brokerage commissions come to the forefront of the asset management industry's response to Paul Myners' review of institutional investment in the UK.

TRANSPARENCY: A DOUBLE-EDGED SWORD

The annual reports of most hedge fund managers do not reveal much about their underlying investments. Getting an insight into a hedge fund's strategy is difficult as managers guard their positions fiercely. In a world of easy replicability, and with markets that discount all strategies within shorter time cycles, holding on to any single strategy is doomed to underperformance from time to time. For some managers, this lack of transparency with hedge funds means that such vehicles will not be popular with pension fund trustees. For Crispin Odey:

> The primary reason for running a hedge fund is that you want to run your own money. So what you want is to have as much of your own money and as little of other people's money under management. Actually, it does not matter whether you operate in an institutional or retail environment. While ten years ago I would have said that the most important thing in this business is performance, now I would say that it is the funding. Make sure that you do not have what I call 'aspirational' clients who not only have high expectations in terms of your performance but they also have high aspiration in wanting to know how you make your decisions and run your business, etc. When you are in a marketplace, it is difficult enough to be independent of that

> market without having others second-guessing you or pulling the plug if they do not like what you are doing. We are guilty of terrible style drift; we respond to the market. Most institutional investors would find that unacceptable. So the funding issue is critical. Thus, knowing your client is vital. Transparency is a big issue but you cannot afford to show your hand if you are a big player and operating in a tight market. If you are small, then nobody is interested in what you do and you can afford to be more transparent.[29]

That partly explains the secrecy which shrouds most hedge funds and the almost cult status of their managers. The lack of transparency also stems from the enormous variety of strategies inherent in the blanket term 'hedge fund'. The *Financial Times* may list some 4,000 unit trusts but most of these tend to invest in one way only – buying shares (or bonds) on a long-only basis – and can only make money when the prices go up. However, no two hedge funds are alike. Pension fund trustees in rightly wanting to know what is going into their portfolio, what the risks are and what leverage is being used, are only fulfilling their fiduciary responsibility. But such scrutiny can also prevent managers from investing blindly. For Nicola Meaden, it was the lack of information that prevented their firm from investing in LTCM.[30] With $7 billion under advice and management, Tremont has invested in over 250 hedge funds. Through its American Masters Fund Series, Tremont offers a select number of single-manager and fund-of-fund products for investors.

For those hedge fund managers who do not wish to be subject to the scrutiny of pension fund managers and their consultants, it can prove to be a barrier. Lack of transparency and effective regulation remain key barriers to the flow of investments into the asset class. For those investors who do not currently invest in hedge funds, significant improvements in transparency and regulation will be required before they change their views. For Tim Gardener: 'If the transparency issue is not dealt with, then it is not a suitable asset class. I am not convinced that pension funds have to be invested in hedge funds. They don't need to be in hedge funds, as they need to invest in bonds and equities. They also don't need absolute returns, as they are more long-term in their focus. If hedge funds want to sell to pension funds in a meaningful way, then they must come up with the products and address the concerns of the pension fund trustees.' The issue of transparency also reflects the nature of the market in Europe. According to Tim Gardener:

> The advice we give is consistent with the marketplace, i.e. the culture of the underlying investor, the liabilities involved and the sophistication and knowledge of the investor. In the US they don't have trustees. The decision-makers or the fiduciaries could be in the treasury department. We would feel more comfortable recommending hedge funds to the chief financial officer (CFO) or next to the CFO of a large company than to a group of trustees in the UK with no financial expertise. Another example would be Hong Kong, where investors are far more concerned with capital loss than their British counterparts. So, recommending absolute return strategies to them makes more sense. The European market is very diversified. You have very sophisticated investors and others less so. Some of them use hedge funds and others are very concerned about risk and remain invested in bonds. Thus, on the question of transparency, the less sophisticated the client base, the more transparent the investment needs to be.[31]

If hedge funds wish to attract the interest of retail investors or pension funds in Europe, then the whole issue of transparency has to be addressed. The complicated nature of the product is a natural barrier to investment, particularly when information is difficult to access. The increasing demand by investors for transparency and consistent risk-return analysis means that for quantitative managers, measuring and reporting risk in a meaningful way will be an added advantage. Technology makes it easier for managers to slice and dice data in various ways and it can be done very quickly. So it certainly has the potential to improve the delivery of information. More important is getting some consensus on what the content and quality of that information need to be. The International Association of Financial Engineers (IAFE) has been doing some work in this direction. They have got managers and investors together in producing an initial set of principles to guide transparency. The next step will involve being more specific about what information is relevant for particular strategies, which is less straightforward.

> Investing in hedge funds is about investing in manager skill. Some managers can and will define what their skill is in very precise terms. In these cases it should be possible for investors to monitor what is happening and ensure that the manager is sticking to his knitting without jeopardising the strategy. Other managers may see their skill as being market opportunists. In these cases you cannot and by definition do not want to pin them down too much. This does not mean they shouldn't be offering investors some transparency but it does make it more difficult to know just what information is actually useful.[32]

While technology helps in delivering information, the problem is more fundamental than that. From the hedge fund managers' viewpoint, the main concern is, Do I want to let the market know what my positions are? And, if I do so, what is going to be its impact on my performance? If the market knows where the manager is short then, depending on the size of the position, it can destroy the manager. However, most hedge fund managers offer transparency on a select basis. Some offer total transparency if you are a client and go into their office. Others offer comprehensive information on a time-lagged basis, as most hedge fund managers are highly sensitive to letting the market know what their investment positions consist of. Managers sometimes can't afford to show their short positions as they could easily be cut off from their source of information, the companies themselves, quite apart from the market consequences. This is true not only of hedge funds and proprietary trading desks, but of large money managers as well. However, according to Nicola Meaden:

> There is more transparency today than there ever was before. The important thing is to have comprehensive information regarding concentrations, exposures, leverage, and so forth. This is as, if not more, useful than daily portfolio downloads. It is really a double-edged sword. We as investment advisers are quite happy to have it on a time-lagged basis – one month old or three month old – to be certain that the manager has complied with what they told us they were doing. One of the major questions for institutional investors when making an allocation to hedge funds is their fiduciary role in ensuring

that managers comply with certain mutual agreements. If managers do not, then it puts both the investor and the manager in a difficult position. Information on a real-time basis tends to complicate matters further.[33]

While pension fund trustees rightly demand greater transparency from hedge fund managers, the irony is that many pension fund managers do not themselves publish annual reports and accounts, nor are they made available to their client members. The uncertainty surrounding the fate of pension policyholders with companies such as Equitable Life is sufficient evidence of lack of transparency and information to their individual members. The corporate sector also does not believe in providing adequate information on its pension funds to its shareholders. The whole issue of the ownership of pension fund surpluses means that sponsors currently do not have an incentive to take an interest in the efficient management of the scheme's investments, as it is difficult for them to benefit from any investment gains. Besides, leading corporations regularly penalise analysts and fund managers who write sell recommendations or short-sell their stock.

There are some traditional fund managers whose annual statements to their individual investors regularly include the names of only the top five holdings in the portfolio.[34] While cost and lack of investor understanding of the full implications of their investment strategy are often cited as reasons, letting the market know their positions is also a concern. It is not that they do not believe that investors are entitled to a fuller disclosure of their holdings, but they also argue that such disclosure may have a detrimental impact on their investment strategy. As investors need to know what they are invested in, transparency is a major issue whether one is investing in traditional funds or hedge funds. Institutional investors actually do have a significantly higher level of access to information than their retail counterpart. If one is not clear about the rationale for investing in an asset class or has doubts about the underlying strategy, it is wise not to proceed with it, however attractive the historic performance figure may appear.

THE TECHNOLOGICAL BARRIER

The implications of investors' growing access to vastly increased computing power aligned with the use of non-linear applications are indeed profound within asset management. From enhanced indexers to hedge fund managers, the use of technology forms the basis of their investment decisions and trading strategies. Qualitative decisions are premised increasingly on quantitative models. As one prime broker pointed out, 'We are just a technology company that happens to do prime brokerage.' The prime brokerage business has been around for almost half a century, but thanks to developments in the industry, its traditional role of providing services such as clearing, securities lending and margin loans has evolved into more specialised ones including technological support, real-time portfolio accounting, marketing and website management. The making and use of mathematical models for derivatives risk management requires a significant amount of skill in the new technologies, not just in mathematics.

The barriers to entry are high; a strong balance sheet, the willingness to invest in technology on a continual basis and the desire to change as you learn are the major drivers for success today. While access to technology has lowered entry barriers in the indexed sector, the ability to invest heavily in the state-of-the-art technology remains critical to the prime brokerage community because it supports the skill factor of their hedge fund clients. A good prime broker offers value-added services such as research, online analysis, margining and portfolio accounting. Analysis of data as an investment tool has become important. The idea of data warehousing is powerful; there are risk, performance and attribution tools. Hedge fund managers want information flowing quickly on their computer screens, as they are supersensitive to potential changes in prices and are highly geared in using the information in their trading strategies. The challenge for the prime broker is to deliver actionable 'intelligence' to the client on a real-time basis. According to Charles Cortese, head of IT at Lehman Brothers: 'The new technology has enabled brokers to deliver superior transaction cost management to our clients mainly through online interaction between buy and sell side. It is predicted that spreads will narrow as new off-exchange liquidity pools develop. The development of consortia's such as Trade Web, BrokerTec and CoreDeal are allowing cheaper access for clients to sell-side firms or sell-side firms to brokers. In both cases these provide for better liquidity and cheaper execution costs.'[35]

Enhanced trading capabilities have saved investors billions of dollars annually in commissions, spreads, market impact and market exposure costs. For any IT specialist in finance, technology has had a major impact over the last few years. One obvious example is the use of market risk systems. Most investment banks are now comfortable managing significantly more market risk than they would have dreamed of 10 years ago. These systems allow for aggregation of various risks on a near real-time basis. Firms are now able to leverage their capital and thereby have more products on hand to offer than ever before. The other example is the major growth in volumes, particularly for listed products. The ability to trade various baskets of securities efficiently has allowed investment banks the opportunity to offer extremely customised indexes to meet the most varied of customer needs.

The evolution of global straight-through processing (GSTP) is yet another example of how technology has enabled the automated processing of a transaction from the point of sale through settling with the client. Many firms have this process for limited types of transaction but its applications are wide-ranging. The ability to allow retail brokers to enter listed equity orders through a web interface, have the order validated and sent to an exchange to be executed automatically and then to confirm and ultimately settle the trade without human intervention will be a massive step forward. Within a few years, most sell-side firms will extend this capability to most products (listed and over the counter) in which they make markets. Even buy-side firms are beginning to appreciate that greater investment in systems is ultimately a more cost-efficient way of running a business due to its superior ability of controlling risk. Technology has shortened settlement cycles and created a demand among investors for more real-time information.Thus, the role of technology in delivering products and services on a timely basis will continue to be fundamental to the asset class.

Nicola Meaden believes that hedge funds will become part of mainstream fund management within a decade. Traditional investors will develop their own hedge fund departments, although boutiques will also thrive. This is made possible by rapid advances in technology.

> You are already seeing a move by prime brokers to support the industry in a big way. The reasons why talented traders leave firms such as Goldman Sachs or Schroder have to do with issues surrounding investment freedom, lifestyle and compensation. As these fund managers get more senior, most of them end up doing a lot of people management and administration, which is a distraction from what they really enjoy doing, i.e. managing money. Also, success within the hedge fund sector means that financial rewards are considerable. And technology is making all that possible. We, for example, would not have been able to do our business without technology. Thus, we see an increasingly important role for technology in all aspects of the fund management industry.[36]

THE RISE OF CAPITAL-PROTECTED PRODUCTS

During the last three years, the market environment has been dominated by uncertainty. We have travelled from one scenario, where growth estimates were being lowered, to another where recession is a reality and recovery a long haul. Interest rates have been cut, aggressively in the US and the UK, albeit not so dramatically in Europe and Japan. Stock markets have been bearish and volatile. Cash and bonds provide security. It is therefore not surprising that capital-protected products (CPPs) or principal-protected products (PPPs) have been introduced to the marketplace during this period. For a new generation of investors, enriched by the rise of stock markets in the second half of the 1990s, the bursting of the asset bubble since March 2000 has been a rude awakening. The continuing problems in the global economy, as a result of the terrorist attack on the US, have posed an additional burden on governments. In such an unsettled climate, CPPs provide the guarantee that investors need.

For Fred Siegrist, head of investment strategy and risk management at Swiss Life Insurance, 'Low interest rates and high valuations in the stock market prompted us to look at how to increase our return potential without increasing the risk profile of the portfolio.'[37] This was during the late 1990s. Subsequent falls in market valuations led to a rise in the demand for investment products capable of generating market-independent, absolute returns. The advantage of the CPP is that, while the product has volatility inherent in it, investors are able to get their capital back, with the bank that structures the product taking all the risk, albeit at a price. CPPs have been in circulation historically in the form of bonds, Treasury bills or gilts and other fixed-return investments.

Traditionally, banks and insurance companies have been the major providers of such investments, particularly in the life sector but also in the mortgage and endowment sector. Investments that offer a secured capital return are not exactly new; in Japan or India they have been popular with retail investors for decades. The major difference with the latest products in the developed markets, and those in the less developed markets, is the level of sophistication of the financial instruments used to secure the guarantee. The rationale behind the creation of structured products in Europe is also linked to accessing alternative investment products, such as hedge funds.

It is not just retail investors who find these products attractive. Institutional investors, under pressure to maintain their rapidly eroding profit margins, are examining alternative investment techniques for better diversification and risk control in their search for the elixir of superior performance and lower costs. The recent convergence of banking and insurance has also enabled the creation of exotic investment products in the alternative risk market. The other major factor contributing to the evolution of CPPs is the rapid development in technology making it easier for issuers to analyse their risk portfolio as well as to price these products more commercially.

The creation of the euro-zone has been an additional spur to the proliferation of CPPs as investors are able to buy and sell structured products within the euro-zone. Not only are pension assets low as a percentage of GDP in European countries, such as France, Spain and Germany, these assets are also primarily invested in bonds. With the increasing 'equitisation' of Europe, there has been a recognisable shift towards investments in equity. However, a 'protected' return offers the best of all worlds. Investment bankers in Europe, freed of major regulatory constraints, have discovered their métier in the structuring of highly innovative CPPs. According to estimates by various market participants, there are some $10–15 billion of CPPs in issue today.

These figures are set to grow dramatically as institutions are using structured products as a way of learning about absolute return strategies without exposing themselves to the risk of investing directly in hedge funds. 'It enables the traditional institutional investor to participate in hedge funds in a risk-responsible manner,'[38] confirms Rob Leary, managing director and head of the pensions group at AIG Financial Products. Swiss Life's joint venture company, Swiss Life Hedge Fund Partners, two-thirds owned by Swiss Life and one-third by RMF Capital Partners, was created primarily to gain direct experience in hedge fund investing. 'The reason for creating the joint venture with RMF was to have quick access to the industry, and the possibility for a transfer of know-how,'[39] confirms Fred Siegrist. The institutional investment community's increasing aversion to risk has made them re-examine the merit of hedge funds, which now have better access to modern tools of hedging risk. The absolute return constructs of many innovative alternative investment strategies provide diversification with added return potential that few traditional investment strategies can match.

The involvement and backing for CPPs by major investment banks as structuring parties ensures that these products bring alternative investment strategies within the accepted structure of the traditional investment community. If CPPs have found a growing investor base in Europe, particularly in France and Switzerland, they have also been a lucrative source of income for investment bankers who structure these exotic products. Many of these innovative products have been able to create a win-win situation for all concerned. In using their balance sheet to provide the 'guarantee', banks have secured an additional revenue stream from that asset. In providing such protection, banks can safely charge a higher fee: 1–2% for the guarantee and often 15–20% of the performance, although this fee structure has been under pressure recently due to increased competition among providers. The guarantee provided is also limited to a set time period, typically 3–10 years. The other factor for the investor to bear in mind is that there are reasonably high penalties for redeeming the investment during the lock-in period. These exit fees can be as high as 5–6% initially, declining over the life of the structured investment.

Are hedge funds and CPP wrappers too expensive? The median management fee for hedge funds is 1% of fund assets and the median incentive fee is 20% of profits. Most investors comfortable with hedge funds prefer performance-linked fees to fixed fees on returns, which are not secured. If a hedge fund delivers a return of 10–15% annually, then an annual management fee of 1% with a performance fee of 20%, above the hurdle rate of return, does not pose a problem for investors. Some firms, such as BGI, aim to return 5% per year above the cash return (3-month sterling LIBID for UK investors) after all fees. The performance hurdle is usually linked to total return, which is based on Treasury bill/long bond plus risk premium. Hedge funds with a high water mark do not charge incentive fees until the fund is profitable. Thus, fees are paid on the basis of not only the current year's performance but also that of the previous year's performance.[40]

Due to a different regulatory environment in Europe, some of the most efficient principal-protected structures in the industry have been developed by the major European banks and insurance companies. The equity derivatives group of Société Générale (SG) is the largest in the industry, employing over 850 staff in Europe alone, and has been in existence since the mid-1980s. Zurich Capital Markets (ZCM), the special structuring unit of the Zurich Financial Services Group, was established in 1997. Along with AIG, SG and ZCM, BNP Paribas, Credit Suisse First Boston, Deutsche Bank, UBS Warburg and Swiss Life are among the top providers of guaranteed investment products in Europe. These firms have been particularly successful in acting as principal in the delivery of products in areas such as alternative investments, enhanced-return investments, structured finance, combined risk and securities lending.

The main instruments used in structuring CPP include true call options, widely accepted in Europe on indexes, stocks and funds, or the dynamically hedged principal guarantee strategy, also called the gap structure or dynamic hedge. All capital-protected structures include a fixed return element that protects the capital till maturity with an absolute return element to enhance the total return of the investment. The price paid by the investor in such a vanilla option structure is that the participation rate in the absolute return product is never 100%. The absolute return structure can take many forms, such as exposure to high-yield bonds, an equity index, or investment in one or a pool of investment managers, typically hedge funds. It is intuitive to seek performance enhancement, so the creators of these products seek out the most qualified market practitioners to provide not only superior returns, but more importantly, risk-adjusted returns.

In its simplest form, within the dynamic hedge structure, the guarantor monitors a reference curve illustrating the amount of capital that would have to be invested in zero-coupon bonds at each point of the curve, during the investment period, to achieve a 100% payout at maturity. As long as the net asset value (NAV) of the hedge fund portfolio is well above the reference curve, then 100% of the capital will be invested in the underlying portfolio and the investor will continue to benefit from full participation in the underlying fund. However, if the investments do not perform well and the NAV drops towards the reference curve, then the guarantor will need to divest the portfolio proportionately to allocate more capital to the zero-coupon bonds. The advantage of such a structure is that it allows the investor full capital protection. The rate of investor participation also rises with the performance of the fund. However, if the fund performs poorly, then deleveraging the portfolio results in a lower rate of participation for the investor.

The trigger structure is also used by AIG Financial Products Group. Here the trigger is based on a Treasury strip to the maturity date plus a buffer reflecting the volatility and liquidity of the underlying investment. The investor reaps all the upside as long as the trigger is not hit. If the trigger is set off, then the fund is liquidated and the proceeds are used to buy a zero-coupon note to the stated maturity. If the proceeds exceed the cost of the note, the excess is returned to the investor.[41] Whatever structure is used in devising a CPP, the ability of the guarantor to fully understand the risks associated with the underlying investments is central to the completion and cost of the product.

SG offers its clients a multitude of choice in the use of derivative instruments in the delivery of their ideal capital-guaranteed product.

Table 5.8 *Capital-protected products: mix and match*[a]

Wrapper	Underlying[b]	Type of index
OTC contract	Single index	Calls, puts
Swap	Single share	Call spreads
Bond	Basket of indexes	Barrier options
EMTN	Basket of shares	Asian options
Fund	Single fund	Multi-asset options
Life insurance policy	Basket of funds	Best of, worst of
Warrant	High-income products	
	Correlation products	
	Managed accounts	
	Multi-underlying[c]	

[a] Source: Société Générale, Equity Derivatives Group, Paris
[b] On 90% of the world stock market capitalisation
[c] Best of equity and inflation, interest rates or currency

According to Stanislas Debreu, global head of sales and marketing, equity derivatives at SG:

> We can structure derivatives products, including capital-protected products, with any kind of 'wrapper' suitable to our client – OTCs, swaps, warrants, bonds, funds, life insurance policies or euro medium-term notes (EMTNs). The underlying choice of investments can be benchmarked on an index, a share, a basket of shares, a fund, a basket of funds, or managed accounts. We have the ability to capture 90% of the world's stock market capitalisation in the creation of our underlying structures. The type of indexation used can also vary from ordinary calls, puts to barrier options, multi-asset options, Asian options along with best-of, worst-of type of strategies.[42]

Thanks to such highly innovative product structures, the chance of the investor receiving only the original capital at the end of the investment term is low. With SG's Altiplano structure, for example, investors have the option of either tripling their invested capital over a 10-year period or securing a guarantee on their original capital and participating in 70% of the positive performance of the portfolio. A similar product was created by SG for one of its major insurance clients in Europe. The product was based on an underlying basket of 10 stocks: Diageo, GlaxoWellcome, L'Oréal, CGNU, Royal Dutch, Coca-Cola, LVMH, Deutsche Bank, Bayer and General Motors. The wrapper used was a life insurance product with a 10-year maturity and the benchmark was the Altiplano exotic option. The flexibility of the multi-manager, multi-asset approach offers superior diversification across strategies and styles along with higher returns. The portfolio mix ensures exposure to investment opportunities in all asset classes: equities, bonds, currencies and commodities. SG's Equinox II fund, offering such a mix, provided a return of over 25% (in US dollar terms on a 12-month rolling period basis) between April 1995 and 2000.

One of the more popular hedge fund structures devised by SG is called the managed account approach. Rupert Allan, a director in the bank, explains it like this:

> What it essentially means is that we open an account with a prime broker in SG's name. We then allow the hedge fund manager to trade the account's assets as s/he normally would. But what this approach means is that we know at all times what is in the portfolio; we don't have to rely on what the manager is valuing it at, nor do we have to rely on what the prime broker is valuing it at. We can independently value the assets in the portfolio, which is done on a daily basis. It is also important to note that these activities are conducted by an independent company, Lyxor Asset Management, to ensure that the appropriate Chinese walls are strictly enforced; positions taken by the hedge fund managers are not accessible to the bank's traders.[43]

As well as being able to value the portfolio, SG provides due diligence on the manager; for example, monitoring that the manager is not putting distressed securities into what is meant to be a long/short equity fund. Not being restricted by the prospectus and redemption clauses, the bank can offer investors better liquidity (typically weekly dealings) along with greater flexibility and transparency. SG assesses the risk characteristics of the investment vehicle. The bank takes the position of principal in the hedge fund, and having assumed lending risk (particularly in a leveraged investment), it therefore has a very real interest in the performance of the underlying fund. The bank performs a thorough due diligence function in monitoring the investment portfolios and demanding transparency and accurate risk control. The structures, participation in the upside, percentage of guarantee, tenure and leverage all vary, as do the fees in packaging these products. Market conditions including prevailing interest rates, underlying assets, currency, duration and pricing of derivatives all impact on the structure. But investment profiles can be individually tailored to meet the investors' needs by making use of the myriad vanilla and exotic derivatives available.

According to Andreas Ritzi of RMF Capital Markets, 'it is critical that the client's investment objectives are not compromised by structural limitations. It is important to get the best quality of hedge fund portfolio because with a low-quality portfolio there is a danger that the institutions get stopped out if they are using a dynamic hedged structure, which will mean that they may finish up with limited upside, as their money is sitting in zero-coupon bonds.' Most providers resort to some form of trigger structure in issuing CPPs. 'I cannot recommend one technology above the other. What is really important is to match the capital guarantee technology to the underlying and the requirements of the client. Depending on the characteristics of the underlying and the objectives of the client, we select the mechanism, which achieves the goal with the least restricting factors,' confirms Ritzi.[44]

Over the past few years, CPPs linked to unit trusts entered the market offering investors a guarantee on their capital with the added exposure to a rising market. The number of suppliers of the underlying capital guarantees has exploded, with investment banks, insurance and reinsurance companies joining the growing market. According to Antony Stack, managing director at NDF Administration in Ireland, the joint launch with CSFB of a protected hedge product for the retail investor in the UK 'is the most significant development in the UK market for many years. It will open up a whole new asset class for many investors for whom hedge funds were previously out of reach. The ability to take the Plan within an ISA offers the extra valuable attraction of a tax free vehicle in which to shelter investments.'[45] Since the launch in 1994 of the CSFB/Tremont hedge fund index, which has become established as an industry benchmark for measuring hedge fund performance, CSFB has become one of the leading providers of hedge-fund-linked products for institutions throughout Europe.

CONCLUSION

The creation of Europe's first academic centre for research into absolute return strategies in the London Business School, with funding provided by Fauchier Partners, Merrill Lynch Investment Managers, BNP Paribas and Deutsche Bank, indicates that the hedge fund sector is gaining acceptance by mainstream managers as a well-established investment strategy worthy of serious scholarship. Its growth potential is such that some hedge fund strategies could gain acceptance by traditional fund managers. As equities already comprise the dominant asset class, the transition from long-only to absolute return strategies is not a difficult one. Thus, there is need for independent research in the area. 'Understanding the different investment philosophies is becoming increasingly important as more and more beta merchants camouflaged as hedge funds without an edge in that discipline of exploiting market inefficiencies and without serious risk management capabilities are likely to tumble as did most copy-cat hedge funds in the early 1970s when markets reversed.'[46]

The outlook for the hedge fund sector will be driven largely by the overall performance of the market as well as the scope of corporate activity. Market volatility, liquidity and regulation will also impact on future growth. With major restructuring ahead in Europe, Asia and emerging markets, there will be a corresponding rise in corporate activity around the world, including the issuance of equity, debt and equity-linked debt. With developments in derivatives markets and securities lending, the scope for hedge fund activity seems reasonably secure. While volatility is good for the hedge fund industry, it is not essential to market efficiency. So if market volatility were to fall back to the mid-1990s level, opportunities for some hedge fund strategies might decline or disappear. Liquidity is the key to the growth of the sector, although some of the best opportunities also arise in highly illiquid markets.

Regulation is the sword of Damocles hanging over the hedge fund industry. Many analysts believe that the attractive risk-return combination in the industry is derived from regulatory arbitrage. If traditional managers were not as regulated as they are today, markets would be more efficient. However, that would also mean fewer opportunities for hedge funds. Inability of many traditional investors to sell short, for example, is one of the reasons for market inefficiency today. Thus, investors realise that stocks are overpriced, but when there are significant obstacles to short selling or costs attached to trading stocks, these traditional investors are not able to use that information efficiently. Hedge funds, on the other hand, due to their regulatory status, are able to use this information with greater efficiency, hence they are better able to capture alpha.

The attractiveness of capital-protected structures investing in hedge funds or direct investment in hedge funds will depend largely on the trade-off between transparency and costs. If the sustainable long-term target for a diversified hedge fund product, after the hedge fund managers have taken their fees, is around 10% then the cost of the guarantee is not onerous in light of the fact that they are also buying a product with a completely different risk-return profile from a normal portfolio and have eliminated the risk while retaining most of the return. A similar argument can be made for funds of funds in the hedge fund sector. If markets continue to be difficult, then investors are more likely to turn to absolute return strategies, except these strategies may also fail to deliver. Although hedged strategies and products have long been the domain of institutions and wealthy sophisticated investors, an increasing number of retail products have been introduced to the market. While investors would be well advised to perform extensive due diligence and gain full understanding of all implications of their individual strategy or group of strategies, it cannot be argued that capital-guaranteed products have many attractive features and could become an integral part of the retail sector, as they offer the investor a more secure rate of return than traditional investments.

For many institutional pension funds and most retail investors, monitoring individual hedge funds is not viable as there is very little information publicly available. Investment consultants have found it equally difficult to come to grips with the infinite diversity of styles involved in the sector. The fund-of-funds route is evolving fast as an option for investing in a diversified hedge fund portfolio. According to the Hennessee Group, funds of funds now handle one of every five dollars invested in hedge funds. However, the availability of good analysts in the sector is a major constraint. Due to the high demand for hedge funds, most managers are actively managing their own funds. There is little incentive to become an analyst and cover a sector where the major players are reluctant to share any relevant information to third parties.

Although there is no lack of choice in hedge fund managers, the real challenge lies in understanding the underlying investment strategy well enough to be able to assess the risks associated with such an investment. Theoretically, a fund of funds should provide the necessary diversification for an investor when choosing such a vehicle, but it is not cheap. In addition to the fees of the underlying hedge funds – typically 1% annual management fee with 20% performance fees – there is the cost of the fund-of-funds manager, which is a further 1–2%. While some believe that in adding a layer of fees, you also add a layer of skill, others are of the opinion that you are adding a layer of risk and costs with the extra fee. The problem with a fund of funds is determining what combination of risk the investor wants. It is difficult enough measuring risk in traditional portfolios, but trying to gauge the risk in hedge funds is just not feasible. While firms like Measurisk.com in New York are enhancing transparency by providing fund-of-funds managers with detailed reporting on individual hedge fund risk exposures, the lack of transparency in the underlying investments poses a real problem for investors.

For veterans of the investment world such as John Bogle, founder of the Vanguard Group, who has spent almost 50 years working towards indexed strategies and lower costs, the fee structure of the hedge fund industry is a no-win situation for the investor: 'It is inconceivable that you could take $500 billion run by 6,000 different managers and expect these managers to be smarter than the rest of the world.' If the market goes up 10%, he calculates, then hedge fund operators would need a 17% return to beat that, given a 20% carry, a 2% annual fee and other taxes. "I don't think that $500 billion has a remote chance of beating 17%.'[47]

As the quality of the data on the performance of hedge funds remains poor and is costly to obtain, it is difficult to refute Bogle's argument. The lack of transparency in the data means information flow is far from efficient. Thus, it remains a risk to investors outside the information loop. Information and high-quality data constitute the competitive advantages of the fund-of-funds manager. So the solution is to choose a good fund-of-funds manager simply because statistically the odds are stacked against the investor in finding the right active manager, be it in the traditional sector or the hedge fund sector. Besides, an industry without adequate regulation is a haven to a lot of rogues who can easily defraud their investors with false statements and accounts. So, if you turn to your trusted friends or relatives, a word about luck. As one Harvard professor put it, he backed his brother-in-law three times and thrice his ventures failed. The fourth time, his brother-in-law understandably approached investors outside his circle of family and friends to back him, and they all became millionaires. As with a lot else in life, good luck makes a difference; although those who succeed in life often do not believe that to be the case.

CHAPTER 6

Private Equity

INTRODUCTION

Private equity encompasses a wide range of investments made by specialist managers using share capital that is privately held and not publicly traded. The illiquid nature of private equity investment and the difficulty in pricing the underlying assets along with the complexity involved in appraising the sources of advantage in the investments involved make it an unconventional asset class. However, it has been widely recognised that such a form of investment is better able to provide the necessary combination of capital, business mentoring and financial discipline that are critical to fostering private enterprise. It also enables investors to access emerging trends in the economy efficiently. Companies such as Microsoft, Compaq, Intel, Yahoo, Amazon.com and Vodafone, among others, were all venture-backed.

One-third of the total investment in European private equity during 1999 and 2000, for example, was in the technology sector, with the largest number of investments being devoted to high-tech ventures (Table 6.1). Funds earmarked for high-tech early-stage and expansion investments rose by 81% to €15.2 billion in 2000, although funds for buyouts also increased 106% to €24.3 billion.[1] In an economic climate dominated by stock market turmoil and uncertainty about the prospect for global growth, venture capital continued to play its role in financing the economy. The single most important asset for a top-performing venture capital fund will be access to scarce resources. In Europe the largest threats are perceived to be the ability to adapt to the speed of change, access to relevant networks and the scarcity of talent.[2] However, much of the

Table 6.1 *Allocation of European private equity funds raised in 2000*[a]

Investment by stage	Allocation
Buyouts	50.7%
High-tech early-stage	18.0%
High-tech expansion/development	13.8%
Non-high-tech expansion/development	11.8%
Non-high-tech early-stage	2.5%
Other	3.2%

[a] Source: EVCA Yearbook 2001

capital raised during the past years has yet to be deployed, leaving ample risk equity capital for entrepreneurs with compelling project valuations. Venture Economics estimated that as of 30 June 2001 the 'overhang' – the amount of venture capital raised but not yet invested in projects – is over $45 billion for the US market.

With the fall in the NASDAQ since March 2000, companies experienced difficulty in securing funding from public markets; IPO market (initial public offerings) in particular dried up, leaving many investors with huge losses as exit opportunities disappeared. Now the hype about venture capital funding has ceased, it can only help to foster a healthier market driven by genuine business innovation and sustained by committed private equity investors. Mere access to capital and the ability to broker a deal are not prerequisites for a genuine entrepreneur. Many venture capitalists too became short-term in their orientation, and a combination of lower selectivity of investments, portfolio concentration and attraction to big names resulted in low returns. A lot of capital was poured into a small number of deals, driving prices up and creating asset bubbles. In 2000 about $200 billion was committed to private equity funds worldwide; in 2001 this number should be closer to $100 billion.[3]

Since 1995 the private equity market in North America and Europe has grown significantly. Global private equity investments rose by 65% to $136 billion in 1999, representing 0.5% of global GDP. Between 1994 and 1999, private equity investing grew at an annual compound rate of 40%.[4] The global private equity market is dominated by the US, which remains the largest market, with over 70% of total investments made in 2000. Europe has registered strong growth since 1997, and remains a key growth market as corporate restructuring and industrial rationalisation, fiscal and regulatory reform, technological innovation along with greater convergence between 'old economy' and 'new economy' firms generate a stream of investment opportunities. The Neuer Markt established itself as the most important financial trading centre for the technology market in Europe. While the global slowdown threatens all investors and the technology sector has been facing a massive cut in investments, many still believe that the merger of old economy values such as profit orientation and new economy visions such as rapid leader placement and fast growth will lead to new organic corporate structures that will provide fresh opportunities for venture capitalists.

A massive €48.0 billion was raised for investment in European private equity during 2000, an increase of 89% on the previous record of €25.4 billion raised in 1999 compared to €5.8 billion in 1989. And €34.9 billion was invested in 2000 compared to €25.1 billion in 1999, with the UK contributing the bulk of the funds raised and investments utilised. On a pan-European scale, pension funds overtook banks in 2000 as the largest capital donors, contributing 24% of funds raised, registering an increase of 125% in funding over the past year (Table 6.2). Banks contributed 22% of the total funds, an increase of 29% over 1999, having accounted for 30% of funding in

Table 6.2 *Sources of investment in European private equity: figures are percentages*[a]

	2000	1996–2000
Pension funds	24.2	24.3
Banks	21.7	27.0
Insurance firms	12.9	13.5
Fund-of-funds	11.4	5.4
Corporate investors	10.9	10.5
Private individuals	7.4	7.0
Government agencies	5.6	4.8
Capital markets	1.3	0.6
Academic institutions	0.4	0.5
Other	4.2	6.4

[a] Source: EVCA Yearbook 2001

1999 and for 27% of funds between 1996 and 2000. Insurance firms also raised their stake to 13%, an increase of 70% in their contribution over the previous year. Pension fund investors in the UK do have a track record of investing rather late in the cycle within other asset classes as well. However, due to the nature of private equity funding, not all their additional investments in 2000 would have been deployed the same year.

Table **6.3** *European private equity: funds raised by country of origin in 2000 and expressed as a percentage*[a]

UK	15.8
Germany	12.0
France	10.6
Netherlands	5.5
Sweden	3.5
Switzerland	3.2
Italy	3.1
Belgium	2.4
Spain	2.4
Denmark	2.3
Finland	1.6
Norway	1.4
Austria	0.5
Greece	0.5
Ireland	0.4
Portugal	0.4
Iceland	0.3
Czech Republic	0.1
Poland	0.1
Other European	1.1
Unknown European	6.2
European total	**73.1**
US	20.2
Asia	3.1
Canada	1.1
Other rest of the world	0.3
Unknown rest of the world	2.1
Rest of the world total	**26.9**

[a] Source: EVCA Yearbook 2001

Over the past few years, the development of the European private
equity industry and increased interest from domestic sources
contributed significantly to the fund-raising effort. Europe
accounted for 73% of funds raised in 2000, while the US accounted
for 20%, an increase from 16% of overall funds raised in 1999. The
UK's proportional contribution remained stable at around 16%,
although in real terms there was a 79% rise in funding from €9.8
billion in 1999 to €17.6 billion in 2000. The changing environment
in Europe for private equity investing has certainly helped the fund-
raising effort. Major tax reforms in Germany, France, Spain and the
UK are expected to unlock investment opportunities across Europe.
Increasing liberalisation of pension fund legislation with a focus on
promoting pensions as a vehicle for individual savings is also

Table 6.4 *Private equity investment (as percentage
of GDP in 2000)*[a]

Iceland	1.497
Sweden	0.924
UK	0.859
Netherlands	0.480
Europe	0.383
France	0.379
Finland	0.291
Czech Republic	0.265
Italy	0.255
Switzerland	0.240
Germany	0.234
Belgium	0.231
Ireland	0.221
Spain	0.186
Norway	0.181
Denmark	0.165
Portugal	0.163
Greece	0.162
Poland	0.133
Hungary	0.121
Austria	0.079

[a] Source: EVCA Yearbook 2001

expected to impact positively on the supply of funds to private equity over the years. The European Union's 'financial services action plan' to create an integrated financial services market by 2005 will also help reduce the cost of capital and widen access to pan-European fund-raising. Currently, most of the fund-raising is done on a country basis (Table 6.3).

Despite this substantial increase in funding, as a percentage of GDP, private equity investments in Europe remain small (Table 6.4). The average for Europe is less than 0.4% of GDP; even the UK invested less than 0.9% of its GDP in private equity. Thus, even a doubling of investments flowing into the sector will still represent a tiny proportion of GDP. There is ample scope for growth in private equity investing in Europe.

DEFINING PRIVATE EQUITY

Private equity refers loosely to a broad asset class, the main feature of which is the private nature of the share capital ownership. It is covered under terms as diverse as hybrid investments, alternative investments, venture capital or non-venture private equity. The categorisation may range from the injection of a small amount of seed capital for the formation of a company up to large, billion-pound corporate restructurings. According to the British Venture Capital Association (BVCA), which follows the broad approach taken in the US, there is a distinction between venture capital and non-venture private equity.

Within the ambit of venture capital (VC) investing, there are stages of funding. Seed capital involves funding at a very early-stage of development of the project, followed by start-up financing, which is provided to companies for use in product development and initial marketing, where companies have not yet sold their product commercially. Then, there is 'other early-stage' financing, which is provided to companies that have completed the product development stage and require further funds to initiate commercial sales. At this stage, the companies are still not generating profits. The next stage up the ladder is expansion financing, which is provided for the growth and expansion of an established company. Capital provided for rescue/turnaround situations is also included in this category.

Refinancing bank debt refers to replacing existing liabilities with a mixture of debt and equity, giving the recipient company greater flexibility in its financial planning. Secondary purchase financing is the purchase of existing shares in a company from another venture capital firm or other shareholders.

Non-venture private equity refers to management buyouts (MBOs), whereby funds are provided to enable current management to acquire an existing/operating business or product line. Institutional buyouts (IBOs), public-to-private and similar financings are included under MBOs. Management buy-ins (MBIs) make available funds to an external manager or group of managers to buy into an established company. Public-to-private funding enables the purchase of the equity of publicly listed companies, which are then delisted, to become private entities. Private equity financing is provided to finance the development of the private company with a view to subsequent listing or trade sale.[5] Private equity investments therefore play a strong role in the creation of and support for very small companies that generate economic growth and have been responsible for pioneering technological development.

Limited partnerships account for the bulk of private equity funds in the UK, US and Europe. Like hedge funds, private equity firms act as the general partner responsible for managing the fund and providing the key expertise. Institutions and other investors become limited partners, and the returns to all the participants are defined in the partnership agreement, which typically involves an annual management fee of 1–3% to the general partner and a share in the capital gain of the fund of around 20%, once it has reached a threshold return.[6] Such a structure has advantages for both the manager and the investor as the tax aspect is passed on to the end investor, which is important to tax-exempt pension funds. Besides, the partnership arrangement can be flexible; it also has a fixed term. With capital gains being shared by manager and investor, their aligned interest provides the incentive for the manager to be focused on performance. The main disadvantage of limited partnerships is that there are limited exit opportunities as there is no secondary market in such an investment product. Also, English law governing such partnerships, enacted in 1907, limits the number of partners and imposes constraints on their ability to act as investment advisors.

Investment trusts are used in the private equity sector, but the rise of limited partnerships has eclipsed the growth of investment trusts. The major difference between the two structures relates to the time-limited nature of limited partnerships, although a few investment trusts have also become time-limited. Investment trusts traditionally were evergreen vehicles where capital gains were reinvested rather than returned to shareholders, who in turn received dividends and capital gains on trust shareholdings. Investment trusts also tend to be fairly tax-transparent to end-investors as long as the trust complies with the UK's Inland Revenue rules for the distribution of income to investors. Being publicly quoted vehicles, investment trusts offer greater liquidity and they can access capital from a wider range of investors, both institutional and retail, via public offerings. Investment trusts also have the unusual flexibility of gearing. The sector is dominated by the 3i group, Europe's leading venture capital firm, with a market capitalisation of some £8 billion, compared to others such as Electra and Schroder Ventures, which are significantly smaller in size (Table 6.5). At the end of December 2000, the total assets of the top 11 UK-listed investment trusts focusing on private equity amounted to some £11.4 billion.[7]

The main disadvantage of the investment trust structure is that the share price does not reflect the net asset value of the trust's underlying holdings, as price is determined by supply and demand. Thus, if the sector/country in which the trust has investments is popular, then the shares tend to trade at a premium. Equally, they languish at big discounts when demand is indifferent. The incompatibility in the timing between the raising of capital, which dilutes the returns, and its investment can put pressure on the manager towards early or untimely investments. The other limiting factor is that while the trust structure is tax-transparent for domestic investors, it is not so for the overseas investor. Many of these weaknesses are being addressed; for example, allowing trusts to buy back their own shares to lower the discount. Better independent analysis of private equity investment trusts will also help in addressing some of these issues. However, expertise in the sector is a limiting factor. As with the hedge fund sector, individuals with an above average level of expertise are engaged actively in the management of funds. Due to a skills shortage, there are not enough practitioners in the field who specia-

Table 6.5 *Market position and sector bias of UK investment trusts[a]*

3i Group	Early-stage and development capital, and small to medium buyouts Pan-European with strong focus on growth and technology
Candover	Medium to large buyouts Media, manufacturing, engineering, financial services, chemicals, support services, consumer products, IT
Dunedin Enterprise	Smaller buyouts Generalist with a bias towards manufacturing, services, financials
Electra	Medium-sized buyouts and development capital Generalist with a bias towards support services, financial services, communications and consumer products
F&C Enterprise	Development capital and small to medium-sized buyouts UK generalist with bias towards financial services and IT
Kleinwort Development Fund	Small to medium-sized buyouts and early-stage and development capital Growth bias via IT, media and publishing, healthcare, engineering and manufacturing
Martin Currie Capital Return	Fund of funds with a bias towards medium to large buyouts (via Candover Funds) and mezzanine investments Fund of funds with 40% exposure to Candover Funds
Mercury Grosvenor	Medium-sized buyouts and development/expansion capital Focus on medical, healthcare, business services and distribution
Pantheon	Balanced fund of funds with a bias towards development capital Diversified fund of funds
Schroder Ventures	Fund of funds with a bias towards medium to large buyouts with a weighting in development capital Consumer products, services, engineering, healthcare, life sciences, IT
Thompson Clive	Early-stage and development capital within technology IT, life sciences, healthcare

[a] Source: Dresdner Kleinwort Benson Research

lise in research and analysis of the sector for the benefit of the investment community.

However, the performance of investment trusts in the UK compares favourably with that of the FTSE All Share index as well as the Small Cap index (Table 6.6). Short-term investment performance has been even more attractive.

The fund-of-funds approach to investing in private equity funds is widely used in other asset classes such as hedge funds, which have a similar problem with transparency. Funds of funds are structured as investment trusts or limited partnerships and invest in other partnerships or trusts to provide the end-investor with a diversified portfolio, albeit at an additional layer of management expense. Although there are a growing range of investment vehicles through which investors can benefit from private equity exposure, the structure, taxation and regulatory issues surrounding these opportunities may still exclude some investors. In the final analysis, the high returns during the past decade or so of private equity compared to public equity may prove to be the overriding factor in banishing investor indifference to the sector.

Needless to remind seasoned investors that the past is no guarantee of future performance and all returns should be seen in the context of the overall economic and stock market cycle as much as the investment and realisation cycles of the underlying companies themselves. Private equity has more beta risk and more stock-specific risk than ordinary stocks. There is a degree of cyclicality, and the attendant issue of illiquidity in private equity investing is an additional source of risk. Hence the importance of selecting managers who are experienced in diversifying their investments and holding on to their investments over a longer period, thereby smoothing out the cyclical nature of the industry. Patience is a great virtue in the investment business. The third-generation wireless licence auction, which has come to haunt the telecom operators, will provide opportunities for buyouts as recent disposals by BT (Yell) and Ericsson (the direct sales force) illustrate. Recessions often offer great long-term buying opportunities.

Table 6.6 *Long-term performance of UK investment trusts (compound annual growth rate expressed as a percentage)[a]*

	10 years to	NAV	Price	FTSE All Share[b]	FTSE Small Cap[b]
F&C Enterprise	30/06/2000	20.9	24.7	10.0	8.0
Thompson Clive	30/06/2000	18.3	20.4	10.0	8.0
3i Group	30/09/2000	17.9	N/A	12.1	10.9
Pantheon	30/06/2000	16.8	18.9	10.0	8.0
Candover	30/06/2000	16.4	15.3	10.0	8.0
Electra	31/03/2000	12.2	15.0	10.8	8.1
Kleinwort Development	31/07/2000	12.1	11.9	10.3	8.2
Dunedin Enterprise	30/04/2000	10.1	13.1	11.2	8.4

[a] Source: Dresdner Kleinwort Benson Research
[b] Excluding investment companies

AN INTRODUCTION TO THE MARKET IN THE UK

A history of mixed investment returns along with a wide dispersion in the performance of the different partnerships traditionally discouraged UK institutional investors from taking a more active role in the sector. However, the recent shift from using peer group benchmarks to customised benchmarks, the abolition of the minimum funding requirement (MFR) – the widely criticised solvency test for pension funds which leads to a bias in favour of mainstream asset classes – and the availability of reasonably long-term performance data on the sector, not to mention the stellar performance record, may all conspire in influencing pension fund trustees and their consultants in structuring a more diversified portfolio of assets that would include alternative investments, such as private equity and hedge funds. US pension fund exposure to alternative investments has been significantly higher at 6–7% of their total portfolios, compared to just 1% for the UK.

What has been puzzling UK private equity industry experts is the willingness of US institutions to invest in UK private equity, which provides a striking contrast to the relative reluctance of UK institutions to invest in the same opportunities. In 1999 overseas investors provided around 70% of the UK private equity industry's funding.[8] Overseas pension funds were responsible for 29% of the UK private equity market. During 2000, once again, overseas investors committed substantially more than UK sources to UK private equity funds (73% more) with US pension funds being the largest contributor (Table 6.7). During 1996–99 overseas investment in UK private equity assets tripled while the level of annual investment by UK pension funds in the same asset class declined. However, 2000 witnessed the reversal of this trend, with almost a 70% increase in funding from domestic sources. Thus, domestic investors also got in at the peak of the investment cycle.

Until 1996 UK institutions provided 57% of the funding, with pension funds contributing 30% and the insurance sector 9%. Since 1996 overseas investments in UK private equity rose at a much faster rate than the domestic rate of investment in the sector. According to the BVCA, UK pension funds invested £817 million in private equity or venture capital in 2000, compared with £437

Table **6.7** *Sources of investment in UK private equity*[a]

	Value (£m)			Percent share	
	1999	2000	Change (%)	1999	2000
Overseas pension funds	1,610	2,759	71.4	27.7	30.7
Overseas banks	786	575	-26.8	13.5	6.4
Overseas corporates	447	414	-7.4	7.7	4.6
Overseas insurance	383	931	143.1	6.6	10.4
Overseas individuals	100	211	111.0	1.7	2.3
Overseas funds of funds	352	427	21.3	6.1	4.7
Overseas government agencies	122	288	136.1	2.1	3.2
Overseas other	237	179	-24.5	4.1	2.0
UK pension funds	437	817	87.0	7.5	9.1
UK banks	350	332	-5.1	6.0	3.7
UK corporates	138	299	116.7	2.4	3.3
UK insurance	533	457	-14.3	9.2	5.1
UK individuals	175	363	107.4	3.0	4.0
UK funds of funds	58	799	1,277.6	1.0	8.9
UK government agencies	29	19	-34.5	0.5	0.2
UK other	56	125	123.2	1.0	1.4
Total	5,813	8,995	54.7	100.0	100.0

[a] Source: BVCA

million in 1999, £533 million in 1998 and £622 million in 1997. One could argue that institutional investors in the UK have been bearish about markets since 1997 and so invested less in high-risk investments such as private equity, while an oversupply of capital in the US caused falling yields, prompting managers to diversify overseas. However, the 87% increase in funding in 2000 from UK pension funds does not support such a view. It can be argued that the Myners Report, along with the London Business School/NAPF/BVCA report on UK private equity investing, had a positive impact on sentiment. However, the driving factor was most likely to be the long-term performance record of the asset class as it became more transparent by 2000.

Overseas pension funds' investment in 1999 had gone up by 310% compared to its 1996 level. However, UK pension funds' commitment in 1999 stood at only 60% of its 1996 level. It is arguable that US interest in UK/European private equity was driven by the inflated asset valuations in the US market. It provided the necessary diversification for the US investor. Note that, according to research by Professor Joshua Lerner of Harvard University, the pooled average return on all US private equity funds over a 20-year period ending March 1999 was 17.1%, which was lower than returns on public equity markets. However, US investment in venture capital has been in a different league altogether, as individual funds fared significantly better than the average fund. The success of the endowment fund of Yale University, which showed an astonishing annual return of 29.6% on private equity between 1973 and 1997 is well publicised. Yale attributed its success to the choice of hands-on managers who excelled at exploiting inefficiencies in an illiquid market.[9]

Pension funds, endowments, individuals and families and corporations in the US account for the bulk of this funding and, unlike the UK, 94% of this capital is secured from domestic sources (Table 6.8). The transformational impact of venture capital on the US economy alerted governments, corporations and investors in Europe to the advantages of private equity investments that are capable of delivering high absolute returns for both investor and entrepreneur. Although the historical development of US private equity was similar in the UK, strong emphasis on venture capital, diversity of the sources of funding and a sustained high level of return enabled the US private equity sector to take a major leap forward. During 1990–98 anywhere between 20% and 30% of the funding raised was exclusively for venture capital investments. In 1999 the total funds raised for private equity investments in the US amounted to $122.7 billion

Table 6.8 *Sources of US venture capital, 1999*[a]

Pension funds	23%
Individuals/families	22%
Endowments	21%
Corporations	15%
Insurance companies	13%
All overseas sources	6%

[a] Source: NVCA Yearbook 2000

with 48.7% aimed at venture capital activity alone. In 2000 a staggering $164.5 billion was raised, with 56% of that being targeted at new venture investments.

This trend towards higher distribution of funding into venture capital activity continued in the first half of 2001, with $26.4 billion being raised for new ventures compared to $18.6 billion for the buyout/mezzanine sector (Table 6.9). Data also suggests that first-time funds found the investment climate more difficult during 2001, but the more experienced venture capitalists were in a stronger position in attracting new funds. Thus, firms such as Kohlberg, Kravis, Roberts & Co. accounted for more than half of the second quarter 2001 buyout/mezzanine volume, with $4.9 billion raised for its KKR Millennium Fund, which has a target of $10 billion. Institutional investors recognise that experienced private equity investors have the ability to outperform public markets through various business cycles and economic conditions.

Although venture capital investing evolved early in the UK, it had greater success in the US due to an array of reasons. The Industrial and Commercial Finance Corporation, now called 3i, was set up in 1945 in the UK. And in the US, the American Research and Development Corporation in Boston was created in 1946. It was during the

Table **6.9** *Distribution of private equity fund-raising in the US[a]*

	Venture capital	Buyout/mezzanine	Other	Total raised ($bn)[b]
1990	3.1	7.6	0.04	10.7
1991	1.7	4.1	1.10	6.9
1992	5.0	12.0	0.92	17.9
1993	4.5	17.6	0.03	22.1
1994	7.6	20.4	2.50	30.5
1995	9.7	26.9	4.90	41.5
1996	11.7	32.9	3.30	47.9
1997	17.0	48.1	6.40	71.5
1998	29.1	62.5	5.40	97.0
1999	59.8	61.8	1.10	122.7
2000	92.3	71.0	1.24	164.5

[a] Source: Venture Economics and NVCA
[b] Totals do not include fund-of-funds data

1980s and 1990s that the US witnessed explosive growth in venture capital investing as well as non-venture private equity funding. This was triggered by a virtuous circle of factors – the liberalisation of pension fund legislation, reforms in capital gains and share option taxation, buoyant performance of the US equity markets and development of the NASDAQ market – creating a strong climate for nurturing enterprise.[10]

During the 1980s and early 1990s, the sector experienced a high level of consolidation in the UK. The level of investments made by the BVCA, founded in 1983, rose to £1 billion by 1987 and stagnated at that level until 1994. Investments started to pick up after 1996. By the end of December 2000, capital raised and investments made by UK private equity funds between 1980 and 1996 stood at £8.3 billion and £7.9 billion respectively. The number of 'independent' UK private equity funds had also risen to 244 in 2000, representing some 95% of the total funds managed by BVCA member firms raising money from institutional investors. In the US, independent partnerships have dominated the sector, providing 80% of the funds under management, with financial firms accounting for 18% of the remaining funds. There are some 620 firms in the sector and the net rate of creation of new venture firms has also risen, from 32 per year in the 1980s to 73 in 1999. Despite such levels of growth and entrepreneurship, the industry model has remained remarkably stable over this period. Each firm has an average of six investment principles, although average investment capital per principal had risen from $6 million in 1980 to $16 million in 1990 and $37 million in 1999.[11]

The relationship between the private equity sector in the UK and that of the wider capital market is not under question. ICFC/3i, for example, was owned by the UK banking sector for a long time. Since the 1980s, the bigger clearing banks such as Barclays and National Westminster operated their in-house private equity firms. So did the major insurers such as Prudential and Legal & General. However, the focus of these firms' investment activity was directed mainly towards management buyouts/buy-ins (MBOs/MBIs). In the mid-1980s venture capital consisted of over half of UK-managed private equity investments; by 2000 that had fallen to 27%.[12] Major fund management houses also developed in-house expertise in private equity, often on a global basis, making use of their corporate finance departments worldwide.

The major difference between the evolution of the UK and the US model was linked to the captive or semi-captive nature of the private equity firms in the UK when compared to the independent nature of firms in the US. During the 1990s the number of independent firms in the UK, structured as limited partnerships, has been on the rise. Some commentators considered this as a structural limitation in the UK private equity sector responsible for the poor investment returns. 'Channelling institutional investment via in-house funds may have hindered the development of a diversified private equity portfolio and reduced competition between private equity firms and investment approaches.'[13] The trend in the UK is changing towards more independent structures. Recently a number of captive fund management groups have bought themselves out, and thus become independent entities. Captive and semi-captive funds accounted for almost one-third of the flow of private equity investments in 1997; by 2000 this flow had declined to 17% of the total.[14]

As the venture capital model in the US made it possible to sell a concept rather than a fully-fledged company, the exit routes for start-up, high-tech companies fell from about 80 months in 1996 to a little over 20 months in 1998 and to less than 18 months in 1999. The dotcom mania provided easy pickings for those who were quick enough to join the game and sell the concept, at a huge profit. Speaking in May 2000, Alan Greenspan warned that inflated private equity portfolios accounted for up to one-third of regulatory Tier One capital in the largest US banks. Not only had US banks invested billions in venture capital funds, but their own internal funds had also poured millions into the so-called new economy. At one point, Chase Manhattan's private equity division, Chase Capital Partners, valued itself at $20 billion. Clearly this level of investment was not sustainable. The NASDAQ index, feeding on this investment frenzy, surged from 1,400 in October 1998 to 5,100 by early March 2000 before falling back to 1,650 in April 2001. In the words of Robert J. Shiller:

> Irrational exuberance continues to pose hazards for business decision makers as well, despite the correction of many excesses with the end of the dot-com bubble. Companies should be wary

of looking to the market for guidance about business decisions. Companies still must remember that they have to produce a valuable product, control costs, and make a profit.

The dot-com crash was a useful warning and reminder of some of these basic facts, but the warning has not always been heeded sufficiently. We do have the willingness as a society to give an awfully long leash to many startups, and one of the consequences of this willingness is that money has been free for risk-insensitive entrepreneurs to try creating firms with a low probability of success but a high upside potential. An abundance of capital gives a lot of people a chance to take such a bet, and some will succeed. But, when the market becomes irrational, the same willingness can create incentives for some firms to look not so much at the probabilities of genuine business success but at chances for short-run success in the stock market.[15]

In fact, it was the investment-led boom in the US economy that caused such concern among investors, as it was clearly unsustainable. Markets tend to react negatively to any form of uncertainty. Considering the prospect for global economic growth was at best slowing and at worst in a recession, markets have been volatile for some time. As the rest of the world – including Japan, Europe and emerging markets – except the UK has also been experiencing a difficult time, the US economy was single-handedly driving the global economy, and investment in technology was driving the US economy. All this investment was also aimed primarily at the US consumer, who plays a God-like role in ensuring that the world goes round. This level of dependence on the US consumer was also unsustainable, in light of events since 11 September 2001.

The surge in popularity of corporate venturing, with the likes of Intel, Microsoft, General Electric (GE), Lucent Technologies and Nokia managing investment funds that dwarfed the biggest funds of independent venture capitalists, played a vital role in keeping this investment bubble afloat. It channelled the high level of liquidity in the US economy into investment channels, which were clearly overpriced. A record number of corporations in the US had venture investing programmes in place by 2000. GE had 95 venture capital deals in 2000 compared to Intel's 176. Portfolio gains in 2000 soared to $3.7 billion from $883 million in 1999 for Intel, comprising some 30% of its earnings in 2000. Corporations accounted for $17 billion, or some 17% of venture capital funding in 2000, compared to $1.3 billion (8%) in 1997.

Although maintaining this level of investment was unsustainable, it did support higher output of innovative activity, albeit at higher cost. A surge in investment from the late 1970s onwards in the US brought in its wake a rise in patenting rates. It is estimated that venture capital accounted for 14% of industrial innovations by 1998. US venture capitalists were also better able to feed off a fertile base of technology emerging from the universities and research institutes. The development of Hewlett-Packard and its impact on Silicon Valley is a classic case in point.[16] High-tech companies treat venture capital investments as an extension of their internal research and development (R&D) activity. While corporate venturing will not replace R&D, it played a strategic role in business development along with alliances, acquisitions and enhanced collaboration with universities. In the UK, venture capital has achieved some successes among technology investments, such as ARM Holdings and Autonomy in Cambridge, but has yet to achieve critical mass. Of the £8.3 billion raised, just £656 million was for the technology sector (Table 6.10).

Private equity investing in the UK had not reached the level of asset inflation witnessed in the US. Technology-related investments delivered decent returns. Early-stage funds showed the highest value as a percentage of paid-in capital at 246% followed by the technology sector. Thus, of the £633 million paid-in capital in the technology sector, 164% had been returned to investors by the end of December 2000, and 67% was still retained within the portfolios. Compared to other industry sectors, technology funds delivered a higher return to investors. Generalist funds showed the highest returns already distributed to investors at 189%. Individual private equity funds in the UK historically produced positive cash flows after 3–5 years. Before this incubation period, the funds invested are in a highly illiquid form. During the 1990s, as investment returns improved, many funds were able to show positive cash flows before

Table 6.10 *Capital raised and realised by investment stage in the UK (to year end December 2000)[a]*

	No. of funds	Capital raised (£m)	Paid-in capital (£m)	Distribution[b]	Residual value[b]	Total value[b]
Early stage	22	388	372	156	90	246
Development	35	488	480	151	19	170
Mid MBO	38	1,511	1,458	130	39	169
Large MBO	29	4,353	4,167	143	41	185
Generalist	34	1,528	1,495	189	41	231
Total	*158*	*8,268*	*7,972*	*151*	*42*	*192*
UK	140	6,822	6,571	150	35	185
Non-UK	18	1,446	1,400	151	75	227
Europe	16	1,384	1,339	150	78	228
North America	2	62	62	177	27	204
Technology	36	656	633	164	67	231
Non-tech	122	7,612	7,339	149	40	189

[a] Source: BVCA Private Equity and Venture Capital Performance Measurement Survey 2000
[b] As a percentage of paid-in capital

three years, though this period was even shorter for buyout funds than for early-stage venture capital funds. Although the illiquidity of specific private equity investments and volatile cash flows can affect individual funds, from the institutional investor's perspective, a diversified portfolio has the potential to generate decent returns over the medium term.

The European private equity market is dominated by the UK's MBO/MBI market (Table 6.11). Of the €25.1 billion invested in 1999, 46% went to the UK. Buyouts accounted for €13.3 billion, or 53% of the total investments made, of which €8.7 billion went to the UK. The picture was similar in 2000 but was influenced by significantly lower buyout activity. Of the €34.9 billion invested in private equity, 38% went to the UK. Buyouts accounted for 41% of the investment, of which €6.9 billion went to the UK, and this was 48% of total buyout investment in Europe.[17] However, taking the size of the economy into account, the UK's investment in the private equity sector as a percentage of GDP trails behind that of Sweden and Iceland, although the UK is ahead of the rest of Europe. Europe's record of early-stage investment remains poor. There is a greater concentration of investment going in at the 'expansion' and 'buyout' stages rather than private equity investments providing a more even distribution of funding through all the stages.

In early-stage investing, the UK fared worse than its peer group in Europe. Early-stage investment per head ranked tenth in the EU and below the EU average in 1999.[18] According to Myners, the main reasons for this development were:[19]

- Initial UK experience with early-stage and particularly technology venture capital produced poor investment returns, leading to a migration of skills and investment capital away from this sector of the market. Higher returns from later-stage venture and MBO funds reinforced this as the focus of UK private equity development.
- The late development of the sector in Germany, Netherlands and Scandinavia may have enabled funds there to learn from the UK experience.
- The governments of these countries have also been active investors in programmes to commercialise technology emerging from

Table 6.11 *Private equity investment record in Europe[a]*

	1996	1997	1998	1999	2000	5-year total
Seed (%)	1.0	0.9	1.2	1.9	2.3	1.8
Start-up (%)	5.5	6.5	10.2	11.0	16.7	12.2
Expansion (%)	40.0	35.0	30.0	29.6	37.1	33.9
Replacement cap (%)	7.1	7.6	7.5	4.7	2.7	4.8
Buyout (%)	46.4	50.1	51.2	52.8	41.2	47.3
Total investment (€m)	6,788	9,655	14,461	25,116	34,986	91,005

[a] Source: EVCA Yearbook 2001

universities and public sector research laboratories. The greater role that the banking sector plays in these countries has also helped in supporting small and medium-sized enterprises to stimulate early-stage venture capital developments.

• Exit routes for venture capital investments improved substantially in the late 1990s with the creation of the Neuer Market in Germany; other new exchanges were set up across Europe, facilitating access to public markets by young, technology-based firms.

An analysis of the distribution of investments made within Europe in 2000 (Table 6.12) confirms that seed-capital and start-up investments in the UK lagged behind that of Ireland (50%), Belgium (47%), Austria (37%), Finland (35%), Norway (35%), Germany (35%), Iceland (27%), France (22%), Poland (21%), Netherlands (19%), Italy (18%), Spain (18%), Portugal (17%), Czech Republic (13%) and Denmark (12%).

In terms of divestment strategies for private equity investors in the UK, public offering was not the most popular exit route in 2000 (Table 6.13), although in 1999 divestment by IPOs accounted for almost 18% of exit options for investors and sale of quoted equity for an additional 8%. During 2000 a better exit strategy was offered by trade sales and repayment of principal loans. Write-offs as a divestment remained steady at 5% of the divestment amount during 1999 and 2000, although the ratio is much higher in terms of company numbers – 17–21% were write-offs.

Successful markets are all about liquidity, flexibility and transparency, which in turn attract successful companies seeking a listing. One explanation for the low representation of IT companies in the FTSE All Share index is that technology and other venture capital investments in the UK sought a listing in specialised exchanges that were set up to facilitate investment in that sector, such as the NASDAQ in the US. In Europe, EASDAQ (now taken over by NASDAQ) and the Euro-NM group did just that. The Neuer Markt (Frankfurt), Nouveau Marche (Paris), Nuevo Mercado (Madrid) and Nuovo Mercato (Milan) were all able to attract high-growth, high-tech companies. Many UK private equity financiers considered the London Stock Exchange (LSE) not sufficiently supportive of various

Table 6.12 Stage distribution of investments in Europe[a]

Country	Seed (%)	Start-up (%)	Expansion (%)	Replacement (%)	Buyout (%)	Total (€m)
Austria	7.1	29.8	54.2	0.0	8.9	163.1
Belgium	14.1	32.7	46.2	1.0	5.9	564.8
Czech Republic	0.0	12.9	71.4	15.7	0.0	121.5
Denmark	0.5	12.0	46.1	11.4	30.0	273.6
Finland	5.9	29.4	29.3	1.0	34.5	384.2
France	1.3	20.4	35.5	4.6	38.1	5,304.1
Germany	8.2	26.5	44.9	2.8	17.6	4,766.6
Greece	0.0	4.7	56.6	38.7	0.0	195.0
Hungary	2.1	1.2	56.2	0.0	40.5	51.3
Iceland	0.7	25.8	49.5	0.0	24.0	138.0
Ireland	0.7	49.3	44.9	2.5	2.7	223.4
Italy	4.4	13.7	32.6	3.3	45.9	2,968.5
Netherlands	0.0	19.4	54.5	7.4	18.6	1,916.5
Norway	1.8	33.4	63.2	0.1	1.5	296.1
Poland	1.4	19.3	78.3	1.0	0.0	201.6
Portugal	0.0	16.8	56.7	1.7	24.7	183.2
Spain	0.3	17.5	50.5	3.7	28.1	1,126.8
Sweden	1.2	8.7	14.5	0.1	75.5	2,299.8
Switzerland	0.4	8.9	20.0	2.0	68.7	626.4
UK	0.5	11.7	34.0	0.8	52.9	13,179.8
Total	2.3	16.7	37.1	2.7	41.2	34,985.8

[a] Source: EVCA Yearbook 2001

Table 6.13 Divestment strategies in the UK[a]

	2000			1999		
	Amount of divestment (%)	Number of divestments (%)	Number of companies (%)	Amount of divestment (%)	Number of divestments (%)	Number of companies (%)
Trade sale	24.4	22.4	22.4	22.1	27.5	26.1
Public offering	6.9	17.1	16.1	26.0	25.0	19.8
of which IPOs	2.9	4.2	4.2	17.8	2.6	2.1
Sale of quoted equity	4.0	12.9	11.9	8.2	22.4	17.7
Write-off	5.0	16.8	16.9	5.2	17.2	21.1
Repayment of principal loans	34.6	19.7	20.7	32.2	N/A	N/A
Sale to another venture capitalist	18.1	2.2	2.1	4.4	3.9	3.0
Sale to financial institutions	2.9	1.0	1.0	3.9	1.3	1.4
Other	8.0	20.9	20.9	6.2	25.1	28.5
Total	£2618.8m	1,226	1,167	£2283.4m	1,261	919

[a] Source: EVCA Yearbook 2001

candidates for flotation, thereby driving listings abroad, as was the case with Autonomy, Dialog Semiconductor and QXL, among others. The demutualisation and flotation of the LSE is therefore a move in the right direction, as the best UK technology companies have historically tended to take their business overseas. Many of the larger private equity investors in the UK experienced a lack of support from the LSE. The launch of the FTSE techMARK All Share index, along with the techMARK 100 index, has partly addressed exit strategies for nascent technology companies.

INVESTMENT PERFORMANCE

Due to the nature of private equity investment, it is important to look at medium-term returns when assessing individual managers as short-term returns can be influenced by a few attractive divestments or constrained by fresh investments. Private equity returns, being linked to public equity markets, tend to be cyclical. There is also a higher level of correlation with the performance of the small-cap sector. In fact, the peaks and troughs of the public equity market are magnified in the private equity sector, due to the illiquid nature of the asset class. Returns from buyout funds, which are linked to valuations at both entry and exit, are directly based on the valuation level of the public equity market. However, 'skilled and highly motivated private equity managers, given discretion over sector, stock selection timing of investment, and able to play an active role in the strategic development of investee companies, have shown themselves capable of generating good returns over a medium-term horizon.'[20]

This is illustrated in the net annualised returns from UK managed private equity funds raised between 1980 and 1996, whose returns have been calculated up to the end of 2000. UK private equity outperformed public equity markets over 1, 3, 5 and 10 year periods. The overall net return to investors since inception, up to the end of 2000, was 16.4% per annum. Over the past 10 years, private equity outperformed UK equity returns within UK pension funds by a margin of 510 basis points on annual returns; over five years this margin rose to 1,260 basis points and over three years to 1,880 basis points (Table 6.14). In making such comparisons, remember that the return quoted for private equity funds is the internal rate of return

Table **6.14** *Performance of key asset classes within UK pension funds (% per year)[a]*

	2000	3 years	5 years	10 years
UK equities	−4.1	10.1	13.8	15.3
Overseas equities	−6.7	15.1	11.0	14.2
UK bonds	9.4	9.2	10.2	11.9
Overseas bonds	14.6	6.7	3.9	10.1
UK index-linked	4.3	9.5	9.8	9.4
Cash	11.5	8.5	7.8	8.6
Property	10.1	12.3	12.3	8.9
Total assets	−1.3	10.9	12.0	13.6
Total UK private equity	25.6	28.9	26.4	20.4
Margin of outperformance[b]	29.7	18.8	12.6	5.1

[a] Source: BVCA Private Equity and Venture Capital Performance Measurement Survey 2000
[b] Between UK private equity and UK equities

(IRR) to investors, net of costs and fees. Returns for the pension fund universes and indexes of company WM are gross, time-weighted returns. The WM All Funds universe represented over 75% of the UK segregated pension fund industry and consisted of over 1,200 funds in 2000 with total assets valued at more than $527 billion.

UK private equity also comfortably outperformed all the relevant equity indexes over one, three, five and ten year periods (Table 6.15).

Table **6.15** *Performance of private equity versus select indices (% per year)[a]*

	2000	3 years	5 years	10 years
FTSE All Share	−5.9	10.0	13.9	15.4
FTSE 100	−8.2	9.1	14.3	15.5
FTSE Small Cap	5.5	14.3	13.5	14.3
FTSE 250	4.0	13.9	13.6	16.2
FTSE World (ex UK)	−4.1	15.5	13.2	15.1
FTSE Europe (ex UK)	1.7	17.0	17.9	17.7
Total UK private equity	25.6	28.9	26.4	20.4

[a] Source: BVCA Private Equity and Venture Capital Performance Measurement Survey 2000

As one-year returns tend to be volatile for all asset classes, the emphasis has been placed on long-term performance figures to arrive at a more realistic picture of the returns on investments made in various asset classes.

However, this overall performance of private equity funds masks variation during the years in which funds were raised (known as the 'vintage year' in the industry) as much as by investment type and individual skill of the fund manager. There is also significant divergence in returns available between the various stages of the investment cycle (Table 6.16). In the UK, the buyout and generalist sectors of the industry outperformed early-stage and development sectors over the long term. However, the past five years witnessed a sharp improvement in returns from early-stage investments. In the 1990s, the margin of outperformance that private equity developed over public equity was largely driven by sustained high average performance of the MBO segment. Non-UK investments also delivered superior returns to investments in the UK and the technology sector outperformed non-technology investments.

Table 6.16 *UK private equity returns by investment stage (% per year)*[a]

	No. of funds	2000	3 years	5 years	10 years
Early stage	47	78.9	48.8	41.3	24.5
Development	48	−0.5	15.6	21.4	14.2
Mid MBO	54	22.8	17.0	17.6	18.0
Large MBO	47	26.6	27.6	25.2	21.4
Generalist	48	13.6	42.9	34.0	20.9
Total	244	25.6	28.9	26.4	20.4
UK	205	13.6	23.1	23.9	19.8
Non-UK	39	47.6	41.1	32.1	22.2
Technology	60	78.3	47.7	37.5	22.4
Non-tech	184	21.5	27.2	25.3	20.1
Very large MBO	22	33.2	33.6	29.6	23.3
Investment trusts	21	17.0	33.5	25.5	19.9

[a] Source: BVCA Private Equity and Venture Capital Performance Measurement Survey 2000

It is worth comparing the returns made by the US private equity sector to highlight the differences in investing skills and emphasis on early-stage venture financing (Table 6.17). Early-stage venture capital funds in the US delivered excellent returns, 47.9% over a 3-year period and 46.6% over a 5-year period. The average return for all venture capital funds was 33.7% over a 3-year period and 35.2% over a 5-year period. Over a 10-year period, returns were lower but similar to the return for UK private equity funds over that period. While the US has excelled in early-stage financing, the UK has done much better with buyouts.

The cyclical nature of private equity investment impacts on its overall performance. As with investing in public equity markets, the timing of the investment can influence returns. Thus, 10-year overall annual private equity return for UK funds raised in 1990 was 12.3% compared with 26.5% for funds raised in 1989 and 20.8% for funds raised in 1988. Since inception to December 2000, the best year to invest in UK private equity was 1994, when returns have been 36.9% per annum. The worst year was 1987, with annual returns registering 8.3%. Thus, the range of return varies according to investment stage and vintage year. Over 5 years, for example, 1994 had the strongest performance, returning 45.2% per annum. The best-performing vintage year was 1985, returning 85.6% per annum over a 3-year period, while 1992 showed the poorest return at 13.6%, though this was ahead of the WM total pension fund return

Table 6.17 *US private equity returns: net IRR (%) per year to end of September 1999*[a]

	1 year	3 year	5 year	10 year
Early/seed	91.2	47.9	46.6	24.5
Balanced	50.2	28.2	30.1	18.5
Later stage	55.5	28.4	34.8	25.4
All venture	62.5	33.7	35.2	20.8
Buyout funds	15.2	16.6	16.7	16.7
Mezzanine debt	15.3	9.5	10.6	10.6
All private equity	28.7	22.3	22.7	18.4

[a] Source: NVCA Yearbook 2000

of 10.9% per annum and the FTSE All Share and FTSE 100 returns of 10.0% and 9.1% respectively.

The performance of the top 10% of the funds in the survey over a 10-year period was 31.4% per annum with higher returns from early-stage (38.4%), mid MBO (35%), large MBO (56.9%) and non-UK (38.2%). However, the bottom 10% of the funds delivered significantly poor returns: -12.0% per annum in total and similar losses for investments in early-stage (-12.1%), development (-15.3%), generalist (-13.2%), mid MBO (-7.4%), UK (-12.4%), non-UK (-6.7%), technology (-11.0%) and large MBO (0.5%). Thus, the bottom 10% of funds performed badly in all sectors. The range of returns by vintage year, over a 10-year period, is also revealing. Out of the top 10% of the funds surveyed, 1985 was the best year (IRR 55.4%) followed by 1987 (IRR 49.4%). However, the bottom 10% of the funds in 1985 delivered a loss of -65.3% per annum, and the figure for the bottom 10% of funds surveyed for 1987 was 0.6%.[21] This clearly illustrates the need for manager selection and manager diversification.

UK private equity failed to outperform other UK asset classes during the 1980s and early 1990s. This was also the period when returns from UK private equity significantly lagged US private equity returns. The overall net annual IRR of the private equity industry in the US has been 17.6% over the past 20 years. The dispersion in the rate of return between the various categories was small: buyout funds returned 19.3% and early-stage venture funds returned 18.9%.[22] With the exception of 1987, the FTSE All Share index outperformed annual private equity returns every year until 1993. From 1993 onwards, annual returns from private equity investments exceeded the FTSE All Share returns. By 1998 the cumulative average annual returns for private equity investments overtook those of the FTSE All Share for the first time, using 1987 as a base year.[23] This gap in performance increased further during 1998 and 1999. For the year ending 1999, 10-year annual returns from the FTSE All Share were 14.9% while for private equity they were 20.0%. Individual funds delivered even higher returns. This trend continued into 2000, with a 10-year annual return of 15.4% for the FTSE All Share and 20.4% for private equity.[24]

As with any other business, the key to maximising return depends on the ability of the manager to buy assets when they are given a low value and in selling them when they are in great demand. Venture capital funds are able to do this better as to some extent they are able to operate outside the market. Thus, a large bulk of their early-stage investments are treated as 'bags of assets' whose true value is realised over time, usually at a large premium to their present carrying value. However, in reality, these companies are live enterprises with specialised skills and unusual business dynamics. Therefore they have a future value as investments that are capable of generating ongoing returns, most of the time significantly ahead of their original cost of capital. It can be argued that in some cases the present embedded value is being bought at a discount (or sometimes at a small premium) and the appraisal value or the future value is a bonus.

THE ECONOMIC IMPACT OF PRIVATE EQUITY

In the US, where venture capital is regarded more as a mainstream asset class and a key driver in raising productivity and economic growth, the success of the sector has begun to attract attention across the rest of the developed world. In a report entitled *The Opportunity in Private Equity Funds*, Paul Gompras and Joshua Lerner of Harvard University estimated that US private equity capital firms as a group created $2 trillion of value over the past two decades. They highlighted three key factors driving this value addition: the acceleration of technological innovation, development of exit routes (via access to public markets for new stock offerings) and a growing pool of managerial talent opting for the entrepreneurial work environment; in brief, a willingness to take risk and not be deterred by failure. Thus, the growth in the asset class has been a virtuous cycle: 'the growth in activity of the venture capital industry has enhanced the conditions that drive the long-run value creation of this capital, which has in turn led to more capital formation.'[25]

It has been widely recognised that private equity financing and the resulting business development process supports overall economic growth by enabling structural change and redeploying capital rapidly to new businesses in new sectors.[26] The relationship between economic growth and overall business entrepreneurship has long been established. For a niche activity, private-equity-backed enterprises appear to have a significant impact on national productivity gains, employment creation and technology diffusion. Various UK surveys estimate that only 9% of small and medium-sized enterprises (SMEs) sought venture finance during 1995–97 and less than 5% obtained it. Venture capital consisted of just over 3% of total external finance obtained by SMEs. Twice as many firms received external finance from alternative private sources, such as family, friends and business angels.[27]

Theory suggests that equity financing is the most expensive form of funding for growing ventures, and most entrepreneurs do have concerns about the possible dilution and attendant loss of control.[28] But sound venture capitalists also provide mentoring and networking support to investee companies. There is evidence to suggest that investee firms value private equity investors primarily for their role as a sounding board for ideas, for challenging the status quo, providing financial advice, and for corporate strategy and direction.[29] According to the *Global Entrepreneurship Monitor* (GEM), sponsored by Apax Partners, the UK ranked behind America, Canada and Israel in terms of entrepreneurship but was ahead of France, Germany, Italy and Japan. This report identified four variables that drive entrepreneurial activity and the UK was ranked accordingly: [30]

- The perception of opportunities
- The capacity of the population to be entrepreneurial
- The infrastructure supportive of enterprise in the country
- Attitudes towards entrepreneurs

Entrepreneurship is defined by this report as 'any attempt at new business or new venture creation, such as self-employment, a new business organisation, or the expansion of an existing business, by an individual, a team of individuals or an established business.' On that count, of the 10 countries included in the report (G7 countries Canada, France, Germany, Italy, Japan, US and UK plus Denmark, Finland and Israel) efforts to initiate new business were the lowest in Finland (1 in 67 adults, or 1.4%) and highest in the US (1 in 12, or 8.4%). While measures of competitiveness and entrepreneurship may vary, sizeable differences in ease of business formation and protection of investors do exist among OECD countries.

The GEM report also suggested that variation in the rates of entrepreneurship accounts for as much as one-third of the variation in economic growth. There are no countries with high levels of start-up rates and low levels of economic growth. It is probably appropriate to assume that one-third of national economic growth is related to the activities of established firms, one-third to the entrepreneurial sector and the rest to the interaction between these two sectors.[31] In the highly entrepreneurial economies – US, Canada and Israel – new business creation was an integral and accepted feature of both economic and personal life.[32] The study also revealed that UK attitudes are among the least supportive of entrepreneurs and that respect for innovators is lower in the UK than in any country except Japan. Most pressing issues for the UK are inherent in the cultural and social norms, which tend to be anti-enterprise, and in the education system, where entrepreneurship is not encouraged. Other relevant issues for the UK include low levels of technology transfer and underdeveloped networks between entrepreneurs, potential entrepreneurs and resource providers.[33] According to Ronald Cohen, chairman of Apax Partners:

> Beyond maintaining sound management of the economy, the Government can improve the UK perception of opportunities by maintaining a stance that is clearly free market, pro-competition, anti-regulation and pro-small and growth business.

> The entrepreneurial capacity of the population must be increased by lower taxes on capital gains and stock options, to encourage the perception that work and risk taking deserve financial reward. It is also increased by teaching entrepreneurial skills as part of a normal education, making it easier to consider starting a business successfully in adulthood.

> But perhaps one of the most telling conclusions is that the right entrepreneurial infrastructure must also be in place, if substantial numbers of companies are to be created. This infrastructure comprises access to capital (i.e. 'angels', venture capitalists, stockmarkets, banks and specialist government-sponsored institutions), technology clusters, companies and centres of higher learning, and programmes to channel government R&D expenditure to innovative smaller companies. There is still a lot to achieve in the UK in comparison with the USA.[34]

Indeed, the UK has a long way to go before it can think of itself as the fifty-first US state, although some commentators do refer to the City as 'a branch office of New York with no control over its destiny.'[35] If that is the case, only the City of London has itself to blame. For Philip Augur, the amateurish nature of management before the 1986 Big Bang was a contributing factor in the death of gentlemanly capitalism. Gordon Brown, UK Chancellor of the Exchequer, has plans to free business by promoting enterprise and competition; nevertheless, there are still major differences between the UK and the US. It is true that the chancellor has already made a few changes; freeing the Bank of England was a revolutionary step forward for a Labour government in the conduct of monetary policy. But the US and German central banks were already doing that. The UK government's reductions in the long-term rate of capital gains tax and the introduction of tax-advantaged stock option schemes are perhaps the most noteworthy changes made in the last few years. The US has cultivated four important attributes over several decades, but these things are still lacking in the UK, the rest of Europe and various other parts of the world:[36]

- Immigration: 45% of US employment growth in the 1990s has been through immigrants
- University–business link: the best and brightest go into business
- Shared compensation and decision-making
- Ease of bankruptcy and access to venture capital financing

In the modern world, where capital, products, raw materials and ideas are being exchanged on a global basis, labour markets have remained excessively restrained by governments. Even data on international migration of labour is not easily available. In 1996, global exports of goods accounted for 29% of the world's gross domestic product. But total global migrant stock rose from 75 million in 1965 to 120 million in 1990 (or 2.3% of the world's population), 1.9% annual growth compared with 1.8% population growth (Table 6.18). Economic migration is frowned upon in the UK and the rest of Europe, and the entrepreneurial spirit of the economic migrant is also looked down upon, although 39% of UK employers recently reported that their business performance was being affected by severe shortages of skilled labour. It is important, therefore, to put labour migration into measurable context.

Table **6.18** *Countries with foreign workers:
percentage of workforce in 1999*[a]

Australia	24.8%
Canada	19.2%
Switzerland	17.3%
US	11.7%
Austria	9.9%
Germany	9.1%
Belgium	8.8%
France	6.1%
Sweden	5.1%
UK	3.9%

[a] Source: OECD

A recent discussion paper issued by the Paris-based Organisation for Economic Cooperation and Development (OECD) emphasises the benefits to be had from a more open labour migration policy. About 30% of software engineers in California's Silicon Valley are estimated to be of Indian origin and over 750 companies in that region are run by professionals from India. Not only has the US economy benefited from this migration, India's IT exports have risen from a mere $150 million in 1990 to around $4 billion in 2000. And in 1996, home remittances by India's overseas workers totalled $7.6 billion, an amount significantly higher than foreign direct investment into India. The US is the largest export destination of India's IT services. During the 1990s, Indians made up more than one-third of total immigrants admitted to the US who became permanent residents, and they also accounted for more than 15% of the temporary workforce in specialised occupations.[37]

It is not surprising that venture investments in the US are concentrated in California, accounting for 45% of total US venture investment in 2000, followed by Greater New York (17%), New England (15%), and the Mid-Atlantic (6%).[38] These are also the areas of higher concentration of Indian communities in the US. It is not just supportive of Indian professionals but professionals from across the world. In the UK, private equity investment is concentrated in London and the South East. Having symbiotic relationships in a network of professional executives, advisers and investors within the same area is essential to the nurturing of entrepreneurs. In Europe there is no single innovation hotbed; Benelux, Ireland, Germany and Scandinavia lead the way as early-stage investment regions. Private equity investments are more evenly dispersed when compared to the US or the UK. However, investing on a pan-European basis is not common. Also, overseas workers have not contributed to or participated in the growth of venture investments in the UK and the rest of Europe, although skilled IT workers do comprise one of the largest components of the overseas labour force.

On the link between universities and business, here too the US model is quite different than the UK model. For a start, academics in the US are significantly better paid, at least in certain disciplines. While academics don't always do it for the money, universities in the UK are under increasing pressure to retain their key brains. The concept of 'collegiality', which underpins the academic system in the UK, conflicts directly with the market model. The concept of a market rate of pay in academia is fraught with difficulties, although the discriminatory, market-driven pay practice is centuries old and has been prevalent in most parts of the world. At Magdalen College, Oxford, the theologian lector was paid twice as much as the logician, and half as much as the lectors in moral and natural philosophy in 1481. Today lecturers in business studies would command a significantly higher salary than an English don. According to Professor Anthony Hopwood, director of the Said Business School in Oxford: 'If you pay people a percentage from the core activities of a university, whether through full-time course fees or research grants, you make universities into very calculating places. Universities need a cooperative ethos to generate ideas.' Fostering that net of intellectual relationships is what matters, and if individuals become entrepreneurs, seeking competitive advantage, the net can easily break.[39] The key lies in building bridges between the source of funding and a stimulating environment for the generation of ideas.

Due to the increase in the amount of funds seeking higher private equity returns and the creation of an artificial scarcity of skilled private equity expertise, the average size of private equity deals has gone up in the UK. As private equity managers are rewarded in such a way that investing larger funds with the potential to deliver higher returns is more remunerative, it is not surprising there has been an incentive to maintain the status quo rather than share that largesse with, for example, academic institutions which are crying out for funding. While financial engineering may be one of their requirements, venture investments need a lot more expertise than just that. One of the key factors driving the success of the sector in the US has been the role of scientists, engineers, doctors, academics and entrepreneurs whose networks and mentoring skills are invaluable to a young firm.[40] Compared to the US, fewer new firms have entered the UK private equity market from technology and industry backgrounds. And the links between business and academia are not as strong as in the US. Ironically, instead of strengthening such links, this has encouraged UK institutional investment in US venture funds rather than in domestic funds.

When assessing the performance of private-equity-backed firms, it is important to distinguish between venture capital and MBO/MBI activity. As finance is applied to investee companies at different stages in their development cycle, it creates different opportunities and challenges when realising their potential. MBO/MBI activity has come to dominate the UK private equity sector, responsible for taking some 75% of total investment in 1999 and 71% in 2000. While it helps businesses to restructure, it does not necessarily ensure the sustainability of returns. A more competitive corporation transactions market (where more deals are auctioned) in an overall environment where substantial restructuring is the norm, this has not been the ideal means of value addition to the investee companies, which demand a greater diversity of expertise among private equity managements. However, buyouts do create value in the investee company rather than simply transferring it to the investors.[41]

A stable macroeconomic environment plays a vital role in supporting the private equity market as it encourages greater risk-taking among investors. If the macroeconomic environment is uncertain or difficult, there is a natural investment flight to safety or quality. In the US, greater economic stability and the strength of the market during the mid to late 1990s did act as a spur to greater risk-taking by venture capitalists. Pension funds, endowments and other investors were also more willing to accommodate the higher risk associated with private equity. The greater uncertainty currently inherent in the global economic environment has resulted in significantly lower investments in private equity as in all other risky asset classes, including public equity. The other factor worth considering when assessing the higher exposure to venture capital among US pensions is their size. US pension funds are typically larger than their UK counterparts. US venture capital funds are also larger than their European counterparts. In fact, there were some 19 venture capital funds in the US that were over $1 billion in 2000. There are some 65 pension funds in the US with assets over $15 billion, but less than 15 UK funds of comparable size. Larger pension funds may have greater propensity to invest in private equity as they have more management resources at their disposal and a higher capability to bear risk.[42] However, trustees of pension funds in the US also played a critical role in investing early into the private equity cycle.

Trustees and their advisers in the UK need to play such a role by considering a full range of investment opportunities, including private equity. The decision to invest in private equity is made at the strategic asset allocation level, so it requires greater investment of time and resources into the asset allocation decision process. An overall, liability-related investment objective is more conducive to private equity investment than a peer group benchmark or an asset allocation driven by a statistical modelling process. Ensuring that decisions are made by those best placed to make them will assist specialist asset classes. Efforts to involve a wider range of advisers with specialist skills will encourage pension fund trustees to obtain quality advice on the role of private equity and its application, thereby boosting the demand for information services in the private equity market. Replacing MFR with an approach based on transparency and disclosure would remove a bias towards the reference assets used to calculate MFR funding; at present, this disadvantages investment in private equity. More knowledgeable trustees working in a more business-like fashion with more in-house staff would be better placed to understand the specific issues raised by private equity.[43] As with other asset classes unfamiliar to trustees of pension funds, there is a lag between recognising the opportunity and acquiring the necessary expertise in deploying that investment. Both trustees and their consultants now realise that private equity offers a genuine diversification strategy.

BARRIERS TO INVESTING

While it cannot be denied that private equity is a powerful form of financing in stimulating wider economic growth, it is still only relevant to the establishment or development of a minority of companies with the potential for delivering rapid growth. Of the total 750,000 companies in the UK, only 1,100 (0.15%) received private equity funding in 2000. More UK companies are likely to have secured informal venture financing from business angels, estimated at about 5,000.[44] Interestingly enough, in 2000 some 6,495 companies across Europe received 'initial' investments by venture capitalists, a 25% rise over 1999. And the number of companies in Europe that received 'follow-on' investment rose from 3,320 in 1999 to 3,945 in 2000, a 19% increase.[45] While early-stage financing has been improving in Europe, historically it has been more developed in the US. Around 3,600 companies in the US received venture financing in 1999, a rise from 2,500 firms in 1997 and 1,200 companies annually in the early 1990s. Estimates suggest that about 250,000 angels invest some $10–20 billion each year in the US in over 30,000 ventures.[46]

According to the Myners Report, barriers to institutional investment in private equity can be classified under five distinct headings:[47]

- Perception of UK private equity performance
- Quality of performance information
- Independent information sources
- Costs of private equity investment
- Regulatory constraints

The rise in funding level to the sector during the later half of the 1990s was a source of concern to investors as increased funding does not automatically translate to a matching increase in demand from entrepreneurs able to meet the rising expectations of private equity investors. In short, delivering returns in a market that suffers from a high level of asset inflation and expectation is not feasible. Institutional investors have therefore been concerned about the extent to which the economies of the UK, Europe and particularly the US could continue to absorb the increased funds allocated to this asset class in recent years, and invest them productively, as has also been the case with the public equity markets. The poor showing in the 1980s and early 1990s contributed to the overall scepticism associated with the ability of private equity managers in the UK. However, recent performance data over a 10-year period has allayed such concerns.

The lack of clarity in differentiating between the various stages of private equity investing may not have helped either. This is further exacerbated by the fact that there has been no comprehensive, readily accessible and independently audited reporting on the absolute performance of UK private equity funds. Thus, arriving at an independent judgement on the comparative strength of the individual manager concerned becomes a subjective affair, as most private equity managers would understandably claim to deliver top-quartile performance. In the UK, the WM Company produces an annual performance measurement survey in conjunction with the BVCA and Westport Private Equity, based on the returns of the BVCA members. The voluntary and unaudited nature of these returns has led some institutions to question the validity of the results. It has made comparison between the various subsectors both difficult and unreliable.

Making a decision under such circumstances involves the sort of risk that no trustee in the UK would like to take, at least voluntarily. Trustees are legendary for their aversion to risk. However, many reject the view that the trustees of pension funds, who ultimately determine where their members' money is invested, are as risk-averse as they are portrayed to be. Phillips & Drew surveyed 202 big pension schemes; it found 31% of them had invested in venture capital and 32% would do so if they could find the right projects to back. The National Association of Pension Funds (NAPF) is also of the opinion that there is a shortage of home-grown entrepreneurial talent. Speaking in response to Prime Minister Tony Blair's call in July 1999 for pension funds to boost their investment in venture capital, Dr Ann Robinson, NAPF's director general, pointed out that UK pension funds are unable to invest as much as they want in the sector because they cannot find enough worthwhile opportunities.[48] In another speech to the International Centre for Business Information, in Frankfurt, she pointed out that 'a robust, variegated and competitive private equity capital industry is essential if pension funds are to be attracted to and to invest in private equity.... It cannot be stressed too often that a strong supply of money into private equity and venture capital from pension funds is dependent on the existence of a robust private equity and venture capital industry.'[49]

Trustees would like their investment consultants to help in establishing a private equity portfolio. However, the advisory and fund management contracts operated by many pension funds have historically tended to produce generalist mandates. When decision-makers are heavily dependent on their advisers, no one in this situation has a clear mandate for taking decisive action or changing direction. According to the Myners Report:

> Trustees tend to feel that they lack the expertise to do so, and advisers that they lack the power to make decisions. The result can easily be inertia. Investment in private equity by pension funds is probably an example of this. Trustees have tended not to consider investing in the asset class because it was not raised as a possibility by their advisers, and advisers in turn say that they have not recommended investment in private equity because trustees have not been interested in it.[50]

There is no peer group pressure as there is among the larger pension funds in the US. Also, trustees in the UK do not have the resources to invest in the necessary due diligence process. Most importantly, private equity is not part of any benchmark against which they ultimately measure their own performance, not just the performance of their managers. It is true that the benchmark is created by the trustees, but they tend to use indexed, scheme-specific or peer group benchmarks, and in none of these benchmarks does private equity appear. However attractive may be the return from an asset class, if it is not reflected in the benchmark or index there can be high penalties for investing outside the prescribed parameter. And considering that long-term returns from private equity investments were not particularly attractive just a few years ago, it is understandable why trustees shied away from taking such risks.

The lack of transparency in the reported statements by private equity managers is also the reason for investor concerns over the product pricing. Institutional investors share strong concerns about the costs of investing in private equity, which like hedge funds incur not only fixed annual management charges but also a performance-related fee, over which most pension fund managers seem to have little influence. Greater transparency may help to alleviate this concern, if applied across the board from performance measurement to the 'carried interest' parameter in the sharing of returns between investors and the private equity firm. While no regulatory constraint per se is imposed on pension funds and their ability to invest in private equity, the introduction of the MFR acted as a barrier for many trustees in their asset allocation decision. The illiquidity of private equity, the lack of adequate pricing mechanisms as well as exit strategies, not to mention the extra costs involved, all act as deterrents to investing in the asset class. Investing in limited partnerships for pension funds raises additional issues under the Financial Services Act 1986 and its updated version, the Financial Services and Markets Act 2000. Under the 2000 act, trustees themselves must become authorised to engage in investment activity or they must appoint an authorised person to act on their behalf. As consultants continue to operate outside the remit of the Financial Services Authority (FSA), trustees have to bear an additional cost in complying with such a structure. Changes to this act were recommended by the Myners Report and were accepted in the 2000 pre-Budget report. Thus, where an investment is made in a limited partnership solely for the purpose of investing that money in private equity investments, it is exempt from the prohibition in the act on unauthorised persons engaging in investment activity.[51]

According to the Myners Report:

The most serious drawback for institutional investors in private equity limited partnerships is the uncertain legal status of limited partners engaged in overseeing investment activity. This is often a requirement for institutions, but there are concerns among private equity lawyers that such activity may be deemed to be management of the limited partnership, which could expose institutions to legal risk. The other drawback of UK limited partnerships is the 20-partner limit: in the US the limit is 500. Private equity funds often need to establish parallel partnerships at some legal cost in order to take investments from more than 20 investors. So the current legal restriction serves only to raise business costs without in practice adhering to the obscure historical rationale for a 20-partner limit.[52]

Insurance companies also have tax considerations and regulatory hurdles to overcome when investing in private equity limited partnerships. Partners including life insurance firms are taxed on their individual share of the income and gain of the underlying assets. Thus, any change in the partnership can trigger a tax liability even though no cash gain is realised. Apart from generating a tax compliance liability, it is a financial burden for the life insurance firms, especially the smaller ones. The Myners Report also recommended a change in the taxation of capital gains on insurance companies' limited partnership investments by moving from taxation based on capital gains at partnership level to taxation of the gains as distributed from the fund.[53]

FSA rules for 'with profits' life funds also specify that no more than 1% of assets be invested in a single unquoted security, such as a limited partnership interest in a private equity investment, and that the total exposure to unquoted investments should not exceed 10% of the fund's assets. While these requirements do not prevent life insurance companies from investing in private equity, they do create the need for greater monitoring of these investments, purely for the purpose of better compliance. Investment in private equity or unquoted securities by pooled investment vehicles is also restricted to 10% of the fund's assets. However, the true obstacle is the lack of liquidity as it impacts on the pricing of the pooled vehicle product. Investment trusts are in a better position to invest in private equity. Considering the global remit of private equity investments today, the Myners Report also recommends that regulatory bodies, such as the FSA, develop 'a centre of expertise'[54] in the asset class.

The EVCA believes that much remains to be done to help develop Europe's entrepreneurial potential. Policy-makers could facilitate the creation of an entrepreneurial environment in many ways:[55]

- More entrepreneurial-related education
- Harmonisation of registration of intellectual property and licensing rights
- More flexible labour and entrepreneurship environments (less bureaucracy for company formation, adapted bankruptcy laws, etc.)

- Favourable treatments of stock options for those who choose to work in smaller, non-listed companies

CONCLUSION

As an alternative investment class, private equity funds like hedge funds have significant barriers to overcome in accessing a wider pool of funds. The main constraints relate to issues surrounding liquidity, costs, performance and transparency. While the retail investor may have had limited opportunities for investing in private equity, the government has taken steps in promoting such investments. One of the key attractions for private investors in venture capital trusts is the tax benefit attached to investing in such vehicles. Investors get upfront income tax relief of 20% up to £100,000 a year. Such investments also enable the deferral of 40% of capital gains tax on gains reinvested. In effect, for each £100 invested in venture capital, there is a rebate of £20 and an interest-free loan of £40. The only catch in securing these tax breaks was that the investment had to be held for a minimum period of five years, reduced to 3 years in April 2000 for those investors who apply for shares at the primary placing. On top of all these incentives, dividends are tax-free as are gains on the sale of the venture capital trust (VCT) shares. Since 1980 well over 200 VCTs have been launched in the UK, many of which have focused on technology-related ventures.

However, the nature of private equity funding is such that liquidity is a key constraint for all types of investor. As with traded portfolios, the starting point for risk management of private equity portfolios is risk measurement. However, standard 'value at risk' techniques are meaningless when applied to private equity portfolios. The key issue is liquidity; for unlisted investments, the opportunities to buy or sell a position are both difficult and expensive. If a price cannot be attached to an investment and marked periodically, then assessing its risk, volatility, standard deviation, correlation, etc., is meaningless. Also, return distributions in private equity portfolios tend to be highly skewed, determined by the exit strategies used. Hence private equity funds are considered highly risky and perhaps not for orphans and widows. For long-term institutional investors, on the other hand, such vehicles can be the ideal high-risk, high-return investment alternative.

If the private equity sector is keen to enhance its influence in the market, organisations such as the BVCA and the EVCA need to step up their efforts in educating potential investors about the role and contribution of private equity to the growth of the economy. At the same time, for an enterprising culture to take root, risk-taking should not be punished or failure should not be stigmatised. It is better to have taken a few risks in life and failed rather than not to have taken any risks at all. In fact, the very act of investing involves taking a few calculated risks. The boom in private equity investing during the late 1990s, unfortunately, did not foster a spirit of true enterprise. It rewarded deal-making rather than nurturing innovativion. Nor did it have an impact on overall job creation in the economy, as a large proportion of venture capital investments backed small enterprises employing family and friends.

However, in the modern world, commercialism is often confused with enterprise. Innovativion and risk-taking are not necessarily linked to a commercial mindset. Understanding the commercial opportunity of a research-driven innovation and recognising what it takes to move innovation from the laboratory to the marketplace are two distinct skills, and they are rarely found together. Bill Gates may not be an exception, but he is definitely not the rule. What society needs is the ability to utilise equitably the totality of skills available in the economy on a global scale. Thus, societies that have the capacity to accommodate the volatility and turbulence involved with entrepreneurship by continually replenishing the stock of new firms, ideas, people and jobs, these are the societies best able to compete effectively in the constantly changing global marketplace.

CHAPTER 7

Socially Responsible Investing

INTRODUCTION

Whether we are Warren Buffett, a trustee of a pension fund in the UK or a housewife in Japan, we are all involved in allocating capital, some of us more efficiently than others. The Taj Mahal and the Sistine Chapel, Oxford and Harvard, Microsoft and Genetically Modified (GM) foods are as much the products of our imagination and aspiration as of a conscious business decision. Regardless of which group of people influence the investment process – governments, non-governmental organisations (NGOs), multinational companies (MNCs), banks, insurance companies, pension funds, private investors – we all share the legacy, albeit unequally, as the spate of floods, cyclones, droughts and earthquakes in some of the poorest parts of the world illustrate. However, the events of 11 September 2001 in the US confirmed that the world's richest nation is all too vulnerable to terrorist attacks. The ramifications of an attack on the twin towers of capitalism and freedom may yet change the world. If the loss of lives on that day brings global understanding of social, ethical, environmental (SEE) issues and with it greater cooperation among nations in addressing such issues, then the terrorists will be marginalised. But if it ushers in division among nations, then the terrorists will continue to prevail. Thus, there exists a clear choice that, as enlightened human beings, we should be capable of making.

As international capital flows have a significant impact on development, the environment and ultimately the kind of society we create, it has become increasingly important to examine our priorities in investing and gauge its long-term impact on societies around the world. The price of globalisation is greater engagement in issues such as poverty, education, health and the environment on a global basis. Unfortunately, concerted involvement has not been forthcoming, although many companies have extended their activities globally. Over the past decade, many MNCs appear to have enriched themselves and their shareholders significantly, but left the job of implementing the SEE agenda to governments and other NGOs. Environmentally responsible and socially inclusive wealth creation has not been the forte of MNCs. This is not to suggest that corporate social responsibility (CSR) and socially responsible investment (SRI) are new concepts or new problems. The Universal Declaration of Human Rights goes back to 1948 and in 1976 the OECD Guidelines for Multinational Enterprises was adopted by 33 countries.[1] These guidelines cover a wide range of issues, including disclosure, employment and industrial relations, environment, bribery, consumer interests, science and technology, competition and taxation.

However, developed countries have not invested adequately in the monitoring of CSR or SRI issues. In developing countries, investment in people and public services has been poor. Mismanagement, corruption and internecine warfare resulted in the squandering away of meagre financial resources. Poor people across the globe have not had a stake in wealth creation. On the contrary, environmental degradation, decline in public services and social welfare – in many cases the non-existence of public services and social welfare – along with the lack of opportunity in general to improve their lot has dented their confidence in the efficacy of global markets. Shareholders recognise the urgent need for a 'new development architecture' to match the new global financial system. But they do not have an effective mechanism for implementing it. The International Monetary Fund (IMF) and the World Bank claim integration of concepts of equity and sustainability to ensure development and the alleviation of poverty in their funding policies. The openness revolution and the anti-globalisation backlash have brought such hallowed institutions' poverty reduction mission under intense global scrutiny - and it has been found wanting.

Institutional investors as well as private investors, in constructing efficient portfolios, aim to maximise return at any given level of risk. In doing so, they fulfil their fiduciary duty. While investment return is easy to measure, there is a lack of consensus in the definition of risk, simply because risk is defined individually. Besides, institutional investors have no mechanism through which they can factor in the rise in global poverty, environmental degradation or violation of basic human rights as a direct risk to the businesses they invest in. Most investors also do not have access to the required information to be able to quantify such a risk, in any meaningful way, into their asset allocation decisions; although they agree that an integrated SEE and financial vision is greatly in need. Corporate reports do not include a proper assessment of non-financial risks they may be exposed to. While insurance may cover some of the non-quantifiable risks as far as the company is concerned, it is by no means clear to what extent an investor may be exposed to them.

Lack of relevant data remains a significant barrier to our ability to value things. GDP, the most visible economic statistic, is the sum of an economy's money transactions, but it does not reflect broader economic health, welfare or environmental issues. While some countries are producing 'satellite accounts', measuring housework, social work and the environmental impact of activity, there is little evidence yet that such statistics have any impact on policy. At the micro level, the list of most balance sheet's blind spots are impressive: they seldom include brand values or account for intangible assets relating to research and development (R&D) and related intellectual capital, and certainly never provide a capitalised value for human assets or for enterprise value. Annual reports fail to account for stakeholder relationships that underpin a company's long-term sustainability as an economic entity and consequently fail to disclose the true sources of corporate value as measured by the stock market.[2] There is no reason why such evaluation should not be undertaken more rigorously. Bridging the existing gap in the evaluation of social and environmental issues within financial analysis in the investment process is the challenge that analysts and investors face.

285

It is true that businesses are ultimately interested in generating profits. That is why we invest in them – we hope to share in that profit. When businesses realise that treating their suppliers, customers and staff fairly, having a CSR policy in place or being environmentally more responsible has a positive effect on their profits, they will embrace such practices voluntarily and competitively. Otherwise, it is difficult to see how they will become more responsible if they view CSR simply as an additional cost. Companies and their shareholders must realise that there is a compelling business case for greater social responsibility. Evidence suggests that a positive attitude to CSR brings benefits in terms of a company's reputation, the morale of its staff and overall profit growth, while a negative attitude to CSR may result in serious damage to reputation and other negative consequences for a company and consequently to its shareholders.[3] Studies also suggest that 'stock prices rose when companies announced they were the recipient of an award for managing and promoting diversity. They fell when companies announced discrimination suits.'[4] As leadership companies develop CSR, pressure for international regulation is likely to rise, if only to discourage free riders.

CHALLENGES OF GLOBAL INVESTING

The last decade delivered a dramatic reversal of fortunes for people and companies in various parts of the world. Although the average per capita income in the US and Europe has risen, most parts of the emerging markets (EM) universe witnessed an unprecedented level of wealth destruction. The point is illustrated by the disparity between the $400 billion market capitalisation of Microsoft, the largest company in the US, and the $10 billion market capitalisation of Hindustan Lever, the largest company in India, one of the more populous countries of the world. Wal-Mart's sales at $140 billion and General Electric's profits at $12 billion raise questions about the efficacy of stock markets in nurturing 'sustainable development' when market valuations of EM countries have been decimated on a global basis. In 1998, for example, total government revenues in Bangladesh amounted to just $3.9 billion for a population of 125 million. The global distribution of income has created more inequalities over the last decade and that should cause real concern.[5]

Less than three decades ago, some of the highly capitalised technology companies of today did not exist. Even a couple of decades ago, the reach of companies such as Wal-Mart, Coca-Cola, Philip Morris, Gillette or GE were limited mostly to the US and the disparity between the largest companies in China, Russia, Brazil, India and the US were not as great as they are today. Market valuations aside, even when one examines return on investment or the ability to generate cash flow, the difference could not be more obvious. Considering the US has transformed itself into the enterprise economy of the world, credit is certainly due to its institutions and policies. But even in the world's richest and most efficient economy, the poor have in absolute terms become poorer over the last two decades, where for much of the twentieth century the gap had narrowed. In America, between 1979 and 1997 the average income of the richest fifth of the population jumped from 9 times the income of the poorest fifth to around 15 times. In fact, the average real income of the poorest fifth fell by 3% during 1979–97. In 1999 British income inequality reached its widest level in 40 years. The poorest fifth enjoyed real annual income growth of 1.9% under John Major's leadership and 1.4% during Tony Blair's.[6] This does not demolish the argument that globalisation has also been a great benefit to individuals worldwide.

Markets work better in societies where advancement is based on merit and ability, regardless of an individual's race, class, sex, age or creed. Markets do not deliver such societies, they only function better under such conditions, as the various participants compete in arbitraging away inefficiencies. Thus, markets need to be regulated, monitored and supported in myriad ways to ensure their proper functioning. From human rights to environmental protection, investors must set the agenda as they essentially define the market. The market's self-adjusting process creates volatility that can wipe out weaker participants. Markets also do not reflect the inability of those participants who cannot access it, creating a high level of inequality. The challenge of globalisation in the new century is 'not to stop the expansion of global markets,' the UNDP Human Development Report 1999 stated: 'The challenge is to find the rules and institutions for stronger governance – local, national, regional and global – to preserve the advantage of global markets and competition, but also to provide enough space for human, community and environmental resources to ensure that globalization works for people – not just for profits.' The underdeveloped markets of the world need better access to the developed markets, not just the other way round.

Capital markets help finance development only under certain prevailing conditions; otherwise, they are more likely to foster what has been dubbed as 'crony capitalism'. Even medium-sized economies experience severe volatility when large financial institutions make relatively small adjustments to their global portfolios. The availability or otherwise of capital by itself is not decisive in determining a company's or a nation's future growth prospect. History is replete with examples of wealth destruction not just by individuals, but also by companies and nations. What is important is the availability of the necessary infrastructure to facilitate the efficient flow of capital. The poor returns on investments in Asia in the early 1990s were due to policy failures triggered by inadequate assessment systems and other factors such as poor project implementation, inadequate monitoring, lack of training and incentives, not to mention nepotism and corruption; in other words, lack of transparency in the system. Thus, governments have a key role to play in shaping policy, along with NGOs and the vigilance of the public at large.

In order to invest effectively today, one must take into account the profound changes that our world is undergoing; not just in the economic arena, but, across a broader range of issues within society, including the global environment. The economic, political, social and religious dislocation is more severe than we have seen before, partly because of the far greater interdependence today between financial institutions, companies and nations.[7] Unfortunately, the militancy of a core group of protestors against globalisation at various global economic forums, from Seattle to Genoa, has distracted attention away from the genuine problems associated with globalisation. Nor do these protestors use soundly researched arguments in favour of their cause. Much of it is simply not based on facts because globalisation has been beneficial on many counts. The protestors have their blind spots and whatever they may or may not have achieved in support of their cause, they have used the global media and the new technology effectively in registering dissent. If institutional investors and governments demonstrated their ability to act affirmatively with regard to issues surrounding equity and sustainable development, even within their own countries let alone the world, then the news of global terrorism would not be centre stage today.

What global investors face is an array of complex issues, which are difficult to implement and often challenge traditional methods of analysis. For example, how does one evaluate a company that uses child labour? Should such practice be abolished altogether? If so, how do shareholders ensure that? More importantly, what is the most appropriate course of action for investors, engagement or exclusion? A majority of investors advocate a strategy of active engagement rather than imposing outright investment sanctions against companies or regimes. While such decision is up to the individual investor, these issues need to be debated rationally and on a global basis, with the viewpoint of the child or slave labourer being taken as much into account as the shareholder and the consumer. The National Garment Workers Federation in Bangladesh, for example, has not had much success in defending the rights of its women workers who work at various sweatshop factories in the Dhaka Export Processing Zone, where human rights are consistently violated, and the women workers earn less than half the national wage. A similar situation exists in the 'maquiladoras' or the assembly plants along the US–Mexico border. These plants are mostly owned by US corporate giants that pay a fraction of the US national wage to their workers, who are mostly women and whose human rights are daily violated.

There is a growing awareness of unacceptable corporate practices within MNCs, although investors have been slow in developing an efficient global forum for raising such issues directly with the offending companies. It is not simply an inability to arrive at ethical or moral decisions, which can be very complex indeed. 'Do investors avoid companies that use sweatshops because such practices are immoral, or because they think they are a risky investment? If the only values that underpin the investment process are financial ones, where does that leave ethical investment?' enquires the *Ethical Investor*.[8] However, the ethical issue is not clear-cut. Most people would agree that children should be in school and not at work, and certainly not earning less than the national minimum wage in their country. But if the child is the sole earner in the family, then who will bear the cost of sending that child to school when the child loses his/her job? Even if we argue that governments should provide universal primary education, how is that to be enforced by investors? And who will monitor the government? Thus, like many other contentious issues that have yet to be resolved, the barriers are often economic ones, if not political, social and religious.

Governments could legislate that companies benefiting from cheap labour must invest in the child's future. Thus, a company can employ a child provided the child is educated at the expense of the employer. But how will that be effectively monitored? When the US government feels the need to take Microsoft to court for anticompetitive practices, how are the governments of developing countries, such as Bangladesh and Mozambique, to resist powerful MNCs when they lack the resources to invest in basic human development of their people? The case of young women workers in Bangladesh who are not even paid the national wage, which is a fraction of the wage in the US for a company like Wal-Mart, is just one example. Of the $12.7 billion earned in 2000, General Electric (GE) contributed $100 million to support education, the arts, environment and human service organisations worldwide. Companies such as GE and others can afford to do significantly more, particularly when it is tax efficient to do so. Even the world's richest countries contribute less than 0.7% of their GDP as overseas aid towards the development of some of the poorest nations in the world.

While the world has become more global, institutions to deal with issues arising as a result of the consequences of globalisation have yet to evolve, particularly at the local, grass-roots level. Unless such participation is effective, democracy as we know it is bound to suffer. Politicians such as Tony Blair convey the impression they would be willing to usher in a Third Way, but in a fractured society there is little consensus as to what that might be. In September 2000 the Global Partners for Corporate Responsibility Research, an international network of corporate research organisations including the Ethical Investment Research Service (EIRIS), issued its 'ten demands for a higher standard of disclosure in the global economy of the 21st century.' Among the proposals was mandatory corporate disclosure of core social and environmental information.[9] It is not as if the consciousness is not there, it is simply that we have not placed enough emphasis on it, or directed sufficient resources in addressing the underlying issues. At the end of the day, we as individuals determine such issues, although we may not realise that is indeed the case. If we as a society continue to accommodate injustice and behave irresponsibly, then we have only ourselves to blame.

In the UK, according to one survey, 77% of the people surveyed indicated that they would like their respective pension fund to embrace an ethical policy, 'on the condition that this can be done without spoiling financial return.'[10] Another survey suggested that three-quarters of those contributing to pension funds would like their trustees to use voting rights in order to pressure companies on their SEE performance.[11] While surveys are far from conclusive and do have their limitations, we acknowledge that there is a dilemma inherent in trying to do the right thing, without having to pay too much for it. Such an attitude puts pressure on companies to be efficient, yet even efficiency can go so far and no further and may prove to be unsustainable in the long term, not only in SEE terms but also financially. In the name of efficiency, cost-cutting has become the new mantra of our times, leading to the exploitation of those who are least able to protect themselves. However, as there is no such thing as a free lunch, someone has to pay; it just may not be us, today. Hostility towards the profit motive is not conducive to wealth creation; nor is greed and the lack of CSR and the awareness of its long-term cost. The skill lies in striking a balance and evolving sustainable policies, in SEE and financial terms. Thus, financial performance includes SEE performance, and the two cannot be disassociated. Over the past few decades, financial performance has failed to account for SEE factors.

It is indeed heartening news that the British public are warming up to business success; it would be better if they demanded such success to be achieved within SEE norms and that such opportunity be available to all, regardless of race, sex, creed, age, etc. A recent edition of MORI's Corporate Image survey suggests that two decades of British animosity towards business success may be coming to an end. In 1970 some 53% of people agreed that big companies' profits helped 'make things better' for everyone, and fewer than 25% disagreed. By early 1999 the proportions had reversed, with 25% supportive of profits and 52% against. However, the proportion that backs profits is now up four points to 29% and the proportion against is down nine points to 43%. According to Brian Gosschalk, MORI's chief executive, increasing boardroom awareness of corporate social responsibility was probably playing a part.[12] If indeed that is the case, then it is good news for the government, which believes that the rate of growth can be boosted if US-style enterprise becomes more prevalent among the UK public. However, support for profit-making was at its peak, at 56%, in 1980 when Margaret Thatcher led the Conservatives to the first of four consecutive general election victories and ushered in a market-driven economic model that introduced privatisations and changed the corporate landscape irrevocably.

Keeping the balance between the profit motive of the private sector and investing in essentially the non-profit-making public sector enterprises is the key challenge for governments in developing policies. It is ironical that our unwillingness to pay for better education, health and transport, which are non-profit-making sectors of the economy, has led to declining investment in these vital sectors. Better utilisation of funding is not under question. Along with efficient management of funds, there is a clear need for increase in investment. It appears that we want it all – we expect governments to invest more and yet we are not prepared to bear the cost. Poor countries have an even greater problem in confronting these issues as corruption and nepotism stand in the way of development. Thus, bringing about change can be deceptive and often very difficult to perceive, particularly when institutions have to be altered radically. It takes decades to build any sort of consensus. While reform can be imposed from above, anybody who has any experience of radical change will know that it is more efficient if it evolves organically from within. Revolutions, the world over, have been bloody simply because one set of ideologies has been imposed by one dominant group upon others. Democracies do not work in such a manner.

Capitalism has been largely embraced by large parts of the world without any force. Unfortunately, it has been seriously corrupted in the process of implementation due to the lack of adequate infrastructure in terms of political, social, financial and regulatory institutions. Even when they do exist, they are not effective; they lack power. Arguing his case for greater empowerment and participation by the poor in decision-making as a panacea for reducing poverty, the chief economist of the World Bank, Nicholas Stern, presented his personal viewpoint in the *Financial Times* with the following observation: 'Recent history has taught us that market liberalisation can fail dramatically if responsible government, sound financial systems and the rule of law are lacking.'[13] Global institutions such as the World Bank and the IMF are themselves the targets of various protests as they have failed consistently in their obligation to provide support to nations in financial distress.

The moral hazard problem will not disappear when one institution is saved for fear of contagion of the rest and another is allowed to sink or swim, as it does not pose such an outright threat. Thus, salvation appears to lie in size and ability to upset the status quo, but nothing to do with efficiency, integrity, transparency and other such sound business principles. Fund managers have a fiduciary duty to their clients and MNCs are accountable to their shareholders, even though it is difficult sometimes to enforce these obligations. Although all these groups should have similar long-term interests, conflicting short-term interests usually blur that vision. While the collective decision of managers of pension funds, banks, insurance firms and MNCs is critical to the future of the world, these powerful institutions have feet of clay and often cave in easily to pressures from the media, mainly due to the lack of greater transparency in their corporate decision-making. The hallmark of civilisation is to what extent society caters to the needs of its weakest members while enabling its more talented individuals to maximise their gifts.

RISE OF SHAREHOLDER ACTIVISM

A socially responsible investment strategy takes into account the SEE record of any company one invests in and incorporates that into its long-term financial performance. Investors recognise there is a corporate governance dividend attached to firms; they usually command a higher market valuation, have cheaper access to capital and benefit from a strong shareholder base. This premium is lower in developed countries but can rise to one-third of a company's value in developing countries as well as in some European countries. It is increasingly evident that the market recognises the SEE performance of a company in valuing it, although it is not a transparent process.

The low valuations attached to companies do reflect poor financial and growth prospects. Unless the industry in which the company operates is undergoing a major restructuring, poor ratings often reflect poor corporate management. Sometimes a change in top management is enough to be reflected in a company's market value. An effective board is essential in delivering shareholder value.

One of the major duties of the board is to define corporate strategy. The composition of the board is vital to ensuring that no individual or small group of individuals dominate the board's decision-making. The Combined Code recommends that non-executive directors should comprise not less than one-third of the board with a minimum of three, as they have the independence and the ability to look at the long-term interests of the company. This requirement aims to reduce conflicts in the governance of companies, where non-executive directors in poorly managed, dysfunctional companies may not have a mechanism for handling disagreements. Independent directors play an essential role by using their unfettered judgement on the issues of strategy, performance, resources, key appointments and standards of conduct. Such independent assessment of strategic direction is probably the greatest value to be derived from a non-executive director.[14] The lack of the independence of non-executive directors is an ongoing issue in the UK, where such directors are drawn from the ranks of lawyers, accountants, ex-politicians, consultants and independent advisers who may have never had any experience in running large corporations.

CSR is increasingly recognised as a commercial imperative that yields competitive advantages by building the business, the people and the trust. Reputation is as much about actions and attitudes as about products and services. Smart companies recognise that a company that actively commits to improving its impact on the environment and building trust with its customers, its employees and the community is better able to gain a competitive edge in the marketplace by building the 'reputation' value of its brand. Obviously, it can also work against the brand if there is negative media coverage. However, on balance, CSR attracts favourable media coverage for the company involved along with sustained investment, helps in retaining talented employees, creates new ways of sharing knowledge in promoting innovation, develops strong, reciprocal relationships with the communities with whom they do business and builds the competitiveness of their local communities.

In a study by Charles J. Fombrun, published in 1996 on the value attached to reputation and corporate image, he attempted to put a figure on the 'reputational capital' of major companies and came to $52 billion for Coca-Cola, $12 billion for Gillette and $11 billion for Eastman Kodak. A higher 'reputational capital' for a company resulted in higher than average stock value, easier recruitment, and the ability to charge premium prices. Inevitably, reputation matters more for a retailer than for a manufacturer. Besides, reputations can be fragile. It may take years to establish a reputation, but this can be easily tarnished by negative headlines and unfavourable media attention, especially for major brand names. In a recent study by *US Chief Executive* magazine, 96% of CEOs said they believe that reputation is very important, and 65% dedicate more time to this subject than they did five years ago. Failure to protect reputation can be considered a management failure by institutional investors who seek out companies with demonstrable good governance structures. Unexpected and unwelcome media attention can be interpreted as poor management.[15]

Over the past couple of decades, the Bhopal, Chernobyl, and *Exxon Valdez* incidents, along with better information about ozone depletion and its consequences have alerted the seriousness of environmental issues to investors. Adherence to superior ethical business principles and overall corporate performance are correlated. Investors understandably demand greater transparency from companies about their corporate governance principles as well as their environmental policies and practices, their record of protecting human rights and a respectable record of involvement in the local communities they operate in. Some investors opt to screen out offending companies from their portfolio – the Church Commissioners have avoided companies whose income is derived from businesses associated with armaments trading, alcohol, tobacco or gambling – and some prefer to engage or intervene in the management of companies in which they own shares. But the ultimate effect is greater scrutiny of the investment process. Socially responsible corporate managemers have internal procedures and disciplines to minimise uncovered risks that can erode shareholder value. Fund managers sensitive to SRI issues take into account such procedures in the identification of companies in the implementation of their SRI policy, followed by monitoring, reporting and enforcement of declared SRI principles, their own as much as those of the companies they invest in.

The National Association of Pension Funds (NAPF) advocates better analyses, engagement and ultimately influence on corporate policy-making by institutional investors. On 23 November 1999, the then pensions minister in the UK, Jeff Rooker, expressed his views on SRI: 'the outmoded negative screening method.. is both unattractive and impractical from the point of view of the institutional investor.... Our focus is on engagement, corporate governance, sustainability and the environment.'[16] NAPF's guidance on engagement offers investors and companies a better understanding of SRI issues. For those who do not know where to start, the NAPF recommends the GoodCorporation's 21-point Charter, developed with the assistance of the Institute of Business Ethics (IBE), which was established in 1986 in the UK for the sole purpose of encouraging a high standard of corporate behaviour. According to NAPF, engagement has two distinct advantages:[17]

- It is a way of finding out directly what a company says are its social, environmental and ethical policies and practices.
- The process can bring to the attention of senior executives issues which concern institutional investors and pension fund trustees.

Not investing in companies, on account of SRI reasons, is less efficient than talking directly to firms about their questionable policies, as that creates a relationship between investor and investee, with the possibility of bringing about change. If there is a process of constructive engagement in place, SRI issues can be raised with the company's management. If matters cannot be resolved by engagement, active investors have the option of withdrawing from the investment. However, such an option is not available to indexed fund managers. Thus, a number of managers of passive funds place significant reliance on engagement processes to enhance the long-term performance of equity investments held within their portfolios. Hermes Pensions Management, for example, sets out clearly what is expected from the companies in its annual report on SEE issues, with emphasis being placed on the management of risks associated with SEE matters. Due to the increased number of requests for information on SEE issues by investors, it is worth 'considering the benefits of working with a consortium of other like-minded investors.'[18] Voting collectively on SRI issues offers such an option rather than simply exiting from the investment.

Traditionally, shareholder actions have been classified into two categories: corporate governance issues and corporate social responsibility. Corporate governance resolutions address issues such as the composition of the board, confidential voting, independence of non-executive directors, compensation of directors and executives. Social responsibility resolutions encompass corporate policy issues on environment, health, safety, gender, sweatshops and other human right issues. According to the Interfaith Centre on Corporate Responsibility (ICCR), in 1999 socially concerned investors in the US filed approximately 220 resolutions with more than 150 major companies. Of the issues raised, 24.5% dealt with environmental issues, 18.6% with global corporate accountability, 17.2% with equality, 14.0% with health and tobacco-related issues, 14.0% with corporate governance and executive compensation, 6.3% with global finance and 5.4% with militarism and violence.[19] According to the Social Investment Forum's 1999 report on socially responsible investing trends in the US, among funds that screen for SRI, a policy prohibiting investments in tobacco is universal. Over 96% of socially screened portfolios avoid tobacco. In addition, the majority of assets are screened for gambling (86%), alcohol (83%), weapons (81%) and the environment (79%). Other screens include human rights (43%), labour issues (38%), birth control and abortion (23%), and animal welfare (15%).[20]

Controversies surrounding shareholder activism arise when investors start to define areas of concern which extend across a wide range of issues: advertising, abortion, alcohol, animal testing, corporate governance, directors' pay, environment, employment, equal opportunities, fur, gambling, genetic engineering, global warming, greenhouse gases, health and safety, human rights, intensive farming and meat sale, military production and sale, mining, nuclear power, ozone-depleting chemicals, pesticides, political donations, pollution, pornography, sweatshops, Third World issues such as commodity extraction, debt, baby milk marketing, pharmaceutical and tobacco marketing, tropical hardwood, tobacco, etc. Today there is lack of consensus on what is 'ethical'. Hence the rise of single-issue protestors who buy a few shares in a company for the sake of registering dissent. As we live in a society that also believes in individualism and freedom, we are legally free to engage in activities which might appear 'unethical' from someone else's perspective. From time to time, society converges on some issue or the other, sometimes on a global basis.

Such an event was the war in Vietnam and the rise of social, ethical considerations in investments can be traced back to the 1960s. There were serious concerns within churches and universities that they might be benefiting from the war effort. The first socially responsible shareholder resolution in the US, submitted in 1969, questioned the morality of Dow Chemical's production of napalm. The following year, General Motors received various proxy resolutions critical of its safety record. Another such event was apartheid in South Africa and once again it was the US taking the lead. Shareholder action helped in waging war against apartheid in South Africa through direct corporate disinvestments. One of the more recent victories of the 1998 proxy season was the withdrawal from Burma, now Myanmar, of Atlantic Richfield (Arco). A growing movement by shareholders, students, human rights activists and Burmese citizens in exile succeeded in forcing such corporate withdrawals. Shareholders also challenged Caterpillar and Unocal about their operations in Burma, where the military dictatorship has become notorious for human rights violations and repression of democracy. Holdings in companies such as Petrofina and Elf Aquitaine were sold after their takeover by the French oil company, Total, as investors did not wish to receive Total shares due to its involvement in Burma.[21]

Other notable recent victories achieved by shareholders include an announcement in August 1999 by Home Depot, the world's largest seller of old-growth timber, of its intent to phase out the sale of wood products from 'endangered forests' by 2002. Baxter International, the world's largest healthcare products manufacturer, also agreed to phase out polyvinyl chloride (PVC) materials in its intravenous products. PVC is one of the most toxic substances when manufactured and incinerated but appears in 25% of healthcare products. In October 1999 GE agreed to spend $150–250 million in cleaning up a stretch of the Housatonic River in western Massachusetts that was polluted by the company decades ago.[22] Today there are outstanding shareholder resolutions requiring companies such as Sara Lee to examine the risks and impact of the continued use of GM foods, for ExxonMobil to invest more in renewable energy technologies, Wal-Mart to produce a report on vendor standards (sweatshops) and Citibank to review its predatory lending practice. Ten international labour and human rights proposals received 10% or more support from US shareholders. In 2000, resolutions on GM foods were filed with 21 companies, including Monsanto, Coca-Cola, McDonald's, Campbell, Heinz, General Mills and Kellogg, to stop the sale of products with GM ingredients pending further safety tests.[23]

Organisations such as Shareholder Action Network (SAN), founded by the Social Investment Forum (SIF), ICCR and the As You Sow Foundation in the US, have been rapidly expanding the coalition of institutions, organisations and financial professionals participating in shareholder action. The various organisations and NGOs which operate in this sector, such as SIF and its subsidiaries, Business in the Environment (BiE) and Business in the Community (BiC), Investor Responsibility Research Center (IRRC), OECD Anti-corruption, International Business Leaders Forum, Social Account-ability International, along with others such as Oxfam, Christian Aid, Médecins sans Frontières, Global Treatment Access Campaign, Greenpeace, Friends of the Earth, Fairtrade Foundation, Grassroots, Ethical Trading Initiative and other pressure groups, including the Free Tibet Campaign, Human Rights Watch, International Alert and Amnesty International, have also become more global in their orientation and approach to tackling issues.

Thus, pressure groups and ethical investors helped to claim a victory in South Africa, where the world's largest pharmaceutical firms dropped their case against the government over intellectual property rights. At the same time, GlaxoSmithKline agreed to publish a detailed policy on Third World medicines so that institutional stakeholders can assess the firm's commitment and performance. At the 2001 AGM of BP Amoco, a coalition of UK and US investors and human rights and green pressure groups linked up to submit shareholder resolutions to the company relating to its carbon transition strategy, a risk assessment on drilling in the Arctic National

Wildlife Refuge and the sale of the company's 2.2% stake in Petro-china, the state-owned Chinese oil company active in Tibet. While active SRI investors, such as Friends Ivory & Sime, continue to moni-tor the situation with regard to BP Amoco, they also concluded that with its exemplary human rights policies, BP is well placed to raise the issue of improved human rights with the board of Petrochina.[24]

Despite the rising influence of shareholders on corporate policy in the US, the major institutional investors or the largest asset managers in the world do not participate in such a form of investment activity. The undisputed focus for asset managers is on ways of securing superior investment returns. Companies with poor corporate govern-ance records would be excluded on financial grounds alone, not because of their weak policies on various SEE issues. SRI investments comprised $2.16 trillion in 1999, or just 13% of the total assets managed professionally, up from 9% in 1997. Of the $2.16 trillion of SRI assets, 70% used screening as an investment strategy, i.e. exclusion as an investment method rather than direct engagement. However, the fastest-growing component of SRI, in the US and the UK, is the growth in portfolios that use both screening and share-holder advocacy. Shareholder activism in the US and increasingly in the UK is becoming a popular means of influencing corporations in addressing their social and environmental policies.

In the UK, such a level of organised intervention has been slow in taking hold of the institutional shareholder community, although the potential for change in corporate behaviour as a direct result of such intervention clearly exists. Paul Myners, in his review of institutional investment in the UK, was 'not making a public interest argument about shareholder responsibility. The most powerful argument for intervention in a company is financial self-interest, adding value for clients through improved corporate performance leading to improved investment performance.'[25] According to the BiE 2001 survey on City attitudes to environmental and social issues: 'All respondent groups gave high rankings to factors such as quality of management, financial status and growth prospects when evaluating companies. Environmental and social issues come in further down the scale with only 3% of analysts, 4% of investors, 3% of journalists and 13% of investor relations managers mentioning them of their own volition.'[26]

It appears that legislation and public pressure are considered by institutional investors to be important factors in pushing the environmental and social performance of companies up the business agenda than purely financial factors. According to the BiE 2001 survey, all respondents attached a lower level of importance to financial factors as being a reason to move social and ethical issues up the agenda,[27] although attitudes have changed since 1994, when only 20% of analysts believed environmental policy of companies were 'fairly or very' important in their evaluation of companies. In 2001 some 33% of analysts believed that to be the case. There is also a rise in the importance attached to the social policy of companies from 12% to 34%.[28] Analysts and investors are influenced in their perception of environmental, ethical and social issues if they are presented as a defining element of the quality of corporate management. The 2001 BiE survey suggests that the mainstream City institutions are taking their time in integrating non-financial criteria into their analysis of companies, although UK companies themselves seem to place a higher level of importance upon environmental and social performance than their institutional shareholders.[29]

One of the main reasons for the inability of investors to integrate social, environmental and financial strategies is the lack of 'independent', verifiable analysis of SEE data as well as the availability of long-term data on the subject. Institutional investors are notoriously slow to respond to issues when they are unable to justify their action to their clients. Annual reports of companies remain the major source of information used by the financial community. It was therefore appropriate of the UK government to request the chairmen of the FTSE 350 firms to voluntarily produce an annual environmental report by the end of 2001.[30] The new pension legislation on SRI will put additional pressure on trustees of pension funds in defining their investment principles, while proposals in the *Company Law Review* for mandatory reporting on social and environmental issues along with the pending guidelines for investors from the Association of British Insurers will collectively increase the need for sustainability reporting. In the UK, the annual Environmental and Social Reporting Awards of the Association of Certified Chartered Accountants (ACCA) puts a spotlight on poor performers and is an extra incentive for companies to improve their SEE reporting.

The Global Reporting Initiative (GRI), which has been driving the corporate sustainability reporting agenda, is due to become formally institutionalised in 2002. The rolling out of the social and environmental accounting, auditing and reporting (SEAAR) standards internationally, supported by the Institute of Social and Ethical Accountability, can only reinforce what appears to be a slow but steady work-in-progress. Unless the information provided is directly relevant to the City, it cannot be effectively included in assessment methodologies. Environmental expenditure data – such as capital/ operational costs, contingent liabilities, provisions – risk ratings and management procedures, non-compliance details including fines and penalties, preparations for future legislation and R&D-related information are all financially tied and may have an impact on the bottom line.[31] For example, waste minimisation is a bottom line issue as well as an environmental issue, and good environmental performance is one indicator of future competitiveness. According to Sir John Harman, chairman of the Environment Agency:

> We already provide data on emissions for the biggest process industry sites such as chemical factories and power stations on our Pollution Inventory, as well as flood risk maps for all of England and Wales on our Internet site. We now also produce an annual spotlight on company environmental performance giving 'league tables' of pollution incidents, prosecutions and fines and indicate those organisations that have made significant environmental improvements. We plan to improve and develop these influencing tools.

> For example, we intend to expand our Pollution Inventory to cover other sectors such as major sewage treatment works, plus nuclear and landfill sites by 2003, and the food processing industry by 2007, and to agree environmental performance indicators with key sectors. We are also intending to publish our own risk assessment banding of regulated sites, something which would be of very great interest to investors.[32]

Lack of established social and environmental performance indicators, along with the uncertainty surrounding the definition of such issues, remains a major barrier for investors. So better information on SEE issues along with regulatory pressure on business, e.g. from EU directives, will also assist analysts and fund managers in their due diligence. Transparency of information and easy comparability of data are equally important for the investing community. One could argue that investors' lack of interest in such data has resulted in its non-availability, and vice versa. However, increased awareness of corporate responsibility has been instrumental in producing UK legislation ensuring that both investors and the companies they invest in are mutually aligned in reviewing their performance in an integrated manner, so that SEE returns are reflected in financial terms.

Some fund managers, such as Dresdner RCM (DRCM) Global Investors, evaluate companies fairly rigorously on the implementation and observance of an effective environmental management system (EMS), which includes the ISO 14001 standard of the International Organisation for Standardisation and the Eco-Management and Audit Scheme (EMAS), which aims to identify and manage the environmentally driven financial risks. These risks include market risk, balance sheet risk, operating risk, capital cost risk, transaction risk, eco-efficiency and sustainability risk. Disclosure and reporting of such risks are as important as a company's compliance record. DRCM Global Investors do not invest in companies that repeatedly violate essential international environmental agreements, such as the UN Convention on Biological Diversity, UN Montreal Protocol on substances that deplete the ozone layer, UN Framework Convention on Climate Change, the Kyoto Protocol and the Cartagena Protocol on Biosafety. DRCM takes United Nations (UN) and International Labour Organisation (ILO) principles and guidelines on various human rights and environmental issues and then incorporates them into its stock selection process. The fund manager applies positive and negative screens in identifying the universe of high-quality companies that demonstrate effective SRI policies across their activities, products and services. However, the DRCM screening process does not specifically adopt a 'best of sector' investment strategy.[33] Rather than eliminating a whole sector of industry from a portfolio simply because it does not stand scrutiny under certain ethical criteria, some fund managers tend to resort to a 'best of sector' approach in their stock selection.

In addressing the complex nature of selecting the SRI criteria, EIRIS in the UK launched the Ethical Portfolio Manager (EPM) software that assesses how some 1,500 UK and European companies are responding to investor concerns about the environment and human rights and how they manage their relationships with stakeholders.[34] BiE has also come up with an annual index that ranks companies according to the quality of their environmental management. BiE's index of corporate environmental engagement and performance is gaining recognition as a leading benchmark of corporate environmental engagement. The index reflects the extent to which a company understands and manages its environmental impacts in a consistent fashion and brings together all the elements of its various environmental programmes as an integral part of its business strategy. Performance measurement reflects the extent to which companies are measuring their global environmental impacts in key areas and setting specific targets to reduce them.

Similarly, Friends of the Earth published a league table naming and shaming UK insurance companies that ignored environmental and social issues, had no sustainable development policy and invested in environmentally and socially destructive companies. A similar survey of UK pension funds has also been produced. There are several other providers of corporate governance and SRI research services, such as Manifest, Institutional Shareholder Services and Global Risk Management. Established in 1996, the Safety and Environmental Risk Management (SERM) Rating Agency Limited is a UK-based financial rating agency which aims to quantify companies' safety, environmental and social risks and thus to enhance shareholder value while cost-effectively leveraging continuous business improvement. SERM also specialises in measuring and benchmarking companies' ability to manage the potential SEE risks arising from their operations, relative to their financial strength. It provides a financial assessment of over 1,600 UK-listed companies, with rating varying from AAA + to C − . SERM works together with the London Environment Centre (LEC) and Bureau Veritas (BV), a company that conducts the verification visits. SERM's rating outputs are supplied to organisations such as ABI, Manifest Proxy Voting Services and NAPF. SERM is also developing BV-SERM Ratings Outputs to be used as a portfolio management tool.

In light of the complexity and range of issues involved, both institutional investors and their advisers face an impossible task in implementing a strategic SRI policy. Tim Gardener of William M. Mercer sums up the issues like this:

I do think the industry should be more proactive on SRI issues, because the underlying issues are serious and affect us all and also because governments increasingly find it harder to govern multinational companies. I do not believe in unelected and ungovernable institutions. The owners of companies can govern and so pension funds can be more active in their governance and should take such a stance at the macro level.

The problems arise at the micro level, where you are not concerned about 'saving the world', but are more concerned about what's right for a particular company and there are significant dangers to the layman becoming involved. How do you demonstrate that 'involvement' with a company has improved your return? And if it does not, how can you justify it when the law is quite clear that your primary duty as a trustee is to enhance your return? So there is a conflict between what is right at the industry level and what the individual scheme can do. I'm afraid the government is going to have to legislate on that if it wants greater action on the part on institutional investors.

Investment managers can adopt a policy of engagement. It is simple. It may not get the headlines, but it is actually a powerful way of going forward. For example, they can make it a requirement that the companies they invest in include a statement on their SRI policy in their annual reports. Then, at least, one small step would have been taken in raising standards. My personal view is that a policy of engagement on SRI issues is good and also for the industry in the long term.

If you start from the basis that SRI is the right thing to do, then you want a common process to be adopted and not an individual one. The industry needs an approach which is sufficiently non-confrontational that the majority can adopt it. Engagement by the fund managers fits the bill and if you can get the major fund managers who control the bulk of the wealth (Fidelity, Capital, BGI, etc.) singing off the same hymn sheet, positive social change can be achieved.[35]

SOCIALLY RESPONSIBLE INVESTMENT

The amendment to the Pension Act 1995 requiring trustees to indicate their approach to a socially responsible investment (SRI) strategy is significant in terms of its potential influence on corporate behaviour. The UK government has been unique in its stance on SRI. The appointment of a minister for corporate social responsibility demonstrates the government's increasing concern about SRI issues. On 3 July 2000 an amendment made to the Pensions Act 1995 required all pension fund trustees to record in their statement of investment principles (SIP) 'the extent (if at all) to which social, environmental and ethical considerations are taken into account in the selection, retention and realisation of investments' and 'their policy (if any) in relation to the exercise of rights (including voting rights) attaching to investments.' Other European countries such as France, Germany, Switzerland and Austria are debating similar legislation along with other countries such as Australia and Canada. In the US, the Department of Labor interpretative bulletin relating to statements of investment policy clearly stipulates the fiduciary obligations of managing plan assets that are shares of corporate stock. This bulletin, issued in 1994, spells out clearly the fiduciary obligations of prudence and loyalty to plan participants and beneficiaries.[36] SRI issues are included in the fiduciary obligations of plan sponsors and managers.

In the UK, occupational pension schemes are now accountable for their ethical and voting policy as much as for their fund's financial performance. Most schemes will satisfy this requirement by confirming that their investment policies do not include special consideration of SRI issues. Trustees that adopt SRI policies then face the problem of funding the cost of achieving their SRI goals without breaching their fiduciary duty to treat the interests of beneficiaries as paramount. According to Frank Russell Company, 'the legislation is important not for what it requires trustees to do, but for what it allows them to do. It allows trustees to specify that fund holdings must meet explicit SRI criteria that traditionally have not been part of the security selection process. However, the legislation does not remove the requirement that trustees must also make decisions that are in the best interests of the plan beneficiaries.'[37] For example, John Denham, the government minister who first proposed that pension funds be required to disclose their SRI policies stated, 'As the law stands, nothing can detract from the primary responsibility of pensions trustees, to place the financial interests of the beneficiaries first.'[38]

According to the UK Social Investment Forum, there are three approaches to pursuing socially responsible investment polices:[39]

- *Ethical screening*: the inclusion or exclusion of stocks and shares on ethical, social or environmental grounds.
- *Shareholder influence*: seeking to improve a company's ethical, social and/or environmental behaviour as a shareholder by means of dialogue, pressure, support for responsible management and voting at annual general meetings.
- *Cause-based investing*: supporting a particular cause or activity by financing it by investment. Cause-based investors may seek a financial return at market rates, or they may take a lower return in order to achieve a particular 'social return' for society from their investments.

Engaging to improve a company's SEE policy is considered a superior SRI strategy to ethical screening, as ethical screening tends to result in the exclusion of a range of companies and may even result in a bias towards medium and smaller capitalisation policies. As explained by Frank Russell Company:

This type of bias introduces an element of additional risk into a portfolio and will lead to periods of underperformance against the broad market even if there is no loss of long term expected return. In the face of this underperformance, trustees could find themselves under pressure to unwind an SRI strategy, even if it is well-designed.

Trustees should apply the same on-going administrative due diligence to their SRI holdings as they do to other investments. This means verifying regularly that the portfolio is being managed within its guidelines – both the conventional risk guidelines and the SRI guidelines.

Trustees should also monitor performance and take care to distinguish between the success of the policy and the success of the agent retained to implement the policy. This may prove difficult in practice. Because policies differ so widely, it is difficult to foresee how any one index can serve as a useful benchmark for all ethical and socially responsible investments.[40]

According to Penny Shepherd, executive director of the UK Social Investment Forum (UKSIF), a study of the top 500 pension funds in response to their SRI policy indicated that 59% of pension funds, representing 78% of the assets, incorporate SRI principles into their investment process, through their fund manager, through engagement or through both. Almost half of those responding to the survey, representing some 69% of assets, indicated that they delegated their fund manager to take account of the financial impact of environmental, social and ethical concerns when investing. Some 71% of local authority pension funds preferred to retain direct ownership of their SRI policy and favoured 'engagement' as an approach to SRI, as opposed to just 23% of company pension funds.[41]

The BiE 2001 survey on City attitudes to environmental and social issues, based on responses from 93 analysts and 50 investors, suggested that 44% of investors and 35% of analysts indicated that the introduction of SRI legislation changed the way they 'engage' with companies. Seeking discussions with companies on issues of concern was the most popular method of engaging with the company by both analysts and investors. Even prior to the SRI legislation, such a form of engagement would be normal among analysts and investors. It is also understandable that investors are in a stronger position than analysts when seeking improvements in company management. It is also not surprising that more investors sought third-party verification compared to analysts, who are supposed to provide independent advice. Trustees of pension funds are obliged in any event to base their investment decision on appropriate and independent advice. What is revealing is that more trustees indicated a need for better information on a company's environmental record compared to analysts. Like analysts, fund managers are routinely subject to conflicts of interests. If fund managers find themselves having to engage with a company whose pension fund they manage or would like to manage, they may not have the independence they need to successfully engage with companies in bringing change.

What is hugely significant is that 46% of investors and 57% of analysts indicated that the introduction of legislation on SRI matters made no difference to their work, and a further 10% of investors and 8% of analysts did not know if it had changed the way in which they appraised companies (Table 7.1). Thus, legislation has yet to feed its way into investment behaviour or the way in which the investment community relates to the corporate sector. It is too early to judge the impact of such legislation, except that it has raised investor and corporate awareness of SRI issues.

The UK's first ethical unit trust, the Friends Provident Stewardship Fund, was launched in 1984. SRI has attracted considerable investor attention at the retail level. There are more than 50 retail ethical funds in the UK. Ethical funds have grown from £199 million in 1989 to £3.7 billion in 2000. During 2000 alone, a 42% rise in the value of ethical funds was registered. Retail ethical funds under

Table 7.1 *Impact of SRI legislation on investors and analysts: percentage of respondents*[a]

	Investors	Analysts
Sought discussion with companies on issues of concern	34	24
Sought improvement in company management	26	20
Sought third-party verification and company statements	24	14
Sought improvement in company environmental reporting	18	8
Sought improvement in company social and ethical reporting	8	6
Other	2	3
None	46	57
Don't know	10	8

[a] Source: BiE and MORI

management are projected to grow steadily; some estimates put it at £10 billion by 2003. In performance terms, there is relatively little difference between the ethical universes and the All Share index. Ethical funds tend to be less volatile, as investors take a relatively longer-term view of their investments. A study by EIRIS indicates that annualised volatility was 10.4% for ethical funds in the same sector compared to 10.9% for non-ethically screened funds.[42]

SRI is far from a new concept; its origins can be traced back to Quaker and Methodist movements in the eighteenth and nineteenth centuries. In his sermon 'The Use of Money', John Wesley emphasised the difference between proper and improper use of money.[43] Ethical specialist managers, such as the Central Finance Board of the Methodist Church (CFB), have incorporated SRI criteria into their investment policy for some time now, as they believe financial and ethical performance to be indivisible. In 1992 they began to publish their investment portfolios, making them available to their members. Their ethical review takes into account a wide range of issues, including alcohol and tobacco, armaments, corporate governance and business ethics, debt relief and fair trade, environment, gambling, human rights, medical and food safety, and pornography. Their portfolios are also independently scrutinised by EIRIS. They also incorporate the corporate governance service provided by the pension investment research consultant PIRIC. Innovest's environmental rating service further helps in flagging up problem areas in investment policy-making. For Russell Sparkes of the CFB, all this helps provide a level of objectivity in assessing investment performance, just as the Combined Actuarial Performance Service (CAPS) provides an independent view of financial returns.[44]

In recent decades, the work of the Cadbury, Greenbury and Hampel committees, which culminated in the publication of the Combined Code of the Committee on Corporate Governance in the UK in June 1998 towards the implementation of an activist stance on certain corporate governance issues by institutional investors, has helped enormously in progressing with such matters. 'These developments have brought a variety of benefits for shareholders and for the economy at large. Nevertheless, while helpful, these initiatives are not always sufficient. It remains widely acknowledged that concerns about the management and strategy of major companies can persist among analysts and fund managers for long periods of time before action is taken.'[45] Most financial analysts emphasise the importance and value of good corporate governance, and investors realise the importance of non-quantifiable factors when determining shareholder value. However, analysts do not currently provide any valid measure of non-financial risks that firms, and investors, may be open to.

Other government-inspired initiatives have played their part in progressing the ethical investment agenda. The Turnbull Committee, the latest addition to the Combined Code, advised in its final guidance to UK companies that board members must take account of 'environmental, reputation and business probity issues' when considering internal controls. This advice was formally adopted by the London Stock Exchange (LSE) in 1999 when the LSE wrote to all the UK listed companies telling them to implement the Turnbull Committee's guidance. Elsewhere within the government, the Foreign and Commonwealth Office drew up a best practice manual to help UK companies invest in a more ethical manner overseas, while the Department of Trade and Industry (DTI) pushed on with its review of company law, offering hope of more companies reporting on their social and environmental performance. Several of the larger consultancy firms have also launched 'reputation assurance and social and ethical auditing services.'[46] Thus, greater attention is being paid to SRI. The decision by Marks & Spencer to join the Ethical Trading Initiative was seen as a boost to the wider campaign to improve working conditions throughout the world. In the UK alone, there exist a host of organisations to assist companies and investors in their SEE policy; some examples are Transparency International, Investors in People, Business in the Community, and the Prince of Wales Business Leaders Forum. However, according to Paul Myners, 'fund managers remain unnecessarily reluctant to take an activist stance in relation to corporate underperformance, even when this would be in their clients' financial interest.'[47] The performance of a small number of specialist funds targeted on identifying and investing in underperforming companies in the UK provide evidence of value opportunities being foregone as a consequence of inaction by other investors.[48] A Wiltshire Associates study identified that the California Public Employees' Retirement System (CalPERS) generated some $150 million annually in additional returns to its pension fund as a direct result of its active approach to corporate governance. Such quantification of the benefits of intervention is difficult to find in the UK. It is by no means axiomatic that investor intervention always adds value, as was the case with Vodafone's takeover of Mannesmann. Foreign institutional investors delivered Mannesmann to Vodafone. It is not clear that this shareholder decision genuinely added value, although SRI considerations were not even in the investors' radar. However, Vodafone is popular with ethical fund managers in the UK.

If they perceive a problem, the vast majority of institutional investors do not intervene in the management of companies in which they are shareholders. Historically, selling shares has been considered the better part of intervention. In most cases the issue revolves around purely financial considerations. Even when the issue is transparent – as with executive compensation, particularly when top executives today regularly reward themselves for failure or simply for pulling off a corporate deal – there is not enough coordinated action taken by institutional investors against such blatant violation of shareholder value, although recently eight leading pension funds and fund management firms did come together and wrote to 750 quoted UK companies asking them to give shareholders an annual vote on the size of their directors' pay packets.[49] The concept of buying shares at what can be called a discount for poor governance and then putting pressure on reforming these companies so that the discount disappears is not actively employed as an investment strategy.

NAPF does not shirk in criticising large UK firms for poor corporate governance, but unless a more activist stance is taken, it may not achieve the desired outcome. According to the annual 'proxy season' analysis conducted by NAPF's Voting Issues Service (VIS), of the top FTSE 350 companies (excluding investment trusts), around 18 companies (5%) of the monitored group in 2000 failed to comply with the LSE's combined code of recommended behaviour on arranging for the notice of the AGM and related papers to be sent to shareholders at least 20 working days before the meeting. This figure was down from 10% in 1999. Some 54% of the companies did not ensure the independence of remuneration committees and 16% failed to establish a majority of independent non-executive directors for their audit committees. Of the companies surveyed, 7% had a combined chairman cum chief executive, and among them were firms such as Anglo-American, Amvescap, PowerGen, Bass, EMI Group, Old Mutual and ARM Holdings.[50] Intervention in the form of voting levels has risen in recent years in the UK, but they still remain rather low in absolute terms.[51] Also, votes against a board remain rare.

A report by Friends Ivory & Sime (FIS) and the Ashridge Centre for Business & Society concluded that there is considerable scepticism that SRI would become much more prevalent, and that if the UK government wishes to use investment practices to influence corporate behaviour, more robust action will almost certainly be required. The message from this report was that 'by not clearly defining the key terms, "social, ethical and environmental" and by not looking at the issue of trust law in tandem, the industry has found it difficult to deal with the issue.... It appears that many pension schemes will side-step the issue because neither they, nor their advisers, can see a clear, meaningful, solution within the current legal framework. In this sense, market systems are like rivers – they will generally find the path of least resistance.'[52] This is because the government only requires trustees to disclose the extent to which SEE considerations are taken into account in the investment process. It does not require any SRI action, give any definition or clarification of these terms, and critically, does not require any proof that the stated policy is in fact being carried out, or that the stated policy is not misleading pension members.[53]

FIS, the UK's market leader in SRI, uses an internally developed investment process called Responsible Engagement Overlay (REO), which is structured to include a large number of companies in its universe. This process has been questioned by investors who favour negative/positive screens. However, an inclusive approach is also favoured by many investors. FIS seeks to engage in a dialogue with companies at the highest level, to make the case for positive change across a range of key issues such as labour standards, human rights, climate change, forestry and other aspects of sustainable development. There are no perfect companies, but institutional stewardship can support companies that are committed to adopting a more active CSR policy. The FIS process of using its influence as an investor to encourage companies in improving their management of key SEE issues is now widely recognised within the investment community. However, that was not the case when the stewardship concept was launched in 1984.

Investment in companies operating in sectors that have an exceptionally high negative impact on society and the environment is only considered if they demonstrate a commitment to improvement. Investments are not made in companies that derive any revenue from military activity. Further, serious concerns arise when selecting companies if 3% or more of their revenue comes from gambling, alcohol or nuclear production. When 10% of a company's revenue is from the sales of tobacco products, distribution or manufacture of strategic military goods or services, or ownership or operation of nuclear power stations, the FIS Stewardship fund excludes investments in such companies. Alcohol retailing, in the hotels and leisure sector, is accepted as a special case because much of the consumption is with food. So in that sector alone, revenue from the sale of alcohol of up to 33% is permitted. The ethical policy stance of the Stewardship fund means that around 40% of the companies in the FTSE All Share index are considered acceptable for investment.[54] The focus has been on smaller and medium-sized companies because many large companies fail to comply with FIS ethical requirements. This has impacted on the fund's performance. As at the end of June 2001, the £1.3 billion Stewardship fund grew by 38% after charges compared to 51% return from the UK All Companies Pension Fund sector average and 71% from the FTSE All Share index.

Fund managers can often encounter a real conflict of interest. 'Fund management firms may be keen to attract or to keep a contract to manage the pension of the company in question – or they may be part of a wider financial organisation, which wants, for example, the investment banking or insurance business of that company.'[55] Like analysts who seem to have lost their independence at the alter of the potential bottom line, fund managers are reluctant to be seen as 'troublemakers' in the interests of attracting new business. The *Company Law Review* makes similar arguments in its consultation document 'Completing the Structure':

If the managers manage a company pension fund, anything less than unquestioning support for that company's board may lead to loss of the business, since a majority of the trustees are usually directors or former directors of the company. If the fund manager is part of a banking or financial services group, the company management may threaten to terminate banking or other relationships.

But the most common agency problem arises from fund managers' own business interests. At any time some sponsoring companies of pension fund clients may be underperforming. Directors are unlikely to welcome shareholder activism from the manager. Even those doing well may be hostile to such activism as future discipline.[56]

What is worth mentioning in this context is that by definition 50% of the 'active' fund-managers underperform regularly, or at best, periodically. So fund managers are equally concerned of their own underperformance and losing business as result. Active intervention in a company by fund managers may boomerang in a higher level of scrutiny of their own business practices, which fund managers are not prepared to face. 'Clearly, where managers were failing to take an activist stance because of their wider business interests, they would be illegitimately subordinating the interests of their clients to other aims. Management firms have a responsibility to ensure that the reality as well as the appearance of effective Chinese walls is established, protecting their clients' interests in improving the performance of companies they own, from their wider business interests.'[57]

For many institutional investors, such as Hermes Pensions Management's Alastair Ross Goobey:

Corporate governance is not a moral crusade but is part of our fiduciary duty to our clients in identifying the business risks, financial and non-financial, to enhance our investment process accordingly. If in the process it makes companies think more carefully about their total risk, then the outcome is likely to be better for everybody. As Anthony Cleaver said, 'What can be measured, gets managed.'[58]

315

It will therefore become increasingly important for companies to measure their bottom line in a more inclusive manner and to report that annually, as shareholders will increasingly demand access to such information. The current trend towards cutting costs via M&A activity, increasing margins and delivering higher profits and dividends deliver short-term benefits, but may not prove to be the most sustainable way of maintaining shareholder value. The focus has been on containing costs and boosting profits rather than on investing in improving the environment or developing other socially responsible relationships. As the World Business Council for Sustainable Development – a coalition of some 120 companies from 33 countries covering 20 industrial sectors – aims to emphasise, there is a strong correlation between ecological and economic efficiency. Investors, including companies, need to appreciate the long-term drivers of commercial success rather than focus on narrow financial measures in the short term. Forward-thinking companies are engaging beyond the short-term profit and loss numbers and looking at the need for implementing an added-value strategy as investors are under greater pressure to factor wider considerations, including ethical considerations, into their investment decisions.

In his report on institutional investment in the UK, Myners proposed that trustees should agree with both internal and external investment managers an explicit written mandate covering a wide range of issues, including activism. 'The mandate should incorporate the principles of the US Department of Labor Interpretative Bulletin on activism. Managers should have an explicit strategy, elucidating the circumstances in which they will intervene in a company; the approach they will use in doing so; and how they measure the effectiveness of this strategy.'[59] As active intervention can be in the best financial interest of intermediaries, it can be argued that fund managers are legally obliged to follow such a course of action to fulfil their fiduciary duty. The US Department of Labor's 1994 interpretative bulletin makes it clear that activism, where it might add value, is part of the fiduciary duty of an investment manager.[60] The Myners review recommends that all pension fund trustees should incorporate the principle of the interpretative bulletin into fund management mandates. It goes further in recommending that the principle should in due course be more clearly incorporated into UK law.

The advantages of shareholder advocacy are many. Often investors do not need to formally introduce a resolution for their concerns. Management, aware that investors have access to the shareholder resolution process, agree to discuss issues with investors in order to avoid a formal shareholder proposal. Thus, the decision to file a shareholder resolution can trigger a mutually beneficial dialogue between shareholder and management, which is generally the most effective way to encourage change. As a result of improved communication, shareholder advocates often withdraw their resolutions before having them presented to the body of the company's shareholders through the proxy ballot and at the annual meeting. Thus a successful shareholder process can lead to the company's agreement to improve a practice or policy without the shareholder proposal needing to undergo a general vote.

Besides, proxy voting is not like electoral politics. Success is not measured through the attainment of a majority vote. In fact, a shareholder campaign may achieve its goals by having obtained a relatively small number of votes. Managements know there are a number of factors that often limit the votes attained. Many large institutional investors tend to vote only if they have researched the issues involved, a process which may take more than a year and extend beyond the initial vote. Also, investors who own stocks through mutual funds do not have the ability to vote their shares. Therefore, even relatively low votes through the proxy process often indicate real and increasing concern among shareholders, and reflect interest on the part of the public and press. This combined level of interest is often enough to encourage management to enter into a dialogue and to consider changing its practices or policies.

Engagement also enables asset managers to enlarge the universe of companies they can invest in as opposed to screening companies on any predetermined criteria. The most powerful argument for intervention in a company is financial self-interest, adding value for clients through improved corporate performance leading to improved investment performance. One would expect that for institutional investors with long-term liabilities, such an approach to investing would appeal.[61] Firms such as Hermes Pensions Management in the UK have taken an activist stance for some time now. According to Alastair Ross Goobey:

Social, ethical and environmental (SEE) matters take a high profile in our investment process. We believe that companies need to take into account the long-term financial cost of their SEE policy. Sooner or later, someone is going to have to pay for it. We participated in a committee of institutional investors that drafted guidance on SEE matters that we would find helpful from companies. For example, has the board considered the non-financial risks associated with their business? The Turnbull Report has made more companies look at these risks; and we, as investors, want to know what the big business risks are for the firms we invest in. We suggest companies include more measures of that sort, which are independently audited, in their annual reports. We don't want to make it statutory nor do we want companies to be overburdened with having to provide such information. As the same time, understanding the big risks from the standpoint of the company as well as for the shareholder is very important.

The Hermes Focus funds grew out of our involvement in corporate governance issues, which if you are not careful could turn into a box-ticking exercise. The question is, What do you do when you come across governance you don't like? You need some way of altering that. While we are happy to facilitate change in governance, it is not a cheap thing to do. We have individuals here who do the research, which has to be paid for. We have to pay for strategic research and that's where the value addition lies. We have to do much more in-depth research than an average fund manager has to for this specialised product. But how do we justify to our trustees the cost of doing all that? We needed to prove that this work was saving them money, if not directly making them huge returns. The Focus funds thus came into existence; we believe that everybody has benefited from it – from the companies themselves to shareholders and investors. Even society as a whole, as you have better-managed companies.[62]

Unfortunately, not all their investments are managed in such a way. In fact, Hermes are among the largest indexed managers in the UK.

Hermes closed their UK Focus fund to new investors, as it is already about £700 million, and in order to add value they believe the fund cannot grow beyond a critical size, although they have never found a shortage of candidates to invest in. The UK Focus fund, set up in October 1998, invests in some quite large companies that are part of the UK index portfolio but which have underperformed vis-à-vis their peer group due to poor management strategy, governance or capital structure and where Hermes believe that an active share-holder involvement can help release the higher intrinsic value of the company. Hermes would have significant holdings in these firms – 5-10% of the firm – to have more clout in stimulating change. 'No action is no option,' confirms Alastair Ross Goobey. 'When we don't like what the firm is doing, we try to change things. We also persuade our institutional colleagues to buy into what we want to do. It is cheaper than getting investment bankers involved and arranging bids.'[63]

The style of investing has proven to be very beneficial for the pension scheme. The fund's return for 2000 was 9.7% compared to the FTSE All Share, which fell by 5.9%. 'I don't think there are many funds that have outperformed the index both in 1999 and 2000, as they were such different market environments. We are therefore beginning to realise that it is not just a statistical fluke,' confirms Ross Goobey. Recently, Hermes launched a European Focus fund with a view to creating a strategic alliance with Relational Investors in the US, who undertake similar shareholder programmes in North America. 'We are marketing worldwide in this area and believe ourselves to be pioneers in this field in the UK. The fee structure for our Focus funds is such that if we outperform, we get a decent performance fee. The business is marginally profitable without performance fees. But if the fund performs well, fees can be quite attractive. And nobody complains about paying fees based on performance.'[64] Thus, activist investing is good business.

For years, Hermes has worked closely with international institu-tional investors to promote improvements in corporate governance in specific companies. They were also instrumental in creating the Global Institutional Governance Network (GIGN), which provides a forum for exchanging information on poorly performing companies, and where feasible, exercising constructive influence. As an investor, they prefer to 'engage' with companies in influencing their SEE outlook rather than 'screening' out of the investment process firms that, for example, invest in Burma or profit from the sale of arms to suspect regimes. The trustees of CalPERS, with whom Hermes have a voting alliance, elected to sell all their tobacco shares against the advice of the professionals for the same reasons that Hermes did not invest in South Africa when apartheid was on because they believed there was substantial risk involved. Hermes simply did not feel comfortable with the business risks involved where there was the possibility of losing all the initial investment. When political, social or environmental actions are going to have a deleterious effect on your investment, one has to take that into account. Premier Oil's investment in Myanmar is a very interesting case at the moment. The company's involvement in a part of the world with a very poor record in human rights is clearly affecting its share price, although it remains a profitable investment.

From child labour to human rights, Hermes aim to be pragmatic about these issues and not be too ideological about them:

> The greatest threat to portfolio investment is the emergence of 'single-issue activists' working outside the political system, who are obsessed with one particular agenda. We have seen these protestors in Seattle, Prague, Montreal, etc. We think it is perfectly reasonable for people to ask BP, for example, what their plans are to meet the challenge of global warming, but it is unreasonable to ask them to submit a timetable for withdrawing from carbon-based fuels altogether. It is unrealistic, as BP cannot be expected to provide a timetable for not producing oil.

> The situation with Huntingdon Life Sciences is a case in point. It is better for us to test our drugs on animals than on human beings. The protestors are not simply saying that the company's standards have slipped in some way, that the firm was testing cosmetics on animals, etc. These protestors do not want animals to be used in any experiments at all. That will be terrible not only for the progress of medicine but also for the whole world. We are not talking of one or two issues; what one has to contend with is any number of issues. This is a challenge inves-

tors face as we are in the front line. People can easily identify us as shareholders and then threaten us, even when we do not have any interest in the company concerned. The Department of Trade and Industry in the UK is trying to find ways of protecting shareholders in such ventures. However, the creation of such nominee companies can be abused by less scrupulous firms.[65]

It is not yet clear how exactly SRI will alter the way in which pension fund trustees and their fund managers determine asset allocation and stock selection. However, SRI is here to stay. With increasing demand for ethical products, mainstream index providers such as Dow Jones and FTSE now offer corporate social responsibility (CSR) indexes – the Dow Jones Group Sustainability Index (DJGSI) and the FTSE4-Good Index. Working in association with EIRIS, the function of the newly launched family of ethical indexes in the UK, called FTSE4-Good, is meant to fill the gap in this market. These indexes – FTSE4-Good UK, FTSE4Good Europe, FTSE4Good US and FTSE4Good Global – aim to be both benchmark and trading indexes and they are based on internationally accepted codes of conduct. The starting points for the FTSE4Good indexes are the FTSE All Share, Developed Europe, US and Developed indexes excluding investment companies. The SRI screening then excludes:

- Tobacco producers
- Companies providing strategic parts or services for or manufacturing whole nuclear weapon systems
- Manufacturers of whole weapons systems
- Owners or operators of nuclear power stations and those mining or processing uranium

This results in the basic eligible universe for arriving at the constituents of the FTSE4Good indexes. The application of first principles includes:

- The Universal Declaration of Human Rights 1948
- The OECD Guidelines for Multinational Enterprises 1976
- The UN Global Compact 1999
- The Coalition for Environmentally Responsible Economies 1989
- The Amnesty International Human Rights Principles for Companies
- The Caux Round Table Principles for Business 1994

- The Global Sullivan Principles 1977
- The Ethical Trading Initiative – Base Code 1998
- The Social Accountability 8000 of 1997
- The Global Reporting Initiative (GRI) Sustainability Guidelines 1999

The amalgamation of first principles creates what is known as the Core Themes of Corporate Social Responsibility and they cover the following areas:

- Working towards environmental sustainability
- Developing positive relationships with stakeholders
- Upholding and supporting universal human rights

Building on the principles and on the experience of companies committed to CSR, their adherence to the Best Governance Practice Framework is integral to the selection criteria for inclusion in the index. Understandably, it is intended that the selection criteria will evolve to reflect mainstream social thinking and changes in levels of information disclosure. However, no system of selection is perfect; the FTSE4Good indexes may include companies that are involved in controversy surrounding their CSR policy. The advisory committee intends to examine such companies at its regular meetings and act accordingly.[66] While it is hoped the creation of such an index may help some investors, it is not at all clear how FTSE4Good will benefit the institutional sector. Considering that the job of FTSE is to provide benchmarks for different classes of investor, the launch of FTSE4-Good makes sense. There is a lack of SRI-specific benchmarks and thus FTSE's attempt at creating one is understandable. The problem lies in the fact that there is no clear definition of a 'good' company.

A comparison between the top 15 companies in the FTSE All Share index and the FTSE4Good UK index is revealing, as the difference between the top 15 companies in the two is minimal (Table 7.2). The difference lies mainly in the weightings; the FTSE4Good has 283 companies with a market capitalisation of £1,178,831 million compared to 759 companies in the FTSE All Share with a market capitalisation of £1,571,282 million. Some 67% of the FTSE4Good UK index is represented by the top 15 companies, while that figure for the FTSE All Share is understandably lower at 52%. However, the

Table **7.2** *A comparison between the top 15 index constituents as at 29 June 2001*[a]

	FTSE4Good		FTSE All Share	
	Rank	Weighting	Rank	Weighting
BP	1	11.2	1	8.41
GlaxoSmithKline	2	10.55	2	7.92
Vodafone	3	9.07	3	6.81
HSBC	4	6.67	4	5.00
AstraZeneca	5	4.96	5	3.72
Shell Transport & Trading	6	4.93	6	3.70
Royal Bank of Scotland[b]	N/A	N/A	7	2.67
Lloyds TSB	7	3.32	8	2.49
BT	8	3.23	9	2.42
Barclays	9	3.06	10	2.29
Diageo	10	2.27	11	1.70
CGNU	11	1.88	12	1.41
Halifax	12	1.57	13	1.17
Tesco	N/A	N/A	14	1.13
Abbey National	13	1.51	15	1.13
Unilever	14	1.48	16	1.11
Prudential	15	1.45	17	1.08

[a] Source: FTSE

[b] Royal Bank of Scotland was admitted to the FTSE4Good UK index in September 2001

stock- and sector-specific risk in the FTSE All Share is already cause for considerable concern among investors. In terms of diversification, the high level of concentration of the FTSE4Good index makes it even less usable.

The Frank Russell Company developed five tests that trustees can use to ensure their SRI policy does not subordinate beneficiaries' interests:[67]

- The SRI policy does not reduce the expected return on the plan's assets.
- Restrictions imposed by an SRI policy should not be so constraining that a fund is inadequately diversified.
- Implementation of the policy should not introduce unacceptable risk exposures or burdensome administrative procedures.

- The policy should be acceptable to members.
- Trustees should maintain proper records of their decisions and the grounds on which they were made.

Although FTSE has appointed EIRIS to source company data, the current level of information companies publish makes it impossible to compare their performance. This is certainly reflected in the data, when the FTSE All Share and the FTSE4Good are set against each other. The impression one gets is that over half the FTSE All Share is ethically sound. In which case, surely the aim should be to make the rest comply with SEE standards rather than create a separate ethical index, unless the purpose is simply to name and shame the companies concerned. In reality, of the 759 companies in the FTSE All Share only 283 are ethically sound, or just 37%. If that is indeed the case, there is genuine cause for investor concern. FIS suggest that around 40% of the FTSE 100 satisfy their ethical criteria. Thus, there is little consensus even among specialists as to what constitutes an ethically sound company.

Does the creation of the new ethical index mean that the UK pension assets that are currently indexed vis-à-vis the All Share have to switch to the FTSE4Good UK index to claim SRI status? That would be highly risky and would indeed be heavily opposed by both investors and the companies concerned. In the long term, SRI must embrace all companies in an index, otherwise 'indexers' or 'trackers' based on the FTSE All Share will not qualify as socially responsible investments. Currently, passive investors can justify themselves as SRI compliant by 'engaging' with companies. In many ways, the creation of the FTSE4Good contradicts the whole rationale behind the SRI legislation. If the government is keen to bring the influence of institutional investors to bear on the companies they invest in, active engagement is a preferred method. In any event, as indexers comprise almost one-quarter of the pension assets in the UK, the question of shifting assets from the FTSE All Share to the FTSE4Good simply does not arise. That then begs the question, What exactly is the purpose of the FTSE4Good? The investment issues that the FTSE4Good raises are encapsulated in this editorial from the *Professional Investor*:

On 1 July FTSE4Good will be launched, a series of 'socially responsible investment' (SRI) global indices, constructed in association with the ethical investment research service EIRIS. The SRI element is defined as protecting the environment, good stakeholder relationships, or the promotion of human rights, while some 'controversial activities' will be banned, resulting in about half the All-Share being excluded.

FTSE4Good has provided few details of its SRI criteria, or its basic philosophy (engagement versus exclusion) – successful indices need rigorous and transparent index construction methodologies. The target market for the new index is not clear. While retail ethical unit trusts have grown rapidly, they are still quite small. UK pension funds are increasingly considering SRI, but they are unlikely to use an index that excludes half the All-Share.

The aims and objectives of the FTSE4Good index are obviously laudable, even if the name may put off a City audience. However, further thought needs to be given to the aims and objectives of the new index. Is it designed to change corporate behaviour, be an ethical equivalent of the All-Share, or track a few ethical unit trusts? Until these questions are clarified, we may as well call it 'FTSE4What'?[68]

Many investors are reluctant to use negative screening as an SRI approach, as they believe it limits the pool of assets they can invest in, thereby jeopardising returns. Others find SEE considerations too vague to be able to provide any clear and specific policy guidelines to their members in their SIP. Thus, according to one anonymous company fund: 'The Directors believe that ESE (ethical, social and environmental) considerations in relation to investment are important, but are impossible to define to everyone's satisfaction, and that any attempt to reflect them in the mandates given to the investment managers may, from time to time, lead to a conflict with the trustee's duty to act in the best financial interests of the members, and may result in a detrimental effect upon investment returns.'[69]

CONCLUSION

The concept of SRI is not new. The basic principles of CSR have been refined over decades, if not centuries, and are based on internationally acceptable standards of corporate behaviour. These principles are not set in stone and are very much in the process of evolution. It is true that companies which are not included in one of the various indexes being created on the basis of SEE performance are more likely to be exposed to greater scrutiny by investors, government and other stakeholders. Even Michael Meacher, Secretary of State for the Environment, is targeting companies to be included in the BiE Index, for example. Emerging trends from this index are to be fed into the UK's sustainable development indicators. While it is true that methodologies used in the creation of such indexes will develop in time, the important fact is that attention is finally being paid to such issues, and SEE factors are beginning to be accounted for. It is clear that as company accounts start to reflect in more tangible ways the financial outcome of their SEE policies, investors will be in a better position to incorporate it into their investment decision-making.

A word about the pitfalls of relying too much on our ability to quantify and measure intangible outcomes, as such processes clearly do not exist. It may drive individuals and companies with the responsibility of doing so to simply adopt a fairly superficial tick-the-box approach to the issue rather than devote genuine thought in addressing the problem. It is true that, for fund managers, the ability to measure SRI will help them in their asset allocation and there is every reason to believe that even companies will benefit from such information. The devil is in the detail. If companies and their shareholders get bogged down in gathering so-called data to justify their CSR/SRI status, then we have a problem, as that involves an additional layer of bureaucracy to monitor the accuracy and continuity of that data. Reconciling data and ensuring that companies are doing what they say they are doing should not be left to shareholders, although they can elect to do so. Thus, an external body that can audit such data is a better strategy, once there is consensus on the different ways of measuring such outcomes and how exactly to interpret such accounts.

However, as investing has become truly global, CSR and SRI must equally have a global remit. While it may be possible to monitor the implementation of such policies within the UK, or even within the developed world, the problem arises when investments deal with developing countries, where such legislation is weak. Investors expect all companies seeking capital in the public financial markets to institute strong corporate governance and oversight through well-established guidelines and practices. The institution of corporate governance is more critical for smaller and start-up enterprises because investors often view these enterprises as having a propensity towards higher volatility in earnings and less historical information available to assess and value the enterprise. The focus on behaviour and full disclosure, rather than mandated structures, allows for flexibility while enabling shareholders to make better-informed investment decisions. Full disclosure of relevant information is essential in assessing the effectiveness of an enterprise's corporate governance; such transparency, in turn, promotes efficient capital markets.

Unfortunately, it cannot be said that institutional investors have played an active role in achieving that. A study has analysed the monitoring role of pension funds in the UK and their contribution in adding value to the companies they invest in; it came to the following conclusion:

> They [UK pension funds] hold large stakes in small and low value companies, they do not lead these companies to comply with the Cadbury report and, in the long run, these companies under-perform their industry counterparts. Our results suggest that pension funds in the UK are passive investors and they do not monitor companies in which they hold large stakes. There is, therefore, a need for them to be more active to maximise their investment returns and the returns of small shareholders.[70]

If that is the verdict on UK small companies and their institutional shareholders, the prospect is indeed bleak for their counterparts in developing countries. Smaller companies in certain sectors are also the ones most likely to need initial support in putting such practices into place. If their professional investors are incapable of adding value, as is taken to be the case among private equity investors, it is not yet clear what sort of help is forthcoming and who might be willing to provide it, not to mention the costs involved in monitoring it, if governments are equally reluctant to do so. The outcome could

327

be that new enterprises only thrive in certain sectors of the economy, such as the IT sector. While in the short term it may appear to be highly attractive, the longer-term consequences of such a policy may result in the wholesale transfer of certain sectors of the economy to less developed parts of the world, where the legal framework for CSR is less onerous. Already, certain low-value-added sectors within manufacturing, even services, have migrated to developing countries, leading to negative impact on the environment while not necessarily improving the social structures within those countries. In fact, the negative global consequences of such policies are already evident.

It has been argued that the British economy suffers from a complex of maladies known as 'short-termism', or what Will Hutton called the 'liquidity fetish'. It refers to the argument that institutional investors have a systematic bias against companies which invest in long-term growth. In the words of Dominic Hobson:

> Instead of rewarding companies which train their employees well, work patiently to build their market share, and research and develop innovative products and services ... the institutions reward those companies which invest in projects to produce the highest returns quickly. The chief discipline which enables them to impose their will in this way is the stock market. It is fear that institutions will sell their shares, perhaps to a corporate predator, which forces companies to disgorge as dividends to shareholders the earnings which could be reinvested. This raises the cost of capital, discouraging investment in any but the most immediately profitable ventures, reducing the rate of growth of the economy, and lowering the standard of living.

> If it is even half true, it is a devastating critique of the structure of ownership in Britain today. For ultimately it holds the institutional investors responsible for the worst ills of contemporary Britain: ignorance, joblessness and poverty, and the crime which feeds off them.[71]

One could argue that the lack of CSR is a result of such an investment bias. In principle, pension fund trustees are long-term investors. However, their behaviour does not support such a bias. The dissociation of SEE policy performance from the consolidated financial statements of major MNCs remains a critical issue when evaluating them. While active managers and investors in private equity can 'engage' with companies with regard to their SEE policy, other investment styles, such as absolute return strategies, do not lend themselves to such a process. As it is accepted that SRI is an essential part of an investment strategy, it is hoped that in time CSR will become an integral aspect of all annual reports. The problem still remains with regard to MNCs which operate in countries with weak or non-existent laws on CSR or SRI. The tragedy in Bhopal, India, where a whole city was affected by the chemical pollution at the Union Carbide plant is only one example of how irresponsible government action failed to offer its citizens adequate environmental, social and ethical protection from poor management by a large and powerful MNC.

In principle, many developing countries adhere to the UN Declaration of Human Rights, the ILO conventions and any number of environmental management systems. In reality, implementing these measures is an additional cost that governments cannot bear. Charging an SEE tax on MNCs for operating in their countries could be a solution, except that monitoring the utilisation of such income exclusively for investment in improving SEE processes may add to the cost of doing business in the less developed parts of the world, and eventually wipe out the cost advantage of operating in the host country in the first place. Developing countries need the investment and would be reluctant to see business disappearing to less scrupulous regimes. However, if action is taken on a global level, as with combating global terrorism, then institutions such as the World Bank, IMF, OECD and the Commonwealth Association for Corporate Governance can invest in improving the fate of many developing nations where market economics has delivered a greater divide between the rich and the poor, instead of better corporate governance and a better redistribution of the spoils of globalisation.

329

CHAPTER 8

Concluding Observations

INTRODUCTION

The 1990s ushered in seismic change to the world, altering its economic, political and cultural landscape. We saw the economic decline of Japan, having seen its giddy rise during the 1980s. We witnessed the spectacular ascendancy of the US, the dissolution of the USSR and the creation of the euro-zone. The decade experienced the rise and fall of emerging markets, particularly the Asian tigers. We saw the growing power of China and economic liberalisation in India. We also saw a concerted decline in inflation in various developed economies and an attendant fall in government borrowing with improving fiscal management. The increased penetration of technology in industry and society and the high level of global mergers and acquisitions (M&A) activity were matched by the 'irrational exuberance' of the major global markets. This was followed by the long-awaited correction that began in March 2000. Just when the world was waiting for signs of global economic stability and possible recovery in the US, the events of 11 September 2001 tipped the balance, making recession a certainty. Stock markets plunged into an irrational depression and exhibited increased volatility.

Demography had alerted governments to withdraw from the key responsibility of providing retirement benefits to individuals, leading to a significantly reduced welfare system. The 1990s saw a decline in the influence of governments and the extraordinary rise in the wealth accumulated by multinational corporations and pension funds. We encountered a concentration of wealth among the few and a greater acceptance of economic disparity, both among nations and individuals. However, individualism did not filter through to greater participation in society or democracy at the grass-root level, only greater consumption. The economic future of the world, we were assured, depended on the almighty American consumer. The decline in our collective belief in God or any form of shared values was matched by the rise of fundamentalism and fanaticism. The rise in globalisation was matched with the organised and violent nature of anti-globalisation protests. Globalisation delivered some benefits, particularly in the fields of medicine and technology, but also created greater inequality. As the Chinese curse goes, May you live in interesting times. We most certainly do. However, it is not clear whether we are cursed or blessed as a result of all this development. Possibly both.

Demographics aside, not many of the other developments were foreseen even 20 years ago. It was not inevitable that capitalism and market economics would be embraced on a global scale, even by countries opposed to it. Hence it would be foolish to attempt to write about the future of the asset management industry. After all, the Pensions Act in the UK came into existence only in 1995. Although retirement was not invented recently, pensions were. Going back a few hundred years reveals that friendly societies provided de facto pension benefits for its members. However, these liabilities were causing serious problems for the societies by the end of the nineteenth century and members were reluctant to increase their subscriptions to the level necessary to finance old age more securely.[1] History has an uncanny way of repeating itself.

While investing to secure a comfortable old age is a modern necessity, it is reasonable to conclude that individuals today need to plan far more actively for their retirement. Those who have the means of doing so are actively engaged in that pursuit. But there are many who are unable to provide for themselves, and it is unclear what level of support will be available to people unable to help themselves as a result of long-term disability or long periods of unemployment. Who will pay for the safety net of social welfare for those who are unable to help themselves? The legislative changes that are being put into place today will have significant impact on our future economic security. While technology, globalisation and demographic changes remain key drivers of change for all sectors of industry, equally influential are legislation and regulation, fiscal and monetary policies of governments and their willingness to investment in public services.

The aim of this concluding chapter is to highlight certain trends that are in place, and to identify areas within the industry that are already under greater scrutiny, and thus likely to change under pressure from investors and/or legislation. It will be unrealistic to capture all the possible changes awaiting the industry. During the course of my research for this book, including interviews with senior industry professionals, certain issues were universally acknowledged, e.g. the influence of globalisation, technology and demographics, and other issues were raised as secondary drivers of change, e.g. the impact of legislation, SRI, the structure of the industry (including fees, independence of research, creation and distribution of products, etc.), global M&A activity, continuing education of investors, rise of the retail sector, role of consultants. As my interviews with key professionals were not based on a survey-type questionnaire, it was all the more revealing what each one had to say with reference to their vision of the future of the asset management industry. No two people gave the same answer or raised exactly the same set of issues. However, had they been presented with a multiple choice questionnaire, it is likely that most of them would have ticked the same boxes. That is why I decided to allow my interviewees to 'choose' their particular areas of concern or express their perception of issues that need to be addressed, instead of feeding them with a series of options. However, it would also be unwise to attempt to create a theory out of such a random assortment of statements. Some conclusions can be drawn, e.g. how and why some firms are more competitive than others in the same industry. Much of that hinges on the calibre and integrity of people that find favour within organisations as much as the ability of firms to integrate a diversity of views into their decision-making process. Anticipating change is one of the most challenging aspects of executive decision-making. But it is also the most rewarding.

PROSPECTS FOR THE FUTURE

The consensus is that the future of the asset management industry, including the insurance sector, remains secure. Many fund managers feel fairly confident of their own future as well as the opportunity for new entrants and niche players. For William Cotter, the main drivers influencing the future of fund management include

> the rapidly changing demographic profile across most developed countries, the trend towards privatisation of social welfare provision and the emergence of intergenerational transfer of wealth. The combination of these factors will have a profound effect on the way we do business. As more and more people accumulate wealth, live longer and have a higher expectation of living standards, investment managers will face the challenge of providing accessible, uncomplicated and relevant products for this expanding customer group.
>
> Who will benefit in this environment? Certainly good equity managers should thrive. We are also likely to see growth towards multi-product providers, who have good brand recognition and whom customers find accessible. But this will not, in my view, be at the expense of good niche firms. Ours is a talent business and investors recognise this. That's why there is always scope for small start-ups that can demonstrate that they have something of value to offer.[2]

The high level of M&A activity over the past decade wiped out most of the major UK fund managers. Schroder Investment Management remains the largest independent asset manager whose ownership is UK-based. While it is unclear to what extent ownership matters, it remains to be seen whether SIM can become a successful global asset manager via organic growth or will settle to be acquired by a larger group as most of its peers did. In a global economy, ownership of assets matters to the extent that it helps or hinders in building and sustaining a competitive edge. If Warren Buffett had been obliged to work for a large fund manager, his genius may never have been manifested to the world. That does not mean that all those who run their own asset management firms are Warren Buffetts. The

unregulated hedge fund sector, for example, is home to several frau-
dulent ventures. Even in the regulated sector, there are plenty of
examples of the wrong kind of risk-taking that inevitably produce
huge losses, collapses, bankruptcies and closures. Genuine innovation also involves risk-taking, but originality is less difficult to come
by. What distinguishes the original thinker and risk-taker from the
fly-by-night operator is perhaps intellectual honesty and accountability. Management has only itself to blame for failing to nurture
individuals with ideas and originality, regardless of its origin, colour,
creed, etc. The UK is not yet the open society it imagines itself to be.
At the end of the day, a nation, a company, a family is characterised
by the men and women who shape it.

Here is Nicola Ralston's view, in light of the recent developments
in technology and its impact on the future of fund management:

Much of what is deemed the 'new economy' is more about
greater convenience, choice and efficiency for both consumers
and businesses to fulfil their needs rather than fundamentally
changing what those needs are, and it is generally a process of
ongoing development rather than radical changes. The internet
is the best example of this with relevance to fund managers and
their clients. For the latter, it can provide information in a more
convenient manner on potential investments, up-to-date information on their portfolios, etc. Advances in technology used by
various stock exchanges and stockbrokers have made it easier
to invest in additional asset classes (non-domestic equities for
example). For fund managers, the internet should make it easier
to provide a more informative level of client service and allow
clients to extract performance data as they want it. From an
investment standpoint, information gathering on potential
investment opportunities is becoming easier and quicker,
thanks to email, company websites and aggregators of other
economic and company- specific data.

Despite these rapid changes, we believe that the essence of the
fund management industry will not change greatly. Institutional asset management will continue to rely on good relations
between managers and trustees, engendered by good perfor-

mance, accurate assessment of clients' needs and timely reporting of performance. In retail fund management, branding
remains of paramount importance for the fund manager, as
investors have an ever-widening array of funds and providers
to choose from.[3]

This more or less sums up what the majority of senior industry
professionals believe, i.e. whatever the nature of changes that may
overtake the industry in the future, the demand for professional fund
managers will not decline, particularly for the above average ones.
What would be worth highlighting is the increasing concentration
and influence of brands globally. While American firms have established themselves in the UK, the process is still in its infancy in
Europe, Japan and the rest of the world. 'Conventional wisdom has
it that the US model will take over the world. If you believe this then
you can have a vision of what fund management will look like in five
years' time. For myself I am not convinced that the American domination of Europe is a foregone conclusion.'[4] That was Tim Gardener's
viewpoint when asked about the future of asset management in
Europe.

For Alastair Ross Goobey, on the other hand: 'Technology has
already affected the fund management industry, but going forward
I think individuals will take greater control of their pension decisions. We will follow the American example of monitoring our
investments online. More and more people will be forced by government policy, through tax breaks, and by the providers to go down
that route. The changes in the distribution of products will mean that
there will be a tendency to brand products and relatively unknown
firms' products will be sold via the branded channels.'[5] The introduction of US-style 401K pension plans for individuals suggests that
the American model has been gaining greater acceptance in Europe.
As the US model has been stable for some time now, there is no
reason to question its efficiency in enabling individuals to provide
for their old age, particularly in light of serious mismanagement
witnessed, for example, within institutional managers in the UK.

Considering the uncertainty surrounding pensions with Equitable
Life, for example, is it fair that the company should accrue management fees while ill-informed investors suffer the consequences of

their decision, which was based on insufficient information in the first place? The whole concept of mutuality and equity has been flouted by the actions of not just the company but also the external regulators, including the House of Lords. Had investors known that a separate group of investors, with guaranteed incomes for which no provision had been made, would get preferential treatment in a crisis, it is unthinkable that any right-minded individual would have invested their savings with such a firm under such inequitable conditions. It is incredible too that no one realised there was a problem – not the auditors nor the company's directors nor the financial services regulators. What is even more shocking is that no one appears to be accountable for perpetuating what effectively amounts to fraud. While there is increasing demand for transparency, it is impossible for lay investors to detect weaknesses in the financial statistics of a company. Investors effectively lent their life savings with the hope of securing a certain level of return, but they were never made aware of the high level of risk inherent in that decision.

THE ROLE OF INVESTMENT CONSULTANTS

Although investment consultancy emerged as a business in the 1980s, it was not until the introduction of the Pensions Act 1995 and the minimum funding requirement (MFR) that gave scheme actuaries a critical role in advising trustees in their strategic asset allocation responsibility. As actuaries were already advising pension funds, the new legislation only enhanced their role. Despite being in business for over two decades, the investment consultancy market in UK is dominated by just four firms. An analysis of a sample of manager selection mandates over a nine-month period in 2000 found that William Mercer handled roughly 26% of such mandates, Watson Wyatt 23%, Bacon & Woodrow 22% and Hymans Robertson 14%, a total of 85% for the four firms.[6] Levels of customer switching are low; many funds retain the same consultant or actuary for 20 years or more. Thus, the role that investment consultants play in the pension fund sector is critical, as revealed in a survey where 78% of trustees indicated that they followed the advice of their investment consultants. It is true that 52% of trustees also indicated that they always questioned their consultant's advice and 77% felt they exerted significant influence on strategic asset allocation.[7]

Investment consultants have established a niche for themselves in the institutional sector. They act as a clearing house of information to their clients and help plan sponsors with other issues such as custody, administration, the education of trustees, etc. But these activities are at the low value-added end of their service. Consultants add value by giving advice on investment managers. Instead of funds having to pick and monitor managers on the basis of past performance, consultants provide qualitative and quantitative inputs. Just as stockbrokers research companies, investment consultants research investment management companies. They add considerable value in that area not only at the selection stage but also in ongoing monitoring. However, as explained by Tim Gardener, global head of investment consulting at William M. Mercer:

> We add the most value in long-term asset allocation advice. Someone has to decide the long-term neutral allocation to various asset classes for the pension fund. All the studies suggest that asset allocation contributes in excess of 80% of the total return of investments. That is a risk/return advice. We add value there. One way of demonstrating that is by comparing the performance of our clients to that of the average balanced pension fund. Over a ten-year period, we have outperformed.[8]

It is widely recognised that in the management of assets, strategic asset allocation plays a vital role in long-term investment performance. However, trustees do not seem to devote as much time and cost in enhancing that process as they do devote to the secondary activity of stock selection, for example. While fund management remains a large, diversified and profitable industry, investment consulting is significantly less profitable, not a large industry and is highly concentrated. According to Myners, 'by keeping profitability low, the low level of resources committed to asset allocation advice appears to be one of the factors driving the concentration of the investment consulting industry. Higher fees could attract a greater and more diverse range of firms into the market.'[9] Tim Gardener arrives at a similar conclusion but also points out that the need for research created a minimum efficient scale:

The nature of the investment consulting business is that it has high fixed costs, principally the manager research, which needs to be global in nature these days. Our database, for example, covers some 1,500 managers with 7,000 products globally. If you are going to research even a small number of those, you need a huge resource. On the basis of the fees consultants get paid, which on average is 1.5 basis points to fund managers' 27, frankly you have three choices:

You become large, so that you can spread the high fixed cost of manager research over a larger client base.

You can be smaller and run a fund-of-funds business in which case you are a fund manager offering some consultancy and paying for your research through the fund management business.

You offer substandard research.

So far most of the firms in the UK have chosen to be large, whereas firms in the US have taken the fund-of-funds route. Maybe the UK will change.[10]

It can be argued that such a practice is a legacy of the tradition of appointing balanced managers in the UK. With the rise in the use of customised benchmarks and the appointment of specialist fund managers, it stands to reason that trustees are in fact spending more time on strategic asset allocation. While trustees have seriously begun to question the fees attached to active stock selection, it is not evident that they have addressed the issue of increasing resources devoted to asset allocation. In his review, Paul Myners wrote: 'We place a heavy burden on the investment consultants who advise trustees. A tiny group of providers, mainly actuarial firms, dominate this small and not particularly profitable market. The result, despite these firms' best efforts – to which I pay tribute – is a narrow range of expertise and little room for specialisation. Nor is the consulting firms' performance usually assessed or measured.'[11] While being part of a concentrated group is one of the inevitabilities of doing business these days, Tim Gardener is of the view that the industry gets what it pays for:

Myners says that the result is a narrow range of expertise with little room for specialisation. I take a different view. These are subjective statements. There are about 300 investment consultants in the UK, but then the industry itself is not very wide. The range of expertise may be narrow, but that's because the business itself is relatively narrow. He is right to the extent that if you want a consultant who knows the entire hedge fund industry, it's difficult to find one. Ultimately it boils down to what people are prepared to pay for.

When Myners says that our performance is not usually assessed or measured, how do you measure the performance of other professionals such as accountants or lawyers? And when you do start, for example, measuring teachers, there is constantly a debate whether it is being done fairly or not. We would love to be measured, because we would love to demonstrate objectively the value we are undoubtedly adding. One of the reasons our fees are so low is because we find it difficult to measure and hence demonstrate objectively the value we add.

Much of our work has to do, in the asset allocation area, with the risk/return advice. You can measure return, but after the event it is very difficult to measure the risk advice. How do you measure advice that has to be given on a probabilistic basis? We can measure whether we rate managers correctly, but that's only part of our business. When you get into the practice instead of the theory, I reckon that, for what it pays, the industry has received a very good service.[12]

One of the reasons why investment consultants remain poorly remunerated for their service is because of their inability to demonstrate the value they add to the overall performance of the funds they advise. This is regrettable, notes Myners: 'Effective assessment of asset allocation advice, while not automatically leading to a greater level of attention and resources being paid to asset allocation, would encourage it by highlighting the value that can be added or lost through these decisions.'[13] The low margins associated with the business act as a major barrier to entry. As asset allocation has a significant impact on a fund's performance, the health of the investment consulting business impacts on the advice that is available to trustees. In the words of Paul Myners:

> The importance of investment consulting advice in the decision-making process calls ideally for a market characterised by a wide range of different firms with specialisms in particular areas, driven by high levels of entry into the industry and high levels of customer solicitation. Instead, the industry is best described as a small, low-profitability market in which a handful of long-established firms offer similar products and limited expertise in some important specialist areas, including private equity. Despite the best efforts of the firms involved, the result is likely to be a narrow range of advice with limited innovation.[14]

It is not helpful simply to blame the investment consulting industry; greater resources need to be allocated towards the sector. Investment consultants can demonstrate value addition via their manager selection process. Mechanisms to measure that process also need to be put in place. A clear definition of objectives, a focus on asset allocation, explicit mandates, appropriate benchmarks, effective performance measurement and greater transparency in the advisory process should help the investment consulting sector. In terms of adding value to a portfolio, asset allocation is significantly more important than stock selection, so it is illogical that trustees are prepared to pay significantly more to their fund managers than their investment consultants, particularly those who help in the asset allocation decision. The power that consultants exercise in the hiring and firing of asset managers is interesting, considering it is the trustees who are primarily responsible for that decision. There are pension funds that do not appoint any investment consultants but that do have actuaries advising them on their liabilities.

Myners concluded that the problem lies with the industry's customers, the pension funds, and he came up with the following recommendations:[15]

- Contracts for actuarial services and investment advice should be opened to competition separately. Pension funds should be prepared to pay sufficient fees for each service to attract a broad range of kinds of potential provider.

- Trustees should arrange for formal assessment of their advisers' performance and of any decision-making delegated to them.
- Trustees should not take investment advice on an asset class from an investment consultant who lacks expertise in that asset class.
- Fees devoted to asset allocation should properly reflect the contribution it can make to the fund's investment process.

The other issue for the investment consulting industry to take on board is the lack of adequate regulation. Fund managers are regulated by the Financial Services Authority (FSA), and trustees are governed by the Trustee Act 2000, which supplements the Trustee Act 1925, but investment consultants themselves are not regulated. The Scheme Actuary may have to report some events to the Occupational Pensions Regulatory Authority. But the investment consultants are not required to report to any authority. As far as the regulation of investment consultants is concerned, Tim Gardener thinks:

> Regulation would result in more conservative advice being given. Until such point as it is demonstrated that self-regulation doesn't work, I do not see the merit of introducing it, as it would deter the industry from doing its job properly and that would be detrimental for the client. One thing that does not exist, and where the Financial Services Authority (FSA) hasn't got its act together, is that anyone can set themselves up as an investment consultant to pension funds.
>
> It is reasonable that the FSA should recognise what we do and put in a barrier of competence for those who wish to call themselves investment consultants. If that is the sort of regulation you are referring to, then it would help. But, if you are referring to the FSA actually regulating the activity thereafter, then I think self-regulation is better. An 'Association of Investment Consultants', for example, to set some standards would be welcome. Something needs to be done in terms of minimum competence levels for quality control purposes.[16]

If pension funds, in having to fulfil their fiduciary duty, are obliged to take a wider range of advice, both qualitative and quantitative, from investment consultants, fund managers and other specialist advisers, then there is no reason why asset managers themselves should not start offering a full range of investment service, including investment consultancy. Firms such as Deutsche Bank already own performance measurement companies like InterSec, which was established by Chris Nowakowski in 1975. The setting up of a Global Investment Analytics division within Deutsche Bank Global Securities Services, confirms this trend. The unbundling of the investment consultant's products into actuarial services and investment consulting services – such as manager research and monitoring of performance – may help in improving the low margins associated with investment consulting.

Investors will continue to depend on financial advisers and professional fund managers to channel their savings into appropriate investments. As far as institutional managers are concerned, the role of investment consultants and specialist fund advisers has increased significantly with globalisation and the emergence of alternative investment products such as property, private equity and hedge funds. Institutional managers have also realigned their investment practices to reflect global standards. As consultants have become more global, they are instrumental in bringing about the changes that result in more innovative and robust investment processes in the UK, as in Europe, that stand scrutiny vis-à-vis US best practice. The global nature of asset management is set to increase with more and more countries adopting globally acceptable and standardised practices. Globalisation has been a positive force for change within the asset management industry, ushering in greater transparency, accountability and competition, thereby lowering costs and improving overall service to customers.

Developments in technology have also delivered dramatic change, with the retail sector being the net beneficiary. According to Stuart O'Gorman, head of technology investments at Henderson Global Investors, 'The internet will lead to a more sophisticated investor base and could lead to more direct investments in the market rather than in mutual funds.' For him, 'the dangers of price wars are not high at the high-net-worth (HNW) end of the market where relationships are more important, but problems could arise for financial intermediaries as they compete for the smaller investors.'[17] The role of intermediaries will undergo change; if they adapt to the new reality by offering greater value addition in their services, then they will survive. Otherwise, with greater availability of information and ease of access, individuals will increasingly be less inclined to pay for a service that has no tangible return.

FUND MANAGEMENT AND THE QUESTION OF FEES

Despite the massive upheavals of the last decade, one constant factor to emerge from this study is the faith that active managers, without exception, place in their individual expertise, skill factor or ability to add value. This act of faith extends to private equity and hedge fund managers. As they earn handsome fees for their ostensible expertise in picking shares, it would be foolish to believe otherwise. At the same time, indexers are equally convinced that they offer a cost-effective investment alternative compared to their active counterparts. As pointed out by William Sharpe over a decade ago, 'Properly measured, the average actively managed dollar must underperform the average passively managed dollar, net of costs. Empirical analyses that appear to refute this principle are guilty of improper measurement.' He went on to add, 'The key implication of this argument is that the ability to identify a winning active fund is likely to be central to the choice between active and passive management – average performance merely incurs the cost penalty of active fund management.'[18]

The salient feature of the performance of active fund management is that the average manager seldom manages to outperform the relevant benchmark over the longer term. Sharpe does not rule out the possibility that certain active managers have the ability to outperform the relevant market index. The problem revolves around successfully identifying them, and even when persistently outperforming active managers can be identified, some of the benefits generated are absorbed by higher costs. Thus, on balance, indexation offers a highly competitive option to the investor. It is therefore important to examine investment returns after fees. In fact, global reporting standards are increasingly advocating performance figures net of fees to make them internationally comparable, as fees vary widely, even within the euro-zone, leave alone the OECD.

However, within the retail sector, major companies have an issue with full disclosure and, as far as performance measurement goes, are in the process of appraising their existing systems. 'We have a problem with using external vendors for attribution analysis due to our disclosure concerns,' explained Fidelity's Simon Fraser. 'Being such a big company, we do have that issue.' Fidelity tends to conduct its performance measurement in-house. 'For our mutual funds we have a strict disclosure bias; we only disclose our top ten holdings for mutual funds for as soon as that happens, it is on CNN. For pension fund clients, however, the process is different; it depends on the client as much as the process.'[19] Transparency and consistency in reporting standards globally can only help in improving standards and investor confidence. Managers who feel unable to disclose their holdings at least once a year in their annual accounts to their customers, even on a time-lagged basis, will increasingly come under greater pressure to do so. Obviously Fidelity has no problem in disclosing its portfolio to its institutional clients; otherwise, they will not be able to win any business at all. There is no real justification for treating individual clients any differently.

Like individual investors, institutional investors also have specific resource constraints, time horizons, cash flow needs, and risk tolerances. Understanding those limitations and objectives provides greater insight into how to invest their funds. Institutional clients appreciate openness and transparency from their fund managers. They need to be kept in the information loop and need to know fairly promptly about changes that affect not just the portfolio but also their investment business. Those fund managers notifying their clients of changes in market direction as well as any loss of key personnel before they read about it in the newspapers score a higher rating than others who are less forthcoming in communicating honestly with the client. As the pension funds are a steady source of income for their managers, they would be very foolish to marginalise their institutional customers and thus jeopardise the relationship. However, individual investors are not treated equally by fund managers, although individual investors pay a relatively higher level of fees compared to their institutional counterparts.

While larger pension funds have tremendous clout over their fund managers, and are even successful in negotiating lower fees as assets under management increase, the fee structure for the asset management industry, including indexation, remains unique. There is no other industry that charges similarly – i.e. on a percentage of assets under management. Lawyers working on a no-win no-fee basis often charge a fee based on a percentage of the compensation won. But then they are seen to be offering a public service instead of a commercial service. The legal profession is perhaps even more culpable in terms of fees charged to clients. Sometimes the fees of the lawyers exceed the compensation won by their clients, i.e. the fee could well exceed 100% of assets won. The major difference between lawyers and fund managers is that as users of their services, we usually tend to leave the assets under management with the relevant fund manager and thus incur a recurring annual fee, for as long as we hire their services. Thus, asset managers accrue a percentage of assets under management as their fee income, regardless of the performance of the funds under their stewardship.

'Fund management, including the insurance sector, is an unusual industry where the pricing of the product is directly linked to the amount of assets. A land agent, for example, charges by the hour; he doesn't charge on the net asset value of the estate under management. Nor do lawyers, doctors or any other profession. Well done, fund management industry.'[20] In fact, hedge fund managers along with private equity fund managers are the most culpable as they charge performance fees on top of normal asset management fees. Retail investors often pay anywhere between 3% and 5% front-end fees when buying a traditional investment product and sometimes a penalty fee when selling the same investment. Various insurance and endowment firms have also imposed punitive fines on those investors who decide to take their investments elsewhere or might even need to liquidate their investments in a personal crisis. When markets are booming, paying your fund manager an annual management fee of 1.5–2.0% may seem acceptable; but when you have lost 15–20% in a year due to falling markets, paying your manager 1.5–2.0% of your diminished fund does appear unjustified, particularly when you remain unaware how that fee was used to enhance the performance of your portfolio.

If research serves as the production machine that drives the asset management business and if identifying market anomalies results in superior performance, then it would be more appropriate if manager fees were linked directly to their performance and not to the underlying assets. Active portfolio managers do not subscribe to the view that markets are efficient, as that would challenge their very existence along with their rationale for charging relatively high fees to their clients. As indexers now own some 25–30% of investments in the US and the UK, there has been pressure on their active counterparts. The rise of hedge funds and private equity funds, with hefty performance fees attached to them, may have lifted the downward pressure on fees for active managers, but it has exerted greater pressure on them to perform. The wide dispersion of fees associated with the various asset classes makes it difficult for consumers to understand their risk-adjusted investment return. Unquestionably, fees will come under greater scrutiny, as will the need to separate them in terms of the individual costs associated with running an investment product.

Tim Gardener raised the compensation structure of the industry when asked about the future of asset management industry. His response was unequivocal:

> There is no doubt in my mind that the investment industry takes a disproportionate and unhealthy share of the wealth of the nation. There are some outstanding people in the City, but not that outstanding and not that many of them either. There is some economic inefficiency in this area. I think that one of the drivers of the fund management industry going forward will be an attack on their wealth. Hopefully, their response will be to become far more efficient. It is true that such inefficiencies exist across the board, i.e. not just in fund management but even more so within investment banking and perhaps marginally less so among corporates.[21]

Some fund managers argue that on the basis of the fees consultants get paid – on average 1.5 basis points to fund managers' 27 – it is understandable that the consulting industry operating in a less profitable market would uphold such an opinion. However, such a view is not necessarily based on the economics of envy. There are many

347

other sectors of society which subscribe to that view – teachers, adult education specialists, nurses and carers, junior doctors, in fact, most public sector workers – but have no way of doing anything about it. The inequitable distribution of income has indeed hurt large swathes of our society; there is an acute shortage of good skilled professionals – not just teachers and nurses, but also scientists, engineers, accountants and economists. The competitiveness of an economy emerges when higher quality is available at a lower cost. It is not self-evident that the high fees charged by the fund management industry are justified.

As consumers of investment products, we continue to accept the high fees and poor performance. Are we really being served any better by the sector despite the high costs? As broking commissions paid by fund managers come under greater scrutiny, thanks to the Myners review, it is time to reassess whether investment bankers, fund managers and the senior directors of MNCs really deserve the sort of compensation they currently earn? As a consumer of investment products, if we do not like the high fees and wish to register our protest by taking our investment elsewhere, the choice is severely limited. Indexation is the only option, and that is not a real one. Bank and building society accounts are not the answer, nor are National Savings Bonds, at least not in the long term. Even the revolutionary 'stakeholder pensions' charge 1% of assets per annum. The only solution is to invest directly in companies, in which case diversification is greatly reduced and stock-specific risk within the resulting portfolio rises. Hence such an option is not optimal either.

Is there any intrinsic reason why fees should be based on a percentage of assets under management? Also, the additional costs associated with buying and selling such products – 3–5% on top of management fees – undermine overall returns to a large extent. If such a practice is to stay, then investors will require a much higher level of additional services, such as full access to information on the portfolio as well as a detailed analysis of costs involved in the management of those assets. Private equity and hedge fund managers would also come under greater pressure to justify their fees. High water mark levels will become more prevalent among hedge fund managers. However, investors still have to pay the annual fees, which remain at 1–2% of assets. The high water mark refers to the agreement that the fund accrues fees only on profits over and above the original investment. Increasingly, individual investors would be prepared to pay performance fees, rather than pay a fixed cost totally unrelated to performance.

FOCUS ON CORE COMPETENCY

The major fear of mega-companies today is 'competition from "virtual competitors" – groups of specialists that could be assembled, using the internet and venture capital backing – to mount a serious challenge. The only thing these groups would not possess would be mega-companies' traditional customer relationship and reputation.'[22] Clearly branding and customer recognition is valuable. However, there is no reason why these supercompanies cannot team up with their virtual competitors in a bid to neutralise the growing competition. The emerging companies may benefit from the brand name and distribution capability. More often these people have deliberately moved away from the mammoths due to their monolithic corporate culture. The mega-companies' worst nightmare may become reality unless they develop ways of partnering these freelance teams. Within the asset management sector, highly profitable independent teams prefer to hold on to their competitive edge. Thus, private equity and hedge fund companies, for example, clearly prefer to operate independently rather than be part of a larger financial service mega-firm.

With increasing emphasis on branding and performance, asset managers have been driven to focus on core competence. In fact, greater competition has driven most sectors of industry into identifying their core competencies and developing those. Being all things to all people is a thing of the past. Even within the hedge fund sector, there is a clear shift to specialisation. Self-knowledge is important in a globally competitive world. Superior product recognition is essential to the distribution edge. The evolution of fund supermarkets indicates that asset managers are only repositioning themselves with regard to their customer base. As far as the institutional sector is concerned, the change from the 'balanced structure' to 'specialist structures' has just been completed in the UK, although it has some way still to go in Europe. With reference to the retail sector, it has not yet reached a critical mass to be able to dictate its unique structure. It is true that the retail sector is set to undergo radical changes in the delivery of the investment product, but as far as the core investment process is concerned, remarkably enough among active managers, there appears to be a high degree of consensus in the stability inherent in the status quo.

The greatest contribution of IT to the fund management industry has been in enabling management to focus on their core competency while outsourcing other non-core aspects of their business. Already, there has been a high level of outsourcing of back-office functions, such as transaction processing or accounting and administration, which are not considered an essential part of the asset management business. Outsourcing has become a powerful strategic weapon in the highly competitive and fast-moving world of finance. As trading, settlement and custody along with sales and distribution are volume-driven and benefit from economies of scale, these functions are set to benefit the most from IT. Even the research and fund management function, driven by timely and superior analysis of a wide range of information, has gained from the new technology. Not long ago, good investment advice was essentially 'inside information' derived from personal knowledge of the company's senior management. It had its merits. Today investment outperformance is no longer driven by 'personal' contacts, although 'relationship management' continues to play a significant role in the new economy.

There have been major changes in the way in which analysts and fund managers access information, interpret it and utilise it. There is a greater level of automation and the introduction of quantitative methods into the overall investment process. But the information still needs to be analysed and the quantitative models fed with appropriate data; a model is only as good as the data it is based on. The skill involved in capturing alpha in their investment portfolios will ultimately distinguish the above average managers from the dinosaurs. With greater emphasis on performance and the need for good, independent research, some restructuring is overdue in that area. If we examine the various functions within fund management (Table 8.1), the front-office functions include the actual activity of buying and selling investments, and various other functions which surround it, such as the formulation of stock selection and asset allocation decisions, and marketing and selling the firm's services to clients. The so-called back-office functions support these front-line jobs, and include custody (safe keeping of the assets); information systems; systems support and administration.[23]

There is not enough synergy between the front-office and back-office functions. Even within the front office, marketing and fund management rarely pull together; their interests are not aligned. Thus, the whole issue of the independence of the fund management side of the business, particularly research, needs to be addressed. As Warren Buffett reminds us: 'To invest successfully over a lifetime does not require a stratospheric IQ, unusual brightness, or inside information. What's needed is a sound intellectual framework for making decisions and the ability to keep emotions from corroding that framework.... Whether you achieve outstanding results will depend on the effort and intellect you apply to your investments, as well as on the amplitudes of stock-market folly that prevail during your investing career. The sillier the market's behaviour, the greater the opportunity for the business-like investor.'[24] Such a mindset is of no use to the marketing specialist, the dealer, or even the portfolio constructor whose job is to create the portfolio that the trustee of a pension fund wants.

What trustees and plan sponsors increasingly want from their fund managers are evidence of a special knowledge and competitive advantage in a specific sector or market. According to Myra Drucker, chief investment officer with Xerox Corporation: 'If we've hired you to manage a value portfolio and you've underperformed the value indexes, we don't want you to come in and say, "Well, value is out of favor and growth is doing better." That is not helpful. What *is* helpful, is demonstrating a special knowledge and competitive advantage in a specific sector or market.'[25] Such competitive advantage is usually derived from people, process and information. However, regardless of the source, the fund manager or fund adviser has to demonstrate that the results were not a fluke, but can be achieved consistently in the future. Such a degree of market specialisation depends on developing core competencies by the fund manager.

As far as the large pension funds are concerned, it is the trustees who make the strategic asset allocation decisions; fund managers

Table 8.1 *Functions associated with fund management[a]*

FRONT-OFFICE FUNCTIONS
Marketing
● *Marketing and sales*: new business and product development

Fund management
● *Strategic fund management*: long-term asset allocation, currency and risk management
● *Operational fund management*: stock selection, decision-making and implementation
● *Research*: fundamental and technical economic and company analysis
● *Dealing*: buying and selling investments; pre-trade broker liaison
● *Cash management*: placing deposits, foreign exchange

BACK-OFFICE FUNCTIONS
Transaction processing
● *Transaction processing and settlement*: deal administration and control, post-trade liaison with brokers and custodians
● *Safe custody*: security safe keeping and control
● *Stock lending*: arranging and processing loans

Systems support
● *Systems maintenance*: operational and technical maintenance of existing information technology
● *Systems development*: planning and implementation of new IT and major enhancements to existing systems

Accounting and administration
● *Investment accounting*: provision of valuations and client reports, tax claims, management information
● *Performance measurement*: provision of investment performance reports, attribution analysis of returns

General
● *Compliance*: regulatory reporting and in-house monitoring activities
● *Financial accounting*: corporate accounting and reporting
● *Corporate management*: training, personnel, staff and premises management

---

[a] Source: British Invisibles, Fund Management, City Business Series 2000[10]

execute their decisions and possess little freedom in exercising their own judgement in shaping that strategic decision. Information and communication technology can well serve to improve the efficiency of information flow and the delivery of products and services under such circumstances. But there is little intrinsic value addition to be had from such an arrangement; the maximum value addition is at the strategic level. Fund managers add value by outperforming the given benchmark and may have some flexibility in tactical asset allocation – currency hedging, market timing, etc. Thus, greater specialisation, and in time fragmentation, will characterise the institutional market.

RISE OF THE INDIVIDUAL INVESTOR

Currently assets under management by institutional investors such as pension funds, charities and endowments dwarf the assets managed by individual investors in the UK. But after two decades of privatisations and the introduction of tax-advantaged investments in personal equity plans (PEPs), now called individual savings accounts (ISAs), venture capital trusts and various other products, the assets managed directly by individuals have risen considerably. Even the trend towards defined contribution pension schemes has altered the profile of the individual investor. However, this is not reflected fully in the marketplace. Individual investors do not have the same access to information and other services as their institutional counterparts.

However, advances in technology are gradually altering the way in which asset managers deliver their products to clients. Web-based distribution has lowered costs and improved service via superior knowledge of the customer. Despite its tendency to 'commoditise' the investment product, the new technology also favours customisation. The net beneficiary of this technological revolution has been the private client or the individual investor, hitherto the poor cousins of institutional investors in terms of service such as research, real-time data and prices. The speed of technological transformation is forcing all participants in markets worldwide to examine their assumptions about conventional business models. New technology has enhanced personal customisation for institutional investors and for individual investors.

Asset gatherers realise that in the emerging retail sector, efficient distribution strategies will determine survival. Individuals are comfortable buying their ISAs via any branded distributor – AOL, Microsoft, Tesco, Asda, Virgin Airlines (in flight), Marks & Spencer, Merrill Lynch or Charles Schwab as easily as via their personal bank, insurance firm or broker. However, individuals tend to attach more value to absolute returns, and thus may prefer managers with consistently superior long-term performance records in the hedge funds and private equity sector, if the fee structure becomes more competitive. Thus, small hedge fund boutiques – or a network of individuals who excel at asset allocation, sector research and stock selection – will be better able to survive by distributing their products through branded channels at low cost, thereby altering the existing profile of investment products.

The ability of financial derivatives to structure virtually any kind of product required by the investor, assuming that markets provide free access, liquidity and transparency, means there is no barrier to investing in a truly global context, as well as in multi-asset classes and multi-managers via funds of funds. The rise of exchange-traded funds (ETFs) is envisioned by many and with it the decline in demand for the services of traditional institutional managers. Direct investment by individuals in markets is also expected to rise exponentially. For veteran investors, such as Dean LeBaron, founder of Batterymarch Financial Management in Boston in 1969, continuing innovation in financial products mean that things such as FOLIO*fn*, where you use computers to provide an individual account, have many advantages over a typical mutual fund: 'I think a mutual fund as an investment structure for individuals is severely threatened because now we can do things much better without passing on the tax liability. Exchange traded funds are one of them, but probably not the most important one. I think folio portfolios, if that's what the word is, are probably better.'[26]

Today pools of liquidity in cyberspace allow shares to be traded outside the restrictions imposed by traditional markets. The new electronic bond trading platforms are expected to transform fixed-income trading over the next few years by increasing efficiency via lower costs and greater transparency. Creation of new indexes, like the techMARK and NASDAQ, also open up investment opportunities for the retail player. Venture capitalists can directly access funds from the retail investor. Innovations such as webcasting have also altered the relationship between investors and fund managers. Retail usage has yet to take off in its Europe, but webcasting is prevalent in the US and is hugely successful in investor education. For Dimitris Melas:

> Asset managers mirror, to a great extent, how society as a whole and the industry in particular evolves. Access to investor information via the website will be the first step in this direction, followed by more specific information on the range of products available and finally enabling clients to deal online and receive reports on their transactions. The process is more evolved in the US, with greater internet penetration and greater individual participation. Europe is moving in that direction. The new technology enables us to communicate more speedily with our distribution channels such as the IFAs, etc. The net beneficiary is the customer.[27]

Technology has developed extremely quickly in certain areas over the past few years, and while the fund management industry has made some changes to adapt to this, it has certainly not done as much as it could have done. The internet has been the major technology advance over the past few years, which has the greatest implications for distribution. This could potentially have a great beneficial impact on the amount of information, which retail investors, in particular, could see for themselves rather than relying on quarterly mailings, and there is also the potential for online purchasing. However, the issue of online distribution remains problematic for both security and regulatory reasons. A lot also depends on the regulatory framework that governments create to monitor these developments and provide investors with a basic level of protection. As these issues are addressed in time, it could indeed change the way in which investors behave.

Investment managers have not even begun to think of the potential uses of the new interactive technology. Internally, for example, they know who visits their website and how long they stayed there. That information is valuable, but still it has not been possible to use that information in any commercially sensible way. 'We realise that we have only scratched at the surface of what we can do in terms of profiling our customers. It is going to be mind-boggling. That is why it is important we invest in technology. Our industry has been pretty slow in deploying technology, particularly in the UK. If you want to remain a mainstream player, you have to invest heavily in the new technology,'[28] affirms Simon Fraser. Thus, 'getting to know your customer,' one of the regulatory mantras, will soon acquire commercial significance in the brave new technological world. It will also mean that companies will need to make sure that all their software is able to interface with the internet, which will have a material impact on their business. Whether products are delivered via the net depends on the client's level of comfort.

The internet may not have changed everything for fund managers and their clients; it has certainly revolutionised the communication cycle. In the opinion of Andrew Skirton, 'there are some great opportunities and challenges in communicating with our existing clients and in gaining new business by winning new clients through the web. Whether it is in sending our reports to existing clients or receiving their orders through the net or in enabling new clients to visit us at our website and look at our products. It is delivering that capability globally to clients so that we can maximise that relationship. It will help in improving communications. In terms of asset management firms, the struggle for survival will focus on excellence; in other words, on consistent long-term performance at low cost and quality service.'[29]

The internet also brings transparency to the relationship. The internet can provide investors with total visibility of their portfolios throughout the day. If a manager claims to have a process, but doesn't actually manage funds that way, it will be clear to their clients. In fact, the transparency created by the internet can provide a platform for risk management. The availability of timely information implies that the opportunity for individual enterprise is huge. But the proliferation of investment products is something that individual investors may simply not have the time, the inclination or the ability to master. Considering that the professionals have failed to 'beat the market' or to foster private enterprise, what evidence is there to suggest that the individual investor or the sole trader will be more able to combine all these objectives and achieve a superior asset allocation strategy? According to Tony Watson:

Technology enhancements in B2B and B2C will make its positive contribution to profitability and client servicing. At the retail level, individuals will buy more of their investments via the Internet. There will obviously be more defined contribution than defined benefit schemes. Whether it is private pensions or stakeholder pensions, technology will be important in record keeping and in reducing paper transactions. But otherwise, what we have seen is more individual day-traders. May be, the rise of hedge funds and private equity funds. It still boils down to finding the right opportunity or making the judgement call by the individual. Why individuals should be any better at it than institutions remains an issue.[30]

As the government and the internet encourage individuals to manage their assets more actively, are we en route to a more equitable society based on transparency and accountability or are we laying the foundations for a society driven by market forces alone? Will the new technology shape a new meritocracy backed by private capital investment and directed by innovative individuals? Will shareholder activism lead to lower business margins and higher investment in research, preservation and development? Will shareholders finally wake up to the fact that the state of the global environment is as much an aspect of investor responsibility as the development of our human resources globally? It may be easier for individuals to buy organic food or eco-friendly consumer goods, it is not necessarily as simple for them to invest in a portfolio of companies whose products they might be inclined to buy. It might lead to a heavily concentrated portfolio that may prove to be risky, in purely financial terms. However, in the words of Dominic Hobson: 'In the twenty-first century, if the government does not stand in his way, the British consumer will overrun the last redoubts of cartelised, paternalistic, institutionalised capitalism, and come into an inheritance which was once the sole preserve of monarchs and barons. He will live, as they once did, "of his own." '[31] The demise of corporate paternalism could remove the obstacle to the restoration of true ownership and capitalism.

WHO WILL PAY FOR INDEPENDENT RESEARCH?

The question of the independence of market research demands a radical change in the status quo. Most industry observers are aware of the various conflicts of interest that arise within the sell side as in the buy side. Various initiatives have been launched by national regulators, and also by the International Organisation of Securities Commissions, whose technical committee has set up a working group to make recommendations by the end of 2001 on conflicts of interest among sell-side analysts. The Association for Investment Management and Research (AIMR) is also concerned that the deterioration of investor confidence in the objectivity of sell-side research could damage the integrity of this research and harm the reputation of the entire profession. The *AIMR Research Objectivity Standards* will complement the existing *AIMR Code and Standards*, which all AIMR members, CFA charterholders and CFA candidates are required to follow.

Most people recognise that efficient markets need transparency and accountability. The question is about finding a consensus on how that is best secured and how to foster and promote 'intellectual honesty' within research. It would be easy to mend the limitation in the current organisational structure of an investment bank, whereby the head of research on the sell side may not always report directly to a main board director with responsibility for research. But it is not clear whether such a reorganisation will ensure independent and objective research. A similar situation also exists on the buy side, and it is also recommended that the head of research should report directly to the asset allocation committee. However, it is not axiomatic that establishing such structures will automatically deliver intellectual honesty and objectivity in research.

It is essential to encourage analysts to be good investigators and use their knowledge and insight to present their conclusions in a format that is simple to understand. A kind of rating mechanism is already used by many companies, and that process can be standardised within the industry. Sometimes analysts will get it wrong and they should not be penalised for making a few mistakes; otherwise, they will be reluctant to take any risks. To be able to support this level of freedom for analysts, it stands to reason that independence can be best secured when the research function is established as a separate profit centre, and not accountable to either the buy side or the sell side. Such a radical restructuring may prove too challenging for the industry to contemplate all at once. Also, unless the link is severed between analysts' compensation and the deals they help bring to the corporate financiers, the analysts themselves would be reluctant to cut off a lucrative source of income. While a good analyst needs to be compensated, it can be done in a way that benefits the industry as a whole.

For large investment banks, such as Merrill Lynch, Morgan Stanley, Deutsche Bank and Goldman Sachs, employing research analysts on both the buy side and the sell side, pooling these resources into a separate research business unit, independent of pressures from corporate finance or fund management, will be a major step in assuring their true independence. Understandably, such an arrangement will involve all users of that research to pay for it. Currently, the research is provided free of charge to the buy side, and they would be reluctant to change the status quo. Buy-side analysts depend heavily on sell-side research, although they use it more as a tool to arrive at an investment opinion. Individual analysts who have established a reputation in their sectors are also highly valued by the buy side. However, there is no reason why the consensus opinion cannot be made available via traditional channels currently provided by I/B/E/S.

If research is valuable to fund management, as they claim it to be, surely they will have no reservations paying for it? Asset managers such as Fidelity and Capital already do so. Perhaps, like fund managers, analysts can charge using a percentage of assets invested, as per their recommendation. The problem will be proving that is the case. Structuring a compensation system for analysts that reflects the quality of research will be more efficient all round than the status quo. There is no reason why analysts should not be allowed to invest in their buy recommendations or short their sell recommendations, after the research is in the public domain. Assuming they report their dealing activity to their line manager and the compliance officer and assuming the research and dealing information is in the public domain, as is the case with company directors' share dealings, there is no reason why analysts should be prevented from dealing in the shares they research in. Preventing analysts from investing in their best ideas is not an efficient way of rewarding enterprise.

In order to improve analysts' ability to do a good job, attention also needs to be paid to the role of accountants in the auditing of corporate accounts. Accountants must be accountable and accounts must be transparent. While 'analysts and journalists must share the blame for a decline in rigorous analysis and fearless questioning,' putting all the 'blame on commentators amounts to shooting the messenger.'[32] It will be easier for all concerned if proposed standards are met in the creation of annual accounts, such as compliance with US GAAP (generally accepted accounting principles) and for companies to reconcile 'pro forma' earnings per share to US GAAP earnings. Accountants play an important role in encouraging their clients to be more open about their figures, including bad ones. Creative accounting often leads to disguising shareholder value destruction. The list of cases where accountants either knew what was going on or should have known better is a very long one, indeed. Investors could have been saved trillions of dollars if accountants had done their job in the first place.

THE COST OF SOCIALLY RESPONSIBLE INVESTING

SRI is in. It is widely recognised that SRI matters and there exist a wider set of stakeholders than just shareholders. There is consensus that something must be done, although there is little consensus as to what constitutes a socially responsible company. If the role of accountants is deemed important in arriving at 'fair' earnings numbers for the companies that we invest in, it is critical that a company's CSR record is incorporated into its account. Thus, accountants bear an even greater responsibility in depicting a company's long-term financial health. Determination of a strong link between financial performance and social, ethical and environmental responsibility will ultimately help in superior asset allocation. If ethical business is believed to be good business, then asset allocation will flow accordingly. Currently, the thinking is that good business rests on lowering costs, enlarging market share and creating new products. The focus is not on how to achieve that without damaging the people involved in the business, preserving the environment for posterity or in improving the condition of those who need greater help. There appears to be no tangible penalty or reward attached to such action.

Like accountants, analysts should be required to include SRI criteria into their research recommendations. While there is no consensus on the ideal company, there is a great deal of commonality between best practice on issues such as corruption, labour standards, human rights, environmental pollution, conflicts, and access to medicines. From the sole standpoint of a company's risk management policy, CSR costs should be reflected in the account and included in the bottom-line earnings figures. It is reported, for example, that firearms manufacturers are making financial provisions in response to threatened litigation over the misuse of handguns in the US.[33] While recent legislative changes have stimulated debate, should governments wish to use investment practices to influence corporate behaviour, and there is potential to do so, far more robust action will be required. Greater government intervention will be necessary because influential institutional investors may have conflicting sets of demands to satisfy, which in the end may paralyse concerted activism. However, the shape and form this intervention should take need careful deliberation.

There is no doubt that when companies fail to quantify their potential CSR liabilities, they are misleading their shareholders and giving a partial view of the business. Long-term CSR is a cost to shareholders, industry, suppliers, employees, and ultimately to society. While shareholder engagement strategies are useful and currently offer the most efficient method of influencing corporate behaviour, engagement is complicated and difficult to measure. More importantly, it is an additional cost in terms of time, resource and the ability to research fairly complex issues. As far as individual investors and small pension funds are concerned, such additional costs may prove detrimental to the financial performance of their pension funds. Trustees of such funds are unable and unwilling to invest time and money on SRI, as there are clear costs involved with no tangible benefits attached to implementing such a policy. Companies do not operate in a vacuum. They have offices, plants or distribution centres within countries and local authorities, etc., and the responsibility of ensuring that firms as well as individuals comply with certain ethical standards falls within the jurisdiction of the authority they function in. Empowering these bodies to do their job effectively is the responsibility of governments not investors.

Existing pension law permits trustees to engage in SRI where there is a will to do so. And trustees of some large pension funds already engage in SRI. The new legislation will help in encouraging companies to disclose their CSR policy. However, unless it can be measured, it will not be an effective tool in asset allocation. While institutional investors can and sometimes do have an influence on corporate behaviour, it would be unrealistic to expect trustees of pension funds to transform themselves into thought leaders and arbiters of values. No group of trustees would willingly expose themselves to accusations of failing to treat the interests of the beneficiaries as paramount. Therefore those who do adopt proactive SRI policies will need to satisfy themselves that their policies do not subordinate the interests of plan beneficiaries.

The costs of implementing SRI and ensuring that the policy will not be challenged may be significantly higher than has been realised. While employers today are regularly taken to court by their employees for various breaches of contract, among other reasons, these disputes are relatively rare in the delivery of pensions. Trustees would prefer to keep things as they are. And those appointed to advise on SRI issues may also need a high level of insurance cover simply to do their job. All costs would ultimately be passed on to consumers. While some costs are definitely worth bearing, consumers need to know what exactly they are paying for. As things stand, there is very little transparency about the cost of running pensions. Individual beneficiaries have very little knowledge of what is involved. Ensuring that an SRI policy has wide acceptance among the plan membership is the responsibility of the plan sponsors. According to Frank Russell Company:

> Without seeking representative member views, trustees run the risk of assuming that their views on social, ethical and environmental issues are shared and supported by the plan membership when in fact they are not.

Member-nominated trustees have an important role to play in the consideration and development of SRI policies. They have the special responsibility to speak for the plan beneficiaries, and to indicate what form of consultation should be made on SRI issues. When SRI is being considered, the voice of the plan membership should be considered fully.[34]

It can be construed that the UK government's intention is not to legislate on the issue but only to inculcate a greater sense of awareness of SRI matters among institutional investors, many of whom will argue that such criteria are already reflected in their investment decision. However, if governments want to exert greater pressure on MNCs to fulfil their CSR, it may be worthwhile urging their governmental counterparts to implement the existing legislation to protect all stakeholders. Industry does not need more legislation that will add to costs, in terms of time, and create a further layer of bureaucracy. We need better and more implementation of existing legislation and agreements on a concerted global basis.

CONCLUSION

In assessing the future of asset management, it has to be acknowledged that one of the major drivers in determining its direction will be the role of government. The introduction of the Pension Act 1995, for example, had a definitive impact on the industry. The rise of indexation, with the introduction of the minimum funding requirement, is one example. The move towards the appointment of specialist asset managers by trustees of pension funds as opposed to balanced managers, the creation of customised benchmarks and a shift away from peer-group benchmarks altered the asset management sector significantly. The introduction of defined contribution schemes and the demise of defined benefit schemes are two further developments. Tax incentives on individual savings led to the rise of mutual funds or pooled investment vehicles such as unit trusts and open-ended investments companies.

Similarly, the introduction of legislation on SRI could impact on investment behaviour, not just at the shareholder level but also at the corporate level. Despite the reduced influence of governments, they still play a strategic role in the quality of our lives. And regardless of the increased wealth of MNCs, they simply do not have the power to determine the level of taxes or level of public spending. Fiscal management, monetary policies and tax incentives have a tremendous impact on the way investments are channelled. Markets help in keeping prices competitive. In any market, prices are best established by open competition between as many buyers and sellers as possible. Distortions arise when fair competition is blocked. Efficient markets tend to be fairly democratic. However, governments and other public sector bodies have a key role in ensuring that markets operate in an efficient environment.

Thus, the important factors when considering the future of fund management is to bear in mind the influence of legislation and regulation as well as inflation and taxation. The impact of legislation, regulation and taxation is self-evident to the extent that they provide clear guidelines about what investors can and cannot do tax-efficiently and legally. Institutional investor behaviour is heavily influenced by such action; so is the behaviour of the individual investor, although many individuals remain surprisingly ignorant of the tax incentives available for their savings. Better investor education can take care of that lack of common knowledge as long as individual investors are also provided with adequate information on the risks associated with these investments and are given the opportunity to consider how well their investments match their own particular requirements. Many individuals end up buying financial products they never wanted in the first place. However, getting compensation for being wrongly sold such a product is far from simple, whether a pension, an endowment or a life insurance policy.

What is less evident in terms of governmental influence on investor behaviour is the role of inflation. It can be argued that in an environment of low inflation and a lower rate of growth in real earnings, bonds are a more attractive asset class. Taking into account the ageing of the population, that will increasingly be the case as investors will depend more on a stable income from their savings as from their annuities. However, with annuity rates being low, personal investment in highly rated corporate bonds or money market funds (most of which are AAA rated) is an option. Unless legislation regarding investment in annuities is changed, pensioners have limited options in the choice of their annuity provider. In a low-inflation environment, it is more attractive to borrow and invest/spend, for companies as much as for individuals. But it also diverts savings from low-interest-bearing accounts into higher-yielding financial products, depending on the individual risk tolerance of the investor.

It can be argued that a long period of low inflation means a lower market equity risk premium. Share valuations tend to be higher as a result. In a high-inflation environment the equity risk premium is higher, reflecting the higher level of risk. The price/earnings ratio tends to be lower as equities adjust more efficiently, reflecting changes in the prospect for earnings along with a host of other factors. Historically the higher level of inflation in the UK can be interpreted as a reason for a higher level of investment in equity. The 'home bias', however, was largely driven by legislation and tax incentives. When the tax advantage was withdrawn and legislative constraints removed, overseas equity investment rose. The conventional view is that, in the long term, equities outperform other forms of investments such as bonds, building society accounts and bank deposits. Historically that has indeed been the case. However, it is not sufficient evidence that the next 50 years will deliver similar returns, if inflation continues to be low.

While it is not proven what causes inflation, excessive liquidity in the financial system is usually a major contributor. Just as excessive demand drives up the prices of goods in any market, asset prices get inflated when there is more liquidity in circulation. This stimulation in demand is sometimes resorted to by governments to fend off a recession. By lowering interest rates, there is less incentive to save. As long as supply bottlenecks are removed and competition is not stifled by the existence of cartels, etc., there is no reason why demand cannot rise without any inflationary pressures building up. As long as the government continues with its responsible and prudent management of economic affairs, there is no reason to believe that significantly higher levels of inflation will suddenly appear. A marginally higher level of inflation than at the present is very likely, as inflation and interest rates are both at their historic lows. But there is no evidence that fiscal imprudence is imminent and that inflation is on its way back.

As the government's public sector borrowing requirement (PSBR) has declined significantly, there is enough scope for the government to raise its expenditure level by issuing bonds to finance much needed investments in infrastructure, for example. However, at the moment, the government seems reluctant to do so. The level of shortage of fixed-income instruments is such that the market can bear a significantly higher level of issuance without causing pricing distortion. The higher level of volatility witnessed in developed equity markets since 1998 suggests that while inflation declined and with it the market risk premium, equities did not start behaving more like bonds. On the contrary, the volatility associated with equities went up. When an asset class has greater volatility, the risk premium should reflect that. Thus, the question of the equity risk premium remains unresolved.

In a world of electronic money and mail, computer-generated actuarial models, breakthroughs in medical research enabling us to determine individual risk profiles, and rapid advances in technological and financial innovations, knowledge management is an integral aspect of risk management. As knowledge is power, knowledge is more powerful today than ever before. Superior asset management revolves around the ability to manage risk effectively. Managing a wide spectrum of risks, some less easy to quantify than others – e.g. risks associated with the environment or terrorism – is no longer the specialist reserve of insurance companies. Asset managers, governments and other stakeholders also share in that responsibility. As more information becomes available, the risks attached to misinterpretation of that information also increase. The ability to manage information and transform it rapidly into actionable intelligence determines success. To sustain excellence, intelligence sharing and the pooling of human resources form the basis of knowledge-based enterprises. While markets work best in a competitive environment, human beings thrive in an interactive one. As individuals take charge of their destiny, knowledge of the 'Other' complements 'Know Thyself'.

Notes

CHAPTER 1

1. Phillips & Drew, *Pension Fund Indicators 2001: A long-term perspective on pension fund investment*, p. 6
2. William M. Mercer, *European Pension Fund Managers Guide*, Volume 1, 1999, p. A-2
3. Financial Times Survey, *Pension Fund Investment*, 17 May 2001
4. In October 2000 Nicholas Applegate Capital Management was acquired by Allianz AG. This transaction was completed on 31 January 2001. As at 30 June 2000, total assets under management with Nicholas Applegate were $44 billion, which is not included in the $781.7 billion under management for Allianz Asset Management. Nor is the $268.5 billion under management with Dresdner Bank Investment Management. On 19 July 2001 the EU Commission approved Allianz AG's takeover of Dresdner Bank. Allianz then confirmed its future stake of 96.4% in Dresdner Bank, which includes its asset management activities. Thus, at the time of writing, total assets under management for the Allianz Group exceeded that of Fidelity
5. Office for National Statistics (ONS), *Share Ownership: A Report on Ownership of Shares as at 31 December 2000*, p. 8
6. ONS, *Share Ownership*, p. 15
7. Leslie Hannah, *Inventing Retirement: the development of occupational pensions in Britain* (Cambridge University Press, 1986), p.ix
8. Paul Myners, *Institutional Investment in the UK: A Review* (HM Treasury, UK, March 2001), p. 76
9. William M. Mercer, *European Pension Fund Managers Guide*, Volume 1, 2001, p. C74
10. ONS, *Share Ownership*, p. 16
11. Tim Gardener, global head of investment consulting, William M. Mercer Limited, interviewed in August 2001
12. Nicola Ralston, head of investment management, Schroder Investment Management, interviewed in August 2000
13. William R. Cotter, chief executive officer, Asset and Wealth Management Services, Bank of Ireland Group, interviewed in February 2001

14. Alastair Ross Goobey, chief executive officer, Hermes Pensions Management, interviewed in May 2001
15. William M. Mercer, *European Pension Fund Managers Guide*, Volume 1, 1999, p. A-2
16. PricewaterhouseCoopers, *Fire on the Horizon* (2000). See also Myners, p. 78
17. Alastair Ross Goobey interview
18. William Cotter interview
19. Myners, p. 76
20. ONS, *Acquisitions & Mergers Involving UK Companies*
21. ONS, *Britain 2001: The Official Yearbook of the UK*, p. 385
22. 'The Britain that is going to be forged in the white heat of this revolution.' Sir Harold Wilson, speech at the Labour Party conference, Scarborough, 1 October 1963. Usually quoted as 'the white heat of the technological revolution'
23. Patrick Young and Thomas Theys, *Capital Market Revolution: The Future of Markets in an Online World* (Pearson Education, 1999), p. xviii
24. *Economist*, 'American productivity,' 11 August 2001, pp. 63–64.
25. Michael Grant, head of Schroder Global Technology Team, Schroder EuroTech Fund, launch brochure, June 2000
26. Professor Robert Wade, 'Global inequality: winners and losers,' *Economist*, 28 April 2001, p. 97
27. Robert Wade, *Economist*, 28 April 2001, p. 94
28. *Economist*, 'A survey of globalisation,' 29 September 2001, p. 9
29. Robert Taylor, 'Job creation the European way,' *Financial Times*, 26 July 2001
30. Robert Wade, *Economist*, 28 April 2001, p. 97
31. *Economist*, 'A survey of globalisation,' 29 September 2001, p. 11
32. PricewaterhouseCoopers, *Fire on the Horizon* (2000), p. 4
33. Mark Rubinstein, 'Rational markets: yes or no? The affirmative case,' *Financial Analysts Journal*, May/June 2001, p. 19
34. Milton Friedman, *Free to Choose* (Harcourt Brace Jovanovich, 1980), p. 16
35. Greenwich Associates, 'North American equity derivatives became hotter market in 2001,' www.greenwich.com, 21 August 2001
36. *Financial Times*, 'Interview: Philip Purcell, Morgan Stanley,' 16 August 2001
37. Paul Platkin, General Motors Asset Management, quoted in *Global Custodian*, Spring 2001, p. 42
38. Myners, p. 82
39. Myners, p. 83
40. *Financial Times*, 'Investors reduce internet trades,' 16 August 2001
41. *Economist*, 'Special report: human rights,' 18 August 2001, p. 20
42. In his book *The Crisis of Global Capitalism: Open Society Endangered* (PublicAffairs, 1998), George Soros provides a compelling analysis of the negative consequences of inefficient global markets. His sequel, *Open Society: Reforming Global Capitalism* (PublicAffairs, 2000), continues to illustrate his views on the subject
43. Robert J. Shiller, *Irrational Exuberance* (Princeton University Press, 2001), p. xxxvii

44. Shiller, *Irrational Exuberance*, p. xxxiv
45. Mark Rubinstein, *Financial Analysts Journal*, May/June 2001, p. 15
46. Rubinstein, *Financial Analysts Journal*, May/June 2001, p. 16
47. To get a fuller understanding of the 'contrarian' investment strategy, read David Dreman, *The New Contrarian Investment Strategy* (Random House, 1980) and *Contrarian Investment Strategy: The Psychology of Stock Market Success* (Random House, 1979)
48. David Dreman, 'Inefficient market,' *Forbes Global*, 6 August 2001
49. Shiller, *Irrational Exuberance*, p. xix
50. British Invisibles, *Fund Management* (City Business Series 2000: Statistical Update), p. 14

CHAPTER 2

1. William F. Sharpe, *Investments* (Prentice Hall, 1985), p. 146
2. Standard deviation is calculated by identifying the set of events that are expected to impact on the price of the security, their probability values and expected deviation. The deviations are squared, thereby making all the values positive and then a weighted average of these amounts is determined, with the probabilities as weights. This result is the *variance* and the square root of the variance is the *standard deviation*.

Event[a,b]	Probability	Deviation	Deviation squared	Probability × Deviation squared
X	0.25	−17.25	297.56	74.39
Y	0.30	2.75	7.56	2.27
Z	0.45	7.75	60.06	27.03

[a] Variance = probability weighted average squared deviation = 103.69
[b] Standard deviation = square root of variance = 10.18

3. The overall risk of a portfolio is not determined by the total risk, or the standard deviation of the constituent securities in isolation, but it does depend on their *covariance*, or the extent to which individual securities respond to events together. The covariance of two securities' returns is a weighted average of the products of the deviations of the returns from their expected values, using the probabilities of the deviations as weights. We simply assume the deviation of returns for securities *A*, *B* and *C* to determine their covariance to each other if events *X*, *Y*, *Z* transpired.

Event	Probability	Deviation of security A	Deviation of security B	Product of deviations	Probability × Product of deviations
X	0.40	1.50	−5.35	−8.03	−3.21
Y	0.30	−2.50	10.75	−26.88	−8.06
Z	0.30	−5.25	−5.35	28.09	8.43
				Covariance	−2.85

Event	Probability	Deviation of security A	Deviation of security C	Product of deviations	Probability × Product of deviations
X	0.40	1.50	−10.90	−16.35	−6.54
Y	0.30	−2.50	11.85	−29.63	−8.89
Z	0.30	-5.25	−5.10	26.78	8.03
				Covariance	−7.40

Event	Probability	Deviation of security B	Deviation of security C	Product of deviations	Probability × Product of deviations
X	0.40	−5.35	−10.90	58.32	23.33
Y	0.30	10.75	11.85	127.39	38.22
Z	0.30	−5.35	−5.10	27.29	8.19
				Covariance	69.73

A positive value for covariance, as in the case of securities *B* and *C*, indicates that the securities are positively correlated. A better than expected return for one is likely to occur for the other as well. It can be compared to investing in two stocks in the same sector, so that a positive outlook for that sector would imply better than anticipated return for most stocks in the sector. A negative covariance indicates that returns could offset each other or cancel each other out. A small value or zero value for the covariance indicates there is little or no relationship between the two returns, as is evident for securities *A* and *B*. When two securities' returns are perfectly positively correlated, portfolio diversification does not lead to the reduction of risk, only risk averaging

4. When calculating a security's beta, an analyst needs to take into account various *scenarios* of the state of the market, economy, politics, etc., that will impact on that security's return.

Event	Expected return of security i	Expected return of market	Covariance
1	20	10	109.12
2	8	4	21.12
3	12	5	16.72
4	3	2	−3.68
5	−5	−15	204.12
Average value	7.6	1.2	65.48
Variance	70.64	72.56	

E_i (expected return of security i)	7.6
E_m (expected return of market)	1.2
V_i (variance of security i)	70.64
V_m (variance of security market)	72.56
C_{im} (covariance)	65.48
Beta	0.93
Security variance	
Market	62.3
Non-market	8.3
Total	70.6
R-squared	0.88
Non-market risk or standard deviation	2.88

Five different scenarios have been identified with a return on security i (E_i) and a return on the market (E_m) given for each scenario. Let us also assume that these scenarios are equally probable. Thus, the expected return on security i is simply an average of the given estimated returns. A similar calculation is provided for the market portfolio. The method of calculating covariance (C_{im}) has already been explained. It is simply an average of the product of the deviation of security i's return from its expected value times the deviation of the market portfolio's return from its expected value for each particular scenario. The average of these values is the covariance between the two returns. The beta value is covariance between the two returns divided by the variance of the security.

Then the risk of the security is broken down to its constituent parts: market risk and non-market risk. To calculate market risk in variance terms, one multiplies the variance of the market portfolio by the square of the security's beta value. The non-market risk in variance terms is simply the difference between the total variance of the security and that of the market. R^2 expresses how much of the security's risk is market related and is arrived at by dividing market risk by total risk. In this example, R^2 is quite high at 0.88; in other words, 88% of the security's risk is associated with uncertainty surrounding the market return. At the portfolio level, the market component of risk tends to be substantially higher than at stock level

5. William F. Sharpe, *Investments* (Prentice Hall, 1985), p. 165

CHAPTER 3

1. Andrew Skirton, chief investment officer, Barclays Global Investors, interviewed in April 2000
2. Burton Malkiel, 'Indexes: why the critics are wrong,' *Wall Street Journal*, 24 May 1999. Burton Malkiel is a professor of economics at Princeton University and the author of *A Random Walk Down Wall Street* (W.W. Norton, 1999)
3. *Hansard*, H.L. Vol. 560, col. 975. Lord Mackay of Ardbrecknish outlining the scheme of the Act in his introduction of the Pensions Bill to the House of Lords on January 24, 1995)
4. Alan Brown, chief investment officer, State Street Global Advisers, interviewed in April 2000
5. Paul Myners, *Institutional Investment in the UK* (HM Treasury, 2001), pp. 5–7
6. *Financial Times*, 'Vodafone pension plan tops list of underfunded schemes,' 16 August 2001
7. Anthony Watson, chairman and chief executive, Hermes Pensions Management, interviewed in June 2000
8. Phillips & Drew, *Pension Fund Indicators 2001*, p. 4
9. Tim Gardener, global head of investment consulting, William M. Mercer Limited, interviewed in August 2001
10. William R. Cotter, chief executive officer, Asset and Wealth Management Services, Bank of Ireland Group, interviewed in February 2001
11. Tony Watson interview
12. William Cotter interview
13. Myners, pp. 4–5
14. Andrew Skirton interview
15. Barclays Global Investors and PricewaterhouseCoopers, *25 years of indexing: an analysis of the costs and benefits*, 1997, p. 26

16. BGI and PwC, *25 years of indexing*, p. 22
17. Myners, pp. 4–5
18. Tim Gardener interview
19. Andrew Skirton interview
20. Andrew Skirton interview
21. Andrew Skirton interview
22. Deborah A. Lamb, *AIMR Advocate*, Vol. 6, no. 5, Sept/Oct 2001, p. 7
23. Deborah A. Lamb, *AIMR Advocate*, Vol. 6, no. 5, Sept/Oct 2001, p. 7
24. Alan Brown interview
25. Tony Watson interview
26. Myners, p. 2
27. Myners, p. 9
28. Myners, pp. 7, 59
29. Myners, pp. 197–98
30. Chris Sutton, head of index portfolio management, Barclays Global Investors, interviewed in March 2000
31. Ken O'Keefe and Khalid Ghayur, 'In pursuit of the superior equity index,' *Professional Investor*, September 2001, p. 22
32. John Morrell, *Professional Investor* (2000)
33. Suzanne Mitchell, manager for performance measurement with Russell/Mellon Analytical Services, interviewed in May 2000
34. Andrew Skirton interview
35. Tony Watson interview
36. Alan Brown interview
37. Myners, p. 81
38. Alan Brown interview; this interview was conducted when MSCI was still in the process of expanding its market coverage
39. Dimitris Melas, global head of research, HSBC Asset Management, interviewed in November 2000
40. Refer to 'The Role of Analysis', pp. 140–166
41. *Professional Investor*, September 2001, p. 2
42. BGI and PwC, *25 years of indexing*, p. 34
43. *Institutional Investor*, August 2001, p. 22

CHAPTER 4

1. John Train, *The Midas Touch* (Harper & Row, 1987), p. 99
2. *Economist*, 'A survey of globalisation,' 29 September 2001, p. 5
3. William F. Sharpe, *Investments* (Prentice Hall, 1985), p. 591
4. William R. Cotter, chief executive officer, Asset and Wealth Management Services, Bank of Ireland Group, interviewed in February 2001
5. J. G. Blease, 'Computers as an aid to investment analysis,' *Double Takes*, pp. 3–20

6. Laurence Fink, chief executive officer, BlackRock Investments, *Global Custodian*, Spring 2000
7. Stuart O'Gorman, head of technology, Henderson Global Investors, interviewed in January 2001
8. Professor Daniel Hodson, Mercers' School Memorial Professor of Commerce, interviewed in March 2000
9. Jill Dodds, director of equities, UBS Asset Management, interviewed in April 2000
10. Simon J. Fraser, chief investment officer, Fidelity Investments in London, interviewed in May 2000
11. Simon Fraser interview
12. Simon Fraser interview
13. Simon Fraser interview
14. Jill Dodds interview
15. Alan Brown interview
16. *Economist*, 'Get a parachute,' 25 August 2001, p. 11
17. Simon Fraser interview
18. Nick Ferguson, Schroder Ventures Holdings Limited, interviewed in May 2000
19. Nicola Ralston, head of investment management, Schroder Investment Management, interviewed in August 2000
20. Dimitris Melas, head of research, HSBC Asset Management, interviewed in November 2000
21. Jill Dodds interview
22. *Economist*, 18 May 2001
23. Steven Wiltshire, director of research at Frank Russell, interviewed in July 2000
24. Simon Fraser interview
25. Nicola Ralston interview
26. Mark Boylan, chairman of UBS Asset Management in London, interviewed in April 2000
27. Simon Fraser interview
28. Jill Dodds interview
29. David Roche, global strategist at Independent Strategy, *Financial News*, April 2000
30. Simon Fraser interview
31. Ole Jacobson, *AIMR Exchange*, Vol. 12, no. 4, Jul/Aug 2001, pp. 3–4
32. Nicola Ralston interview
33. I/B/E/S company brochure, 2000
34. Peter Hopkins, head of quantitative research, Baring Asset Management, interviewed in August 2000
35. Nicola Ralston interview; since the interview in August 2000, SIM's internal technological capabilities have been further enhanced
36. Credit Suisse First Boston Equity Research, *The Euro Q-Book*, prepared by Bill McQuaker and Duncan McCourt, Summer 2001, pp. 24–26
37. Dimitris Melas interview

38. James Morrell, 'Economic forecasting and investment analysis,' in *Double Takes*, edited by John Goodchild and Clive Callow (IIMR/John Wiley, 2000), p. 21

39. James Morrell, 'Economic forecasting and investment analysis,' in *Double Takes*, edited by John Goodchild and Clive Callow (IIMR/John Wiley, 2000), pp. 29-30

40. *Financial Times*, Lex column, 20 May 2001

41. David Dreman, *The New Contrarian Investment Strategy* (Random House, 1982), p. xi

42. *AIMR Advocate*, Vol. 6, no. 5, Sept/Oct 2001, p. 2

43. Arthur Zeikel, *AIMR Exchange*, Vol. 12, no. 4, Jul/Aug 2001, p. 15

44. Alexander M. Ineichen, *In Search of Alpha* (UBS Warburg, October 2000), p. 46.

45. Statement of Thomas A. Bowman, CFA, president and chief executive officer, Association for Investment Management and Research, to the US House of Representatives Committee on Financial Services, Capital Markets, Insurance, and Government Sponsored Enterprises Subcommittee, 'Analyzing the Analysts: Are Investors Getting Unbiased Research from Wall Street?' 14 June 2001. Go to AIMR website at www.aimr.org and see under 'advocacy'

46. '"A precipitous solution is not the answer" Tom Bowman testifies on analyst objectivity,' *AIMR Exchange*, Vol. 12, no. 4, Jul/Aug 2001, p. 8

47. Robert J. Shiller, *Irrational Exuberance* (Princeton University Press, 2001), p. xvi

48. Statement of Thomas A. Bowman

49. *AIMR Advocate*, Vol. 6, no. 5, Sept/Oct 2001, p. 3. See also NASDR website at www.nasdr.com

50. *AIMR Advocate*, Vol. 6, no. 5, Sept/Oct 2001, p. 3

51. *Financial Times*, 16 August 2001, pp. 22, 23, 28

52. *AIMR Advocate*, Vol. 6, no. 5, Sept/Oct 2001, p. 5

53. *Financial Times*, 21 June 2001, p. 1. A similar advertisement reappeared. See 'Oracle quarterly profits reach record levels in tough times,' *Financial Times*, 4 October 2001

54. Eugene F. Fama and Kenneth R. French, 'Forecasting profitability and returns,' *Journal of Business*, Vol. 73, pp. 161-75 (2000)

55. Peter Chambers, chief investment officer, Gartmore Investment Management, interviewed in November 2000

56. Shiller, *Irrational Exuberance*, p. xxxvi

57. *AIMR Advocate*, Vol. 6, no. 5, Sept/Oct 2001, p. 2

58. AIMR's Personal Investing Task Force Report issued in May 1995 clearly sets out the position. It is also summarised in the AIMR *Standards of Practice Handbook*

59. Statement of Thomas A. Bowman

60. Dimitris Melas interview

61. Dimitris Melas interview

62. Derek L. Rice, 'A lesson in time from global investment pioneer Ole Jacobson,' *AIMR Exchange*, Vol. 12, no. 4, Jul/Aug 2001, p. 4

63. David Dreman, *The New Contrarian Investment Strategy* (Random House, 1982), p. xiii

64. David Dreman, *The New Contrarian Investment Strategy*, p. 154

65. Peter Chambers interview

66. Peter Chambers interview
67. Tim Gardener interview
68. *Financial Times*, 5 April 2001, p. 9
69. *Financial Times*, 23 April 2001
70. Alastair Ross Goobey, chief executive officer, Hermes Pensions Management, interviewed in May 2001
71. Dimson and Marsh, *Smaller Companies Effect* (London Business School, 1986)
72. Brian Woods-Scawen, chairman of accountants PricewaterhouseCoopers in the Midlands (UK), interviewed in 1999
73. Prof Mario Levis, City University Business School, interviewed in 2000
74. Peter Hopkins, head of quantitative research, Baring Asset Management, interviewed in August 2000
75. Nicola Ralston interview
76. Fidelity PEP and ISA Investment Review, 31 July 2001, p. 18
77. Fidelity PEP and ISA Investment Review, 31 July 2001, pp. 5–6
78. Dimitris Melas interview
79. Alastair Ross Goobey, *Bricks & Mortals* (Century 1992), p. 18
80. Dominic Hobson, *The National Wealth: Who Gets What in Britain* (HarperCollins, 1999), p. 1022

CHAPTER 5

1. Bing Liang, 'Hedge fund performance:1990–1999,' *Financial Analysts Journal*, Vol. 57, no. 1, Jan/Feb 2001, p. 17
2. Crispin Odey, chairman of Odey Asset Management, interviewed in August 2000
3. The prudent man rule, as enacted by legislation in most US states, holds that a fiduciary shall exercise the judgement and care, under the circumstances then prevailing, which men of prudence, character and intelligence exercise in the management of their own affairs, not in regard to speculation but in regard to the permanent disposition of their funds, considering the probable income as well as the safety of their capital
4. Simon Hopkins, 'On phenomenal growth track,' *Investment & Pensions Europe*, June 2000, p. 40
5. Alexander M. Ineichen, *In Search of Alpha* (UBS Warburg, October 2000), p. 7
6. Liang, p. 15
7. Ineichen, p. 7
8. TASS Asset Flows Report, September 2000
9. Liang, p. 12
10. Ineichen, p. 51
11. Ineichen, p. 53
12. *The Future Role of Hedge Funds in European Institutional Asset Management 2001*, Golin/Harris Ludgate
13. Ineichen, p. 4

14. Alastair Ross Goobey, chief executive officer, Hermes Pensions Management, interviewed in May 2001
15. Kevin Coldiron, head of BGI's market-neutral strategy in London, interviewed in January 2001
16. Kevin Coldiron interview
17. Richard C. Grinold and Ronald N. Kahn, *Barclays Global Investors: Investment Insights*, May 2000. See also Richard C. Grinold and Ronald N. Kahn, *Active Portfolio Management: Quantitative Theory and Applications* (Probus Publishing, 1995)
18. Kevin Coldiron interview
19. *The Future Role of Hedge Funds in European Institutional Asset Management 2001*, Golin/Harris Ludgate.
20. Crispin Odey interview
21. Crispin Odey interview
22. Nicola Meaden, chairman and chief executive officer of Tremont TASS (Europe) Limited, interviewed in March 2001
23. TASS Asset Flows Report, September 2000
24. Crispin Odey interview
25. *The Future Role of Hedge Funds in European Institutional Asset Management 2001*, Golin/Harris Ludgate
26. Kevin Coldiron interview
27. Nicola Meaden interview
28. Tim Gardener interview
29. Crispin Odey interview
30. Nicola Meaden interview
31. Tim Gardener interview
32. Kevin Coldiron interview
33. Nicola Meaden interview
34. Fidelity PEP and ISA Investment Review, 31 July 2001
35. Charles Cortese, managing director and head of IT, Lehman Brothers, interviewed in August 2000
36. Nicola Meaden interview
37. Fred Siegrist, head of investment strategy and risk management at Swiss Life Insurance, interviewed in May 2001
38. Rob Leary, managing director and head of pensions group at AIG Financial Products, interviewed in May 2001
39. Fred Siegrist interview
40. Liang, pp. 15–16
41. Rob Leary interview
42. Stanislas Debreu, global head of sales and marketing, equity derivatives at Société Générale, interviewed in May 2001
43. Rupert Allan, director at Société Générale, London, interviewed in May 2001
44. Andreas Ritzi, RMF Capital Markets, interviewed in May 2001
45. Antony Stack, managing director at NDF Administration, CSFB notes to journalists issued on the launch of the product in 2000.

46. Ineichen, p. 3.
47. John Bogle, 'The $500 billion hedge fund fever,' *Forbes Global*, 6 August 2001.

CHAPTER 6

1. All references to data on European private equity investments are from the Annual Survey of Pan-European Private Equity and Venture Capital Association (EVCA), the EVCA yearbooks for 2000 and 2001
2. Toon den Heijer, executive director, Gilde IT Fund, 'Syndication strategy in Europe,' *EVCA Yearbook 2001*, p. 12
3. Antoine Drean, managing partner, Triago, 'Private equity gets alternative ... again,' *EVCA Yearbook 2001*, p. 25
4. 3i & PwC, *Global Private Equity 2000. A Review of the Global Private Equity and Venture Capital Markets*
5. Paul Myners, *Institutional Investment in the UK* (HM Treasury, 2001), p. 152
6. Myners, p. 155
7. Dresdner Kleinwort Benson, *Venture Capital and Private Equity Investment Trusts*, December 2000
8. Myners, p. 19
9. *Financial Times*, Comment and Analysis, 26 August 1999
10. For a more detailed analysis of the US private equity market, refer to Fenn, Liang and Prowse, *The Economics of the Private Equity Market*, Federal Reserve Bank Staff Papers (1995)
11. National Venture Capital Association, *NVCA Yearbook 2000*
12. EVCA Yearbook 2001
13. Myners, p. 159
14. EVCA Yearbook 2001
15. Robert J. Shiller, *Irrational Exuberance* (Princeton University Press, 2001), p. xxx–xxxi
16. Myners, p. 166
17. ECVA Yearbooks 2000 and 2001
18. EVCA Yearbook 2000
19. Myners, p. 162
20. Myners, p. 176
21. BVCA Private Equity and Venture Capital Performance Measurement Survey 2000
22. NVCA Yearbook 2000
23. Oliver Burgel, *UK Venture Capital and Private Equity as an Asset Class for Institutional Investors* (London Business School, 2000)
24. *BVCA Private Equity and Venture Capital Performance Measurement Surveys*, 1999 and 2000
25. Dresdner Kleinwort Benson, *Venture Capital and Private Equity Investment Trusts*, December 2000, p. 7
26. Paul Gompras and Joshua Lerner, 'Venture capital and the creation of public

companies,' *Journal of Private Equity* (1997). See also the European Commission's *Risk Capital Action Plan* (1998)

27. Cosh and Hughes (eds) *British Enterprise in Transition* (ESRC Centre for Business Research, 2000)
28. Poutziouris, Chittenden and Michaelas, *The Financial Development of Smaller Private and Public SMEs* (Manchester Business School, 1999)
29. Myners, p. 165
30. Apax Partners, *Global Entrepreneurship Monitor* (1999) UK executive report, p. 1
31. *Global Entrepreneurship Monitor* (1999) p. 21
32. *Global Entrepreneurship Monitor* (1999) p. 2
33. *Global Entrepreneurship Monitor* (1999) p. 3
34. *Global Entrepreneurship Monitor* (1999) p. 1
35. Philip Augur, *The Death of Gentlemanly Capitalism* (Penguin, 2001)
36. Richard B. Freeman, 'Institutional differences and economic performance among advanced OECD countries,' Merrill Lynch Seminars, London, 6 June 2001
37. *Rethinking High Skilled International Migration: Some Research and Policy Issues for India's Information Economy*. OECD. Garson@oecd.org. See also Robert Taylor, 'Time to rethink labour migration,' Financial Times, 21 June 2001
38. Venture Economics and NVCA
39. Graham Topping, 'What price thought,' *Oxford Today*, Trinity 2001, pp. 11–12
40. Myners, p. 165
41. Myners, pp. 166–67
42. Myners, p. 175
43. Myners, p. 19
44. Myners, p. 163
45. EVCA Yearbook 2001
46. NVCA Yearbook 2001
47. Myners, pp. 177–78
48. *Bloomberg News*, London, 6 September 1999
49. Dr Ann Robinson, 'UK pension funds and investment in private equity including venture capital,' speech to International Centre for Business Information, Frankfurt, 16 February 2000
50. Myners, pp. 6-7
51. Myners, p. 181
52. Myners, p. 182
53. Myners, pp. 181–82
54. Myners, p. 183
55. Serge Raicher and Emile van der Burg, 'Foreword,' *European Technology Success Stories*, October 1999, p. 5

CHAPTER 7

1. The UN Declaration consists of 30 articles setting out the basic rights of indivi-

Notes

duals and nations. (www.unhchr.ch/udhr/lang/eng.htm). The ILO is an intergovernmental organisation linked to the UN, which specialises in employment matters. It issues conventions setting basic standards of employee welfare, including those relating to safety, child labour, workplace standards and procedures. (www.ilo.org). ILO conventions of various types exceed 180; the core conventions are listed on the Ethical Trading Initiative website (www.ethical-trade.org)

2. Business in the Environment (BiE), *Investing in the future: City attitudes to environmental and social issues*, 2001, p. 18
3. Studies include Charles J. Fombrun, *Reputation: Realizing Value from Corporate Image* (Harvard Business Press, 1996); John Weiser and Simon Zadek, *Conversations with Disbelievers: Persuading Companies to Address Social Challenges* (Ford Foundation, November 2000); *Buried Treasure: Uncovering the Business Case for Corporate Sustainability* (Sustainability, 2001); Mark Mansley, *Socially Responsible Investment: A Guide for Pension Funds and Institutional Investors* (Monitor Press, 2000); Michael Russo and Paul Fouts, 'A resource-based perspective on corporate environmental performance and profitabilities,' *Academy of Management Journal*, Vol. 40. no. 3, June 1997, pp. 534–59, where the authors demonstrate that companies which adopt higher environmental standards than those required by government regulation post higher profits; John B. Guerard Jr, 'Is there a cost to being a socially responsible investor?' *Journal of Investing*, Summer 1997, where the author found that risk-adjusted performance is the same for socially screened funds as for unscreened funds
4. *Just Pensions: Socially Responsible Investment and International Development. A Guide for Trustees and Fund Managers*, May 2001, pp. 5–6
5. 'Does inequality matter?' *Economist*, 16 June 16 2001, p. 11
6. *Economist*, 16 June 2001, p. 11
7. David Dreman, *The New Contrarian Investment Strategy* (Random House, 1982), p. xi
8. Ethical Investment Research Service (EIRIS), *The Ethical Investor*, Summer 2001, p. 3
9. EIRIS, *Annual Review 2000*
10. FTSE, 'Socially responsible investment,' July 2001
11. BiE, *Investing in the future: City attitudes to environmental and social issues*, 2001, p. 27
12. Brian Gosschalk, MORI's CEO, quoted in the *Financial Times*, 'Britain has change of heart on profit,' 16 August 2001
13. Nicholas Stern, *Financial Times*, Personal viewpoint, 2001
14. National Association of Pension Funds (NAPF), *Towards better corporate governance* (2000) p. 4
15. *Just Pensions*, p. 5
16. NAPF, *Engaging for success* (2001) p. 1
17. NAPF, *Engaging for success* (2001) p. 3
18. NAPF, *Engaging for success* (2001) p. 5

19. Social Investment Forum (SIF), *Report on Socially Responsible Investing Trends in the United States* (1999)
20. Social Investment Forum (SIF), *Report on Socially Responsible Investing Trends in the United States* (1999)
21. Central Finance Board of the Methodist Church, *Annual Report 2000*
22. Ironically enough, GE is currently challenging the proposal by the US Environmental Protection Agency (EPA) made during the final days of the Clinton administration to conduct a massive and possibly destructive environmental dredging project in the Upper Hudson River on the ground that it is less effective and more harmful than GE's source-control clean-up program and that such action will cause widespread and potentially irreversible damage to the Hudson's ecosystem.

    According to GE, the EPA's proposal:

    - Is larger than all other environmental dredging projects ever tried;
    - Will increase the levels of PCBs in fish;
    - Will delay the time when people can consume Upper Hudson fish by up to a decade in 70% of the upper river; and,
    - Will remobilise at least 2,200 pounds of PCBs, and possibly more, in the Upper Hudson during dredging.

    GE said that EPA's own data show that GE's source-control program will achieve the same reductions in PCB levels in fish as EPA claims dredging will produce without any of the negative impacts of dredging. EPA's own report shows that unless GE's clean-up efforts are successful, EPA's dredging scheme will never achieve any of its PCB reduction goals in the Thompson Island Pool, where EPA proposes the most aggressive dredging. See GE's website for more information on the subject
23. Shareholder Action Network website, www.shareholderaction.org
24. *Friends Principles: The Newsletter of the Stewardship Trusts*, Issue 11, Summer 2001, p. 8
25. Myners, p. 90
26. BiE, *Investing in the future*, p. 7
27. BiE, *Investing in the future*, p. 19
28. BiE, *Investing in the future*, p. 9
29. BiE, *Investing in the future*, p. 12
30. In 1998, 1999 and again in May 2000, Michael Meacher wrote to the chairmen of the FTSE 350 asking them to voluntarily produce an environmental report. See UK Social Investment Forum, 'Response of UK pension funds to the SRI disclosure regulation,' Eugene Mathieu, October 2000, p. 4. In October 2000 Prime Minister Tony Blair challenged these companies to publish annual environmental reports by 2002. See also EIRIS, *Annual Review 2000*
31. BiE, *Investing in the future*, p. 18
32. BiE, *Investing in the future*, p. 22
33. Dresdner RCM Global Investors, *Socially Responsible Investment Policies under Agreement with the United Nations Association Trust*. The DRCM SRI screening

Notes

process does not carry out corporate engagement (except on specific issues with regard to companies it already owns or plans to invest in), other than through the positive and negative screening processes outlined in this company brochure

34. EIRIS, *Annual Review 2000*
35. Tim Gardener interview
36. Interpretative bulletin relating to statements of investment policy, including proxy voting policy or guidelines, Code of Federal Regulations Table 29 Chapter XXV, 2509. 94-2, 1994. See also Myners, p. 92
37. Bob Collie, Mike Clark and John Ilkiw, *Socially Responsible Investments*, Russell London Monograph, no. 10, August 1999
38. The Rt Hon. John Denham, 'Building a better world: the future of socially responsible pensions,' Lecture at the UK Social Investment Forum annual general meeting, 9 July 1998
39. UK Social Investment Forum website, www.uksif.org
40. Collie *et al.*, *Socially Responsible Investments*, Russell London Monograph, no. 10, August 1999
41. UK Social Investment Forum, 'Response of UK pension funds to the SRI disclosure regulation,' October 2000
42. EIRIS, *Annual Review 1999*
43. John Wesley's sermon 'On the right use of money.' See also Russell K. Sparkes, 'Socially responsible investments in global equity portfolio management: a fund manager's perspective,' 12 April 2000. Russell Sparkes is the secretary of the Joint Advisory Committee on the Ethics of Investment of the Methodist Church. He is also the author of *The Ethical Investor* (Harper Collins, 1995)
44. Russell K. Sparkes, 'Socially responsible investments in global equity portfolio management: a fund manager's perspective,' 12 April 2000
45. Myners, p. 89. The Turnbull Code required UK-listed companies to assess and report on their internal risk management controls from December 2000
46. EIRIS, *Annual Review 1999*
47. Myners, p. 2
48. Myners, p. 89
49. EIRIS, *Ethical Investor*, Summer 2001, p. 3
50. NAPF, Voting Issues Service
51. The NAPF-sponsored report of the Committee of Inquiry into UK Vote Execution found that they had risen to 50% in 1999, from 20% in 1990
52. *Socially responsible investment and pension funds* (Friends Ivory & Sime and the Ashridge Centre for Business and Society, March 2000), p. 1
53. UK Social Investment Forum, 'Response of UK pension funds to the SRI disclosure regulation,' October 2000, p. 5
54. *Stewardship ethical investments: an introduction* (Friends Provident, 2001), p. 11
55. Myners, p. 91
56. Modern Company Law, *Completing the Structure* (2000) p. 72. See also Myners, p. 91
57. Myners, p. 91

58. Alastair Ross Goobey interview
59. Myners, pp. 149, 151
60. Interpretative bulletin relating to statements of investment policy, including proxy voting policy or guidelines, Code of Federal Regulations Table 29 Chapter XXV, 2509. 94-2, 1994. See also Myners, p. 92
61. Myners, p. 90
62. Alastair Ross Goobey interview
63. Alastair Ross Goobey interview
64. Alastair Ross Goobey interview
65. Alastair Ross Goobey interview
66. Information provided by FTSE
67. *Socially responsible investment and pension funds* (Friends Ivory & Sime and the Ashridge Centre for Business and Society, March 2000), p. 15. See also Bob Collie, Mike Clark and John Ilkiw, *Socially Responsible Investments*, Russell London Monograph, no. 10, August 1999
68. 'FTSE for what? Muddled objectives,' *Professional Investor*, Jul/Aug 2001, p. 5
69. UK Social Investment Forum, 'Response of UK pension funds to the SRI disclosure regulation,' October 2000, p. 28. It is worth noting that the Domini 400 index (a screened SRI index) outperformed the S&P 500 between 1Q 1990 and 4Q 2000. Annualized returns between 1Q 1990 and 4Q 2000 were 16.6 percent for the DSI, 15.5 percent each for the S&P 500 and Russell 1000 indices. The DSI had a slightly higher volatility. Annualized standard deviation during the same period was 15.7 percent for DSI, 13.6 percent for S&P 500 and 14.2 percent for Russell 1000.
70. Mara Faccio and Meziane Lasfer, 'Pension fund investments and corporate monitoring,' *Professional Investor*, May 200, pp. 23–26
71. Dominic Hobson, *The National Wealth: Who Gets What in Britain* (HarperCollins, 1999), p. 1113

CHAPTER 8

1. Leslie Hannah, *Inventing Retirement*, p. 6
2. William Cotter interview
3. Nicola Ralston interview
4. Tim Gardener interview
5. Alastair Ross Goobey interview
6. Myners, p. 65
7. Myners, p. 59
8. Tim Gardener interview
9. Myners, p. 60
10. Tim Gardener interview
11. Myners, p. 60
12. Tim Gardener interview
13. Myners, p. 61

Notes

14. Myners, p. 70
15. Myners, p. 72
16. Tim Gardener interview
17. Stuart O'Gorman interview
18. William F. Sharpe, 'The arithmetic of active management,' *Financial Analysts Journal*, Jan/Feb 1991, pp. 7–9
19. Simon Fraser interview
20. Crispin Odey interview
21. Tim Gardener interview
22. Richard Donkin, 'Facing up to a virtual response,' *Financial Times*, 4 October 2001
23. British Invisibles, *Fund Management*, City Business Series 2000: Statistical Update, p. 28. See also Myners, p. 74.
24. Warren E. Buffett, in the preface to *The Intelligent Investor* by Benjamin Graham (Harper & Row, 1973), p. vii
25. Myra Drucker, chief investment officer with Xerox Corporation, quoted in *AIMR Exchange*, Vol. 12, no. 5, Sept/Oct 2001
26. Dean LeBaron, 'Some that worked, others that didn't; Dean LeBaron shares a multitude of outlandish ideas,' *AIMR Exchange*, Vol. 12, no. 5, Sept/Oct 2001
27. Dimitris Melas interview
28. Simon Fraser interview
29. Andrew Skirton interview
30. Tony Watson interview
31. Dominic Hobson, *The National Wealth: Who Gets What in Britain* (HarperCollins, 1999), p. 1183
32. Jane Fuller, 'Search for a new baseline,' *Financial Times*, 4 October 2001
33. *Socially responsible investment and pension funds* (Friends Ivory & Sime and Ashridge Centre for Business and Society, March 2000), p. 11
34. Collie *et al.*, *Socially Responsible Investments*, Russell London Monograph, no. 10, August 1999

Index

Printed and bound by CPI Group (UK) Ltd, Croydon, CR0 4YY

16/04/2025

14658499-0005